FACES IN THE CROWD

Musicians, Writers, Actors & Filmmakers

GARY GIDDINS

DA CAPO PRESS

Library of Congress Cataloging in Publication Data

Giddins, Gary.
    Faces in the Crowd: musicians, writers, actors & filmmakers / Gary
Giddins.—1st Da Capo Press ed.
        p.   cm.
    Originally published: New York: Oxford University Press, 1992.
    Includes index.
    ISBN 0-306-80705-X (alk. paper)
    1. Arts, American. 2. Arts, Modern—20th century—United States. I. Title.
NX504.G5   1996
700′.973′0904—dc20   96-14920
                                                                          CIP

First Da Capo Press edition 1996

This Da Capo Press paperback edition of Faces in the Crowd
is an unabridged republication of the edition first published in
New York in 1992. It is reprinted by arrangement with
Oxford University Press and the author.

Published by Da Capo Press, Inc.
A member of the Perseus Books Group

2 3 4 5 6 7 8 9 10   02 01 00

For Lea Aviva,
a born player

Author's Note

Mencken called one of his earliest and best essay collections *A Book of Prefaces*, a title I was tempted to appropriate. The work gathered here includes essays, reviews, profiles, polemics; all are attempts to convey my admiration for the faces in this peculiarly heterodox crowd. Yet not all of the entries are general enough to qualify as prefaces, and not a few turned out to be more critical than I anticipated when I began writing them—a consequence of the often regrettable distinction between artists and those who package their art or chronicle their lives. Elias Canetti has argued that every group, animate or inanimate, constitutes a crowd, usually a nefarious one. Here is one in which I would be pleased to mingle. It seems unlikely that the writers and players (musicians, actors, filmmakers) assembled between these covers can have much in common beyond my regard for them; some would undoubtedly grouse about the company they are asked to keep. I hope in every instance my enthusiasm outshines my apprehension.

All selections have been revised, many from stem to stern. Yet I have attached to each the original publication date so that the reader can place my comments in perspective. Updates that aren't conceptual or stylistic are confined to footnotes and addenda. None of these pieces has appeared in my previous books, though other accounts of some of the same people have.

I have many people to thank. Ben Sonnenberg, who commissioned "This Guy Wouldn't Give You the Parsley off His Fish" for his incomparable *Grand Street*, is the only editor I have ever known who on reading the submission asked the writer to accept more money than was originally agreed. In the spirit of Jack Benny, I complied. Elizabeth Pochoda, who has been something of a guardian angel to me, requested "Prince Charmless" for the short-lived *New York Post* book review, which sounds like an oxymoron but wasn't. David Hirshey gave me more leeway than I expected when *Esquire* published "Birdman of Hollywood," and Michael Anderson allowed me more words than he expected when the *New York Times* Book Review published "In His Own Write" (Miles Davis). It was a pleasure to work with Katha Pollitt of *The Nation*, which ran "Citizen Cain" and "Scat Song"; Mark Feeney of the *Boston Globe*, which ran "Musicologist" (Gunther Schuller); Louise Boundas of *Stereo Review*, which asked me to honor "The 100 Years of Irving Berlin"; and Erik Rieselbach, gifted editor at Jean Stein's revamped *Grand Street*, which commissioned and ran most of "Dizzy Like a

Fox." Jon Schapiro did the splendid transcriptions for that one, and I thank him for allowing me to reprint them here. "One-Nighter" (Sarah Vaughan) is derived from an article written for *Dial*, a PBS journal; much of "First Lady" originated in an article in *Hifi/Stereo Buyer's Guide*.

Everything else was written for the *Village Voice*, which has given me a free hand for nearly 20 years. Most of those pieces were vetted by the ever-scrupulous Doug Simmons, who has my gratitude and admiration. Other present and former *Voice* editors who provided a sounding board and safety net for the work collected here are Bob Christgau, Karen Durbin, Howard Feinstein, M. Mark, and Kit Rachlis.

As ever, I am grateful to Sheldon Meyer and his staff at Oxford, notably the eagle-eyed Scott Lenz, as well as India Cooper, a most rigorous copy editor. I thank my assistants Amelia Belle and Folly Butler, who helped me keep my desk relatively clear, and my singing pal Mary Cleere Haran who found time to help me with research. I acknowledge with pride the personal support of the Questels, Rothchilds, and Halpers. I bow in devotion to the junior muse to whom this book is dedicated, and to my senior muse and wife, Deborah Eve Halper.

New York   G. G.
October 1991

Contents

IV WRITERS

PART I

SHOW PEOPLE

"This Guy Wouldn't Give You the Parsley off His Fish"

I became interested in Jack Benny in the early 1970s, when I saw him live. The occasion was a New York concert appearance by George Burns, who, after several years of relative inactivity, was embarking on his highly successful comeback. Benny came along to introduce him. It took him about 10 minutes, and I don't remember a word he said. But I've never forgotten that as soon as he walked out—body flouncing, arms swinging to breast-pocket level, eyes glazed with stoic chagrin—I was convulsed with laughter, an effect his TV appearances had never had on me. If Burns was good, Benny was bewitching. During the past year my impressions of that evening have been confirmed almost nightly, thanks to the Christian Broadcasting Network. CBN harvests souls by day, but by night it lures prospective recruits with back-to-back reruns of old programs by those same wily Jewish comedians, Burns and Benny. After a year of late-night viewing, often of shows that I recalled from childhood with a rather indifferent fondness, I've become a Jack Benny zealot, recounting bits and anecdotes, hoarding pregnant pauses and martyred stares, and even composing this tract about a radiantly funny man, whose humor stands up against all odds.

The fact that I can't recall anything Benny said in concert is germane, since he may be the only great comedian in history who isn't associated with a single witticism. He got his biggest laughs with two exclamations—"Now cut that out!" and "Well!"—and impeccably timed silences. When he died in 1974, I watched the news stories for samples of his jokes. There weren't any. The one bit they frequently played came from radio: Benny, out for a stroll, hears footsteps behind him. A holdup man says, "Your money or your life." Benny says . . . nothing, for a very long time. That's the joke. But it isn't the topper. The holdup man repeats his threat and Benny shouts, "I'm thinking it over!" On the original radio broadcast, he followed through with yet a third variation on the theme: The holdup man gets abusive and Benny, a model of agitated innocence, responds, "If you wanted money, why didn't you just ask for it?" Needless to say, none of this is funny if you don't know the character of Jack Benny. What an arduous exercise it would be to try and explain Benny's unprecedented and unequaled success in American comedy to an audience unfamiliar with the sound of his voice or his deadpan face. Happily, that task is not yet necessary.

Everyone I know knows Benny, though the degree of knowledge depends on age. Those under 40 remember him from TV; those over 40 remember him chiefly from radio (specifically, a Sunday-night-at-seven ritual so widespread that in 1943 NBC declared the time slot his no matter what sponsor bought it). Benny was a comic institution for four decades and apparently had no detractors— though Benny wouldn't have been too sure. In his later years, an insurance group eager to use him in its newspaper ads hired a marketing researcher to measure his popularity. The company was elated by the results: he was loved by 97 percent of the American public—a higher number than for anyone else. "What did I do to that three percent?" Benny wanted to know.

Yet the character he created and developed with inspired tenacity all those years—certainly one of the longest runs ever by an actor in the same role—was that of a mean, vainglorious skinflint: a pompous ass at best, a tiresome bore at near best. To find his equal, you have to leave the realm of monologists and delve into the novel for a recipe that combines Micawber and Scrooge, with perhaps a dash of Lady Catherine De Bourgh and a soupçon of Chichikov; or better still, a serial character like Sherlock Holmes, who proved so resilient that not even Conan Doyle could knock him off. The Benny character was no less fully rounded—an obsessed fan, armed with hundreds of broadcasts, might construct a reasonably detailed biography of him. On the other hand, no one believed Doyle was Holmes, while many people believed Benny was "Benny," a phenomenon that amazed the actor as much as a literary parallel would later distress Philip Roth. A lawyer once dunned him with outraged letters for refusing to pay Rochester his piddling back wages (a plot contrivance on radio); the exasperated Benny finally wrote him, "I only hope you're making in one year what Rochester makes in one month."

Many of the veteran entertainers who pioneered on radio, exchanging a string of vaudeville theaters for millions of living rooms, were surprised by the new audience's credulity and its implications. A fan once asked Gracie Allen if Benny was really cheap; she responded, "Am I stupid?" Yet Benny, like Roth, courted trouble by injecting just enough reality into his work to confuse the issue, and by sustaining his conceit—this, perhaps, was his greatest achievement—through all the fashions that attended the Depression, the Second World War, the affluent society, and the switch to television. Once he established his image, he remained intransigently loyal to it. No but-seriously-folks closers or nice-guy apologias for him. Unlike every other comedian you can name, he never stepped out of character. He seems to have sensed early on the new medium's potential as a mirror for the more commonplace foibles of a mass audience. In any case, he emerged over the decades as a comic staple who could bind the sensibilities of several generations.

Meredith wrote of Molière that he "did not paint in raw realism [but] seized his characters firmly for the purpose of the play, stamped them in the idea, and, by slightly raising and softening the object of his study . . . generalized upon it so as to make it permanently human." Benny's fictions evolved so humanly that the actors who incarnated them ended up adopting the names of their roles. Eddie Anderson had many credits before he joined the Benny crew but was thereafter known in private life as Rochester. Owen Patrick McNulty legally changed his name to Dennis Day after his first four years with Benny; his family convinced him to change it back, but he performed exclusively as Day. Sadye Marks, Benny's wife, legally assumed the name of the dumb gentile shopgirl she played and remained Mary Livingstone Benny even after retirement. Benny also underwent a name change, though not to suit a script. During his apprentice years in vaudeville, his real name, Benjamin Kubelsky, prompted two lawsuits: the first from a violinist named Kubelik who thought a violin-playing Kubelsky would confuse people; the second from bandleader Ben Bernie, who complained that the consequent pseudonym, Benny K. Benny, was a deception designed to cash in on Bernie's fame. ("Now Jack Osterman is suing me," Benny used to tell friends, referring to a comic of the day.)

If the Benny character looms as a kind of metafiction, it isn't in Victorian novels that its genesis is to be found. Benny virtually invented situation comedy, and like most significant innovations, his was a natural outgrowth of local traditions: the American stereotypes and modes of entertainment predominant at the turn of the century. When Benny came along, minstrelsy's ritualistic subordination of individual performers to a faceless (or blackfaceless) group was on the wane, but the idiom's conventions had a lasting influence. The minstrel olio was the first American variety show, typifying theatrical fragmentation and creating such enduring specialties as the Irish tenor (who traditionally sang the first solo), the stout announcer and buffoon (Mr. Interlocutor), sketch dialogues (Mr. Tambo and Mr. Bones), and grotesque caricatures of every racial and ethnic group.

Vaudeville, its immediate heir, freed the specialty acts from an oppressive scheme, not to mention blackface, and forced the performers to assume more individual identities. Still, nostalgia for the old minstrel troupes lingered. The first variety show ever broadcast was a 1924 performance by Dailey Paskman's Radio Minstrels, and tributes to minstrel stars regularly turned up on radio and in movies through the mid-1940s. During the broadcast premiere for the 1940 film *Love Thy Neighbor*, the banter between Benny and Fred Allen turned into a kind of minstrel badinage, which prompted Benny to ad lib (and fluff!) a reference to Mr. Tambo: "We'll go right into a black routine," he says, imitating the endmen laugh, "Yuk, yuk, yuk." He had a right to patronize the old style. The best of the untethered, unmasked comics on the vaudeville circuit had long since originated more precise and inventive personae, often working in pairs—a straight man with a laugh-getter. Sketch humor had come into its own.

Into that world, enter Benjamin Kubelsky, a very young and eager violinist manqué. He was born on Saint Valentine's Day, 1894, in Waukegan, Illinois, the son of Russian immigrants who were Orthodox Jews. At 6 he began violin lessons and at 8 was acclaimed a local prodigy; at 12 he persuaded a friend to get him a job in a theater and worked his way up from ticket taker to usher to musician in the pit orchestra. He must have been pretty good, because Minnie Marx tried to hire him as music director when her sons played the theater, an offer his parents made him decline. In 1912, Benny was expelled from high school and went on the road with a flashy pianist and veteran performer named Cora Salisbury. When she retired after the season, he teamed with another pianist, Lyman Woods, and in 1916, "Benny and Woods: From Grand Opera to Ragtime" played the Palace Theater at $250 a week. They did 11 minutes of musical parody, and although *Variety* called it a "pleasing turn for an early spot," they flopped. Yet they toured for nearly five years, until Benny learned his mother was dying and returned home; a year later he joined the navy, where he devised a routine with the famous novelty composer and pianist Zez Confrey. More significantly, he also did his first monologue in a navy show that eventually toured the Midwest. By the time he returned to the civilian circuit, Benny was concentrating on getting laughs while holding on to the violin as a prop. He was billed as "Ben K. Benny: Fiddle Funology," then "Jack Benny: Fun with a Fiddle," then "Jack Benny: Aristocrat of Humor," and finally "A Few Minutes with Jack Benny."

Robert Benchley praised his cool bravado and subtlety when Benny returned to the Palace in 1924, but others panned him for what they construed as egotism and aloofness. Benny was studying other comics to learn how to sustain narratives and raiding joke books for one-liners, including occasional "cheap jokes"—for example, "I took my girl to dinner, and she laughed so hard at one of my jokes that she dropped her tray." Nevertheless, he was regularly employed. Nora Bayes hired and romanced him, and the Shuberts installed him in the revue *Great Temptations*, on which tour he courted and married 18-year-old Sadye Marks. Never a major vaudeville star, Benny appeared in three unsuccessful movies and worked mostly as an emcee during the next few years. Yet he was making good money in 1930—$1,500 a week—as the comic in *Earl Carroll's Vanities*, when he faced up to the fact that vaudeville was through and began looking beyond it.

Ed Sullivan gave Benny his first radio shot in 1932; he opened with, "Ladies and gentlemen, this is Jack Benny talking. There will be a slight pause while you say, 'Who cares?' " No one did, but the following summer his agent got him a job as emcee on a show featuring George Olson's band. Benny experimented with topical humor and began kidding movies and the sponsor ("I was driving across the Sahara desert when I came across a party of people . . . ready to perish from lack of liquid. I gave them each a glass of Canada Dry Ginger Ale, and not one of them said it was a bad drink"). By summer's end, he had made a terrifying discovery. Radio consumed material faster than he could get it. A joke that might have worked for a whole season in vaud was good for only one night on radio.

In 1934, at age 40, Benny saw the promised land. His guide was a writer George Burns had introduced him to named Harry Conn, who seems to have played Herman Mankiewicz to Benny's Orson Welles. Accounts differ about Conn's contribution, since Benny and Conn parted bitterly a few years later, but there is no doubt—Benny himself was emphatic about it—that Conn was instrumental in conceiving the brainstorm that revolutionized radio: situation comedy based on the lives of the performers, complete with sophisticated sound effects. Instead of revue skits and strings of jokes, each show would be a variation on a constant theme: life with Jack Benny. It was Conn's misfortune to underestimate the importance of Benny's delivery, timing, personality, and script editing in making the initial concept work. Once the idea was established, writers could be replaced, as Conn was when his demands grew unreasonable. But before that happened, he and Benny came up with many of the motifs that would become the star's trademarks: the scenes set in his home, the Irish tenor, the jovial announcer, the dumb girlfriend, the obnoxious bandleader, and the *reductio ad absurdum* of shows that depicted only a mock rehearsal for the show on the air. It was not an immediate hit; in 1934, the *New York World Telegram* named Benny the most popular comedian on radio, but two sponsors dropped him. Not until 1936 and 1937, when Rochester and Phil Harris joined the cast, did the Benny magic take hold.

When Benny surpassed Eddie Cantor in the ratings in 1937 as the most popular star on radio—a position he maintained for most of the next 15 years— he rang the death knell, symbolic and real, for vaudeville. Cantor later remarked, "He made all the other comics throw away their joke files." His popularity had no equal in radio, then or ever. Utterly stymied by Benny's success on NBC, CBS produced an ambitious series of topical dramas for the Sunday-at-seven slot, because no sponsor would buy the time. (The notion of combating popularity with quality seems rather quaint today: CBS, which bought Benny's radio show in 1948 and made a fortune with it, canceled him on TV in 1964, when "Gomer Pyle" beat him in the ratings.) As Fred Allen told Maurice Zolotow in 1950, "Practically all comedy shows on the radio today owe their structure to Benny's conceptions. He was the first to realize that the listener is not in a theater with a thousand other people but is in a small circle at home. . . . Benny also was the first comedian in radio to realize that you could get big laughs by ridiculing yourself instead of your stooges. Benny became a fall guy for everybody else on the show." Or as Benny put it, "The whole humor of Jack Benny is—here's a guy with plenty of money, he's got a valet, he's always traveling around, and yet he's strictly a jerk."

Some jerk. Everyone knows a few things about radio's Jack Benny: he was eternally 39, cheap, bald, and self-admiring, drove a dilapidated Maxwell (is there any other kind?), lived with a valet named Rochester, and had irresistibly blue eyes. With the possible exception of the last, none of this was true of the real Jack Benny; in fact, he had to eliminate the bald jokes when he moved to television. Henri Bergson wrote, "The comic comes into being just when society and the individual, freed from the worry of self-preservation, begin to regard themselves as works of art." Benny honed that generalization to a lunatic specificity, making himself a clown by acting the part of an artwork. No matter the humiliations he had to endure, his self-esteem remained untouched; like cartoon characters who fall off cliffs, are momentarily flattened, and quickly recover, Benny and his vanity were emboldened by adversity. The better the audience knew that, the less he had to do for a laugh. *He* was the laugh. A carnival pitchman bets him a quarter that he can correctly guess Benny's age, and guesses 39. Benny simply gazes helplessly, and the audience is right with him, agonizing over his impossible choice between the quarter and his vanity.

He opened one television show by striding center stage and calmly announcing, "Well, here I am again, standing in front of millions of viewers, completely relaxed, and not a worry in the world. Now, some critics will attribute this to my years of experience; others will say it's the temperament of a true artist. Personally, I feel that it's nauseating confidence." Right away, the audience likes him. Yet he continues in a mode of fake candor, as though he were stepping out of character: "My psychology in starting out with a remark like that is to get you people to dislike me immediately. Then when you realize you're disliking a nice, harmless, elderly man, this gives you a guilt complex. Guilt leads to sympathy, sympathy leads to laughter, and laughter leads to applause. And then when the applause is over, you go home and I go to the bank. That's when I laugh."

Money, and Benny's affection for it, was his most successful leitmotif, one that required some courage to pursue, since it underscored the most persistent of negative Jewish stereotypes (and yet another convention of minstrelsy). Of course, by carrying it off so well, Benny helped to dispel penuriousness as an anti-Jewish barb. Still, this was a matter of concern to him. In 1945, at the height of the fad for radio contests, his show offered a prize to listeners who could best complete the phrase "I Can't Stand Jack Benny Because . . ." in 50 words or less. Benny approved the idea but worried about anti-Semitic responses and asked that they be pulled. Of 270,000 entries, only three were offensive. Benny's Jewishness, in the context of his comedy, is a rather complicated issue, and the manner in which he broached it suggests the degree to which the Jews of his generation felt, in Bergson's phrase, "freed from the worry of self-preservation."

Before 1900, Jewish grotesquerie was a familiar ingredient in the entertainment world, but Jewish humor that wasn't self-deflating simply didn't exist on the American stage. "There were plenty of excellent Jewish performers," according to vaudeville's chronicler Douglas Gilbert, "but they were doing Dutch, blackface, or singing and dancing acts. Some of them were good Irish comedians. Indeed, Weber and Fields at one time did a neat Irish act." Gilbert traces the emergence of Jewish humor to the Mauve Decade success of one Frank Bush, whose doggerel included:

> Oh, my name is Solomon Moses, I'm a bully Sheeny man,
> I always treat my customers the very best what I can.
> I keep a clothing store 'way down on Baxter Street,
> Where you can get your clothing I sell so awful cheap.

But no single performer can liberate a people's pragmatic instinct to keep their ethnicity under cover. Something more, a confident sense of assimilation, is necessary. Years later, Al Jolson seemed to personify and answer that need: first he anglicized his name and hid behind blackface, then he wiped it off to emerge as a celebrity whose renown in the Jazz Age was rivaled only by that of Babe Ruth and Charles Lindbergh. As Jack Robin (in *The Jazz Singer*), he was the Augie March of his time—a fast-talking all-American hustler who could discard or employ his Jewish roots with equal facility. Which isn't to say that Jewish entertainers weren't apprehensive about their gradual acceptance as Jews; even in the Hollywood of the '30s and '40s, Jewish producers avoided Jewish subjects, and Jewish actors played Italians.

Benny's ambivalence about Jewish humor runs throughout his program. Mary Livingstone, who variously turned up as his wife, girlfriend, or just another prickly opponent, had no Jewish characteristics. Benny drew directly on his own Jewishness only rarely. In a TV episode, he auditions actors to play his father in a movie to be based on his life. One actor identifies himself, with a thick burr, as Kevin O'Houlihan. Benny stares haplessly into the camera before blurting, "NEXT!" On a radio show, guest star Bing Crosby told of how he'd been rejected by a country club for being an actor. Benny ad libbed, "How would you like to be an actor *and* a Jew?" To his friends, he was the quintessential Jewish monologist. The harmonica virtuoso Larry Adler, who toured with him and considered himself a disciple, told me that Benny "not only epitomized Jewish storytelling and intonation, but showed everyone else how to do it." That intonation comes across more clearly in off-camera interviews and, oddly enough, his highly amusing letters—some of which are collected in Irving A. Fein's *Jack Benny: An Intimate Biography*—than on the air. Nevertheless, the Benny cast included two Jewish dialecticians—Sam Hearn in the early years and later the more enduring Mr. Kitzel (played by Artie Auerbach).

A harmless, middle-aged man who speaks with a chirpy Ellis Island twang and wears a glassy-eyed smile, Mr. Kitzel is the *only* recurring character who doesn't treat Benny like a jerk. No matter how harassed he is, Benny is always delighted to hear Mr. Kitzel's "Hallo, Mr. Benny" and to play straight man for his corny jokes. Mr. Kitzel isn't nearly as funny as the other cast members (especially Frank Nelson as a maddening repertory character with prim mustache and uniquely chromatic way of saying "Ye-e-e-e-s?"), but for Benny he represents one bright moment amid a regimen of humiliations. On an early TV show, Benny takes the

Beverly Hills Beavers, a boys' club, to the carnival. Mr. Kitzel plays a utility man, who keeps turning up in different guises—first selling hot dogs, then in a gorilla suit, and so forth. The show ends when the boys want to see the belly dancer, and Benny says he doesn't think it would be right. We zoom in on the dancer's face and hear Mr. Kitzel's voice as she lip-synchs, "It's all right, Mr. Benny, it's only me." Benny turns an amazed smile to the camera, shrugs his shoulders, and leads the pack into her tent.

Benny was probably wise not to make too many direct Jewish allusions. After all, his alter ego embodied enough standard Jewish stereotypes to effect not only the anti-Semitic backlash he feared but to intimate the self-denigrating humor of early vaud. He toted a violin, postured with the vanity of a young girl, mistreated the help, and hid his money in a dungeon surrounded by a moat. Yet he played the role with such originality and brio that his failings seemed at once too particularized and too broad to represent an ethnic group. His moot sexuality is a good example of his restraint. In a TV episode, he explains to Rochester why the studio wants to film his life: "I wasn't exactly the first choice, but they found out mine was the only life they wouldn't have to censor. [Intent pause.] Darn it!" Though he was eternally youthful (else the age jokes wouldn't have seemed quite so crafty) and, at least in his early years, a great success with women, Benny so convincingly embodied the ineffectual fop that he became a professional neuter—sexless even when playing opposite Carole Lombard in his best film, *To Be or Not to Be*.

On radio, Benny was sexually anchored by Mary; on TV, he became slightly hysterical (Barbara Nichols, in her usual floozy role, played his occasional date). He was surrounded by sexuality that was vulgar (Phil Harris), sly (Rochester), and placid (guest couples such as the Ronald Colmans on radio or the Jimmy Stewarts on TV). But Benny remained a naif, a mama's boy without a mama, or, more precisely and oddly, a mama's boy with a black male servant for a mama. Yet unlike Johnny Carson, who, for all Benny's obvious influence on him, is sexually cold and untouchable, Benny was warm and intensely physical—constantly patting the hands of his female guests and wrapping his arms around the shoulders of his male friends. (Benny prefigured the "Tonight" show host in his movie *The Big Broadcast of 1937*. He played a radio host named Jack Carson, who boosts his ratings by having a couple get married on the air, à la Tiny Tim.)

Most of Benny's character traits evolved accidentally. If a certain joke worked one week, he played a variation on it the next. The age jokes, for example, didn't start until he was 55, and a nurse in a sketch asked him his age; he paused and said 36. It got a big laugh, so he remained 36 for the rest of the season. The following year, he was 37; in the next, 38. He decided to freeze at 39, because it's a funnier number than 40. His most fertile subject was his stinginess, an angle that produced countless variants. Here is a small garland of them:

He pays his agent 9 percent.

He keeps Mary's fur in his refrigerator: it's "a better deal than the storage company."

He plays a $100 Stradivarius—"one of the few *ever* made in Japan."

For 15 years, he drives a 1927 Maxwell—sound effects by Mel Blanc—which he reluctantly sacrifices to the wartime need for scrap metal. Reborn as a bomber, it makes the same sputtering noises.

When traveling, he pawns his parrot rather than leave it at the pet shop at 75 cents a day.

He stays at the Acme Plaza in New York—the basement suite, which "underlooks the park."

The act of pulling a dime out of his pocket produces suction.

He discovers his tux is stained. Rochester: "That's what you get when you rent a dress suit." Benny: "Well, let's be careful who we rent it out to."

When Fred Allen visits him in the 1945 movie *It's in the Bag*, Allen finds a hat-check girl in the closet and a cigarette machine in the living room. "This guy wouldn't give you the parsley off his fish," Allen mutters.

Benny's secretary calls a cab for him and is told it'll take two hours. "Are they that busy?" he asks. "No, they say they'd like time to think it over."

A terrorist throws a rock through Benny's window with a note that warns, "Get out of town before it's too late." "Hmmm," Benny muses, "just a note, no ticket."

At the race track, Benny says, "I hope I win, I can sure use the money." Mary: "Why? You've never used any before."

On TV, Benny lives in characteristic middle-class, sit-com modesty—his house and those of his moviestar neighbors could easily be exchanged for the dwellings on "Father Knows Best" or "Leave it to Beaver." On radio, however, his vault is somehow located in a subterranean passage, protected by a drawbridge, a moat, a creaking door, a guard who hasn't seen daylight since the Civil War, and finally a combination safe. "You must have a million dollars in the vault," Mary assures him when he worries about money. "I know," he says, "but I hate to break up the serial numbers."

Benny's cast of characters was fine-tuned by the same hit-and-miss system that produced his most enduring conceits. Some performers remained with him for decades. The most celebrated was Eddie Anderson, a vaudeville star whose appearance as a Pullman porter in a 1937 episode was so successful that he was brought back as Benny's valet. He continued as Benny's long-suffering but shrewd and frequently impertinent sidekick until he retired 21 years later. As Rochester Van Jones, Anderson delivered a brazenly hoarse counterpoint to Benny's spry chatter, and usually got the best lines. On his day off, Rochester might don an outrageously gaudy smoking jacket and sprawl on a chaise, sipping a mint julep and smoking a cigar, refusing even to answer the phone. But he earned those days. Rochester had to dip his typewriter ribbon in grape juice because Benny wouldn't replace it. When Benny tried to talk him out of install-ing his own phone, assuring him he could use his, Rochester said, "I know, boss, but look at it this way. Suppose the house is burning down and I haven't got any change?" They didn't quite love each other; but they were perfectly at home in each other's company. One Christmas, Rochester asked a department store clerk to help him choose a gift.

> Clerk: What kind of man is your boss? Is he the athletic type?
> Rochester: No.
> C: The intellectual type?
> R: Well, no.
> C: The executive type?
> R: Hmmm, no.
> C: Perhaps the outdoor type?
> R: NO!
> C: Well, perhaps he's the playboy type.
> R: (Laughs.)
> C: I'm afraid there isn't very much left.
> R: That's him!

It was a source of pride to Benny and his staff that when the NAACP and other groups condemned the portrayal of blacks in the media in the 1950s, there was no protest about Rochester. Nor could anyone doubt Benny's personal feelings: in 1940 he refused to perform or board in segregated establishments, and in 1968 he returned $17,000 rather than fulfill a touring contract that would have taken him to South Africa. Yet his public image was utterly nonpolitical. Indeed, his refusal to link his comedy to serious issues made him especially valuable in the 1960s, when everyone else made a show of taking sides. Benny continued to fulfill the comedian's contract to focus on manners rather than morals. I've been able to find only one instance of his making a political statement: "I am neither a Democrat nor a Republican. I'm a registered Whig. If it was good enough for President Fillmore, it's good enough for me. Now don't laugh about President Fillmore. After all, he kept us out of Vietnam."

I don't imagine there will ever be another generation of entertainers who can sustain the loyalties of successive generations as Benny and a handful of his contemporaries did. President Kennedy is said to have been eager to meet Benny because he recalled the Sunday evening ritual in the 1930s when his father made the whole family sit around the radio. The tempo of life, the dissolution of family entertainment, and the increasing disposability of popular culture have imposed new imperatives and standards. Does this mean that Benny himself will simply fade away? Will the very character-induced economy that enabled him to get laughs simply by staring into the camera undermine the effectiveness of his programs when the character is no longer widely known? One innovative cultural critic, John A. Kouwenhoven, has suggested that the strengths of American art lie in its open-endedness, in its fulfillment of Emerson's dictum that man is great "not in his goals but in his transitions." Situation comedies, like other American variations in high and low culture—including skyscrapers, jazz, *Leaves of Grass*, comic strips, the Constitution, and soap operas (to use some of Kouwenhoven's examples)—derive their integrity not from a notion of finalization but from process and continuity. They are designed with interchangeable parts, to be altered and disposed. What survives is the motivating idea, the germinal core.

Benny himself was a remarkably adaptable figure in the entertainment world, taking every technological twist and popular fashion in stride and refusing to wallow in sentimentality and nostalgia. Yet his radio shows are largely inaccessible to contemporary tastes, as are virtually all radio shows from the pre-TV era— except to satisfy those same maudlin longings Benny rejected. The TV shows are another story, primarily because we still live in a television age. Ironically, despite the visual humor and the irresistible physical presence of Benny, they are not as richly made as the radio series. But they will suffice to keep Benny from becoming primarily a show-business metaphor—much as films kept Will Rogers and W. C. Fields from becoming mere metaphors respectively of cracker-barrel wisdom and inebriated impudence. In the relaxed ambience of Benny's TV skits, a singular clown holds his ground—"completely relaxed, and not a worry in the world." The viewer who hasn't been primed on the fine points of Benny's world will pick up on them soon enough; though even a naive viewer may find Benny's preposterous carriage and delivery sufficient to evoke a deeply, perhaps unexpectedly, satisfied smile. It's not the situations in Benny's comedy that compel attention; it's Benny himself—or, more accurately, Benny qua "Benny"—a peculiarly durable character.

(October 1985)

The 100 Years of
Irving Berlin

Irving Berlin—the name radiates pleasure, recollection, and anticipation. We know what's coming: first, a catalogue of songs so diverse and durable that it strains credulity to ascribe them to one soul; then, the most often told yet jealously guarded rags-to-riches saga in American entertainment. As long ago as 1915, the year D. W. Griffith premiered *Birth of a Nation*, a columnist writing in *Music and Theater Gossip* proposed Berlin as the ideal subject for a six-reeler. Imagine a biography of the world's most famous songwriter told in silent images. The columnist had been provoked by the opening of Berlin's first revue, *Watch Your Step*, often cited as the first Broadway score written entirely by one songwriter. At the close of an evening that presented Vernon and Irene Castle dancing to "The Syncopated Rag"; an uncommonly splashy number (17 pages of music) called "Opera Burlesque"; and a new kind of song, "Play a Simple Melody," in which two melodies and two sets of lyrics were counterpoised, the audience cheered, "Composer! Composer!" Berlin, who refused Hollywood's many importunities to film his life, was not yet 26.

Berlin celebrates his first century in May, a blessing on all of us who need to know that giants still walk the earth, and a reproof to the numberless show biz entities who made their swag and disappeared into the vapors of nostalgia. Berlin is with us always. He lives, reportedly alert and crusty as ever, with his wife of 62 years in an exclusive neighborhood on New York's Upper East Side, just a few miles north of the area, once famously poor and congested, in which he was raised and, as a singing waiter, introduced his first songs to the discerning trade at the café-brothels that proliferated below Union Square. There he helped to establish the popular song in all its motley, and set the ground rules that governed American entertainment—its business as well as its style—for generations to come.

To the extent that our lives are measured in song, we live in the Irving Berlin Era. The evidence was more comprehensive in the decades before rock, when we embraced music with the earnest felicity of a people finding its best instincts, hopes, and illusions expressed in song. An indication of how little songwriting

changed between the teens and the mid-1950s can be adduced by the fact that
"Play a Simple Melody" achieved its ultimate success as a million-selling record
(by Bing and Gary Crosby) 36 years after *Watch Your Step*. Yet even the most
benighted members of a generation raised on Top-40 radio and MTV, unac-
quainted with the very idea of "standards," deafened to the seductions of Kern,
Gershwin, Arlen, Rodgers, Ellington, and Porter, can't help but know Berlin
songs, if only the most sentimental and patriotic of them. They're in the air. Like
the anthems of Stephen Foster written before the Civil War, they seem as imme-
morial as folk songs. Can it be that one man collects royalties on so much of our
national birthright—from "White Christmas" and "Easter Parade" to "There's
No Business like Show Business" and "Blue Skies," from "Always" and "The Girl
That I Marry" to "God Bless America" and "Alexander's Ragtime Band"?

Well, not quite. Scratch "Alexander's Ragtime Band," the song with which
Berlin and American popular music first conquered the world. Berlin—who
fought long and hard to help establish the American Society of Composers,
Authors, and Publishers (ASCAP) and an equitable system of mechanical royalties; who mastered every aspect of the business of plugging and publishing his
work; who has gleaned percentages on his songs from the time when they were
marketed primarily as sheet music and piano rolls through the age of phono-
graphs, movies, radio, and television—has been foiled by a copyright law that
grants only 75 years of protection to songs composed before 1978. (Today's songs
are protected for the life of the composer plus 50 years.) "Alexander's Ragtime
Band" has passed into the public domain along with dozens of other early Berlin
songs that aren't as well remembered, among them "Everybody's Doin' It,"
"When I Lost You," "Dance of the Grizzly Bear," "That Society Bear," "Snooky
Ookums," and "When the Midnight Choo-Choo Leaves for Alabam," each a hit
in its day. How must he feel, witnessing the nationalization of his work, this man
who is so often referred to as a national institution?

Berlin's songs crystallized not once or twice but repeatedly the emotional and
historic milestones of the country to which he was brought in steerage 96 years
ago. Like many impoverished Russian Jews terrorized by pogroms, Berlin's family sold its possessions and journeyed from Temun in Siberia to the Baltic coast
where ships were bound for America. The youngest of eight children, Israel
Baline was born on May 11, 1888, to cantor Moses Baline and his wife, Leah.
Twenty years later, Berlin's idol George M. Cohan paid him tribute and got a
laugh with the line, "Irving Berlin is a Jewboy who named himself after an
English actor and a German city." Everyone present probably knew the true story
of how a printer mistakenly changed Baline to Berlin in setting the type for his
first song, in 1907: "Marie from Sunny Italy" by I. Berlin. The young man,
presented with a liberating initial, renamed himself Irving because he thought
Israel too pretentious. By then he had seen a good deal of show business from the
bottom up.

Berlin was eight when his father, with whom he had sung in synagogue, died.

His siblings were already working in sweatshops, and now he too worked, selling papers after school. He began hanging around Bowery beer houses, and his mother was mortified when he announced his ambition to become a singing waiter. One can only imagine the mixture of daring, aspiration, tenacity, and dislocation that propelled him at 14 to leave home and school, to sleep in basements and hallways, knocking about in search of places to sing. He had no musical background other than the synagogue, and his voice was high and reedy, though he could project it well enough. For a while he accompanied a blind street singer, then went solo. The popular songwriter Harry Von Tilzer got him a job reprising songs from the balcony of Tony Pastor's Music Hall on 14th Street. At 18 he finally got his singing-waiter job at a joint in Chinatown called Pelham's Café. After hours, he taught himself to pick out tunes on the black keys of the piano and wrote parody lyrics of songs by Cohan and Von Tilzer. "Marie from Sunny Italy" earned him a total of 37 cents and suggested anything but a natural talent: The man who later chided a lyricist for rhyming "apples" and "Minneapolis" (he told his biographer Michael Freedland that he would have written "God didn't make little green apples and we don't pray in churches and chapels") was once satisfied with "queen/mandolin" and "beauty/suit me."

Still, within two years Berlin was scoring minor hits, writing lyrics to Ted Snyder's music as well as his own, and finding unknown but talented people to sing them. "Next to Your Mother, Who Do You Love?" was introduced at a Coney Island café by Eddie Cantor; "Sadie Salome Go Home," a Yiddish dialect song, was the first comedy number ever performed by a burlesque singer named Fanny Brice. People paid attention when he altered "Spring Song" with syncopation and came up with "That Mesmerizing Mendelssohn Tune." When the up-and-coming Cantor added "My Wife's Gone to the Country (Hooray!)" to his vaudeville act and a recording was made by Arthur Carter, 600,000 copies of sheet music were sold, earning Berlin $12,000 and a commission for new lyrics (he wrote 100 different verses) from the *New York Evening Journal*. He moved his mother and siblings to a larger apartment.

From that point, despite a series of tragedies and even an occasional period of writer's block, Berlin's career appears to have rolled along with the speed and certainty of a locomotive. Nearly every year between 1910 and 1954 saw the introduction of important Berlin songs. Those songs circled the globe as ambassadors of the American temperament; accelerated and in some instances engendered the careers of singers, dancers, and bandleaders; became emblematic of their native turf. One thinks of the parallel impact Louis Armstrong was to have on jazz. The differences between them are interesting but not very revealing: one black, ebullient, true to the aesthetic of improvisation, and unwilling to be bothered by the necessities of business; the other Jewish, reclusive, a stickler for detail, and obsessed with promotion. The similarities are more intriguing. It's one thing to mouth platitudes of the American Dream and quite another to contemplate in the cold light of day the unvarnished facts that the two most influential figures in American music were set on their ways with backgrounds of grinding poverty and minimal education, and that fueled by genius and an utterly furious work ethic that left little time for self-congratulations, let alone complacency, they managed to claim the world.

In 1910, Berlin sang two of his songs in a show in Boston, while the great vaudeville star Nora Bayes introduced three more in her own show. Fanny Brice won a coveted position with Ziegfeld's Follies and asked Berlin for material; his "Dance of the Grizzly Bear" and "Goodbye, Becky Cohen" secured her stardom. In subsequent years, he would write several showstoppers for the Follies, including "Woodman, Woodman, Spare That Tree" and "Ephraham Played upon the Piano" for the master of comic pathos, Bert Williams; "You'd Be Surprised" for Eddie Cantor (his only million-selling record); and the most sublime of chorus-line themes, "A Pretty Girl Is like a Melody." In the meantime, he'd also written a two-step without a lyric, which, in Berlin's words, was "a dead failure" that lay unpublished for six months. Berlin described what happened next in one of the several interviews he gave in and around 1915:

> One day a social organization, the Friars, got up a club show and asked me to sing a song in it. I hastily wrote a lyric, silly in the matters of common sense, and sang it—"Alexander's Ragtime Band"—at the performance. It turned out to be what the vaudevillians call "a riot," both here and in Europe. No one was more flabbergasted than I was at the smashing hit it made. I humbly began to study my own song, asking myself, "Why? Why?" And I got an answer. The melody . . . started the heels and shoulders of all America and a good section of Europe to rocking. . . . Its opening words, emphasized by immediate repetition—"Come on and hear! Come on and hear!"—were an *invitation* to "come," to join in, and to "hear" the singer and his song. And that idea of *inviting* every receptive auditor within shouting distance to become a part of the happy ruction—an idea pounded in again and again throughout the song in various ways—was the secret of the song's tremendous success.

That's probably as good a rationale as any. Yet even after 77 years, one is at a loss to explain why this particular march, ingeniously crafted though it is, should have had so ecumenical and international an impact in 1911. From the moment Emma ("I'm not pretty, but I'm good to my family") Carus, a deep-voiced ragtime singer, introduced it in Chicago, the song was a popular sensation. Within weeks, Al Jolson started singing it with Dockstader's Minstrels, and Helen Vincent and Sophie Tucker installed it on the vaudeville circuit. Though he hadn't written a true rag, Berlin was promptly dubbed "the rag king" and besieged for more of the same. Cultural critic Gilbert Seldes recognized the anthem as a "crystallization" of a hustling new spirit waking in the new world and ready for export. Berlin's lyric refers to the ragging of military music and minstrel songs, and the melody interpolates a bugle call and "Swanee River." "Alexander's Ragtime Band" celebrated a music filled with bravado and the promise of good times—a music "so nat-u-ral that you want to go to war."

Six years before America's doughboys extended the dream of empire to Europe, Berlin's song announced the presence of a powerful new cultural force. The celebrated black bandleader James Reese Europe would soon team up with Vernon and Irene Castle to popularize a dance called the Turkey Trot (which Berlin boosted in another 1911 hit, "Everybody's Doin' It") and other dances considered salacious for the time. In 1919, Will Marion Cook provided Europe with a real taste of African-American music when he brought his Southern Syncopators Orchestra (featuring Sidney Bechet) overseas. But Berlin's Alexander paved the way. It wasn't ragtime, but it was authentic Americana and it did the trick.

Berlin was now famous enough to attract offers from Europe, and he agreed in 1913 to a vaudeville tour of England, where once again he was misguidedly billed as the King of Ragtime. The night before he opened in London, in a panic to present new material, he wrote "That International Rag"; with characteristic dispatch he addressed the marvel of the new music in the opening verse:

> What did you do, America?
> They're after you, America.
> You got excited and you started something.
> Nations jumping all around.
> You've got a lot to answer for.
> They lay the blame right at your door.
> The world's gone ragtime crazy from shore to shore.

In the chorus, he proceeds to explain how all Europe lost its dignity while dancing to "a raggedy melody full of originality," a phrase employing a triplet that Berlin thought gave the song "punch" and made it memorable. The tour was a triumph, but it followed hard on the blackest days of Berlin's young life.

The previous year Berlin had married 20-year-old Dorothy Goetz, and they honeymooned in Cuba during an outbreak of typhoid. Two weeks later she died of it. Berlin expressed his grief in a song utterly unlike anything he'd written before, the waltz "When I Lost You." Though rarely sung today, it was probably as important to his development as a songwriter as the so-called rags. His first ballad of lost love achieved tremendous and unexpected popularity—more than 2,000,000 copies sold (Cohan called it "the prettiest song I've ever heard in my life")—and was a milestone in the genre. Because of it, Berlin is often considered the father of the modern love ballad, though "My Melancholy Baby," also written in 1912 (by Ernie Burnett, who had no other hits), must share pride of place.

Love ballads had long been a staple of minstrel shows and vaudeville, but they rarely displayed original melodies or interesting chord structures. Jerome Kern's "They Didn't Believe Me," written in 1914, has been cited as the first truly modern ballad. Yet it was Berlin who wrote the largest number of successful and enduring love songs, several of them tied to his much-publicized courtship of the telegraph heiress Ellin Mackey, who married him against her father's wishes in 1926. Grace Moore introduced many of those songs in the Music Box Reviews and said she felt like a singing telegram, carrying Irving's laments to Ellin. Berlin ballads and waltzes of the 1920s included "What'll I Do?" "All by Myself," "All Alone," "Remember," "The Song Is Ended," "Always," and "How About Me?" During those same years, he turned out rhythm hits that encapsulated the talents of specific performers—"Heat Wave" for Ethel Waters, "Puttin' On the Ritz" for Harry Richman, "Shaking the Blues Away" for Ruth Etting, "Blue Skies" for Belle Baker, and "Let Me Sing and I'm Happy" for Al Jolson. He even managed to provide Ziegfeld with a festive account of the country that must have filled him with deepest remorse, "I'll See You in C-U-B-A."

Back in 1912, however, Berlin was still known as the ragtime man, and if the world was dancing to his rhythms there were any number of critics who disparaged what they construed as American vulgarity. The same insensibility that would later dismiss jazz as whorehouse music repudiated Berlin's suspicious popularity—and would continue to deny him such conventional honors as the Pulitzer Prize or recognition by the American Academy of Arts and Letters. Since Berlin could play the piano only in F sharp (he used a transposing piano to shift keys, as Cohan and other self-taught songwriters did) and required arrangers to prepare his scores (he would dictate his harmonies through trial and error), derogatory rumors abounded: Berlin had a black man in Harlem turning out his songs; Berlin had a staff of three slaves; and so on. An interview Berlin gave the *New York Herald* in 1912 was bannered with the news that he had made $100,000 in just three years of songwriting. Berlin, the reporter huffed, "has 'ragged' more money from the public's unsentimental pockets than possibly all the writers of real poetry since the days of Thomas Chatterton put together." While musing over Berlin's betters ("I could not help thinking of Richard Le Gallienne"), he decried the fact that "decrepit pianos will jingle [his music] from the banks of the Saskatchewan to the shores of the Yukon; from the shacks of Panama to the remoter homes of Brooklyn and New Jersey."

The reporter concluded with comments on "boosting," an early form of payola: "To have a song introduced by a popular Broadway star may require quite a payment to the idol of the footlights. The songwriter depending on personal suasion will wait at the rear entrance of theaters and buttonhole the noted black face comedian or the pretty lass of the twinkling toes to interest them in a new song." Actually, the stars were beating a path to Berlin, who was never shy about equating songwriting with business. "Success," he explained, "depends on the trick of putting in what we call 'the punch'—that's a swinging melody [this in 1912] or a sudden twist which will make an impression on the public mind." Ah, but will such songs live? "I think so. At least they'll live 10 years—that's long enough for me."

Berlin collaborated with Justus Dickenson in 1915 on an article for *The Green Book* magazine, "Words and Music (How They Are Written)," in which he expounded at length on his craft. Some songs were written in white heat, but most required "torments and tortures." He continued: "So many of my songs are written under pressure that I can't trust to what is called inspiration. I have an expensive publishing and selling organization almost wholly dependent upon me for a product." He attributed his success to the fact that he wrote words as well as music, as though that were simply the most efficient thing to do. "I sacrifice one for the other. If I have a melody I want to use, I plug away at the lyrics until I make them fit the best parts of my music, and vice versa." His primary concern, he said, was phrasing: " 'Easy to sing, easy to say, easy to remember and applicable to everyday events' is a good rule for phrasing."

Melodies, Berlin suggested, should go up on an open vowel (A, I, O) because ascending on a closed vowel (E, U) "makes enunciation difficult." He believed that the rules of marketing were the essence of successful songwriting and that you couldn't succeed if you weren't also a performer of your songs. A lifelong insomniac, he wrote chiefly between eight in the evening and dawn. "When I work in the daytime, I pull down the window-shades and work by artificial light, strumming away by ear in the key of F sharp, or using a transposing keyboard." Nothing is more emblematic of Berlin's influence on the modern song than his belief in short verses and long choruses, the opposite of the 19th century style. He had been warned that "Alexander's Ragtime Band" wouldn't succeed because the chorus was too long, but he argued that short choruses "don't carry enough sustained interest." He concluded, "I know rhythm. Therein is one of the great qualities, for rhythm is a big part of any one-octave song. It's the swing. When I get the swing, songs come easy."

Five years later, in 1920, he gave the *American* magazine his "nine rules for writing popular songs." Briefly paraphrased: (1) The melody must be in the range of the average voice. (2) The title must be strong and effectively planted in the song. (3) The song must be "sexless," or suitable to performers of both sexes. (4) It should have "heart interest." (5) It must be original in "idea, words, and music." (6) "Stick to nature—not nature in a visionary, abstract way, but nature as demonstrated in homely, concrete, everyday manifestations." (7) A lyric should strive to be "euphonious," with lots of open vowels. (8) Keep it "perfectly simple." (9) "The song writer must look upon his work as business, that is, to make a success of it, he must work and *work*, and then WORK." Perhaps it goes without saying that Berlin violated all of those rules, excepting the last.

He was already a legendary character. In 1918, the year Bartók wrote *Bluebeard's Castle* and Stravinsky *A Soldier's Tale*, Berlin was inducted into the army and conceived the idea for a show that would star 350 soldiers, called *Yip! Yip! Yaphank!* The highlights were his songs "Mandy" and "Oh, How I Hate to Get Up in the Morning," which had its genesis in his insomnia. He explained: "There's a song called 'The Star-Spangled Banner,' which is a pretty big song hit, too; but my answer to the question in the opening line of the national anthem is a loud 'No!' I can't 'see' anything 'by the dawn's early light.' My song about hating to 'get up in the mo-o-o-rning' was a protest written from the heart out, absolutely without the slightest thought that it would ever earn a cent." (Berlin withdrew one of his songs from the show because he decided it was rather too shameless a flagwaver; it lay in Berlin's files until 1938, when Kate Smith asked him for a song to sing on her Armistice Day radio show. He dug out the 20-year-old reject, "God Bless America," and, refusing to capitalize on his patriotism, assigned all future royalties to the Boy Scouts, Girl Scouts, and Campfire Girls. His other contribution to the Second World War, the show *This Is the Army*, reunited many of the WWI doughboys.) In 1919, when Berlin parted with Ted Snyder to open his own publishing house, Irving Berlin Week was proclaimed across the nation.

Berlin and producer Sam H. Harris (Cohan's partner for many years) opened the Music Box in 1921; it remains the only theater ever built in New York to exhibit the music of a particular composer. Berlin wrote four annual reviews, including such numbers as "Say It with Music," "Everybody Step," "Pack Up Your Sins" (the wittiest of his contrapuntal songs), and "The Schoolhouse Blues." Oddly, some of his best songs of the period, including the ballads for Ellin Mackay and "Lazy," were not written for the Music Box and had to be interpolated into the shows when they became hits. In 1925, he wrote the score for *The Cocoanuts*, starring the Marx Brothers. In 1927, he became the only composer to score an entire edition of the Ziegfeld Follies, and also found time to knock off "Russian Lullaby," "The Song Is Ended," and "Blue Skies," which quickly made its way to Hollywood and the first musical film, *The Jazz Singer*, starring Jolson.

For Jolson's fourth and arguably best film, *Mammy*, a recreation of the world of minstrels directed by Michael Curtiz, Berlin wrote "Let Me Sing and I'm Happy," a song that served Jolson's fading generation of entertainers as astutely as "There's No Business like Show Business" would eventually embrace the larger aesthetic. A ballad from the same film, "To My Mammy," creaked along with a flat melody but had an idea in the lyric that Berlin would make memorable two years later in one of his finest songs, "How Deep Is the Ocean?": "How much does she love me?/ I'll tell you no lies/ How deep is the ocean?/ How high is the sky?" On Broadway, in *Face the Music* and *As Thousands Cheer*, he unveiled "Soft Lights and Sweet Music," "Supper Time" (a haunting lament about the aftermath of a lynching), "Let's Have Another Cup of Coffee," "Heat Wave," and "Not for All the Rice in China." Two other songs of the early '30s were, like "How Deep Is the Ocean?" reworked from material he had previously rejected— "Say It Isn't So" and "Easter Parade."

The best of Berlin's original film scores was created in 1935 for the Fred Astaire and Ginger Rogers vehicle *Top Hat*, and produced five instant classics: "Isn't This a Lovely Day?" "No Strings," "Top Hat, White Tie, and Tails," "The Piccolino," and, best of all, "Cheek to Cheek," which was equally daring in melody and words. The music begins with the opening strain of Chopin's "Heroic" Polonaise, here relieved of all heroism, and includes not one but two releases. The lyric begins in the middle of a sentence ("Heaven, I'm in heaven") that swallows its own tail after the second release ("The charm about you will carry me through to . . . Heaven"). *Top Hat* was Berlin's personal favorite among his film scores, presumably not least because it was the biggest grossing musical film to date. His second score for Astaire, *Follow the Fleet*, is almost as strong, and includes "Let's Face the Music and Dance," "I'd Rather Lead a Band," "I'm Putting All My Eggs in One Basket," and that incomparable siren call to free spirits (as sung by Ginger), "Let Yourself Go."

By the late 1930s, Berlin had matured into one of the most consistently creative of lyricists, second perhaps only to Larry Hart and rivaled only by the other words-and-music man, Cole Porter. Yet this aspect of his gift has often been overshadowed by the diversity of his melodies and his penchant for unusual song forms. In a 1938 interview in the *New York Times*, he said, "The words of a song are all important, for the melodies linger on, but it is the words that give the song freshness and life." That same month, in the *New York Journal American*, he showed how he wrote songs at his "trick" piano. "I'm a little like a poet who can write verses that people like, but who can't parse the sentences in his poems. Well, he isn't worried. Any high school kid can parse." He played and sang "Alexander's Ragtime Band," using his lever to make the key change from verse to chorus. Asked what the second key was, he said, "Damnfiknow"; he called one of his assistants in and learned that the verse is in C and the chorus is in F. "You see, a songwriter who's a musician is something comparatively new," he observed. "Of course there were men like Jerome Kern and Victor Herbert, but they were few and far between." Berlin probably enjoyed acting the musical rube; he certainly no longer felt impelled to recite the nine rules for successful songwriting.

The triumphs continued with alarming regularity—*Holiday Inn, Easter Parade,* and *White Christmas* in the movies; *This Is the Army, Miss Liberty,* and *Call Me Madam* on stage. Yet even by those lofty standards, one work stands above the rest, effectively personifying his untutored virtuosity. *Annie Get Your Gun* (1946) is built on an ingenious premise that locates the birth of American entertainment in the Wild West shows of the American *fin de siècle*. The book, based on the romance of sharpshooters Annie Oakley and Frank Butler, who starred with the Buffalo Bill touring company, might seem a slim peg on which to hang genesis. Yet the subject explored the truths and illusions of the American west in a setting of genuine spectacle. Buffalo Bill once rounded up the legends of the west for a road show; *Annie* would bring the road show to Broadway.

Annie Get Your Gun was originally intended for Jerome Kern, but Kern died late in 1945. The show was then offered Berlin, who had just turned down a request from the Bernard Shaw estate to adapt *Pygmalion*. Despite the stipulation that his name would not be billed above the title (a spot reserved for the producers, Rodgers and Hammerstein), he hesitated only briefly before accepting, complaining that he couldn't write hillbilly music. But who other than Berlin could have tackled so handily the basic, commonsensical, comic drama of forthright people with limited education and a God-given gift to do what comes naturally?

Who better than Berlin to enlarge upon the theme of feminist moxie, the subject of many of his early songs, or to distill the whole business of show business and its voracious theatricality?

The success of Rodgers and Hammerstein musicals in the 1940s helped bring about the end of the revues that were Berlin's stock-in-trade and restored coherent texts of the sort that had made Kern's *Showboat* an enduring classic of the '20s. Berlin accepted the challenge with extraordinary vigor; hardly a melodic refrain or lyric in *Annie Get Your Gun* fails to deliver something unusual and memorable. With Ethel Merman at her outlandishly brassy best (Berlin, who insisted she play Annie as a precondition of his participation, had her kid "pretty" singing in "Anything You Can Do"), the show was a model of Tin Pan Alley craftiness, an unembarrassed pageant by and about self-made entertainers.

In Kern's hands, *Annie* might have been a classier act with love songs approaching the operatic and a showstopping inquiry into the vicissitudes of trouping. One cannot imagine Kern writing "Anything You Can Do" (one of the best of Berlin's many comic songs) or "There's No Business like Show Business"; nor can one imagine his lyricist Dorothy Fields creating verses anywhere near as sassy as Berlin's. And no other songwriter capable of writing those numbers could also be expected to come up with such purebred ballads as "They Say It's Wonderful" and "I Got Lost in His Arms," or the waltz "The Girl That I Marry," or those remarkably sunny soliloquies "You Can't Get a Man with a Gun" and "I Got the Sun in the Morning," or the loony pseudo-folksong "Doin' What Comes Naturally," which is packed with native horse sense, not to mention a double release to break up the nattering main melody.

Annie is all shameless pretense, all greasepaint and costume. Berlin emphasizes the point boldly, brazenly, brilliantly with the score's most inspired coup, that peremptory round of theatrical savvy "There's No Business like Show Business"—an entr'acte that he almost pulled because the producers didn't seem to like it in rehearsal. Here, for once, a songwriter tells the truth about the vain and insecure people onstage and those others in the audience, "the butcher, the baker, the grocer, the clerk," who are jealous because they never get any applause. The applause junkies on stage get little else. Irving Berlin managed to accrue hundreds of millions of dollars and a Medal of Freedom, but in the enchanting climate of *Annie Get Your Gun*, you get the feeling that those things don't really count, and so you applaud all the harder.

Berlin continued to compose throughout the 1950s. Early in the decade, he reunited with Merman for a stage hit inspired by the career of Washington hostess Perle Mesta. *Call Me Madam* introduced the ballad "It's a Lovely Day Today" and the best-known of his contrapuntal songs, "(I Wonder Why) You're Just in Love," which was an emergency replacement for "Free," a tricky canon of a song that died on the road. Outfitted with a new lyric, "Free" was reborn as "Snow" in *White Christmas*, the top-grossing movie of 1954. Though beset by a pedestrian script that sentimentalizes the Second World War, *White Christmas* offered, in addition to a reprise of the title song (originally heard in *Holiday Inn*) and a medley of Berlin chestnuts, his last great score—complete with singular song structures and surprisingly whimsical lyrics. The highlights are "Count Your Blessings," "The Best Things Happen While You're Dancing," "Sisters," "Love, You Didn't Do Right by Me" (a smoky ballad with which Rosemary Clooney nearly steals the picture), "Gee, I Wish I was Back in the Army" (a three-chorus lyric plus a swingtime finish), and a minstrel production number that satirizes minstrel conventions—and, for the first time, eschews blackface—while partaking of its raucous satisfactions, thereby closing a circle in the song-writer's long career.

After the unsuccessful stage show *Mr. President* in 1962, Berlin, always leery of the obligations of celebrity, dodged the glare of public life. He wrote seven songs for a projected MGM musical (never filmed) and offered his last published effort, "I Used to Play by Ear," on a 1968 television show celebrating his 80th birthday. After that, silence. Alienated by the pop music of the 1960s, and depressed by diminished interest in his own kind of song, he now kept his work to himself. Yet he never stopped working on new songs, or so he has claimed. "I'll continue to write them," he told Michael Freedland, "because songwriting is not just a business with me. It's everything." He is rumored to have hundreds of unpublished songs in his files.

Toward the close of an open letter to Berlin published in *Town and Country* in 1954, Bing Crosby wrote, "Many times I have come to the studio, apathetic, dispirited, unhappy with my work, and after five minutes listening to you demonstrate a song in your something less than adequate demifalsetto, your arms waving and your eyes sparkling, I am back in action again. The material is always good, I know, but it's your enthusiasm that's so infectious and I've just got to go along with you, not only on your birthday, but every day." That same infectiousness, as communicated in the material itself, led the composer John Alden Carpenter to write more than 60 years ago, "I am strongly inclined to believe that the musical historian of the year 2000 A.D. will find the birthday of American music and that of Irving Berlin to have been the same." The truly elite songwriters never die, they just fade into the public domain.*

(February 1988)

---

*Berlin died September 22, 1989, four months after his 101st birthday. Ellin Mackey Berlin died July 29, 1988, at 85.

Sometimes He Wondered

When comfortable Americans talk about folk music—the kind PBS regularly sanitizes of all the political affiliations that gave it heart, while its proponents try to sustain the conceit that American children actually enjoy pizzle like "I Wanna Ride in the Car Car"—they lean to the sentimental left. In that sunny clime, Joe Hill will never metamorphose into Jimmy Hoffa, and the workers' paradise won't stone intellectuals or deflate the Bill of Rights. Since they lean, almost alone, against the prevailing winds, I cheer their perseverance and happily lift my voice in a chorus of "This Land Is Your Land." Yet I'm no longer convinced that folk music is safely defined as the province of two-chord guitar players with social consciences, even those as brilliant as Woody Guthrie. Blues and country have long staked a claim to the territory, and even capitalist pop music has a way of entering the folkscape after it's passed through the purgatory of public domain: consider the works of Stephen Foster, James Bland, W. C. Handy. Many Tin Pan Alley songs will pass that way, too, no matter how apoplectic Irving Berlin gets about it.

At the height of the commercial song factory of the '20s and '30s, there was a small cadre of songwriters who strove self-consciously to be folkish. The three most talented were Willard Robison (born 1894), Hoagy Carmichael (born 1899), and latecomer Johnny Mercer (born 1909). Though they came from diverse points in the heartland—respectively: Peekskill, Bloomington, and Savannah—they had much in common. As white nonethnics in a field dominated by Jewish songwriters and black performers, they began in the throes of jazz (each contributed standards to the jazz repertory) and, almost alone among their contemporaries, managed for much of their careers to bypass the stage (Robison for radio, Carmichael and Mercer for Hollywood). Each sang his own material and dabbled in lyrics and music; Robison wrote both, Carmichael mostly music, Mercer mostly words. Not surprisingly, the last two were ideal collaborators, who reached their apex with "Skylark," a song with one of the most ethereal, jazz-inspired middle parts in all of pop music.

They were witty, learned men who wrote about rural life—of lazy rivers and moon rivers; of peaceful valleys and buttermilk skies; of old folks and lazybones; of sharecroppin' blues, blues in the night, and washboard blues; of Georgia on my mind, the Missouri walking preachers, and the Atchison, Topeka, and Santa Fe. Yet they were virtually bereft of a musical social conscience (there is nothing in their work comparable to Berlin's "Supper Time") and shared a lingering nostalgia for minstrelsy that should cause greater embarrassment than it does. Robison's radio show was called "Plantation Echoes," and Carmichael and Mercer would have been suitable guests. Minstrel echoes resound in their work, from the image of an innocent "colored boy" to the singer-songwriter's "colored" inflections. "I'm goin' down to dat river," Carmichael sang, for no particular reason—didn't white people also get the washboard blues?

It is high tribute to their melodic craftsmanship, to the closely observed images in their lyrics, and the guileless nature of their art that the minstrel echoes can be put to rest, while the songs retain their charm. If a phrase or performance is a bit patronizing, malice is utterly absent. Moreover, though all three owed much of their original success to Bing Crosby, the principal popularizer of pop tunes from the late 1920s through the mid-1950s, numerous black musicians and singers kept them current. Robison's "A Cottage for Sale" is remembered because of Billy Eckstine, and his "Old Folks" is the subject of countless jazz interpretations. Carmichael's enduring reputation is greatly beholden to Louis Armstrong (perhaps his best interpreter overall), Ethel Waters, and Ray Charles. Mercer, the most diverse and worldly of the three, is too ingrained in the jazz repertory to single out specific examples.

On the other hand, it is partly because of those minstrel inflections that they aren't much attended to as singers anymore. Carmichael made hundreds of recordings and achieved celebrity as one of Hollywood's most congenial second bananas in the 1940s, but his singing has dated in a way that his songs haven't. His voice and his piano could be highly effective on his novelties—could *anyone* else do right by "Hong Kong Blues"?—but his folksy nasality undermines the arching melodies and sophisticated harmonies of his grander pieces. That disparity was made especially clear in 1956, when he recorded his songs with the Pacific Jazzmen (among them Art Pepper, Harry Edison, and Jimmy Rowles) and sounded ready for a rocking chair; he offered nothing remotely as impassioned as Pepper's reading of "Winter Moon."

So it's no wonder that a new retrospective issued by the Smithsonian Collection, *The Classic Hoagy Carmichael* (a coproduction of the Smithsonian and the Indiana Historical Society), edited and annotated by John Edward Hasse, includes only nine Carmichael records in 57 selections. Carmichael parented something of a folk tradition of his own, albeit for highly trained folk, as witness the collection's six versions of "Star Dust," which I believe stands a close second to "Body and Soul" (it's three years younger) as the most-performed ballad of the century. As Hasse sees it, Carmichael's career falls into three periods. During his "Indiana tenure," 1924 to 1929, he worked with jazz bands and wrote complicated instrumentals, often with multiple strains, such as "Riverboat Shuffle" as well as "Star Dust." In his New York period, 1929 to 1936, he concentrated on songs to be sung, consisting of verses and choruses, among them "Lazy River," "Georgia on My Mind," and "Old Man Harlem." His Hollywood period began in 1936 and produced (often in collaboration with Mercer) such characteristic movie staples as "Two Sleepy People," "The Old Music Master," "Old Buttermilk Skies," and "In the Cool Cool Cool of the Evening" as well as those exquisite ballads, "The Nearness of You," "I Get Along Without You Very Well," and "Skylark."

Like Crosby and many other jazz fanatics of the '20s who went Hollywood in the '30s, Carmichael became uneasy with the paths jazz took. By the mid 1940s, his songs employed increasingly familiar gambits and lost much of the auto-didactic originality that gave his best work—for all its diversity—an instantly recognizable tang. The Carmichael trademark of discriminating craftsmanship purified by endemic appeal never ceased to foster interpretations. He never had to look far or wait long for assured and colorful readings. Yet after the searing "Winter Moon," he composed little of importance in the quarter-century before his death in 1981, and despite the usual tributes and awards, not to mention various acting assignments and the triumphant rediscovery of "Georgia on My Mind," courtesy Ray Charles, he is said to have become bitter at getting rocked under and rolled over. Most of the selections in the Smithsonian set come from his highly creative two decades, 1925–45, and argue an irresistible case for the enduring nature of his art.

The folksy quality of the songs runs deeper than his own Indiana-accented, back-of-the-beat, wry and whiskey voice, and the references to washin', fishin', and rockin' (Carmichael gets away with those dropped *g*'s, which sound so calculated in the mouths of urban folkies). His folksiness emerges in the quotidian detail that informs his own lyrics and those of his strongest collaborators— Mitchell Parish, Paul Francis Webster, and Ned Washington, as well as Mercer. It peaks in melodies that seem to find their way with the miraculous spontaneity of an improvised solo. Carmichael's craggy, wistful individuality is strengthened by an absolute freedom from pomposity. His homegrown genius for melody and harmony was at the service of a reliably unpretentious ear, so that while he could be memorably innocuous ("Heart and Soul," Hasse reminds us, is second in popularity to "Chopsticks" among novice pianists), he was never showy. Even in songs that are virtually impossible for amateurs to sing, such as the verse to "Star Dust" or the bridge to "Skylark," he gives the illusion of a natural melodic flow. You can sing him in your mind's ear, even if you can't get the notes out.

The Smithsonian selection leans, as it must, in the direction of jazz. It has four performances by Armstrong (including his ecstatic transformation of the bauble, "Jubilee") and two each by Benny Goodman, Mildred Bailey, Ethel Waters, Bing Crosby, Mel Tormé, Frank Sinatra, and Marlene VerPlank. There are some unexpected and particularly adroit choices, among them Hank Jones's lighter-than-air "Heart and Soul," a late Carmichael jape called "Serenade to Gabriel," Jo Stafford's "Ivy," a certain Marcie Miller on "I Guess It Was You All Along," and an insuperably inventive "Star Dust" by Ella Fitzgerald and Ellis Larkins that should move the multitudes to petition MCA for the release of that entire session. None of the inclusions is egregious, though I'd prefer to live without Betty Hutton and Kate Smith, and one VerPlank would have been enough. A few omissions are surprising: Room should have been found for Roy Eldridge's "Rockin' Chair," Armstrong's "Ev'ntide" and his 1947 "Rockin' Chair," and Nat Cole's "Star Dust," which is the purest reading of verse and chorus ever made. And if I were editing a fifth platter, I'd probably add Red Norvo's "I Get Along Without You Very Well," Art Tatum's "Star Dust," Gene Krupa and Anita O'Day's "Skylark," Stan Getz and Jimmy Rowles's "Skylark" (though the included version by Bob Brookmeyer and Getz is fine), Kay Starr's "Lazybones," Helen Merrill's "The Nearness of You," Hot Lips Page's "Small Fry," Bob Dorough's "Baltimore Oriole," Hoagy's 1947 recording of "One Morning in May," and—well, that's the point of collections like this: they make you think of performers as interpreters and every songwriter, folklike or not, as his own academy.*

(January 1989)

*The Classic Hoagy Carmichael is available from the Smithsonian Collection, P.O. Box 23345, Washington, D.C., or from the Indiana Historical Society at 315 West Ohio Street, Indianapolis, Indiana 46202.

Prince Charmless

Samuel Goldwyn, né Goldfish né Gelbfisz, the patron saint of independent movie producers, spared no expense for publicity, especially when the subject was the reputation of Samuel Goldwyn. He was so successful at manipulating his chroniclers that today, 15 years after his death at age 94, he is still remembered— check his entry in any movie reference book—according to his own design: a self-made man who produced distinguished films by unerringly hiring the finest talent; a philanthropist whose humble origins were betrayed merely in a succession of widely quoted malapropisms (Goldwynisms), among them "Include me out," "I was on the brink of an abscess," "She has the face of a spink," and, in response to an adviser who warned that a play was too caustic to film, "I don't give a damn how much it costs, buy it!"

Here's a Goldwyn story from A. Scott Berg's impressively deadpan and immensely readable biography, *Goldwyn*, that isn't part of the lore: the baked potato incident. One afternoon in New York, he took the only child of his first marriage, a nine-year-old named Ruth—whom Goldwyn had neglected for seven years and on whose child support payments he regularly welshed—to lunch. He was feeling sorry for himself over their estrangement and livid at her for failing to show the proper nuance of filial devotion. Fork at the ready, she attacked her baked potato, which Goldwyn, displaying the eye for detail that would soon be vaunted as the Goldwyn Touch, decided was underbaked. He created havoc in the restaurant. Ruth insisted the potato was all right and tried to eat it. He freaked, ultimately cutting off all contact with her for the next 15 years. When, at 21, she wrote to tell him he would soon be a grandfather, he ignored the letter, thinking it was a ruse to distract him from a suit he had been pursuing for several months. The great mogul was in court trying to reduce the sum total of unpaid child support from $25,000 to $20,000.

The neglect he and his loyal second wife, Frances Howard (the pathologically insecure and penurious daughter of a rabidly anti-Semitic mother), exhibited toward his other child, Samuel Goldwyn, Jr., was no less severe, but a good deal more virtuosic, since they lived under the same roof until Junior was sentenced to military school. As for Goldwyn's other relatives: he sent money to his mother in Poland, but made no attempt to bring her over; he offered moderate aid to the brothers who did come over, but refused to visit the sister who settled in Los Angeles, even when she issued a plea from her deathbed. The rest of his relations perished in Treblinka about the same time he attended a speech by Joseph P. Kennedy, who came to Hollywood to warn the moguls not to make any more anti-Nazi movies and to "get those Jewish names off the screen."

Goldwyn's son asked Berg to write this book and gave him unlimited access to the records and to his and Ruth's recollections, as well as the promise of independence. Berg labored 10 years and has produced the most damning authorized biography I've ever read. Goldwyn was no less monstrous to his partners and employees than to his family, and though the biographer makes repeated references to his subject's charm (allegedly reflected in the range of his acquaintances and friends), he is unable to make us see it. Indeed, the mind is taxed at having to recall a more charmless figure in life or fiction. (Well, okay, Harry Cohn.) Yet Goldwyn emerges, miraculously, as an ultimately sympathetic figure, at times a heroic one. Ruth understood him as well as anyone: "The secret of this man is that he always did what he wanted. Once he saw what he wanted to have next, he went in an absolutely straight line to get it." He moves and shakes, overcomes astounding odds, reinvents himself repeatedly, asserts unexpected integrity, makes a few good pictures and a couple of great ones.

Goldwyn is divided into three sections, which slightly overlap three more profound divisions in the story. The first and third elicit admiration. At 16, Schmuel Gelbfisz, with a sense of destiny worthy of the most romantic *bildungs-roman*, left his Hassidic family and walked 500 miles from Warsaw to Hamburg, sailed to England and then Canada, where as an illegal alien he entered the United States on the Maine coast, and continued on to Gloversville, New York, where, despite language and other disabilities, he soon established himself as the leading gloves salesman in a city of gloves salesmen. In 1913, he saw Bronco Billy at a nickelodeon; says Berg, "The same lightening bolt that had struck Zukor and Laemmle and Fox and Loew and Mayer and the Warner brothers now electrified him." He convinced his brother-in-law, vaudevillian Jesse Lasky, and Cecil B. deMille, who had hardly *seen* any movies let alone worked on one, to join him in his new venture. They put up a small sum (Berg puts it at $15,000 on page 35 and $25,000 on page 50), bought the rights to the play *The Squaw Man*, and sent deMille in search of a location. He found Hollywood.

By 1925, Goldwyn himself was ensconced in Los Angeles, one of "a handful of tribal chieftains. Little more than a quarter century earlier, most of them had been wretches living within five hundred miles of each other in Eastern Europe, strangers destined to be forever bound by their common dreams. Surely this was the promised land." (In fairness to Berg, he rarely lets his prose sit in the sun that long, but when he does it oozes with a Hollywoodian smarm: "tribal chieftains" is epic deMille; a description of Lindbergh as "a shy Minnesotan in his flying crate" is sentimental John Ford; infrequent puns—television came "unto" Sid Caesar, whose audiences "hailed" him—are Bob Hopeless.) A heroic quality also resonates through the chapters on Goldwyn's final years, beginning with the production of his greatest film, *The Best Years of Our Lives*, and underscores his stand against HUAC, his rapprochement with his children, and, despite diverse disasters, his refusal to slow down or die.

Yet a chill permeates the long middle act, when Goldwyn accomplished almost everything for which he is remembered. In those pages, he is brutish and distant. It's as though he bartered his soul—not to mention his background—for success (see Dieterle and Benét's *The Devil and Daniel Webster*), leaving nothing for his biographer to work with but an endless string of alternately amusing and appalling anecdotes. Like his fellow chieftains, Goldwyn tried to cover up his Jewishness. Most of the moguls named their sons Junior as a bone to assimilation. Sam Sr. went further and protected Sam Jr. from every shred of Jewish culture.

Perhaps Goldwyn's story should be read as a parable of capitalist ethics. The studio system he helped invent and partly abandoned fostered several of the most barbarous consequences of unregulated enterprise: the monopolistic trusts of production and exhibition that took 50 years to break; a self-imposed censorship that was intended to disarm outside influence but inevitably turned craven when outsiders came looking for blood in the 1950s; the seven-year contracts with extension and suspension clauses that came as close to indentured servitude, if not downright slavery, as 20th-century business would tolerate; and the casting couch that awaited countless young women (mostly fatherless, as Berg takes pains to illustrate) who, lured by a shot at stardom in a medium that was often more enthralled by beauty than talent, provided the most extensive concubinage of modern times. (Like the starlets, the moguls themselves were fatherless. It would appear that Hollywood's vicious patriarchy was in part the response to a despised matriarchy.)

Goldwyn, an independent in need of distribution, fought and finally beat the monopolies. He acquitted himself with more dignity during the HUAC terror than anyone else at his level of power in Hollywood—though he acceded to the blacklist, a fact that Berg uncharacteristically buries in the footnotes. As a studio boss, however, he traded in flesh with the best of them. That in itself isn't surprising, but given the Goldwyn myth, his incompetence in recognizing and exploiting talent is. He was, to be sure, lucky and perhaps even perspicacious in recruiting his workers—cameramen George Barnes and Greg Toland, set designer Richard Day, composers Alfred Newman and Hugo Friedhofer, writers Ben Hecht, Anita Loos, Lillian Hellman, Robert Sherwood, and Billy Wilder, actors Will Rogers, Ronald Colman, Vilma Banky, Sylvia Sidney, Eddie Cantor, David Niven, Dana Andrews, and Danny Kaye, and directors John Ford, Howard Hawks, and, of course, William Wyler, who, more than anyone else, including Goldwyn himself, was responsible for the most appealing qualities of the Goldwyn Touch.

He alienated *all* of them. The list of directors alone who refused to work for him, or refused to work with him again, or achieved a place on his payroll but were never entrusted with pictures, includes Hawks, Ford, Frank Capra, Leo McCarey, Billy Wilder, King Vidor, and John Huston. (Huston, Berg reports, was brought in to make Heathcliff and Cathy a happier pair, something he refused to do—or tell about in his autobiography.) The list of actors he misused is far longer. Most of them achieved stardom on loanouts from which Goldwyn made more money than they did. In the nine years he owned Ronald Colman, he repeatedly miscast him (*Arrowsmith!*), until Colman preferred to retire rather than work for Goldwyn. Only when he got free of his contract did that weary Britisher with the boudoir tonsils make the films on which his reputation now rests. Meanwhile, Goldwyn was gambling and losing a fortune trying to force Anna Sten on American audiences. Practically every mogul had his Galatea. Bedding down would-be stars was too easy—the real challenge was to anoint one, thereby bedding down the entire moviegoing public.

Goldwyn was the kind of filmmaker who believed in uplift. He sought "eminent authors" and borrowed prestige wherever he could. When the Goldwyn Company, which he founded with Edgar Selwyn (he adopted the final version of his name from it), needed a logo, it drafted the lion from the New York Public Library and added the motto *Ars Gratis Artis*. (Goldwyn was booted out of the company before it merged with Metro and his hated rival, Louis B. Mayer. Thus he was completely unconnected to the studio with which most people associate him.) Bernard Shaw refused Goldwyn's frequent blandishments with the remark, "There is only one difference between Mr. Goldwyn and me. Whereas he is after art, I am after money." There was another difference: Goldwyn's sense of realism—*The Best Years of Our Lives* was the exception—deserted him on the soundstage. The Goldwyn Touch too often reflected the producer's obsession with cleanliness, which he confused with class and good taste. And so he gave us a scrubbed ex-courtesan, Merle Oberon, and a happy ending in *Wuthering Heights*; an immaculate slum in *Dead End* (Wyler littered the set with trash, which Goldwyn personally removed, screaming, "There won't be any dirty slums—not in *my* picture!"); the de-ethnicized Damon Runyon crew in *Guys and Dolls*; the blonde Danny Kaye (with his natural coloring, he looked too Jewish); and the spit-and-polish Catfish Row of his disastrous swan song, *Porgy and Bess*.

The man of taste and distinction, in part an invention of public relations innovator Benjamin Sonnenberg, was, in his biographer's persuasive portrait, vain, cruel, capricious, cheap, ignorant, and Philistine. He cheated at cards and croquet and attempted to steal credit from everyone he worked with, including Wyler: "I made *Withering* [sic] *Heights*, Wyler only directed it." But what a spell he cast on the industry, the public, and the press. Politicians kneeled before him; the press salivated. In 1925, the *New Yorker* exalted him as "the Celluloid Prince," an "inspired buccaneer." Twelve years later, the *Saturday Review* compared him with Flaubert, and Arthur Sulzberger of the *New York Times* pulled an unflattering review of a Goldwyn film between editions (toady Bosley Crowther was called in to provide a more favorable one). Sulzberger apologized to his readers, but only after he was upbraided by that paragon of journalistic calumny, Walter Winchell.

Berg has admirably set the Goldwyn story against the growth of the movie business, and he has cogently ordered an enormous amount of research. There are a few missteps (Walter Brennan did not begin his film career with *Barbary Coast*, and the chronology of Virginia Mayo's career is skewed) and omissions, including the anticipated specifics in a tantalizing subplot involving Frances Goldwyn and her lifelong friend, the homosexual director George Cukor, who announced at her funeral, "If circumstances had been different, I might well have been [Sam Jr.'s] father." Goldwyn never knew that Frances arranged for Cukor— apparently the one person outside the family who stuck with her no matter how oddly she behaved—to be buried beside them. The most egregious omission, however, is the general reluctance to discuss the content and value of Goldwyn's films. This failing, all too familiar in contemporary biographies of people in the arts, seems to stem from the assumption that criticism slows down the action, leaving in the cold all those consumers who haven't seen, read, or heard those works that are the only excuse for writing such a biography in the first place.

Most of Goldwyn's silent melodramas and comedies are interesting only as curiosities, but notwithstanding such horror shows as *The Goldwyn Follies*, *The Adventures of Marco Polo*, and *The North Star*, he did have his triumphs in the sound era. Surprisingly, the Eddie Cantor pictures, with their often outrageous subversion of sexual conventions, look more chipper today than ever before, while the Danny Kaye remakes have dated badly. The Hawks films (*Barbary Coast*, *Ball of Fire*, and *Come and Get It*, which Goldwyn ordered Wyler to complete) are not that director's best work, but they add a uniquely rhythmic zest and earthiness to the Goldwyn canon. The William Wylers are admirable. Even the worst are stylish and well made, while the best, *Dodsworth* and *The Little Foxes*, are a good deal more. Yet they lack the bite of *Jezebel* and *The Letter*, both of which Wyler made for Warners. *The Best Years of Our Lives*, particularly the first hour, almost alone embodies what Goldwyn wanted the world to think of him and his artistry and his good taste. For once, he restrained himself from second-guessing his scriptwriter, Robert Sherwood, and gave Wyler a free hand. Berg's refusal to discuss Goldwyn's films may reflect his own assessment of his critical powers, or the publisher's opposition to analytical distractions in a potential bestseller, or both. Whatever the reason, the result is the depreciation of his subject. The hefty volume doesn't even have a filmography.

Berg also omits, strangely enough, one of the most famous and pointed of all Goldwynisms. Told that he would not be able to film Lillian Hellman's *The Children's Hour* because it was about lesbians, Goldwyn is said to have retorted, "Don't worry, I'll make them Americans!"

(March 1989)

Perfect

Splendid, slinky Myrna Loy, of the sloe eyes and disarmingly squeaky voice, finally won the attention of the preposterously named Academy of Motion Picture Arts and Sciences, at the age of 79 and on the 60th anniversary of her first appearance in the movies (as a chorus girl in the 1925 *Pretty Ladies*). Like Edward G. Robinson, she was never nominated for one of their hideous statuettes, though they rushed him an apologetic Special Oscar on his deathbed. Now they have mustered the smarts to acknowledge Loy and her indispensable work with a tribute at Carnegie Hall on January 15—a half measure, since it won't be acknowledged on the Oscar telecast. * I went to pay homage, and left secure in the knowledge that even the most auspicious of Academy-sponsored events will be marred by raffish vulgarity. There was, of course, nothing untoward about the unsinkable Loy, who looked radiantly beautiful in the first balcony, crowned in vigorous waves of bright auburn, safely above the fray and away from the prattling script devised for all the onstage participants.

The Academy's tardy recognition of Loy parallels the belated confidence bestowed on her by the movie studios. She had perhaps the longest apprenticeship in movie history: In the nine years preceding her 1934 star turn opposite William Powell in *The Thin Man*, Loy appeared in no fewer than 80 movies—first as scenery, later as a vamp. W. S. Van Dyke II, known to all as Woody, got the idea to team her with Powell in an adaptation of Dashiell Hammett's novel after directing them in *Manhattan Melodrama*, a film immortalized as the last crust of entertainment permitted John Dillinger. A clip was shown at Carnegie of their first scene together, in a cab, and you could see immediately the magic that she and others have spoken about: Powell and Loy clearly enjoy looking at and listening to each other; the timing is easy and inspired. Still, Louis B. Mayer nixed her for the role of Nora until Van Dyke promised to complete the filming in three weeks; it took him 16 days. The result was a smash, and Loy was no longer asked to play vamps. She was now the Perfect Wife.

That doesn't sound like an especially appetizing tag on which to build a career

---

*It wasn't until 1991 that the Academy finally gave her an honorary Oscar on the awards show of that year.

(except perhaps for someone as pious as, say, Greer Garson), but then it doesn't suggest the irreverent spin she brought to the role. Nick and Nora Charles, as embodied by Powell and Loy, were a gleaming advertisement for the bliss of heterosexual palship; they had a touch of Laurel and Hardy in their souls. Her primary duties were to stay on top of his one-liners, defend him against the police and her in-laws, tackle an occasional felon, and shake a mean cocktail—the very sound of which produced vibrations that could lure him home from a hard day strolling in the park. She appeared with Powell (who was also neglected by the Academy) 14 times, if you include her cameo in the 1947 *The Senator Was Indiscreet*, in which she showed up for a one-line gag.

Lauren Bacall, who served as hostess at Carnegie, identified herself as "an irrationally devoted fan" of the honored guest. Perhaps all such a acoLoytes are a touch irrational, since by most critical standards few of her 124 movies are very good. Loy's career demonstrates more than most the ability of movie stars to rival the most commanding auteurs in subverting the conventions imposed by the movie code. *The Thin Man*, for all its slapdash energy and canny dialogue, would be just another Charlie Chan, complete with drawing room denouement, but for the stars. Audiences were so delighted with the pleasure Powell and Loy took in each other that they didn't worry about the mystery. Despite all the mutations in marital protocol, no other movie couple has come close to incarnating the elusive ideal. Eventually, Nick and Nora became middle-class, visiting Nick's parents, who occupied the same perfect dwelling as Judge Hardy's family; switching from gin to cider; hiring Louise Beavers to look after the kid; taking pratfalls with Asta, the perfect dog. But at the start, they were rich, irreverent, inebriated, and sexy.

Woody Van Dyke was not the first filmmaker to fully gauge Loy's unique appeal, but he was the first to successfully promulgate it. (An earlier champion was Michael Curtiz, who tried to convince the moguls to let him direct her as Emma Bovary as early as 1927.) In the year before *The Thin Man*, Van Dyke billed her second to Warner Baxter in *Penthouse*, an entertainingly inane gangster-romance-comedy; she played the tantalizing whore, Gertie Waxted. In 1933, the Production Code hadn't taken effect, and while the script didn't come out and say *whore*, it did crackle with the kind of racy chat (by Frances Goodrich and Albert Hackett) that would soon disappear from movies. Baxter, as a mob lawyer, asks Loy to dance:

> Baxter: Music is a wonderful thing. I meet you and five minutes later you're in my arms.
> Loy: Do you have to have music?
> Baxter: I don't know, do I?
> Loy: I refuse to answer on the grounds that it might incriminate me.

After he shows her to his bedroom and leaves to sleep on the couch, she muses: "A few more weeks of this and I'll be out of condition." Loy doesn't appear in

Penthouse until 34 minutes into the film, but when she does it becomes her show. Her line readings are concurrently decisive and coy, her voice occasionally cracking midsyllable to underscore the character's winsome wit. "You're not going to disappoint Tony, are you?" he asks, referring to the mobster who asked her to join their table. "I'd be scared to," she says, cracking a note on *scared* and fluttering her eyes. When Baxter finally kisses her, she breaks the all-time eye-fluttering record, shaking her head and batting her lashes no less than seven times (not for nothing do VCRs have slo-mo controls.) After she played Nora Charles, she was rarely cast as women of easy virtue, but, good girl or bad, her work exemplified a unique ability to get the most from a line, often with the help of those alluring eyes.

The one Loy film that bears the burden of Greatness is that crafty behemoth of postwar rumination, *The Best Years of Our Lives.* Loy received top billing, but the picture sags in the last hour because the script loses sight of her character in favor of roles played by sensible Theresa Wright, upright Dana Andrews, and, for ballast, that perfect couple of well-scrubbed sleaze, Virginia Mayo and Steve Cochran.* The movie's most celebrated episode, the one that climaxed the tribute to Loy at Carnegie, is Fredric March's surprise homecoming. Directed with inspired economy by William Wyler, the sequence requires only a few set-ups to get March in the door and greeting his kids, who then frame the deep-focus embrace of March and Loy (naturally, she was in the kitchen when he buzzed). In the close-up, her voice cracks (at this point, theaters are festooned with Kleenex), and then . . . a brainstorm. Instead of advancing to the next scene, Wyler finished this one out with a phone call in which Myrna, weeping with joy, cancels the evening's plans. It's a non sequitur that did little to advance the story and everything to establish Loy as one of the most heart-rattling women in screen history.

I'm not sure why that scene remains so affecting. The fact that it does helps put another patch of film lore in perspective. A decade earlier, Luise Rainer, as Anna Held, Flo Ziegfeld's first wife, won an Oscar for a weepy phone call that may still be considered Great Acting by people who haven't seen *The Great Ziegfeld* in 30 years. Today her throbbing seems laughably overwrought if not downright hysterical, especially as it follows what is probably the most cleverly handled nonmusical scene in the film—Powell's proposal to Loy on a park bench, shot entirely from behind. Loy's small role in that film was rather thankless. She played

---

*What a memorable yet undervalued team they were, with their shiny good looks—he dark, she whiter than white—and brooding desperation. Cochran and Mayo appeared in six films together, descending from Technicolor sunshine into noir gloom. In three Danny Kaye vehicles, Mayo became the ultimate Goldwyn girl, a ravishing if slightly cross-eyed adornment to Kaye whose primary duty was to look earnest and/or appreciative; Cochran was the hood who needed a shave and invariably lost her to Kaye. (Fat chance!) They were far more persuasive in black and white, bringing a wrenching touch of the dark side to *The Best Years of Our Lives* and especially *White Heat*. Yet the payoff was a disarming return to color in the neglected and surprisingly funky backstage musical *She's Back on Broadway*, which has a much imitated audition sequence (see *The Producers*, *The Fabulous Baker Boys*) and a discerning touch of theatrical sadism.

Ziegfeld's second wife, Billie Burke, still a popular performer in 1936. Her effervescence could hardly be captured or abated by another actress. Now that Burke is all but forgotten, Loy's work seems refreshingly understated and intelligent, which is more than you can say for the movie.

But then intelligence is at the core of her art. In virtually every interesting role she played, Loy suggested a thinking being. That's one reason her line readings are so absorbing and so often full of surprises. Another is her inimitable voice, which even in her seventies could suggest the pout of a schoolgirl, the wiles of a siren, the common sense of a schoolmarm, the fatigue of a disillusioned matron—sometimes in the same speech. Pitched just high enough to seem vulnerable, it carried a precise and thoughtful ring that was ideal for wry comedy or brooding histrionics. Her shrewdness is captured in the 1932 movie *The Animal Kingdom*, recently restored by the Academy Foundation and shown as the second half of its tribute. Here is a film with virtually no interest other than the acting, but well worth seeing for that.

Adapted from a smarmy Philip Barry play that was said to be funny onstage, *The Animal Kingdom* sets up a triangle consisting of Leslie Howard as the publisher of Bantam Press, his bohemian artist soul mate, Ann Harding, and his manipulative wife, Myrna Loy. Loy steals the honors with an uncommonly subtle performance that justifies Howard's infatuation and ultimate disenchantment with her. Almost any other movie actress would have made clear from the start that the wife was poison, especially as the script provides her with so little motivation. Loy, however, plays the early scenes walking on eggshells, thinking before volunteering every line; she remains persuasive at the end, too, even when Barry suddenly and anvil-handedly portrays her as a tramp.

The Animal Kingdom represented a significant advance in Loy's career, as it pretty much ended her vocation as a supporting, frequently Asian, vamp. Her previous film had been the unintentionally hilarious *The Mask of Fu Manchu*, which remains palatable because Loy and Boris Karloff, in a wonderfully stylized performance, decided the dialogue couldn't be read straight, no matter what anybody else at MGM thought. Karloff proved his mettle with impossible lines like: "This serum distilled from dragon's blood, my own blood, the organs of different reptiles, and mixed with the magic brew of the sacred seven herbs, will temporarily change you into the living instrument of my will." Loy, mincing around in Chinese pajamas, has one irresistible close-up, when she makes her eyes grow beady.

Two years and 10 movies later, she was cast opposite Powell, and then opposite Gable and Tracy and Grant. Perhaps the funniest of the non–Thin Man films with Powell are *I Love You Again* and *Love Crazy*, made in the early '40s. In the latter, she arranges over the phone to meet with suspicious Donald MacBride. "Say, what do you look like?" he inquires. "I tell you what I'll do," she judiciously replies, "I'll bring pictures." By 1950, when she should have had her pick of the best character parts, she worked less frequently in movies, only 10 times in the past 35 years. She appeared often on stage, including a successful tour as Doña Ana in Shaw's *Don Juan in Hell* in the early '60s. She had other interests as well, including devoted service to the Red Cross during the war. In 1948, Loy was cited as one of eight witnesses friendly to the Hollywood 10; a few years later, she helped lead the attack on McCarthy and was pronounced a Commie sympathizer by the *Hollywood Reporter*. She attended the first sessions of the U.N., was appointed a representative to UNESCO, and campaigned ardently for Adlai Stevenson and later Eugene McCarthy. In 1982 she told a TV interviewer, "I never worked with Ronald Reagan. I'm not happy that he's President. . . . He's destroying everything now I've lived my life for." She's probably not in line for a Kennedy Center Award.

But then, does she really want another tacky affair? Bacall started off by calling her "the perfect vamp, the perfect wife, and the perfect woman"—tough billing to live up to, but I'll buy it. I also believe, though I wonder why Bacall said it, that some of the men who worked with her would like to have had more than a professional connection with her. Sylvia Sidney and Sidney Lumet assured us, before introducing some of her "Oriental clips," that she was a "leading fighter against racial discrimination." Lillian Gish exclaimed, "Myrna Loy! What a joy!"—twice. (This is only a guess, but I don't think she was reading from the script provided by Comden and Green.) Joseph Mankiewicz reminisced about Myrna and Bill and pointedly added, "Our job was to provide reasonable entertainment for a grown-up, undemanding audience. We never expected anyone to write essays on our collective unconscious." Burt Reynolds apparently thought the tribute was to him. Making a peekaboo star entrance, he mumbled incoherently for several minutes, managing to insult Loy's second husband, plug his current movie, complain about directing young punks as compared to "old pros" like Myrna, and asserting that her movies raised the Jewish population of New York 15 percent. No one present knew what he meant, either.

Maureen O'Sullivan and Teresa Wright were charmingly prim, if somewhat ethereal. Robert Mitchum said he felt "about as macho as John Gielgud," but he compensated with amusing anecdotes about the making of *The Red Pony*. Maureen Stapleton and Tony Randall, appearing as fans rather than stars, were funny and generous. Stapleton said of Loy (they worked together in *Lonelyhearts*), "When somebody is that great and kind to you, you learn how to be great and kind to others. . . . I would do anything for her." Randall introduced a winning episode with Loy from his TV show, *Love, Sidney*. Lena Horne dubbed her "the conscience of a nation," and Harold Russell emanated good cheer. The clips were marvelous, and there should have been more of them (no *Libeled Lady* or *Too Hot to Handle* or *Chapter By the Dozen*), especially since much of her work has disappeared from TV. Videocassettes will surely come to the rescue. As uneven as her movies are, they more than adequately preserve the good sense, great spirit, and incomparable talent of Myrna Loy, perfect human.

(February 1985)

Birdman of Hollywood

There's never been a movie like *Bird*—a cinematic pasticcio based on the life of the great jazz saxophonist Charlie ("Bird") Parker. Lurching back and forth in time, it mirrors in its dark intensity Parker's own frenetic vitality and casual mastery, his outlaw irreverance and brazen charm. Seizing energy from his music, *Bird* probes its bigger-than-life hero and draws a bead on themes that American movies usually shun or, worse, patronize: black urban culture, miscegenation, drugs, the vagaries of art. In refusing to mute or romanticize Parker, or to pontificate about the evils that brought him down, *Bird* is remarkably adult and manifestly European in style. Parker's genius is depicted offhandedly—the movie proceeds from the foolhardy presumption that the audience knows him, or should. His life and art are addressed with such poise and affection you'd think Hollywood had been making serious movies about black artists for years. But no, it's taken Clint Eastwood to make that leap.

When Warners announced a year ago that Eastwood's Malpaso Productions was completing preproduction work on *Bird*, jazz fans were mildly stunned. A feature film about Charlie Parker had been rumored for a decade, always as a starring vehicle for Richard Pryor. Jazz movies as a rule are so farcically rotten that any announcement of Hollywood encroaching on the turf is likely to elicit groans from music lovers. In recent years, even Martin Scorcese (*New York, New York*) and especially Francis Ford Coppola (*The Cotton Club*) were defeated by a subject that seems ideal for the movies; French director Bertrand Tavernier brought a sharper eye and deeper respect for jazz to *Round Midnight*, but was undermined by a cliché-ridden script and insufficient trust in the music. But Clint Eastwood—how did he get on this train?

Much of the surprise occasioned by the Eastwood bulletin arose from two widespread assumptions: that country was his musical sphere and that (incidentally, if not consequently) he was a fascist. True, country music scores were used in his most and least commercially successful movies (respectively, *Every Which Way but Loose* and *Honkytonk Man*). But he also commissioned some of the finest jazz scores of the past 25 years (from Jerry Fielding and Lennie Niehaus)—those for *Play Misty for Me* (in which he played a jazz dj), *The Enforcer*, *Tightrope*, and particularly *The Gauntlet*, which boasts extended improvisations by Jon Faddis and Art Pepper. The accusation of fascism proceeds from the assumption that Clint Eastwood *is* Dirty Harry Callahan—a tribute to his acting, perhaps, but hardly defensible in consideration of an oeuvre that includes *The Beguiled, High Plains Drifter, Breezy, The Outlaw Josie Wales, The Gauntlet, Escape from Alcatraz, Bronco Billy, Honkytonk Man, Tightrope,* and *Pale Rider.*

Still, no one could have been more apprehensive than I was when, in the summer of 1988, I flew to Los Angeles to see *Bird* and interview its creator. I've loved Parker's music since childhood, and I'd spent most of the previous two years immersed in his life. In the course of writing the book *Celebrating Bird* and piecing together a documentary film—little footage of Parker exists—of the same name, I had come to harbor my own idea of who he was and how he looked. That prejudice, added to my pragmatic suspicion of Hollywood's motives and my propensity for quibbling over factual inaccuracies, weighed on me during the drive to the Burbank Studios. I was resigned to spend several days grousing with Eastwood.

Turn left after the studio gate, drive straight down, and you see the small stucco cottage that houses Malpaso Productions. The furniture in the front room is adorned with Mexican motifs, and the walls are decorated with a few movie posters, one of them memorable: "Dirty Harry and the homicidal maniac," it trumpets. "Harry's the one with the badge." Two dozen magazines are neatly layed out on the coffee table. I looked them over—*Millimeter, Hollywood Reporter, Variety, Arizona Highways, Traveler, National Fitness Trade Journal* and *Muscle and Fitness* (Eastwood is on the cover of both), *American Film, Guns & Ammo*—before choosing *American Heritage,* which promised an article on jazz. I got no farther than the teaser, which suggested that traditional jazz died "the first time it was played before a seated audience rather than in a whorehouse or dance hall." Eastwood's arrival saved me from apoplexy. Hand extended, he emerged from his office wearing khakis and an unzipped jacket. Tall and trim, the most popular movie star of modern times—a top-10 box office attraction for more consecutive years than anyone in history—does not look like the amoral bounty hunter or cop who kills with impunity and sometimes pleasure. He smiled rather shyly, his pale eyes suggesting a customary warmth, and, as he sat on the couch, displayed the awkwardness of Henry Fonda in *Young Mr. Lincoln* in trying to find a place to store his long legs. After a few minutes of small talk (the ambiguous *Dirty Harry* poster, I learned, was never actually used), he walked into another room and returned bearing a pile of *Down Beats* from 1949 and 1950, saved since adolescence and in mint condition.

We talked music, his expressively whispery voice betraying not a touch of the colorful, often scatological language of his most popular films. At one point, during his lunch break (sushi on a styrofoam tray in an office strewn with exercise equipment), he showed me a newly acquired album of Bix Beiderbecke 78s, carefully sliding them from the jackets to look them over—not a scratch. But, surely, he was a country-western fan, right? "You know, I was once working for a timber company in Springfield, near Eugene, Oregon, and all they played up there was country music, Hank Snow and all that kind of stuff, and I never liked it. I always preferred jazz. I'd stay up all night so I could listen to Jimmy Lyons broadcasting from San Francisco at midnight, playing the hot stuff of the time— Brubeck and Mulligan and all that. My mother had a collection of Fats Waller records, and she played the piano, and taught me. Later on I became interested in the self-destruct kind of country guys—Hank Williams, Red Foley—after I read *Honkytonk Man*. I appreciate it more now than I did as a kid. I like rhythm and blues and pop. I thought rock and roll by white guys was boring—it sounded like guys trying to be black and didn't have it."

The idea of making a jazz film had been with him for years. He'd known about the Charlie Parker project and had tried to get a look at it. Then one day he saw the script at his agent's office. "I said, Let me read this, I'll give it back to you. I really liked it, the way the guy [Joel Oliansky] had laid it out, and I thought, Jesus. Then another script was offered to me at Warner Brothers that Ray Stark at Columbia was dying to have. I said to the heads of the studio, Do me a favor, if they want this script see if we can get hold of the Charlie Parker thing. It had been lying dormant for at least six years that I knew of. So they finally came around and made the trade." At the time, Eastwood had been elected to a two-year stint as mayor of Carmel and had another project on the fire. But he started putting together a crew and proceeded with *Bird*. "I wanted to use unknown players, no name faces. For Bird, I'd seen Forest Whitaker in several pictures, small parts, and I always thought he did a lot with very little. We did a test on him and he was terrific. I found this gal Diane Venora, who plays Chan, in New York, along with Michael Zelniker, who plays Red Rodney, and Sam Wright, who plays Dizzy Gillespie."

Chan Parker, the last of Parker's four wives (two registered and two common-law), shares with the other two who are alive the conviction that she alone had Parker's heart. Joel Oliansky, the scriptwriter, focused on her perspective almost exclusively, which made the complicated entanglement of Parker's affections easier to cut through. Diane Venora, her hair cropped like a bell and her *hey, man*'s drawled with just the right touch of New York exasperation, met Chan when Eastwood brought her to Los Angeles. Eastwood also consulted (as had Oliansky) with Red Rodney—Parker's trumpet player in 1949—and several others who knew him. I became increasingly optimistic about *Bird* when he expressed dismay at Columbia's original intention of using a sound-alike instead of Parker's records. Eastwood would have none of that. He knew about jazz movies:

"I was a Beiderbecke fan as a kid. I had played cornet and Bix was the king. So *Young Man with a Horn* comes out, and the breathing was off, the dubbing was terrible, and the plot line—I thought, oh God, what have they done, and I went out of the theater dejected. I was 16 or 17 and I felt that jazz had never been shown as the real, true American art. The reason wasn't really the story—it doesn't have to be accurate, because the main thing is, it *is* a story—but it has to be told by somebody who really loves the art. I've always felt that a jazz movie has never been made by anybody who really liked jazz."

Jazz and film are about the same age, and each is spoken of (often as if the other didn't exist) as America's sole contribution to the arts. In the 1930s, they defined popular culture; in the 1950s, they accrued intellectual pretensions. Each is a product of industrial life. Technology made movies possible and ensured the permanence of musical improvisation. Subsequent technological advances governed their growth—the introduction of tape and long-playing records no less than sound on film. Each has struggled for cultural status and received major boosts from Europe. Each is a collaborative art. The fundamental differences are symbolized by the addresses of their most acclaimed artists. Hollywood is the Valhalla of American fantasy; jazz lives on the outskirts of town. They represent the two sides of America's self-image, opulent vanity vs. scuffling hipness.

Although the impact of black American music around the world has been no less profound than that of cinema, its heroes—with the arguable exception of the blues singer Leadbelly, the subject of an underexhibited Gordon Parks film of the same name (1976)—have not been favored with much cinematic flair. A few Hollywood-produced jazz features are redeemed by the presence of Louis Armstrong, whose roles are often incongruous or condescending, and other performers. The contexts remain no more convincing than, say, those of Biblical epics. Even Anthony Mann's *The Glenn Miller Story* (1954), a nostalgic if distorted recounting of a pop musician tangentially related to jazz, expresses its contempt for the music it pretends to memorialize by slowing it down a hair so that it doesn't swing and by occasionally replacing the distinctive sound of Miller's orchestra with an indifferent ocean of strings. The lowest point was *Lady Sings the Blues* (1972), an appalling desecration of the life and music of Billie Holiday, who worked in Hollywood once—as a maid in *New Orleans* (1947). The urban jazz world, with its countless anecdotes of hipster transcendence and artistic triumph, its jam sessions and battles of the bands, has remained practically virgin territory. Until *Bird*.

I asked to see *Bird* as soon as possible. Red Rodney and his son and a few production people were also in the large screening room. The critic Leonard Feather, who knew Parker, was leaving an earlier screening. As we said hello, he brushed away a tear. It occurred to me as the lights went down that I was so steeped in the documented Bird that the thought of a completely imagined one would be disconcerting no matter how good the movie was. Yet the very first shot, which employs a technique—the recreation of an event from a photograph—familiar from Eastwood's other period films, was reassuring: A famous picture of Charlie as a young boy, sitting astride a pony and holding a finger in the air, was brought to life.

For the first hour or so, I noted minor inaccuracies and the careful straddling of life and myth. What's that line from *The Man Who Shot Liberty Valence?*— "When the legend becomes fact, print the legend." Lousy journalism but acceptable filmmaking policy. At the same time, my ears burned at the fullness of Parker's sound as Forest Whitaker mimed him onstage at the Three Deuces, and my eyes popped with pleasure at the garishly accurate rendering of 52nd Street in its heyday. After two hours and 40 minutes, the running time of this low-budget epic, I was fairly elated. I had known Eastwood to be a gifted director, but I was unprepared for the fullness of *Bird*, the largeness of the canvas; the complete trust in the power of Parker's music to make its own case; the avoidance of preaching; the refusal to condescend to the audience; the attention to detail; the wit. You don't need a crash course in jazz to be caught up in *Bird*, though you may not catch all the references—even basic ones. Parker calls Dizzy Gillespie by his middle name, Birks, for example, and the source of his own nickname is unexplained. Eastwood blithely argues, "If they get it, they get it. If they don't, maybe somebody who knows will point it out. I couldn't make it for the lowest common denominator. It'd be nice if you leave the picture and you find out something new about the music or the people."

Charlie Parker was the most authoritative musician in postwar America. The phrases he improvised on alto saxophone altered the rhythms, harmonies, and melodies—the entire language—of jazz and influenced pop music, film and TV scores, and classical composers. He ranks with Louis Armstrong and Duke Ellington as one of the most revered and influential figures in jazz history. Unlike them, he died young, the embodiment of the self-destructive artist who wears himself out (at 34) and never achieves just recognition until after his death. Because Parker was rarely filmed—a single TV kinescope and a couple of minutes of silent film are the only available footage*—the actor who plays him doesn't have to compete with a popularly ingrained image. Dick Gregory credibly played a character based on Parker, called Eagle, in the 1966 potboiler *Sweet Love Bitter*. In *Bird*, Dizzy Gillespie, who with Parker helped create the modern jazz movement in the 1940s, tells him, "I'm a reformer, you're trying to be a martyr. They always remember the martyr longer. They'll talk about you when you're dead, Bird."

Eastwood's film focuses on the decade between Bird's debut on New York's 52nd Street in 1945 and his death 10 years later. Through a complex structure of

---

*The silent footage was part of an uncompleted film on Parker by Gjon Mili, the photographer who had earlier directed the classic jazz short *Jammin' the Blues*. For years, the Parker film was said to have been suspended because the soundtrack was lost; the film's producer, Norman Granz, constantly denied possession of both visual and audio material, beyond a widely circulated two-minute soundless excerpt. But in 1991, Eric Miller, a longtime associate of Granz, told me he had found not only the film (some 20 minutes long), but the soundtrack as well, and was preparing an eventual release. A minute of silent film in which Parker appears has also been found in Europe. Rumors abound about the possible existence of additional kinescopes of Parker performing.

flashbacks, flashbacks-within-flashbacks, and flashforwards, he gives us a Parker whose triumph and tragedy are intertwined and inescapable. A notorious heroin addict, Bird unwittingly attracted dozens of musicians to their doom, much to his horror. Eastwood punctuates the early scenes with a symbol—actually a cymbal, flying through the air and crashing with jarring finality. A flashback details a Kansas City jam session at which the cymbal was hurled at Bird's feet by a contemptuous drummer. The scene is loosely based on fact, and the effect, an idea of Oliansky's that is nonetheless reminiscent of the ominous flashbacks in Eastwood's surreal western, *High Plains Drifter*, ties Parker's humiliating apprenticeship to the hopelessness of his future. It also embodies his achievement, the adversity he overcame.

Eastwood was wary of relating the cymbal, which is the last sound his Parker hears before dying, to rejection metaphors in his other films or to personal experience, but said, "Adversity makes you struggle a little harder. I think everyone is the product of some sort of setback or something—that thing where you snap and say, I don't give a crap what they say, I'm going to overcome this. Adversity pushes you. I don't know if I identify with Bird, I just like him very much."

Clinton Eastwood, Jr., was born in 1930, in San Francisco, at about the time his family, hit full force by the Depression, began moving from town to town. In the late '40s, after his father set up a successful hardware store in Oakland, Clint worked at every kind of job, from logging to digging Beverly Hills swimming pools, while trying to decide whether to pursue a career as an actor or musician. He matriculated at Seattle University as a music major, but left when the draft caught up with him. He was made lifeguard at California's Fort Ord. It was a safe guess that there must have been a cymbal or two hurled at him in the years before he achieved success at 33, and then only in Europe. "Yeah, there was. There's been a lot of them, but I suppose it was after I had acted for a few years and was thrown out of Universal and voted least likely to succeed as a contract player. I did some television and finally a film, an awful western called *Ambush at Cimarron Pass*. Scott Brady was the lead, and it was so bad they didn't even show it to the cast and crew, they just put it out. When I finally saw it I just slid lower and lower in the seat. I thought, I've got to get out of this business, I've got to get out. In the first place, I'm not getting any work in this profession; in the second place, when I do get work, it's this kind of product. So I kind of made up my mind to go back to school and finish my education. My wife at that time encouraged me, so we gave it a little time and just ground away. I finally mustered up the sand and said, I'm going to win this game." A year later, at 27, he was offered second lead in the television series *Rawhide*, which ran seven years and allowed him to learn filmmaking techniques from two generations of directors, from Tay Garnett to Ted Post.

Bird is filled with the kind of invention that mines truths barred to the documentarian. A composite character named Buster Franklin, for example, is a rather sinister musician who haunts Parker's musical progress. He presides over the humiliating jam session in Kansas City, quits playing in disgust after hearing Parker's mature brilliance, and winds up as a successful rock and roll honker making more bread than Bird every dreamed. A more piquant episode, also fictional, conveys Parker's love of modern music, specifically Stravinsky, and the barrier between two cultures. Learning that his California lover and the transplanted Russian composer see the same dentist, Bird has her drive into the area where the famous expatriates live—Huxley, Thomas Mann, Schoenberg, Stravinsky. While *The Firebird* swells on the soundtrack, he rings the bell at Stravinsky's gate. The door opens, and the composer in his smoking jacket peers out; for one moment they stare at each other across the abyss, then the door is shut. As Bird climbs back into the car, Eastwood brings them together on the soundtrack. The opening phrase of "Parker's Mood" floats over *The Firebird*. "What that does to Stravinsky, I don't know," Eastwood says, smiling with pleasure at the conceit. "But here's two different guys from two different worlds, and I thought they should meet."

Some of the liberties taken with history are irksome—not least because they are trite, therefore unnecessary. Bird's childhood doctor calls him Charles Christopher Parker, Jr., though Christopher was his father's middle name, not Bird's. In later years, Bird might have used it to stress his ties to the drifter who abandoned his mother and him—but his family doctor would never have made that mistake. The *New York Daily News* did not flag Bird's suicide attempt on the front page; it didn't even print much of an obit. The jam session in Kansas City is a tad too boppish for the mid-1930s. Bird rode a horse to Chan's door a few years *after* her eldest daughter was born, to impress the daughter, not before, as shown in the film. Bird figured out his style rehearsing with a guitarist, not a pianist. His West Coast lover, a mysterious sculptress, was nothing like the svelte blonde played by Anna Levine. Red Rodney met Parker in New York, not Los Angeles. And Rodney didn't play nearly as large a role in Parker's life as the picture suggests. Similarly, Chan's role is amplified at the expense of another common-law wife, Doris Sydnor, whom many musicians remember being on the scene more than Chan was.

None of this matters much. The scenes in which Rodney arranges for Parker to play a Hassidic wedding (a true story: the other musicians were Thelonious Monk and Art Blakey) and travels with him in the south pretending to be an albino blues singer (true in part, but much overstated) are so forcible and funny that it's impossible to mind the elaboration of his character. Eastwood avoids the cliché of having Rodney serve as a white filtering agent for Parker's black experience. The makeshift marriage between Bird and Chan works as a wholly credible love story, unmarred by the kind of didactic dialogue that turns each participant into a billboard for liberal cant. The quotidian detail that marks their scenes together gives their love a depth and credibility rarely seen in Hollywood movies, most especially in the depiction of an interracial couple.

Eastwood heard Parker three times while growing up in Oakland. The first time was in 1946, when Parker made his debut at the all-star theatrical jam sessions known as Jazz at the Philharmonic. "I had gone to see Lester Young, who was God to me, and suddenly this guy in a pinstripe suit steps forward playing, and I'm not sure what it's all about, but there's a lot of things going on here. It's unexplainable—there was nobody like him. At Jazz at the Phil, he was standing there with real heavyweights—Coleman Hawkins, who was still playing well, and Lester Young, and the more show business guys like Flip Phillips. I didn't even know who Bird was. But there was something about his music that was just unbelievably well played. And he looked like somebody special, different from the other guys. They were great, they were giants, but here was somebody different. It was like four Joe Smiths and Gary Cooper or Clark Gable. Just something about the guy."

One of the chief pleasures of *Bird* is the attention to period detail. Parker died in 1955, while watching the Tommy Dorsey show on television in the hotel apartment of Baroness Nica de Koenigswarter. Eastwood managed to find a kinescope of the actual show. After talking with the Baroness, he located the precise segment—a juggling act—that Bird was laughing at when he keeled over. "I sent her the pages of the script about his death. She said, it wasn't quite like that, it was like this. She told me about how he stood up and started laughing, and so I took it down and did it like she said. I told her, if you don't mind, I'll just portray it like that." He took equal care with the distraught telegrams Bird sent Chan when he learned their infant daughter had died. "We even reshot one because the spelling wasn't exactly as on the original wires."

Perhaps the most impressive attempt at recreation is the facsimile of 52nd Street, a block-long bazaar of nightclubs and bars, reproduced from a famous photograph and brought to life with the teeming energy of musicians, milling servicemen, and the phony doorman, Pincus, a fixture of the street, who pretended to work for all the clubs and would take tips for opening the door or pointing out a parking space. As we drove over to see the set where the 52nd Street scene was shot, Eastwood remarked, "Usually I prefer not to be anywhere near soundstages. My whole career as a film director has been, Take me elsewhere. *Pale Rider* was done in Idaho, up in the Sawtooth area. *Josie Wales* was done in Lake Powell, Arizona. Whatever places work. The climbing scenes in the *The Eiger Sanction* were done on the Eiger, which I wouldn't do again because we lost one of the climbers. One sequence was done in Monument Valley. I was shooting it, and this old-timer out there tells me, 'This rock, this is John Ford's rock, John Ford always made a shot from this rock.' I said, 'Really? I'm not going to try to improve on Ford, let's run out there.' So we ran out and made a shot from it."

We reached a street of dour brownstones, false fronts for the most part. "This is called the Annie Street, because it was built for *Annie*. We had the Deuces over here with the big long dolly shot, and then all down the street. We backlit the street so that it would have depth, and we had the awnings on and the neon and all that kind of stuff. Did it all in one shot. We picked up a high shot—an establishing shot—of Chan lighting a cigarette as she walked by a fruitstand, and backed up to reveal the whole street."

Eastwood's New York of the 1940s is new to movies. You realize you've never seen it before, never seen wartime New York pulse with as much life—never seen it racially integrated. Not in wartime movies, at any rate, though Vincente Minnelli took care to place occasional black extras in crowd scenes in *The Clock*. Most location shots used in films of that period suggest the absence of all blacks other than an occasional doorman, shineboy, or porter. Even the independent black films failed to portray the interracial boisterousness that was part of the allure of 52nd Street, Harlem, and Greenwich Village. If Eastwood recreated New York on a soundstage, he did venture slightly beyond the studio for other locations. The scenes set in Kansas City were filmed in bars and theaters in old sections of Los Angeles and Pasadena. He persuasively simulated the deep south in the Sacramento Valley.

Equal care was spent on the music and soundtrack. Indeed, the movie's claim to innovation lies in its use of original Charlie Parker broadcast recordings. "The first question a lot of jazz fans asked when they heard about *Bird* was, 'Is this going to be another one of those films where they play a two-bar intro and then people talk over all the music?' And I said, 'Well, I don't think so. You're talking to a fellow aficionado.' " Instead of using Parker's famous records, Eastwood purchased rights to the relatively little known cache of concert recordings, most of them privately taped by Chan on a machine Bird bought her for her birthday. That decision makes perfect musical sense, since Bird's live performances have a vivacity and expansiveness lacking in his often punctilious studio recordings. The problem was poor sound and abrupt editing: Chan would turn off the machine as soon as Bird finished his solo.

To build up the sound of the recordings, Eastwood's technicians cleaned up the tracks, separating the alto from the accompanying instruments, which were then wiped away. Musicians were brought in to overdub drums, bass, piano, and trumpet. The results were laid out in stereo. "We brought in Monty Alexander, Ray Brown, John Guerin, Walter Brown, Barry Harris, and Ron Carter and others. Dizzy wasn't available, so we had Jon Faddis play Dizzy's solos and a pretty good imitation of Howard McGhee, too. I thought, What is a guy like Ray Brown going to think? But they had a ball, they were all misty-eyed. Ray said he felt like he was 19 again. Red Rodney played his own solos and coached Michael Zelniker. For the incidental music, we had James Rivers, who played the title tune in *Tightrope*, and Charles McPherson. For the scene when Bird sends the telegrams, I had McPherson just stand there and watch the screen to try and get into Bird's head and play something, using 'Parker's Mood' as a theme." Lennie Niehaus, himself a formidable saxophonist, taught the instrument to Forest Whitaker, who, his hairline shaved back and a false plate on his teeth, repro-

duced Parker's playing stance down to the hunched shoulders, though the pis-
tonlike activity of his fingers is exaggerated.

Eastwood decided that Bird, who traveled with a small ensemble of strings in
the early '50s, would have enjoyed playing with a fuller complement of strings,
and had Niehaus score "April in Paris" for 20 violins and cellos. Bird is shown
playing it during a triumphant tour of France in an especially deft sequence.
While Parker's solo continues on the soundtrack, the film cuts to the end of the
performance, as Bird bows and a cheering audience pelts him with flowers.
Then, viewed from the rear of the stage, Bird lifts a rose to his lips and consumes
a petal. That night an expatriate musician, loosely based on the New Orleans–
born Sidney Bechet, who became a national hero in France, tries to convince
Parker to leave the United States for good. "I'm not running from my own
country," Bird says. "Your country?" "Mine! whether they like it or not, mine."

The turning point in Eastwood's own career came in 1964, when he left his
country to shoot a western in Europe for an unknown Italian director. "I had a
few months hiatus from *Rawhide*, and the guy at my agency said that the Rome
office wanted me to do a film in Spain. It was an Italian-Spanish-German
production. I said, No way, I'm not interested. I do a western every week here in
this country. He said, Do me a favor and just read it. I said okay, figuring I'd give
it 20 pages. I started reading it—it was called *The Magnificent Stranger*—and I
said, Gee, I know this story. At about page 30, I realized it was *Yojimbo*, which I
had seen a few years before down on Western Avenue at a theater that specialized
in Japanese films. I thought, This is good, the way they changed it from the
samurai, and I told the agent to see what he could find out about the director.
They negotiated with the Japanese, because it was a dead steal, and it became *A
Fistful of Dollars*."

From the beginning, Eastwood took control of his character, cutting out
dialogue "by the carload, big paragraphs." Sergio Leone, the director, was puzzled but finally came around, though the producer thought Eastwood was mad:
"Sergio and I agreed and we philosophized about it, but the producer thought,
My God, this guy isn't saying anything. But I was trying to build something. I
thought that my character should be a figure of mystery and let everybody else
talk and ramble about him." He made two sequels with Leone, *For a Few Dollars
More* and *The Good, the Bad, and the Ugly*, which were international box office
hits. But it wasn't until he returned to America that he began to shape the details
for a new kind of film hero—a laconic, invariably homeless (when he does have
a home, it is soon defiled) avenger, capable of murderous zeal and seductive
tenderness, doomed to haunt—quite literally, in some instances—a treacherous
land.

There is no bleaker view of the mythic American west than the trilogy of
westerns Eastwood directed: *High Plains Drifter*, *The Outlaw Josie Wales*, and
Pale Rider. They constitute, along with Robert Altman's *McCabe and Mrs.*

Miller and *Buffalo Bill and the Indians,* the one significant contribution to the genre since Sergio Leone and Sam Peckinpah (*Ride the High Country, The Wild Bunch*) replaced the twilight westerns of John Ford and Howard Hawks with visions of crazed hired killers and balletic bloodbaths. Eastwood's films, with their religious symbolism and moral quandaries, depict communities rotting from the inside, presided over by lethal hucksters who justify every atrocity with acclamations of free enterprise. Leone's westerns made Eastwood famous as a bounty hunter, the epitome of capital gone sour, but as Josie Wales he is the quarry of bounty hunters. Edward Fitzgerald wrote, "I sent my Soul through the Invisible,/ Some letter of that After-life to spell;/ And by and by my soul return'd to me,/ And answered, 'I myself am Heav'n and Hell.' " Eastwood's Drifter from the high plains is a hellhound; his avenger in *Pale Rider* is heaven-sent.

"There are two American art forms," Eastwood says, "the western and jazz. It's funny how Americans don't support either of them anymore. My westerns are the way they are because of the point in history where I picked it up. John Wayne once wrote me a letter, and he wasn't very pleased about *High Plains Drifter.* He said, 'That isn't what the West was all about. That isn't the American people who settled this country.' I told him, 'You're absolutely right.' It's just an allegory, and it wasn't intended to be the west that's been told hundreds of times over by many players through the years, about pioneers and covered wagons and conflict with the various Indian nations. *High Plains Drifter* was a speculation on what happens when they go ahead and kill the sheriff and somebody comes back and calls the town's conscience to bear."

Eastwood represents something of an affront to profligate Hollywood. He started Malpaso Productions in the 1960s to counter the conspicuous waste he'd experienced while making *Where Eagles Dare* and *Paint Your Wagon,* and he's famous for bringing his films in under budget. *Bird* was shot in nine weeks and cost $10 million. In an age when most of the reigning film stars spend years cutting deals before making a picture, Eastwood is a prolific and devoted film-maker. Despite two years as mayor of Carmel (he took office for the most Eastwoodian of reasons: to get revenge on bureaucrats who used zoning laws to try and stop a building project), he has made 35 films in 25 years. He starred in 33 of them and directed 13, beginning with *Play Misty for Me,* which stands up extremely well, especially when compared with the hysterical remake, *Fatal Attraction.* He knows what his audience wants, but he hasn't let commercial pressures limit the range of his work.

Graham Greene used to insist on distinguishing between his serious novels and those he called "entertainments." Eastwood makes a similar distinction between what he calls "Clint Eastwood persona" films and personal ones. A glance at his filmography shows that he's always paired the release of his most ambitious films with those that could be considered relative sure things. The superb sex allegory *The Beguiled* was followed by *Dirty Harry;* the idyll *Breezy* by *Magnum Force;* the epic and highly successful *The Outlaw Josie Wales* by *The Enforcer;* the splendid comedy *Bronco Billy,* which won him the admiration of many skeptical critics, by the second of his blockbuster orangutan movies, *Any Which Way You Can.* While editing *Bird* in San Francisco, he spent his days starring in the fifth Dirty Harry movie, *The Dead Pool.** Yet you can't separate his works with too heavy a hand, because—as with Greene's novels and entertainments—the themes, successes, and failures overlap. Eastwood's work is remarkably consistent, and surprisingly diverse. Because he has developed an unmistakable persona, he gets away with things that few American filmmakers attempt: the sexual obsession of *Tightrope,* the depiction of cops as mindless brownshirts in *The Gauntlet,* and the Roy Rogers–Dale Evans parody in *Bronco Billy.* Even his barroom-brawler movies display a hunger for moral alternatives in a dissolute community. "I don't mind being pessimistic at times," he says. His best films have in common an underlying wit that counters pretension and vanity. He does not hesitate to bend his "persona" out of shape from time to time.

Yet, not unlike Charlie Parker, he has taken a continuous battering from American critics and enjoyed enthronement by French ones, and though he says he doesn't take the attacks personally, he's clearly pleased by the "hindsight reviews" he gets now: "It's the same with awards. I love to see people get them, and I suppose I'd be just as happy as all those people who get up there—though I don't think I'd say, You love me, you love me. But how many did Howard Hawks or Raoul Walsh get, or Edward G. Robinson and Cary Grant? Look at the reviews of a lot of classic films, even *The Wizard of Oz,* and they were scathing. But that's fine. I'm not in the award business. I'm in the movie business. My life is making movies. It's not about whether you get some stuff in the bag."

A few days later, Eastwood would be leaving for Cannes to show *Bird* at the film festival. Did he expect to take home a prize? "No, I can't be that way. There's always so many elements that come into it. I mean, you've got a film before a jury—who knows what those people will think of you? Or whether they want an American film. This is the first American film with a major studio attached to it, and that might be a bad statement." A week later the news came from Cannes. *Bird* won two awards: Forest Whitaker was named best actor, and Eastwood was given a special prize for the technical quality of the film. According to newspaper accounts, members of the audience groaned when he didn't win the director's award.

Reading about the festival, I was reminded of Eastwood's musings on the period when he returned to America after his success with the Leone trilogy. He was one of the highest-paid actors in the world, but the studio didn't want him to do anything but westerns. "It took a long time for the prejudice about me to break. I was never a product of a big flack campaign, never part of the prestige depart-

---

*Most recently, *White Hunter, Black Heart,* in some ways his most impressive film to date (he wickedly impersonates John Huston in a caustic fable about moviemaking, filmed on location in Africa), was followed by the violent cop-comedy *The Rookie.* Neither one made money.

ment of the studio. I wasn't supposed to do anything by expert predictions. There was doubt about whether I should be where I was. Then a few reviewers started saying, Don't overlook this, maybe there's something here. Maybe he's not conventionally what we consider a great performer, but there's something unconventional in what he's working at. Let's take a look at it. But most people didn't." Which was perhaps just as well. Had too many people—beyond his millions of fans—looked too closely, Eastwood might have been too self-conscious to cover as much territory as he did. His personal films continue to stand up and, in fact, look better with age. Unlike Bird, Eastwood has paced himself for a long run at his art. The day after Parker died, the phrase "Bird Lives" began appearing in subways in downtown New York. In a sense, Eastwood's film is an elaboration on that scrawl—a fan's notes, a promise fulfilled.

(October 1988)

Spiked Jazz

Spike Lee is as adept at provoking controversy as he is at self-promotion, a talent that may or may not qualify him as an endangered species in the Schwarzenegger Era, but is surely rare enough to generate protective instincts among serious filmgoers. At a *fin de siècle* tea party presided over by such mad hatters as the Diceman and Senator Helms, an artist who offends by pressing the nub of sensitive issues yet stays afloat in the mainstream seems so vulnerable to the temptations of commercialism, on the one hand, and censure, on the other, that you want to shield him from such relatively marginal distractions as philistine carping.

Lee's craving for media attention provides plenty of ammunition for his detractors. Though he eschews the normative methods of self-promotion practiced in the '80s (e.g., substance abuse, followed by visits to Betty Ford and a televised confessional; indiscreet philandering; ineffectual political posturing; rudeness to the press), he persistently invites scrutiny with intemperate interviews, pompous souvenir books, and a Keith Haring–type store devoted less to Spike's art than his logos. Yet his effusive ego seems a small price we have to pay for the films themselves. Lee is the first American filmmaker since Melvin Van Peebles to force a reckoning with black culture that goes beyond the stereotypes of victimhood, and perhaps the first since Robert Altman whose work repeatedly stimulates debate about the proprietorship of America's soul.

Lee has been willing to play the pariah à la Philip Roth—or Chester Himes—in shining light on aspects of a minority experience that the minority would rather keep to itself (especially in the relatively clumsy *School Daze*, which addresses the touchy issue of skin tone in the African-American community), and he's redefined the agenda by which whites address the culture within the culture. The *New York* magazine seer who warned that *Do the Right Thing* would stimulate race riots was the film's perfect target; the only race riot that took place was in his head and in the heads of people like him, as intended. Still, Lee's films are discussed almost exclusively in terms of what they say, while the reason audiences come alive to them has as much and probably more to do with the intrinsic pleasures of spirited moviemaking.

The look and the rhythm of *Do the Right Thing* and now *Mo' Better Blues* are rousingly individual. With cinematographer Ernest Dickerson and production designer Wynn Thomas, Lee has created a partly real, partly fabulist world of primary colors and fluid camera movements, with enough leeway to accommodate not only a diversity of ethnics and acting styles, but characterizations that range from realism to travesty. Because he sets up scenes that have the austerity and vividness of a cartoon strip, the emotions he dredges up—and underscores by elaborate tracking and odd angles—are that much more intense. Much has been made this summer of the color-coordinating in the disastrously wooden *Dick Tracy*, but the deployment of color in Lee's two most recent films is far more affecting and was achieved on a fraction of Warren Beatty's budget.

Mo' Better Blues lacks the sizzle of *Do the Right Thing*, but advances a more capacious view of community. Its uncommon theme is that of the artist who can't act beyond the obsession of his art until tragedy brings him back to the familial womb his art had helped him escape. *New York* will have to warn its readers against the movie's potential for inciting a wholesale return to middle-class values. Unhappily, *Mo' Better Blues* has been merchandised as a jazz movie, as though that were a genre onto itself. But as a movie about jazz, it is only marginally more persuasive than *Round Midnight* and not as savvy as *Bird*—to pick the two films Lee slams at every opportunity. As the son of Bill Lee, who wrote much of the score, Lee boasts that he has no excuse not to do the right thing by jazz, yet his film is knee-deep in corn: The key dramatic scene is played in the rain (as in *Round Midnight* and *Bird*); the music is invariably cropped or shortchanged (as in *Round Midnight* and *Bird*); the hero is deeply troubled (as in *Round Midnight* and *Bird*).

There is a difference, though, and it is a profound one. Along with Frank Gilroy's delightful Catskills anecdote, *The Gig*, this is a rare contemporary jazz movie that isn't about alcohol and drugs. Bleek Gilliam (Denzel Washington) is a product of Brooklyn's middle class, a serious trumpet player and composer whose world is ruled by tenacious discipline. The only complication in his life is the juggling he must do with his two lovers, the beautiful, ambitious Clarke (Cynda Williams) and the more conventional if independent Indigo (Joie Lee). Bleek is charming, but not entirely sympathetic. He's more frivolous with the women than necessary, cool to the needs of the musicians in his quintet (a mutiny ensues), yet oddly loyal to his childhood friend and inept manager, Giant (Spike Lee), a compulsive gambler. The film, which is as much about loyalty and betrayal as it is about art and obsession, tracks the unraveling of Bleek's closed world and—in an audacious montage that telescopes his reawakening as well as the conception and birth of his son—his return to the middle-class hearth. It opens and closes with parallel scenes: young Bleek forced to practice the trumpet under the acid eye of his daunting mother (Abbey Lincoln), and Bleek's son practicing under the more forbearing eyes of Bleek and his wife.

Mo' Better Blues is kept percolating by Lee's dry comedy. He is at his best directing partly improvised scenes of loud dispute. *Do the Right Thing* is a sustained showcase for droll squabbling, masking genuine dissension, which bursts to the surface in the harrowing climax. The new film is somewhat similarly constructed. The early backstage arguments over the habitual lateness of pianist Left (Giancarlo Esposito) or the long solos of saxophonist Shadow (Wesley Snipes) or Giant's incompetence are lively and funny. Those involving Giant always include references to his height. "What's size got to do with it?" he asks Shadow. In a moment of inspiration, Shadow responds, "You're always coming up short!" and the camera wheels back to catch a perfectly blocked tableau of the musicians, disgruntled and laughing. Soon enough the disputes become poisonous. Shadow's on the make for Clarke. Bleek incurs the wrath of both women when they enter the club on the same evening wearing the same red dress he'd bought them. Giant is pursued by a loan shark's enforcers who giggle insanely while breaking his fingers and worse. The exploitative club owners, Moe and Josh Flatbush (John and Nicholas Turturro), threaten suit. Finally, while belatedly coming to Giant's aid, Bleek is nearly killed by the enforcers.

The first time I saw the film, I found the violence of that last scene excessive and misplaced; the slo-mo shot of Bleek's shattered mouth spewing blood and teeth is an overt homage to Martin Scorcese, and it seemed too disruptive of the general tone of affirmation. It smacked of the familiar jazz movie convention—something terrible always happens to the man with a horn before he comes to his senses. On a second viewing, it worked for me. The central figures in *Mo' Better Blues* are rats in a maze: Catharsis leads to an exit, and not only for Bleek. Clarke succeeds as a singer, teaming up with Shadow; the punctilious Bleek emerges from a year of unruly self-pity to start anew with Indigo. Only Giant remains trapped: As best man at their wedding, he brandishes a newly broken arm. The violence also explodes the pervasive obsession with detail and numbers. This is a film in which Moe and Josh do a vaudeville tribute to the reliability of math; the loan shark Petey (Rubén Blades) and Giant are locked in a deadly embrace of wins and losses; Bleek's days are ritualized by his fanatical organization of time. The beating breaks through all the systems and the complacency they engender.

The movie's several lovely visual conceits are testimony to Lee's practiced eye: a blindingly sunny afternoon with the street covered in maple leaves in the opening and closing frame shots ("The End" is painted bright red on the street by a little girl, an epiphany in itself); exteriors with a backdrop of the Brooklyn Bridge; the wishful design of the jazz club (called unconvincingly, considering the nature of the Flatbush brothers, Beneath the Underdog); the camera whizzing between the women in red seated in the club; the cutting between Bleek and first Clarke, then Indigo, when he inadvertently calls one by the other's name in bed (in his confusion, he ultimately turns away and reaches for his trumpet); and the bravura child-is-father-to-the-man montage, including detailed obstetrics. The musical score is most effective in the later scenes. Bleek's only really cogent solo (Terence Blanchard plays the trumpet parts) is played during the attack on Giant; a superb reading of Ornette Coleman's "Lonely Woman" by Branford

Marsalis on the soundtrack gives immeasurable weight to his rapprochement with Indigo. The long closing montage is set to the first movement of Coltrane's *A Love Supreme*.

With one exception, the performances are admirable. Washington, who may be incapable of indifferent work, isn't given the star treatment here; he's usually photographed in ensemble style with the other actors, and though he exerts considerable control through the force of his talent, he doesn't dominate the film, much to his and the director's credit. Esposito, a Lee regular, creates an amusing characterization as pianist Left Hand Lacey, who sports a porkpie hat, spectacles with a dangling ribbon, an earring, slicked hair, and a grin that could cream cheese. Dick Anthony Williams (whose lead performance in Joseph Dolan Tuotti's *Big Time Buck White* was a theatrical cause célèbre in the '60s) has one of his most nuanced and moving roles as Bleek's father.

Yet the actor likely to get the most mileage from *Mo' Better Blues* is Wesley Snipes, who gives Shadow a powerful presence throughout; he looks more comfortable on the bandstand than the others, and is equally compelling loosing rage or spinning flattery. The late Robin Harris is on hand as the intermission comedian, Butterball, and though his shtick is old, his execution is winning. (Lee wisely thought better about adding more old shtick. According to the published script, which differs greatly from the film, he wanted the bassist and drummer, played by Bill Nunn and Jeff Watts, to do an ancient black vaud routine, in which each answers the other's phrase. The threadbare punch line is "That's what I like about you and me. We complement each other like the drum and the bass.") Only Cynda Williams's Clarke disappoints; she looks fine in her big scene as a singer, but her line readings are fatally coy, whether she's on her feet or back.

Mo' Better Blues is flawed, and one of its central failings is musical. Why did Lee write a movie about a trumpet player when he obviously idolizes Coltrane and allows tenor saxophones to dominate the soundtrack? Since Bleek is never allowed to manifest a really potent musical personality, he remains at more of an emotional distance than he should. "I've got my own voice," he insists at one point (shades of Jimmy Stewart's Glenn Miller), but too often he picks up the trumpet just to have the camera cut away before he can play anything. When he finally unleashes a bursting solo, during the scene in which Giant is pummeled in the alley, you wonder why he hasn't been cutting loose like that for the past 90 minutes. At one point, he makes an elaborate bandstand introduction to an alleged blues, but the piece he plays is 16 bars of church chords, and only Shadow gets to embellish it.

The movie opens with an ominous theme for strings that suggests nothing of the jazz ambience to follow, and closes with a group called Gangstar doing a stale rap number about famous jazz musicians. I was reminded of the closing credits of *The Glenn Miller Story*, in which the big band themes are played by Hollywood strings. A jazz equivalent of the exhilarating dancer who opens *Do the*

Right Thing would have been more in keeping with Lee's professed devotion to the music. Mo' better jazz would have made this a mo' better movie—none of the bandstand numbers has anything like the kinetic excitement of the "Lester Leaps In" in *Bird*. When it comes to trusting the music to tell its own story, Lee has more in common with Bertrand Tavernier and Clint Eastwood than he wants to admit. The one extended performance is a parody of radio-play music, called "Pop Top 40"—fine for what it is, but out of character for the movie. It's the one scene in which you know you're watching Denzel Washington, gifted actor, and not Bleek Gilliam, uptight trumpet player with a control problem.

There are minor problems in continuity as well. At a party, Bleek goes off on a tangent about the low turnout among blacks at jazz clubs. That's true of life, but not of the movie. Every time the camera pans the audience at Beneath the Underdog, we see a predominantly black crowd. Also, we never learn what Bleek does to support himself after he leaves the jazz scene. Does he write arrangements, compose, teach, live off his wife? A single line of voiceover dialogue in the wedding scene could have cleared this up.

Finally, there is the crude characterization of Moe and Josh, which is bound to bring accusations of anti-Semitism for the good reason that the portrayal is undoubtedly anti-Semitic. The insult is amplified by the fact that the actors are Italian, as were many of the jazz club owners in New York, from the Harlem Renaissance to 52nd Street to the heyday of the Five Spot and the Half Note. What is gained by pointedly characterizing them as Jewish? The most widely known Jewish club owners—Max Gordon, Art D'Lugoff, and Barney Josephson, who opened the first integrated nightclub in the country in 1938 and was red-baited for it—are not generally thought of as shekel-counting vampires with pallid skins and a vocabulary of *doo-doo* and *ca-ca*. Lee ought to ask his friend Max Roach, who spoke so eloquently at the memorial service for Gordon, about the dangers of stereotyping, though I'd have thought he could figure that out for himself. And what are we to make of the name Flatbush, which doesn't exist as a patronymic, only as a neighborhood in which many Jews reside? Nevertheless, I confess the Turturros are so good at what they do that I didn't mind the intended offense as much as I should. *Mo' Better Blues* remains a foxy, original, and moving film.

(August 1990)

ADDENDUM: Accusations of anti-Semitism followed with predictable speed and overstatement, and my review was occasionally quoted as an example of someone who recognized the slight yet forgave the movie. I don't for a minute believe Spike Lee is anti-Semitic. But I do think he cringed from dealing seriously with an issue that causes great consternation yet is studiously avoided by the very artists who might illuminate it. The subject of black anti-Semitism might make a powerful movie for Lee—better for him to explore it in depth than to cultivate smug caricatures.

Because of recent eruptions in New York, lovingly fanned by nihilistic activists (an oxymoron, true, but a fair enough characterization of the Reverend Sharpton and his Rosencrantz and Guildenstern legal aides) and an obsequious press, the assumption is widespread that black resentment of Jews is a new wrinkle in the barbarous history of racial and religious distrust, a perversion of the historic solidarity between two aggrieved minorities. Yet the one novel to shrewdly and imaginatively assess the problem is Chester Himes's *Lonely Crusade*, which was published in 1947 and was condemned so heatedly by blacks, Jews, labor leaders, Communists, industrialists, and everyone else that Himes was ultimately hounded out of the country. His book was virtually unavailable in the United States for nearly 40 years.

More than 20 years later, the subject was raised tenuously on the Jewish side by Saul Bellow, who, in *Mr. Sammler's Planet* (an otherwise providential comedy), caricatures the new black as a menacing enigma brandishing his cock; and by Bernard Malamud, who, in *The Tenants* (another comedy, though less effective), pairs an educated Jewish writer with a self-taught and possibly crazed black writer. In both instances, the Jew had better watch his back. Which is pretty much what Lee Gordon, the protagonist in Himes's novel, feels about the Jews. Himes examines Gordon's paranoia in a canny dialogue with the communist Abe Rosenberg (Rosie) in chapter 13, but also points toward reconciliation in the penultimate chapter 31. The crux of his explanation for black resentment is economical. "Just what is back of all this growing anti-Semitism among the Negro people, anyway?" Rosenberg asks.

> "Now I can answer you," Lee replied, "and frankly, Rosie, just two things—contact and attitude. Most of the Negro contact with the business world is with the Jew. He buys from the Jew, rents from the Jew, most of his earnings wind up, it seems, in the Jew's pocket. He doesn't see where he's getting value in return. He pays too much rent, too much for food, and in return can't do anything for the Jew but work as a domestic or the like."
> "That is only in cities and—"
> "That is only where anti-Semitism exists among Negroes, also."

In 1970, Himes, interviewed at length at his home in Spain by John A. Williams (see Williams's impressive essay collection, *Flashbacks*), elaborated on his own ambivalence about black anti-Semitism: "Most of the white people I do business with, who help me, whom I love and respect, are Jews. But that doesn't negate the fact that the Jews are the ones who had contact with the blacks and took advantage of them. Now the gentiles had enslaved the blacks and worked them as beasts, but when they were freed, the gentiles didn't want to have a damn thing to do with them. They left the blacks without food or shelter. They worked them for a pittance and that was all. Whereas the Jew realized that to house and feed the freed black man was a business . . . because where else could Jews, who were in a ghetto themselves, open up any kind of business and have customers, other than in the black ghetto."

In short, as Williams himself suggests, a certain amount of familiarity bred contempt. Yet I suspect that the facile black anti-Semitism observed in recent flare-ups, not unlike the empty-headed racism of white youths who taunt black protesters with watermelons, has less to do with historic grudges than with the peculiar role Jews and African-Americans play in the urban media. Each group brandishes its historic victimhood as a means of warding off all criticism, thereby inviting the louts to thumb their noses. Jews are better at it, of course, having the Holocaust as an all too recent, if sadly fading, memory with which to allay dissent. But Jews also have thinner skins (absence of melanin?), and as such are ideal targets for nihilistic black activists. Attack the tribes of D. W. Griffith or John Ford for spreading racism in the movies, and nobody stirs. Attack the Jews for the same crime, and you get your picture in the papers for days.

All of which might add up to a terrifying comedy thoroughly suited to the talents of Spike Lee. He might even find his script in *Lonely Crusade*. With the Flatbush brothers, though, he doesn't address the issue. He merely snickers—not unlike those pitiful young gentiles in Brooklyn who greet African-American protests by hoisting watermelons.

Buffalo Bob and
the Van Goghs

Perhaps no decade in American film is so identified with one filmmaker as the '70s are with Robert Altman, notwithstanding his conspicuous dearth of blockbuster hits. He was a 45-year-old director of TV episodes with a generally unimpressive résumé in the movies (only the 1968 *Countdown* suggests something of what was to come) when he and scriptwriter Ring Lardner, Jr., conjured *M*A*S*H*, a blistering antiwar comedy in which irreverence borders on misanthropy. It was in every sense a director's film, and a stylistic coup at that. Altman guided a large and idiosyncratic cast through a beguiling whirl of roving cameras, multiple soundtracks, and precipitous gore, at a tempo that seems less a corollary of film-and-edit craftsmanship than of free-falling spontaneity. It was the right film at the right time, a prize-winning smash that in effect sponsored the more rewarding Altman audacities that followed. With rare exceptions, he was the one filmmaker who sustained the rage and satiric howl of the '60s in an age of alfalfa sprouts and EST. He undermined genres and revitalized them, inventing at least one of his own in the process.

In *Nashville* and *A Wedding*, he perfected the movie equivalent of the discursive fable—the apologue, to borrow a term the critic M. M. Liberman resurrected in describing Katherine Anne Porter's *Ship of Fools*. "As an apologue," he wrote, "it not only has the right, it has the function by its nature to 'caricature' its actors, to be 'saturnine,' to have a large cast, to be 'fragmented' in its narration, and above all, to quote [Wayne] Booth again, to achieve 'unity based on theme and idea rather than coherence of action . . . [to have] no steady center of interest except the progressively more intense exemplification of its central truth.' " I know of no better description of the Altman method, which for me reaches its most satisfying fruition not in *Nashville*, but in the gamier alternate worlds of *McCabe and Mrs. Miller, The Long Goodbye, Thieves like Us, California Split*, and the curiously neglected *Buffalo Bill and the Indians*.

The problem Altman posed for audiences, beyond the insolence of adducing new contexts for vintage presumptions, was a way of looking at dramatic action without the reassuring cause and effect of conventional plotting. His work is often faulted for a lack of narrative tension, much as Ornette Coleman's improvisations are assailed for the absence of predetermined harmony. The comparison, I think, is apt: Plot and harmony are the requisite ingredients—schemes that keep you on track even when your attention fades—that make movies and music relatively easy pleasures. The only way to listen to Coleman is to follow him note for note, because there are no fixed resolutions to anchor you. The only way to watch Altman is to immerse yourself in his busy textures, scene by scene, trusting them to exemplify a central truth.

It amuses me that Altman affects a goatee not unlike Buffalo Bill's. In his film about Colonel Cody, he is as absorbed in the birth of "the show business" as he is in debunking Bill, which had already been done, not least by e. e. cummings. Just as there is something of the Wild West Show in Altman's films (sets that are virtually jerrybuilt communities), there is something of the irascible faker in Altman, who strives for the illusion of reality while luxuriating in the expression of sheer invention.

The films that apparently ended Altman's '70s roll were the twin dinosaurs of 1980: *Popeye*, a technical exercise bound to an insubstantial idea that was spurned by the critics but embraced by a large public, and the more interesting *H.E.A.L.T.H.*, spurned by everyone and barely released, which comes to fleeting comic life only in the performances of Carol Burnett and Alfre Woodard and is otherwise mired in a tone of curdled satire, or contempt. Altman's subsequent decade in the wilderness is not so bleak as is generally thought. He turned to the theater and the opera and filmed a series of plays, some to little effect, others with sufficient bravura to successfully enliven restrictive material, notably his one-man Nixon rant, *Secret Honor*. In TV, however, he found himself again, applying the real/fake techniques of video news to resuscitate *The Caine Mutiny Court Martial*, and bringing off the compulsively watchable six-hour saga of a presidential campaign, *Tanner '88*. Here is Altman revived—the shifty camera, the multitrack soundboard, the tiers of activity, the fierce wit moderated by a sympathetic tone, the indisputable control of his material.

Now we have his first feature film in three years, which appears to be something of a love child of TV and the movies. *Vincent & Theo*, a study of the van Gogh brothers, was conceived and executed as a four-hour miniseries for television, but Altman accepted the project with the stipulation that he could cut a feature film at the same time. It was broadcast in London in August, two months after the theatrical version opened. Though the film is intended to stand on its own, the question remains—and will remain unanswerable until the TV version is shown here in a year or two—as to how marginal the missing footage is. What can be said with certainty is that Altman has managed to be Altman, and that his take on the most familiar story in all of art history is original, mystifying, often sumptuous, and generally fascinating. The themes of madness (*Images*), commerce (*McCabe*), friendship (*The Long Goodbye*), alienation (*Brewster McCloud*), art (*Nashville*, *Buffalo Bill*), and obsession (*California Split*) are familiar enough, but the style is one of methodical intimacy—as though the bad boys of the art world put Hollywood's bad boy under a spell.

All but a handful of scenes in Julian Mitchell's script are structured around two or three characters, and most of the film (this is strictly true of the first hour) alternates episodes from Vincent's life with those from Theo's. Their infrequent confrontations usually end in arguments. It's a nervous, quirky film (dilatory scenes are juxtaposed with terse ones) and strangely subdued. The camerawork is full of fluid moves, casual passes, and unassuming zooms (Jean Lepine is the cinematographer), yet a mood of deliberation is constant, as though Altman were listening past the myth for a clue that might make sense of the tragically bound brothers. When the prostitute Sien (Jip Wijngaarden) walks out on Vincent, the film repeatedly cuts between her leavetaking and the dissolution of Theo's affair with a woman. Similarly, Vincent's disastrous break with Gauguin (Wladimir Yordanaoff in a cagey and original performance) is set against Theo's marriage to Jo Bonger (Johanna ter Steege, who looks like a Vermeer come to life). Each, in extremis, screams the other's name.

The focus on Theo is Altman's central contribution to the story. As the frustrated, syphilitic curator of a gallery, Theo barely ekes out a living for himself yet supports his older brother, whose work he cannot sell. As played by Paul Rhys, Theo is effeminate, high-strung, devoted. When he's most restive, Vincent is oddly serene. But there isn't much serenity in either of their lives, and perhaps the most disturbing element of *Vincent & Theo* is the reluctance to extend any hope to them. Theo died a few months after Vincent, and Altman represents his final moment as a desperate cry from what appears to be a madman's cell. (So far as I know, Theo died in a hospital; if Altman intended the final image as a metaphor, it's an unsettling departure from the general verisimilitude.)

The film's primary focus is, as it must be, on Vincent, though less as an artist than as a man with a monumental gift. There is a difference: Kirk Douglas's Vincent was violently antisocial, but everything about him—especially his yearning—was bigger than life, so while he and Vincente Minnelli kept faith with the facts in *Lust for Life* (more than Irving Stone had done in his novel), the character loomed as a tortured genius with all the romantic implications.

Tim Roth's Vincent is, by contrast, as small as one of van Gogh's harvesters making his way across the horizon. His eyes are darting bullets, his teeth and tongue blackened by paint (his Vincent moistens the brush with his tongue), his pipe a kind of doorstop that helps him keep his temper when he can. Kirk Douglas once outraged Hollywood publicists by declaring his motivation to be repressed homosexuality. Altman, repressing nothing, has Roth kiss Gauguin in his desperation to keep him in the yellow house. This Vincent slips determinedly into madness, sucking up turpentine, agonizing over the pain in his ears, cutting off one lobe and flirting with the idea of amputating the other.

By the end of the film, Altman has created such distance between Vincent and the audience that he seems to be insisting on the right of an artist to go to hell by any route he chooses and declaring absolute discontinuity between the man who makes the art and the art itself, which ultimately has a separate life anyway. *Vincent & Theo* begins in 1987, with an actual film clip of the auction of *The Sunflowers* for £22,500,000, and fades back to Vincent's decision to become a full-time painter. In a different kind of film that might make for hamfisted irony, but in light of the world Altman (who shot on location at the appropriate sites in France and Holland) unveils, the auction looms even larger as a sign of a madness that all but dwarfs the agonies of the van Goghs.

Although Altman devotes much time to the breaking off with Gauguin (the anecdote is probably a precondition for any van Gogh dramatization), he generally targets different aspects of the life, as well as of the art, than Minnelli. Minnelli's art direction strove for a world that mirrored van Gogh's paintings; time and again, he shows you a model or a setting designed to remind you of a famous painting—the implication is that all Vincent needed was good draftsmanship to get it all down. Altman tends to ignore the paintings—we see them almost exclusively in the background, on the walls of Theo's gallery or in Vincent's house. A couple of instructive scenes, including a pan of the students' work at the Atelier Cormon, where van Gogh studied in Paris, place Vincent in opposition to the conventions of the day, but the film exhibits a nearly chaste refusal to presume on the privacies of art. Like Clint Eastwood's much-maligned *Bird*, it presumes the audience's sophistication.

Vincent & Theo also ignores information that would provide a deeper understanding, all of it covered by Minnelli. We hear little of the van Gogh parents, and nothing of Vincent's ruinous love for his cousin Kee or his ministerial labors in the Borinage. I'm more surprised that Altman, like Minnelli, ignored the Parisian affair with a barmaid that led to van Gogh's most erotic work, though we do see Vincent in a brothel, confessing his impotence to a whore. And I'm bewildered by Altman's decision to ignore the letters, much referred to but never quoted, which convey almost as great a generosity of spirit as the paintings. Perhaps all of that is covered in the miniseries. The acting is generally convincing, and much of it is striking, though the sound mix and motley of accents (Roth's near-cockney is startling at first, but you get used to it) obscures a few lines. Jean-Pierre Cassel is memorable as Dr. Gachet, displayed here as a pontificating bourgeois who stockpiles art in a vault.

It may be said that *Vincent & Theo* is less concerned with stockpiling facts than canvassing an accumulation of insights through the crafting of a time, place, and mood that allows the van Goghs to leap out of history in all their ungainly glory. Altman's comment on the inability to tether genius to its human form is suggested in the painting with which the film opens and closes. The camera advances resolutely (Gabriel Yared's percussive music thunders on the soundtrack) into the brush strokes surrounding Vincent's signature, until all narrative meaning is left behind and all that is retained is a fury of activity, unknown and unknowable.

(November 1990)

PART II

DIVAS

Lady Gets Her Due

Lady Day is unquestionably the most important influence on American popular singing in the last 20 years.
                                                                Frank Sinatra, 1958

And yet the matter of influence seems almost academic today. Sinatra was speaking a year before Billie Holiday died, at 44, when countless singers considered themselves directly in her debt, and when her gutted voice, drawled phrasing, and wayworn features were widely construed as evidence of a self-immolating decline. Now the verdict is less dependent on what we know of her story and more on what we perceive in her music. Now it's obvious that, like Lester Young, whose career closely paralleled hers, Holiday managed to achieve two discrete musical styles in a short, calamitous life. That their later styles were forged in reaction to outrageous fortunes is a fact that continues to offend naive listeners who look to art for limitless innocence and youth. Holiday's later recordings are all the proof we need of her ability to transfigure hurt and confusion into theme and variation. Had she been able to sing "What a Little Moonlight Can Do" at the end of her life as she did at 20, she wouldn't have been much of an artist—she'd have been what Young contemptuously called a "repeater pencil."

Holiday's influence can be calibrated in the language of musical technique: in her use of legato phrasing, ornamentation, melodic variation, chromaticism. But musicology doesn't suggest the primary impact of her singing, which is emotional. Even in her apprentice years as the golden girl in a man's world, taking no more than the single chorus allotted each instrumentalist and transcending the material no less completely, her technique was limited by any conventional standard, blues or bel canto. As Paul Bowles wrote in 1946, "One of the chief charms in Miss Holiday's art is that she makes absolutely no attempt to approach any of the elements of art singing, at the same time cannily making the most of all the differences that exist between that and her own quite personal style." Despite a thin voice and a range of about 15 notes, she overpowered musicians and listeners with multilayered nuances: She embellished melodies, tailoring them to her own needs and limitations; lagged behind the beat, imparting suspense; harmonized well beyond the ground chords of the composition, projecting a bright authority; and inflected words in a way that made even banal lyrics bracing. Bessie Smith and Louis Armstrong adapted blues and improvisational devices to pop songs, but it was Holiday who pushed their achievement into the realm of unmitigated intimacy. Hers was the art of reflection.

Holiday's craftsmanship rarely failed her, but her subjects—the world and her appetites—often did, and latter-day Holiday was formed in part by those failings. Some of her last records, recorded when her instrument was worn to the nerve endings, are disastrous, yet the overwhelming body of work from her last 15 years is as rewarding as jazz singing gets. The early records expel a golden-age sheen of sunny rhythms and instrumental bravura; later records are built entirely around the singer. The tempo is slower, the ambience more conversational. But her alterations remain provocative and full of surprise; her enunciation is, if anything, more compelling, the emotions urgent. The differences between early and late Holiday are illuminated by a comparison of the Columbias (1933–42), many of them contracted and originally released under pianist Teddy Wilson's name, and the Verves (1952–59); each series evokes a dramatically different mood. The Verves are by no means a qualitative reduction of the Columbias, and a listener could no more confuse their respective values than those of Beethoven's early G-major and late A-minor string quartets. The artist has *changed*, no matter whether the cause was heroin addiction or deafness.

The change in Holiday's case took place during the decade between those two major label affiliations, beginning in 1942. That was the year she apparently began using hard drugs to alleviate difficulties with her first husband, an addict she had married the previous year. It was also in 1942 that she worked two months at Billy Berg's Trouville Club in West Hollywood with the brothers Lee and Lester Young, during which gig she first met Jimmy Rowles, the group's pianist and sole white member (Lester had to assure her "this cat can blow"), and the young producer of the club's jam sessions, Norman Granz. After recording "Travelin' Light" with Paul Whiteman, a major hit from which she received no royalties, she spent a few months in Chicago and had her first encounter with the police. Those events set the pattern for the rest of her life—triumph alternating with catastrophe.

She recorded for Milt Gabler, first at Commodore with written band arrangements, then at Decca, where she became the first jazz singer to use strings, a gamble that paid off handsomely in such milestone performances as "Lover Man," "Good Morning, Heartache," "Don't Explain," "No More," "Ain't Nobody's Business if I Do," and "God Bless the Child." Underappreciated (she never won a *Down Beat* poll) and underpaid, Holiday may have felt that the complement of strings flattered her desire to climb a few rungs in the status of mainstream show biz. In any case, the Deccas can be seen today as transitional recordings. Her voice, still in full bloom, met the challenge of the imposing repertoire, but the staid settings diluted the expressive content of her singing.

The addiction began to take over. Her marriage broke up, and she canceled engagements, yet she remained unbowed. Although she seemed to be retreating from life, she asserted herself in ever bolder directions—embarking in 1946 on her first solo concerts (the second of which was recorded as part of Granz's Jazz at the Philharmonic package); undertaking an acting role in the disgraceful 1947 movie *New Orleans* as a maid (she walked out in the middle of filming); and hooking up with the superb accompanist Bobby Tucker. In 1947, she took a voluntary cure for addiction, but a few weeks after her release she resumed her habit and was arrested in Philadelphia and sentenced to a year and a day at the Alderson Reformatory in West Virginia. She served nine and a half months.

Upon release, she returned to New York for a glorious concert at Carnegie Hall. Newspapers that previously ignored her singing now sensationalized her troubles, a few radio stations blacklisted her, and New York City refused her a cabaret card (Mayor La Guardia's odious cabaret law remained in effect until 1967), which meant she could never again sing in a New York room that served liquor. The only work she could get was on the road or in theaters. More arrests followed, though none of them stuck. The bad publicity tripled, then quadrupled, her salary; yet in 1950, a *Down Beat* hack referred to her as "Lady Yesterday." She continued to cast dangerous playmates in the role of Lover Man, resulting in betrayals and beatings; her second husband, the unmourned John Levy (not to be confused with the respected bassist-turned-manager of the same name), framed her on a drug rap, which she beat—though the cost was permanent insolvency. After Decca dropped her in 1951, she made one session for Aladdin, which yielded the sublime torment of "Detour Ahead," and drifted until Norman Granz signed her to his Mercury label (the parent of Clef and Verve) a year later. Except for one Columbia album, Granz supervised her records for the remaining seven years of her life.

Since 1970 a producer named Akira Yamoto has worked with the Japanese affiliates of American labels to release every record Billie Holiday ever made. None of these issues has been imported to the United States; the Commodores and Deccas are available anyway, many Columbias aren't. Yamoto recently completed his project with *Billie Holiday on Verve 1946–1959*, a box of 10 records that PolyGram is importing at a retail price of about $100. I have some quibbles about presentation, but this is one of the most satisfying compilations ever produced. Its 135 performances, which constitute an anthology of Holiday's favorite songs, are extremely uneven, including much of her best work, along with painful sessions recorded when she could barely summon the energy to enunciate or stay in tune. Despite all the lapses, mannerisms, and clichés—at least 25 songs end with her most overworked tic, the interval of a ninth or major second down to the tonic—there isn't a side I'm not pleased to have. Nor do I feel morbid or sentimental in saying that. The musical elation she affords is often inseparable from the tension of hearing a great artist wrestle with and frequently surmount technical and personal cumbrances. The great thing about Billie Holiday is that she never stopped wrestling.

Consider two performances: the 1952 "These Foolish Things" (which André Hodier singled out for praise) and the 1956 "All or Nothing at All" (which John Chilton singled out as "the nadir"). In the earlier recording, her voice is strong and the inspiration of the opening paraphrase is sustained throughout the chorus; in the later one, she's hoarse and her variations are occasionally tremulous. Yet in both instances the overriding impression is of a singer intent on making the songs her own, of an artist refusing to accede to what Holiday called "close-order drill." She feels her way through both songs, refurbishing melodies and lifting rhythms, and if her artistic control is indisputable in "These Foolish Things," as it surely is, "All or Nothing at All" is compelling as well—she consistently takes risks, as in the extremely legato swing of the release.

For all but one of the Verve albums, Holiday returned to a setting that superficially resembled her Columbia recordings. Once again she was surrounded by an intimate coterie of brilliant improvisers. The resemblance stops there. The tempos have stalled to a medium nod-time, fit for ruminating, often sensuous. The singing is economical, and so are the arrangements, which were mostly improvised. Instead of a couple of wind instruments escorting her through the harmonies, as on many of the Teddy Wilson classics, she is most frequently heard in dialogue with one soloist. (Harry Edison's obbligati throughout are beyond praise.) Holiday draws you into these songs: They are translucent baubles held to the light and languidly examined. And whereas once she transcended silly lyrics with the intensity of her rhythmic and melodic skills, now she makes them work for her. Every stanza seems autobiographical. When she was 20, in 1935, she made "What a Little Moonlight Can Do" a rowdy jaunt, precocious and exhilarating; 22 years later, worn down by numberless ills, she makes a valiant and winning effort to sing it for the crowd at Newport, and for the first time you hear the words and suddenly what is banal on paper—"You only stutter 'cause your poor tongue/ Just will not utter the words/ I love you"—is jarring in performance.

The earliest session, her 1946 appearance at a JATP concert in Los Angeles, represents Holiday at her best. Her conceits on "The Man I Love" are as ingenious as those on the Columbia version, although this time Lester Young's contribution is confined to an obbligato in the second chorus. Listen to the way she glides over "seems absurd," or rushes "someday, one day," or bends "my" over two notes. The 1952 and 1954 studio sessions are ornamented with masterly work by Charlie Shavers and Flip Phillips, though the heavy-handed Oscar Peterson is inattentive to her needs. It hardly matters; nothing could bring Holiday down when she was singing this well. In 1955, she was chaperoned by a more orderly Tony Scott ensemble (with Shavers at his peak) and consistently worthy material. She freely reharmonizes key phrases in "Always" and "Ain't Misbehavin'," italicizes the witty lyric of "Everything Happens to Me" (note the inflection on "measles" and the percussive push on "thought you could break this jinx for me"), adds the verse to her classic "I Wished on the Moon," and debuts the first of two sublimely personal versions of "Do Nothin' till You Hear from Me," on which Budd Johnson perfectly echoes her disposition.

Perhaps the best sessions are those with Jimmy Rowles, Harry Edison, and either Benny Carter (his "What's New" improvisation is a song in its own right) or Ben Webster (wailing on the second and superior "Do Nothin' "). In the '70s, a small label released a taped rehearsal conversation between Holiday and Rowles; she exclaims, "It's a pleasure working with you again. Jesus Christ! I've been with some pretty big shots, and they don't dig me no kinda way." On the Verves, Rowles trails her like a bloodhound, his footing as savvy and sure as hers—for examples, "Day In, Day Out" and "I Didn't Know What Time It Was" (with verse). Edison (who was Sinatra's preferred trumpet player during the same period) is startling, booting her final chorus on "I Get a Kick out of You," feeding her shots on "One for My Baby," answering her every phrase on "Do Nothin'." Holiday occasionally sounds exhausted, but she regularly comes up with fresh twists, such as the curtailed rest at the opening of a shyly romantic "Isn't This a Lovely Day?" A 1956 session with Tony Scott and Wynton Kelly is sluggish, and the big band album with Ray Ellis, recorded four months before her death on July 17, 1959, can be a trying experience. The voice is haggard, though its soulful cry still penetrates. I find several of these performances deeply moving.

Billie Holiday on Verve comes with a 39-page booklet that includes the most comprehensive discography to date, plus a list of album compilations and four cardboard facsimiles of 10-inch album jackets designed by David Stone Martin. This is the kind of loving production that gives a remarkable artist her due even as it shames the relative negligence and unimaginativeness of American labels. Still, I mentioned quibbles, and they include the singular unattractiveness of the box (the drawing of Holiday has a nose that more closely resembles her Chihuahua's); countless typographical errors; the senseless segregation of her live performances on two final discs (the other sessions are presented chronologically); the deletion of Gilbert Millstein's fine readings from her autobiography at the 1956 concert (you have to buy *The Essential Billie Holiday* to hear them); the absence of a song list with dates and personnel (you have to annotate the booklet to keep from constantly flipping its pages); and poor liner notes rendered poorer by a pidgin English translation—surely PolyGram could have justified the expenditure of a few hundred dollars for an English-speaking proofreader.

When it comes to jazz, domestic indifference has rendered the United States a colony of Japan—and of England. Last year, the BBC broadcast a 98-minute documentary called *The Long Night of Lady Day* that is far and away the best film ever made about her. A wave of interest in Holiday crested in 1972 with the release of Hollywood's unspeakable and slanderous *Lady Sings the Blues*. Diana Ross won't be around to confuse the issue, should that tide return in the wake of the BBC film and the Verve project. Perhaps the recent homages to Edith Piaf on TV and in the theater will now spill over to our own diva of vernacular heartaches. I've often suspected that Piaf was an easy object of mawkish veneration because her problems reflect on another country. Holiday's tragedy reflects the racist Philistinism of our own time and place. Her mature recordings remain controversial not least because they vividly incarnate her indictment of the world, as well as the spirit and dignity she sustained through all its blows. *

(October 1985)

*Recently Columbia issued all the Holiday records from the years 1933 to 1942 on nine compact discs. The sound of the early ones is icily inexpressive but improves as the series continues. A three-CD Holiday compilation was subsequently released by the label as *The Legacy*. The selections, originally masterminded by John Hammond for the juke-box trade, are largely indispensable and include most but not all the high points ("When You're Smiling," "Sugar," and "It's a Sin to Tell a Lie" have been passed over for inferior performances). A few oddities are included—an excerpt from Ellington's film short "Symphony in Black," containing Holiday's first recorded vocal—as well as two 1958 songs and the 1957 "Fine and Mellow," taken from a recording session and not the superior telecast, *The Sound of Jazz*, as claimed on the box. The compiler's notes are tastelessly autobiographical, but he is not the first and will not be the last adult reduced to a howl of reflective longing by this incomparably seductive music. The complete Verve recordings, discussed in my essay, were scheduled for release on CD in 1992.

First Lady

Ella Fitzgerald is one of a handful of preeminent jazz performers who have become public monuments, emblematic of an unquestioning national pride. She embodies jazz as a positive force even for those who pay no attention to jazz. Yet not unlike Kate Smith's or Mahalia Jackson's, her enduring authority may have more than a little to do with an image of youthless (which is to say ageless) maternalism, sturdy and implacable. Large-boned women tend to intimidate their potential detractors. Unlike Smith, whose voice was without direction or artistry, or Jackson, whose euphoric artistry was narrowly directed, Fitzgerald is principally an inspired and readily accessible entertainer—robust and swinging, if rarely cathartic. She is often exhilarating (her voice still has much of its girlish purity, stretching over a perfect two-octave midrange, and her rhythms are irresistible), but one attends her performances expecting to be moved less by introspective drama than by the contagiousness of her joy in singing.

Fitzgerald's long career is a tangle of paradoxes. The pop and songbook records notwithstanding, she is determinedly a jazz singer, yet she cannot sing the blues and tends to embroider them into banality. She is an irreproachable connoisseur of ballads, but has little talent for histrionics: The stilted Bess she presented to Armstrong's effulgent Porgy is a case in point. She is a product of the Swing Era ("A-Tisket, A-Tasket," recorded with her mentor Chick Webb, remains the biggest hit of her career) who became associated in the public's mind with bebop-inflected scat singing. (Although she makes melodic references to bop, her time and phrasing have more in common with the even 4/4 rhythms of swing players like Lionel Hampton, Coleman Hawkins, and especially Roy Eldridge, whose cross-octave improvisations may well have influenced her.) She is a black singer who names the white Connie Boswell as her primary model. She is a peerless "straight" interpreter of pop songs, and also a willful embellisher who can attack songs as though their lyrics had no more significance than scat syllables. She does not make hit records, but she works exclusively in the world's great concert halls.

In recent years, she has been ill, and her voice has lost some of its luster, its purity. The plush falsetto, once as solid and flexible as mercury, has been raked by time. At several concerts, I found myself growing impatient and leaving early. So I was caught entirely off guard by her stupendous performance at a Pablo Jazz

Festival concert at Carnegie Hall last weekend. The material was without exception superb, and the asides brief and charming. The ballads were thoughtful, the
swingers galvanizing, and the voice was brighter than I'd heard it in several years.
On a recklessly fast "Lover, Come Back to Me," she chugged along like a well-
oiled engine, roaring into a high-note conclusion with a majestic aplomb that all
but announced, renascence.

You expect to hear her in optimum circumstances—in Tommy Flanagan's
trio, she has the best accompaniment in the business. But she was additionally
inspired by the presence of the Count Basie band (without Basie). The nasal
entrance of the reeds on "My Old Flame" goaded her, and on "Mr. Paganini"
(how she makes that musty warhorse hustle!) she traded fours with Jimmy Forrest
and Al Grey, holding her own with tremendous wit and assurance. She affected
Grey's plunger sound and Forrest's grit, matching their every conceit, and when
all three began riffing in tandem and the orchestra added gleaming staccato
exclamations, the Swing Era seemed fully and unequivocally revived. There
were quieter moments, too—gentle duets with guitarist Joe Pass, as well as
selections with the trio, including two elegant and overlooked gems by Benny
Carter ("When Lights Are Low") and Duke Ellington ("I Ain't Got Nothing but
the Blues," which, of course, is not a blues). When Fitzgerald is at her most
monumental there is nothing of the monument about her.

In the beginning, no one would have thought to characterize her as, or predict
for her the status of, an icon. She was too much the lively young girl, precocious
but vulnerable, looking for her little yellow basket. Fitzgerald's performing ven-
ues and salary didn't begin to reflect her cross-generational prominence until the
mid-1950s, when she left Decca Records after a 20-year association and—under
the tutelage of her manager and producer, Norman Granz—embarked on a
series of lushly orchestrated "songbooks," each devoted to a single songwriter, for
Verve. She insisted on being recognized as an artist who sang jazz and pop, as
opposed to a jazz singer who sublimated pop to jazz biases. Some critics faulted
her versatility, complaining that she lacked Billie Holiday's uncompromising
Angst. But if she transcended the jazz audience, she never abandoned jazz
principles. The main reason the songbooks stand up so well is the rhythmic lilt
and telling embellishments with which she intuitively edits the material.

It would be a mistake, however, to assume that the more than 300 sides she cut
for Decca (about 40 of them as the vocalist with Chick Webb's orchestra) were
more rigidly conceived within the jazz idiom. Indeed, the Deccas were the most
commercially designed recordings of her career, save the dim exploitation albums of the late '60s and after, made for Capitol and Warners (i.e., Ella sings
country, Ella sings the Beatles). The first half of her career is a reflection of the
prevailing attitudes—the imaginative strengths and limitations—of the producers who operated Decca, as well as her extraordinary rapport with the musical
climate of the Depression and war years. Fitzgerald became the most popularly

acclaimed jazz singer of all time during the age of Eisenhower, but it was during the era of Little Orphan Annie that she scored her biggest hit record.

The Fitzgerald story has been told often, if elliptically. Briefly, she was born in Newport News, Virginia, in 1918, and taken to an orphanage in Yonkers, New York, after the death of her mother in the early 1930s. (Considering her renown, one can only be astounded at how little is known of Fitzgerald's early years. Her ability, shared by Armstrong and Ellington, to control the dissemination of biographical material is perhaps the one advantage to the invisibility syndrome addressed by Ralph Ellison.) In 1934, Benny Carter heard her at an amateur contest at Harlem's Apollo Theater and recommended her to several influential men in the music business, including Fletcher Henderson and John Hammond, who were unimpressed. Drummer and bandleader Chick Webb, a dwarfed hunchback, agreed to give her a try and soon assumed total responsibility for her. He became Ella's legal guardian even as he reorganized his trailblazing orchestra around her unfledged 17-year-old voice. His faith paid off three years later when her adaptation of a nursery rhyme, "A-Tisket, A-Tasket," put them on top of the heap. During the summer of 1938, that recording was omnipresent. When Webb died the following summer, Fitzgerald confirmed her loyalty by fronting the orchestra—she kept at it for three years, before going out as a single.

Except for a couple of sessions with Teddy Wilson and Benny Goodman, all the records she made between 1935 and 1955 were for Decca, a label subsequently assimilated by MCA, which allows all but a handful of its treasures to repose in its vaults. * Decca's base commercialism was typified when it induced Jascha Heifetz, during his brief sabbatical from RCA, to cover "White Christmas," the label's all-time bestseller as recorded by Bing Crosby. It was Decca's policy to integrate jazz and pop—prefiguring the present crossover cancer. The results were often charming, and just as often detestable. Fitzgerald's sessions were frequently burdened with contemptible material and banal vocal choirs, which may be why they are no longer deemed worthy of reissue. But that wouldn't explain why the superior sides, which are numerous, are also unavailable.

It's tempting to speculate about the kind of records Ella might have made for

---

*European and Australian companies have done wonders with the Decca catalogue, but in this country MCA has been content to do little more than reissue the same best-of compilations that have been available for more than three decades. Its initial attempt at a new CD series was disastrous, trumping even Sony and Bluebird in the awfulness of the digital sound. You'd think Fitzgerald would have sold enough records to inspire the company to do something worthy of the many great performances in its possession. That responsibility has been assumed elsewhere. A reissue series called Classics, manufactured in France and distributed here by Qualitron Imports, Ltd., has turned up in local stores. They've issued four CDs thus far in a series called *The Chronogical* [sic] *Ella Fitzgerald*, tracing her career from the first recording with Webb in 1935 through the June 29, 1939, session at which she took over the reigns of the orchestra after Webb's death. Excepting "Wake Up and Live" and an alternate take of "I Want to Be Happy," every record she made in that period (including the Teddy Wilsons and Benny Goodmans on Columbia) is here, with the promise of successive volumes to follow. The sound is acceptable—better, in fact, than the MCA Deccas. Grab them while you can.

Columbia in those years, when John Hammond's policy was to present Billie Holiday in small instrumental groups consisting of the most accomplished jazz musicians of the day, usually under the leadership of Teddy Wilson. Early in 1936, Fitzgerald did record two sides with Wilson. "All My Life" is a pleasantly nostalgic ballad, enunciated with a clarity worthy of Ethel Waters, even if the sensibility is relatively naive; "My Melancholy Baby" swings steadily on the beat and is enhanced by good-natured improvisatory touches. Whereas Holiday personalized a song by inflecting every phrase, Fitzgerald conveyed a purer approach, less idiosyncratic and sometimes less discerning. Benny Goodman was so impressed with her that he used her as a replacement for Helen Ward in June of that year. She gave "Goodnight, My Love" a well-phrased but formal, even stiff, reading; "Take Another Guess" unveiled the girlish, swinging Ella, though her vocal quality was thick and clouded, not yet fully formed. In those years, she accented long-vowel sounds with increased vibrato and broke words into staccato syllables to stress rhythmic impact. She had more faith in melody and rhythm than in lyrics.

By the end of 1936, she was emerging as the definitive voice of swing, performing many tunes with the words *swing* or *swinging* in the title. One of them, "Organ Grinder's Swing," was recorded at the first session under her own name—accompanied by the Savoy Eight, a contingent from the Webb band—and proved to be prophetic. It was a novelty with a childhood theme that led to several others, including "Betcha Nickel," "Chew-Chew-Chew," and, of course, "A-Tisket, A-Tasket." Of greater importance, it showed her off for the first time as an aggressively deft scat singer. In the final chorus, she riffs the phrase "Oh, organ" and outswings the band. At her third session, Decca characteristically teamed her with the popular Mills Brothers, an indication of the company's confidence in her growing success. She was still only 18.

Her voice matured greatly during the next couple of years, though her naive, on-the-beat determination abided. More often than not, the material was pitiably weak, but if Fitzgerald could not transcend it like Holiday, she could uplift it with her expressive, trumpetlike delivery—for example, "If You Should Ever Leave" or "Dipsy Doodle." On the latter, she sounds entirely oblivious to the song's abysmal lyric. She could raise temperatures on a worthy swinger like Irving Berlin's "Pack Up Your Sins and Go to the Devil," or fashionable band numbers like "If Dreams Come True" and "Rock It for Me," but she also betrayed awkwardness in those years—a bumptious quality undoubtedly exacerbated by the dire novelties that threatened to become her trademark.

The sensual lilt in her voice became more pronounced in 1939, in such memorable readings as "Don't Worry About Me" and "If I Didn't Care." With "Stairway to the Stars," her characteristic approach to ballads was codified: The first chorus was reasonably straight and the second was an exercise in swingtime, as she transfigured the key melody into a contagiously rocking riff. Yet her improvisations remained fairly predictable, and you can get a fair idea of how much she grew by comparing "Stairway" with "Soon," recorded in 1950. Once again, a forthright chorus is followed by a rhythmic one, but the voice has flowered into the very embodiment of swing phrasing—luscious and effortless.

The 1940s were undoubtedly the period of Fitzgerald's most uneven recordings, a reflection of an in-between dilemma that defined the era. Swing was losing its magic, and bop was little more than an underground workshop. Decca presented her in a series of encounters with the label's black artists—Louis Armstrong, the Ink Spots, Louis Jordan, the Delta Rhythm Boys, Sy Oliver, Bill Doggett, the Mills Brothers (again), and others. These accounted for some of her most successful records of the decade, musically as well as commercially, especially when compared with the numerous ballads she was asked to sing in collusion with lumbering string orchestras and vocal choirs under the direction of Gordon Jenkins. Fitzgerald is frequently miraculous despite the overblown settings, but the dim arrangements engulf her in a period flavor. Her thick delivery had now metamorphosed into a light and pristine style, fully at home in the greater spaciousness of her range. But it wasn't the kind of voice that could always turn dross into gold. Too often, a superficiality set in that matched the material and made her seem a brilliantly equipped hack.

Yet in many scintillating deviations from the stock ballad settings, a mature Fitzgerald was emerging—the queen of scat, the first lady of song. Her 1945 "Flying Home" was an all-scat performance that established her among the jazz modernists. She wasn't born of bop, like Sarah Vaughan, but she was thoroughly accepted into the fold. With her ear and technique, Ella was not likely to be intimidated by a flatted fifth; on the contrary, she was still in her 20s, and the new sounds of Charlie Parker and Dizzy Gillespie were a welcome source of inspiration. She thrived on it, roaring through a lexicon of bop licks on "Lady Be Good," which became one of her most requested and enduring showpieces, and on the more imaginative "How High the Moon," where she followed a straight chorus with a vigorous variation compiled equally of phrases from swing and bop.

Fitzgerald's ballads, too, reflected her enhanced improvisational powers. She displayed a penchant for altering the character of a dull phrase by raising a key note the interval of a sixth. She continued to develop her mastery of portamento, with which she would rise or fall to the proper note or, more intriguingly, begin with the written note and slide into a more colorful interval. She meshed beautifully with the Mills Brothers on a serene and enticing "I Gotta Have My Baby Back"; displayed wonderfully airy highs on "I've Got the World on a String"; exhibited the purest voice ever applied to scat on the extended novelty, "You'll Have to Swing It." It's not at all surprising, given the fullness of her recording regimen, that Fitzgerald could be drearily impersonal even with attractive material (as on "I Wished on the Moon," 1954), but when she was committed to a song ("It Might as Well Be Spring," 1955), she was luminous.

Fitzgerald recorded exclusively for Decca until 1955. The 20 sides she recorded with pianist Ellis Larkins (eight Gershwin titles in 1950, and a mixed bag in 1954) represent the culmination of that long episode in her career. I've heard singers argue that she never surpassed the collaboration with Larkins, and to be sure she achieves a sensuousness and command of the material that is, note for note, enthralling. Her voice had never sounded quite as resplendent before. Few interpretations of popular songs can match her readings of "Soon," "Someone to Watch over Me," "I've Got a Crush on You," and "How Long Has This Been Going On?" although their very excellence heightens the exasperation generated by a survey of her entire output in those years. The Gershwin sides (just enough for a 10-inch album) prefigured the hugely popular if less compelling *Cole Porter Songbook* in 1956.

The gloried monument of popular song that Fitzgerald became after she signed with Verve records coincided with the rise of TV and hi-fi, both of which repeatedly underscored her renown. The successes included eight song-books (the Ellington, Berlin, Arlen, Gershwin, and untypically concise Mercer are especially fine); a triumphant appearance in Berlin (she wore a blonde wig); collaborations with Armstrong, Ellington, and Basie; a few movie roles and frequent guest spots on television; and dozens of albums with large ensembles or intimate jazz combos. She has enjoyed an association of nearly 10 years with the outstanding pianist Tommy Flanagan. A misguided 1963 recording with her old friend Roy Eldridge (*These Are the Blues*) demonstrated her ongoing detach-ment from the funk and drama of the blues. But by then, blues were the last thing anyone associated with the First Lady of Song.

(December 1976)

A Starr Is Reborn

In a 1958 interview, writer Chris Albertson asked Lester Young if he thought "anybody nowadays" could sing like Bessie Smith. He got a surprising response: "Yeah . . . sometimes you think upon Kay Starr and listen to her voice and play one of Bessie Smith's records and see if you hear anything." A similarity? "Yes, very much," Young said. Kay Starr, best known in those days for the oxymoronic "Rock and Roll Waltz," had other admirers in the jazz world, including Dinah Washington, Helen Humes ("I think she swings from way back"), and Bud Powell, who voted her best female singer in a 1956 poll. Five years before that, the traditionalist readers of *Record Changer* voted her number six among female vocalists in its "All-time" poll (after Bessie Smith, Ma Rainey, Billie Holiday, Mildred Bailey, and Ella Fitzgerald). By the time of the Young interview, however, Starr was hardly ever discussed or reviewed in jazz circles; in subsequent years, as she and her best records dropped from sight, she was remembered chiefly for a few hits ("Side by Side," "Wheel of Fortune," "Rock and Roll Waltz") that all too neatly embodied 1950s whitewashed pop—the stuff rock and roll was supposed to puncture and sink.

My interest in Starr was roused a year ago, in Amsterdam, where I found reissues of records she made for Capitol and RCA in the '50s. When I discovered other reissues, pressed in Japan and England, turning up as imports in New York stores, I decided to write a column about her—a historical account of a neglected (and presumably retired) singer, whose most enduring work had been overshadowed by her ephemera. Then a press release arrived, announcing a three-week engagement at Freddy's Supper Club. I attended opening night with some trepidation, wanting her to recapture the prodigious zest and savvy blues-colored phrasing of the radiant and largely forgotten jazz records she made between 1945 and 1961, but fearful of hearing no more than an extended sop to lifeless nostalgia. All doubt was eclipsed about 10 seconds into her opening set.

Starr is an electrifying performer, thoroughly in command of her talent. I don't hear much Bessie Smith in her, but I can understand why Young and many others did in that decade when white girl singers tended to be cool as menthol and cute as high-buttoned shoes. She holds the stage like someone who paid her dues in tent-shows, red-hot and earthy, enthralled to a sinewy beat, unafraid to belt, jolt, wag her finger, shimmy, and tell bad jokes. Nor is there anything faded or ersatz about her exuberance, wit, and musicality. Starr has an open, lucent quality, accentuated by a wide, sexy smile and glittery eyes. For me, she represents a "new" addition to the very small pantheon of great working jazz singers.

Starr is so unabashedly consumed with the pleasures of singing, it's hard to imagine her in premature retirement: She's 63, the age Helen Humes was when she returned to duty a decade ago. Nor has she been entirely inactive. She has sung for corporations, appeared with the Summer Symphony in Los Angeles, and toured for more than two years with the nostalgia revue, *4 Girls 4* (along with Helen O'Connell, Rosemary Clooney, and Martha Raye). In every instance, she was locked by a large band into a rigidly rehearsed repertoire. Her decision to "do something for myself" followed an experience in London two summers ago, when she appeared as part of a Kool Jazz package. She explained, in characteristically breathless fashion, "It was a one-nighter in a little jazz club and when I said I would do it, I didn't know I'd have only three or four musicians. I almost had cardiac arrest. But I was able to get the drummer touring with us, Jerry White, and of course I had Frank [Ortega, her music director of 19 years], and how much trouble can you get into if you've got a good drummer? I sat there singing and before I realized what was happening to me, I felt like I'd been released or something. Just felt so free, singing and soaring and having the best time, and I didn't have anybody in my way. When I came back and started doing the normal kinds of dates, with the 18- and 25-piece bands, I suddenly was boxed in, and I thought, 'What's happening here?' And I sat down with myself and said, 'Look, what's happening is you really want to sing with a smaller group.' So I let it be known and pretty soon I got a bite from Frank Nolan, who owns Freddy's. I was anxious about it, but I don't like to talk about what a good time I'm having—I *really* am."

Except for an appearance in Brooklyn seven years ago ("does that count?"), she hasn't appeared in New York in at least 15 years. The show mirrors her anxiety only in its politic variety, though she abstains from a medley of hits. Backed by Ortega on piano and a pick-up trio (guitarist John Bassili, bassist John Ray, drummer Ronnie Zito), she leads off with a jaunty version of "Love Will Keep Us Together," replete with half-time interludes and the unblushing blues notes that are a Starr specialty. She slides in and out of pitch like a trombone. When I asked her about the song, she said, "That was Toni Tennille. I think Fats Waller or somebody did it first and she found it." As Starr sings it, Waller doesn't seem an unlikely source, but actually Neil Sedaka wrote it. She does the two strongest songs from her *Just Plain Country* album of 23 years ago, "I Really Don't Want to Know" and "Crazy," but with more feeling and invention than in her previous versions. Taking the former as a blues (it isn't), she slows it down to a deliciously sensual plea, twanging upper-register notes against chesty mid-range phrases, and underscoring musical conceits with histrionic ones—expressive mask, imploring hands. The ease with which she switches from country laments to "Honeysuckle Rose" or "Hard-Hearted Hannah" is startling. Like Joe Turner, whose blues style is equally at home in jazz, r&b, or r&r, Starr uses her Oklahoma drawl and superb time to democratize all genres.

Starr still sings Pee Wee King's "Bonaparte's Retreat," her big hit of 1950, because she found it herself in Dougherty, Oklahoma (where she was born), convinced Capitol to let her do it, and credits its success with the company's decision to hand her the aptly named "Wheel of Fortune." It's a trite piece, notwithstanding a hootchie-cootchie middle-strain that lets her sashay. She slows "For the Good Times" to a crawl, paced by Ortega's tremolos, and colors an occasionally stagy interpretation with serpentine portamentos that resemble tailgate glides. Then she rests her chops by turning the stage over to the pianist, who plays a medley of five Ellington tunes, the highlight of which is "Mood Indigo" strummed harplike on the strings.

Starr invariably chooses the right tempo and melodic embellishments, investing her songs with a voluptuous huskiness that can give the illusion of abandon, as on a dramatic "I'm Through with Love," complete with half-yodeled cries and stop-time release. She doubles the tempo on "Lazy River," takes an Armstrongian break, and makes the last note a perfect descending triad. The set begins to unravel toward the end with a travel medley that disappoints because her single choruses of "Going to Chicago" and "Kansas City" make you want to hear more; instead, they're just teasing preludes for the exceedingly anticlimactic "New York State of Mind." She closes with her chartbusters, the insidious "Rock and Roll Waltz" and the inevitable "Wheel of Fortune," rendering them palatable with self-mocking zeal.

Starr's brassy fusion of urban swing and country twang fixed the attention of several bandleaders in the '30s and '40s and later established her as a "utility singer" (her phrase) able to indemnify almost any kind of song against banality. Yet her versatility offended chroniclers of every genre. Though she has recorded some of the most effective swing band vocal albums of the past 30 years, as well as notable efforts in country, gospel, and r&b, she isn't listed in any of the standard encyclopedias for those fields. Her remarkable collaborations with arranger Van Alexander in 1960 were ignored by most jazz magazines. In books on American popular or jazz-related singers she is mentioned parenthetically or not at all. She is listed in Hardy and Laing's *Encyclopedia of Rock*, ironically enough, but is grouped with the likes of Pat Boone and Gale Storm as one of "those whites with no feeling for r&b," who were guilty of "undercutting black performers." Which is triply absurd: Starr had little to do with rock; she's one of the rare "white" singers (she's actually three-quarters Native American) with a profound feeling for rhythm and blues; and her one notorious "cover" was of a white performer. The moral of all this is a variant on Gresham's law: A performer's good records will be driven out of circulation and memory by the bad ones that yield immediate and staggering profits.

When I visited her in the penthouse that Freddy's provided for her stay in New York, Starr was completing a photographic session ("Some photographers make you pose till you feel like drugstore lettuce," she noted) and preparing vodka collinses. The radio was playing singers of her generation, and I was trying to think of a polite way to say that she reminded me of a white Dinah Washington, when she threw up her hands and said, *"There's* my favorite singer." I turned to the radio, and of course it was Washington. "I stood up at her wedding to Night-Train Lane. I think I've known Dinah about half my adult life. I got to meet her on Central Avenue in L.A. when I was with Charlie Barnet, and she'd come to hear me with Charlie's band, and we became really good friends. We'd laugh because she was one color and I was another but we were the same." One of the numbers Starr recorded with Barnet in 1944 was "What a Difference a Day Made," which became Washington's signature song years later. Could Starr's recording have influenced her? "I don't think so, I don't think she listened to *anybody.* She just had it and knew what to do with it." Minutes later: "And that's my other favorite singer"—Ella Fitzgerald, whom Starr slightly resembled on her first recordings, made in 1939.

The question of influence is always nettlesome, and never more so than in the instance of a singer who violates all the usual pigeonholes. Starr was born Katherine La Verne Starks in Oklahoma, in 1922, to a full-blooded Iroquois father and a mother who is Cherokee, Choctaw, and Irish. Since three of the most individual "white" women jazz singers—Mildred Bailey, Lee Wiley, and Starr—are American Indians, I asked if she thought there was an ethnic connection. "I don't have any idea, but it's interesting, isn't it? Red Norvo and Mildred used to come to my house at the beach, but we never talked about it. If you were on a reservation, which is government run, they have Presbyterians and Methodists and people telling you your religion—in order to get subsidized you had to go to church. But those of us who *weren't* brought up on some kind of reservation don't really belong to a church. I go to everybody's church, why not? God is everywhere. But most of us believe in elements, in wind and trees and the earth, and I think we're just children of the soil. I think we three Indians, if you've researched the other two, you've found they've always been honest: They weren't trying to prove anything in particular, they were just doing what came naturally, and rolled with the punches. That's the personality Mildred had, it was mine, and the little bit I knew of Lee Wiley, it was hers. Of course, Indian music has a hell of a beat—it's all drums and chanting. There is not a whole lot of melody to our music."

As a child, she pretended her mother's chicken coop was an amphitheater and was satisfied to entertain the roost until her aunt entered her in a contest. She won third prize for simultaneously singing and working a yo-yo. Most of her childhood was spent on the move: "My daddy worked for a big sprinkler company and was foreman when they put automatic sprinklers in big buildings all over Texas. I've said that I lived in every town in Texas for 15 minutes, because it seemed like that to me. I never really got to know anybody, and my mother was my playmate all my life—she's still the best girlfriend I've got—so it was easy for her to go on the road with me as my sister because we did everything together." She performed on radio with Bill Boyd and his Cowboy Ramblers in Dallas, and the Light Crust Doughboys in Fort Worth. When the family finally settled in Memphis, she repeatedly won a local radio contest and was offered her own 15-minute show three times a week. She was 13. Shortly afterwards, the great jazz violinist Joe Venuti and his orchestra came through Memphis.

"Joe's contract called for a girl singer, and he didn't have one. He thought he could bluff his way through with a boy singer, but towns like Memphis, Tennessee, going through growing pains, weren't having it: The contract called for a girl singer, and where *is* she? They wouldn't let him open. Joe's road manager heard me on this radio show, just me and a piano player, pop songs and a few rhythm songs, because it's hard to sing rhythm songs with just rum-ching rum-ching, but when you're young you're invincible and think you can do anything. So I was trying to do anything, and he heard me and didn't have any idea how old I was. My voice hadn't started to grow up—I sounded like Dolly Dawn, Bonnie Baker, and those other young voices. But I had the feel, and so he called the station and wanted to talk to me about joining Joe Venuti's band. I said, 'Gee, I'm sorry, you're going to have to talk to my mother and dad.' He said, 'WHAT?'—he thought I was at least a young adult.

"So he went up to the house, and my father said okay, because I was going to cry, I was going to throw a fit if they didn't let me. But I had to be off the stand by 12, so I could go to school. They had to buy me two evening dresses, and at 13 I weighed about 165 pounds. Joe thought I was wonderful and took me under his wing, and every summer after that I used to sing with his band. But we had to tell everybody my mother was my sister because those hotels could have been closed with everybody having alcoholic drinks and a 13- or 14-year-old kid on the stage. I guess the person I give the most credit to for anything I've done or ever will do is Joe Venuti. He taught me to sing with authority. He said, if you make a mistake make it loud. When we played places like a hotel in Toledo or Memphis, if someone like Menuhin or Kreisler was in town, they'd be in the dining room to listen to Joe play quiet things like 'Estralita' that are good for the digestion, and I'd sing quiet songs. But after dinner, when they left, he went back to playing jazz, and he played great jazz."

I asked if she had listened to Bessie Smith. "Not until later when musicians made me conscious of her, because I think they could feel that once in a while I had a tendency towards the blues. But in the part of the country I came from there is a great deal of gospel, so I was exposed to all this stuff. The guys in the band used to take me to Beale Street, to those churches and, my God, those holy rollers. You never heard anything like it in your life. I mean those people would start singing and would sing until their voices disappeared, and they broke out in a sweat and fell to the floor, writhing and foaming at the mouth—the goddamnedest thing you ever saw. The holy rollers would start at midnight and sing until noon on Sunday. The worshipers came and went, but the singers just stayed there. It was sobering, I'll tell you that, and all-encompassing, and if you had that kind of feel about you anyway and you didn't know where you were going, it could sure help you to get there. So I loved it."

In 1939, Gil Rodin heard Starr on a Venuti broadcast and recommended her to Bob Crosby, who had just signed with the Camel Caravan. She sang "Memphis Blues" (Crosby's sidekick Johnny Mercer introduced her) on the first show and was pulled. She and her mother returned to the Plymouth Hotel to get their things, when someone from the Glenn Miller band walked in, complaining that Miller's singer, Marian Hutton, had collapsed on stage and a replacement was needed. A musician pointed out "that little round-assed girl" getting in the elevator, and Starr soon found herself doing two weeks at the Glen Island Casino and recording two selections with the Miller band—in Hutton's key. "I sound like Alfalfa," she says. She certainly doesn't sound like Kay Starr on the sappy "Love with a Capital You," though on "Baby Me," an Eddie Durham rhythm tune, she suggests a Fitzgeraldian lilt. If you place all of Starr's early recordings in chronological order, from the Crosby number to her solo sessions in 1945, you can hear her style come into focus incrementally. In five performances with the Barnet band, which she joined in 1944, another with Wingy Manone, and four more with Ben Pollack, you hear her refining her vibrato, dynamics, and time. But the personality isn't there, the husky edge, the rhythmic assurance.

That would come a year later, and seems to have developed at least in part from an inflammation of the throat. Starr contracted pneumonia while touring army camps on transport planes. Forced to leave the Barnet band, she learned that nodes had formed on her vocal chords. Rather than have them snipped off, which, she was warned, might change her range and sound, she agreed to have them frozen for three months. "Every two days they were sprayed, and if you can believe anybody as gabby as me didn't utter a sound for three months, and couldn't even taste what I was eating—well, it was weird. The keys I sang in stayed the same, but it might have made me a little raspier. Everybody seems to think it did."

In March of 1945, producer Dave Dexter called her for a record session at Capitol. "I thought I was in the wrong room and started to back out before anybody saw me. Dave called me, 'Come back, Okie, you're in the right place.' There was Nat Cole, Coleman Hawkins, Benny Carter—I thought I'd died and gone to heaven." She sang on two sides with the Capitol International Jazzmen ("If I Could Be with You" and "Stormy Weather") and at last demonstrated a style that was unmistakably her own. During the next two years, she recorded a series of records for small labels, accompanied either by a band with Vic Dickenson and Barney Bigard or one with Joe Venuti and Les Paul; the rhythm section for both included Red Callendar and Zutty Singleton.

These are the records on which her early reputation as a jazz singer was based, and most of them hold up marvelously well. Performances such as "Sunday," "After You've Gone," "Frying Pan," "I'm Confessin'," "There's a Lull in My Life," and "All of Me" find her phrasing with unaffected proficiency, taking tempo changes and breaks in stride, fully abreast of the demanding rhythms. A 1946 big-band session for Rondolette offers a fully matured "Them There Eyes," and a 1947 Just Jazz concert (with Charlie Shavers and Willie Smith) includes her sensuous "What Is This Thing Called Love?" and a version of "Good for Nothin' Joe" that was withdrawn because she sang the phrase "beats the hell out of me" (you can hear the audience gasp). At the same time, as a direct result of the Dexter session, she embarked on her first, long association with Capitol Records.

In those years, Capitol had a near monopoly on pop singers, and used different color labels for different musical categories. Starr appeared on every color. "I was a utility singer because I had tried country, blues—I could sing with Ernie Ford ["I'll Never Be Free" was a big hit] or I could do Dixieland. They figured that the rest of the girls were so stylized—except Jo Stafford, no matter what she did it was still Jo Stafford. But someone like me could do anything, and they used me as such." The degree to which Starr's country cry and worldly swing confused the company's staff producers resulted in 78s like the one that paired "Bonaparte's Retreat" with "Someday Sweetheart." Consider two imports that anthologize material from the early years at Capitol: *The Fabulous Favorites!* and *The Kay Starr Style.* The first is a collection of relentlessly gimmicky hits that stultify and date the singer; the second offers straight-ahead arrangements of standards, usually in a big-band context. Even when the standards aren't any good, the settings elicit an improvisational spark that makes her performances timeless.

The record that made her a major star and sealed her fate was "Wheel of Fortune," a classic story of a cover of a cover. During Starr's first week at Freddy's, George Weiss, who wrote the song with Ben Benjamin, dropped by to meet her for the first time (they thanked each other for buying each other's homes). He described the genesis of their hit. The song was originally crafted for Johnny Hartman at RCA, whose record went nowhere. In December 1951, Eddie Wilcox, the former Jimmie Lunceford arranger, produced a version for Sonny Gale on the Derby label, which seemed likely to take off. Weiss, however, disappointed with the Hartman record, revised the song and sent it to Voyle Gilmore at Capitol.

The week the Gale record hit the stores, Starr was awakened at night and told to come over to the studio. "I didn't realize there was this big conspiracy going on," she says. "They forced me to learn the song and said it had to be recorded that night. My record was out a week after Sonny Gale's. Her record company was smaller, so mine became the hit. She don't like me one bit, and I'd be afraid to meet her." Starr's million-seller was covered by other singers, including Dinah Washington, whose version was number three on the r&b chart that year. The "drugstore" version was recorded by Marilyn Horne: "She did it to keep herself in vocal lessons, and it's spooky how much she sounds like me. We used to do it together at parties."

In 1955, Starr left Capitol for RCA. "Capitol had been like a family, but then they wouldn't let me have any say. So RCA came along and, though my heart wasn't in it, my heart wasn't in staying at Capitol either. Well, at the first session they gave me 'Rock and Roll Waltz' and I thought it was a joke, because I don't read music and all I could read were the lyrics and I thought, 'Oh, my God, look at this—one, two, and then rock, one, two, and then roll.' I said to Hal Stanley, who was my manager and who had introduced me on Central Avenue, 'Is this a joke?' He said, 'No, this is what they want to do.' I thought, 'Oh, I've left Capitol Records for this!' Because I was used to doing blood and guts, those kinds of songs, and this looked to me like a nursery rhyme. I really was incensed, but Stan said, 'What the hell do you care? Do it.' So I said okay, and the whole time I did it I thought to myself, 'What if this becomes popular? How in the hell am I ever going to present this?' I mean I almost had to take a Dramamine to do it. And oddly enough, nobody ever requested it. Yet I was told that it was the quickest single record to ever go a million at RCA. A writer once called me and said, 'Do you know you had the first rock hit at RCA, the first with rock and roll in the title?' I thought, he thinks that's rock? I don't know *what* it was, but it sure wasn't rock."

Starr's RCA albums are another story—long out of print and deserving of a fresh hearing. Superficially, they fall into categories: jazz (*The One—the Only Kay Starr*), gospel (*I Hear the Word*), blue ballads (*Blue Starr*), and rhythm and blues (*Rockin' with Kay*). In fact, they are of a piece. The arrangements combine a male choir with Ellingtonian brass comments, efficient band riffs, and effective if brief solos, and Starr is riveting. The 1957 *Blue Starr* is perhaps the strongest, from the trombonelike melisma she applies to the word *you're* in "It's a Lonesome Old Town (When You're Not Around)" through the five-minute tour de force version of "I Really Don't Want to Know" to the impeccably modulated "Blue and Sentimental." Like all great interpretive singers, she has a cache of unlikely material that she brings alive by dint of her ingenuity and charm, ranging from Ink Spots hits ("We Three," "Do I Worry") to Hoagy Carmichael's southern cycle ("Lazy Bones," "Rockin' Chair," "Georgia on My Mind"), to which she supplies a definitive tang.

She returned to Capitol in 1959, and during the next three years recorded an extraordinary series of albums mostly in collaboration with Van Alexander. Largely ignored at the time of their release, they are probably her most satisfying achievements. Alexander first made his mark writing for Chick Webb's band in the 1930s (he arranged Ella Fitzgerald's milestone hit with the band, "A-Tisket, A-Tasket") but subsequently busied himself in movie work. The Starr sessions gave him an opportunity to strut his stuff, and he took full advantage of it; these records don't have the usual Capitol gloss, a sound created chiefly by Nelson Riddle and Billy May. "Van Alexander was the sweetest man to work with," Starr says, "but sometimes you'd hear things in his music, raunchy things, and I told him, 'There's a side to you you don't let anybody see, but it's in the music.' The record company people would find new songs—all they thought about was being commercial—but we'd all put in lists for the old standards."

Although Alexander worked with a full orchestra, balancing reeds and brass in standard Basie-out-of-Henderson style, his chief forte was voicing saxophones. On *Movin'*, he uses them for swooning jazz textures and raucous r&b riffs, anticipating Starr's phrasing on "Lazy River" with neatly scored portamentos, and her oscillating between registers on "Night Train." The texture of reeds is alternately rough and smooth on a version of "Swinging Down the Lane" that rivals Sinatra's. For contrast, "Indiana" is swung over a trombone riff. Starr has never sounded more exuberant, leaning into consonants in a way that propels the rhythm, finding just the right blues groove to make the most of "Going to Chicago" and "Sentimental Journey," and driving "On a Slow Boat to China" and (surprisingly) "Around the World" with steamy embellishments and bright tempos.

Movin' on Broadway is in some ways even more impressive. "I decided to do all the songs different than they were usually done—like getting a low, earthy phrasing for 'On the Street Where You Live.' Van said, 'How are we gonna do this?' I said, 'Don't worry, leave it to me.' " "(You Gotta Have) Heart" becomes a blue ballad, complete with sexy reeds, guitar obbligato, piano tremolos, and Harry Edison's pungent trumpet. "Get Me to the Church on Time" is done Basie-style. "I Love Paris," with its vocalized brass, suggests Ellington (only Starr can make the word *sizzle* sizzle). "All of You" is worked out over a sax riff that might be played—no joking—by the World Saxophone Quartet. On *Jazz Singer*, organ is scored with the orchestra, and though most selections are jazz standards, many of them from the '20s, the irresistible ringer is a deep blues rendition of Skillet Licker Riley Pucket's "I Only Want a Buddy Not a Sweetheart," with tenor sax and organ accompaniment. The last in the series, *I Cry by Night*, has Starr making a rare appearance with a quintet—four-man rhythm section plus either Ben Webster (one of his few sessions in this period) or Mannie Klein. The obvious restraint imposed on the musicians is regrettable, but Starr and the material ("Lover Man," "Baby, Won't You Please Come Home," T-Bone Walker's "I'm Still in Love with You") are first-rate, and her interaction with the surprisingly ethereal Webster on "More Than You Know" is sublime.

Starr currently divides her time between Los Angeles and Honolulu, and much of her attention in recent years has focused on Indian affairs. In 1967, she was named to the Advisory Board of the Los Angeles Indian Center, which raised $2 million. In the early '70s, she helped found a scholarship fund and, with Grace Thorpe (Jim Thorpe's daughter), a university in Davis, California, called DQ (for Desanawidah Quetzalcoatl), which recently graduated the first American Indian dentist. Starr and her husband own a tile business, "so if anything happened to me and I couldn't sing, I wouldn't be alone, somebody would take care of me." Presumably she will be sunning herself in the spotlight for some time to come. Now that she's past her commercial prime, she can concentrate entirely on the attributes that make her art an enduring one.

Needless to say, she isn't signed with a record company: "I'd love to record, but it's a different world today, and I'm not really a business-minded person." It seems unlikely that an American record company will present her with opulent band arrangements, but as her engagement at Freddy's demonstrated, she doesn't need more than a good rhythm section and maybe a couple of soloists. That was the setting for much of her best recorded work in the past; it was also the setting for Helen Humes's comeback albums and for the ones with which Rosemary Clooney has been braving new musical heights in the '80s. Starr is in her prime right now; there's no reason she couldn't make some of her best records in the next few years. A retrospective of her past accomplishments, matched by a rash of new ones, will properly define her place once and for all as one of the incomparables. *

(November 1985)

*Despite subsequent tours and exceptional press, Kay Starr was unable to revive her recording career. RCA has not reissued her albums in the United States. Capitol has released a compilation of her hits.

The Once and Future Queen

"I sure miss Dinah." Johnny Hartman's voice, leveled by awe and directed at no one in particular, penetrated the sudden silence at a rehearsal for a concert of jazz singing, at Avery Fisher in 1981. The commotion of musicians and stage-hands had subsided a few minutes earlier for the first time all afternoon, when a clip of Dinah Washington—one of several clips chosen to bring departed singers into the program—was projected on stage. It was from *Jazz on a Summer's Day*, Bert Stern's souvenir of the 1958 Newport Jazz Festival, with Dinah wailing "All of Me," accompanied by a Terry Gibbs quintet. She wore a short, sleeveless, white blouson dress fitted just below the hips with a huge bow that bumped flirtatiously in time, and her face, under closely cropped hair, was a radiant pond of brown and red hues. During the vibes solo she grabbed Gibbs's spare mallets and, with the unrivaled sass that made her a tigress on and off stage, invaded his territory. She didn't play much, but the pleasure she took in hammering along and the wonder that she could play at all (even if she was a skilled pianist) heightened the moment. After Urbie Green's trombone solo, she resumed sing-ing, the cadences glancing upward trumpetlike. Few performers have taken a stage or stormed off one with quite the noblesse oblige of the Queen, who died at 39, in 1963, of an accidental mixture of diet pills and alcohol. In the intervening quarter-century, her reputation has been in serious disrepair.

One reason is that all her recordings except for a couple of sessions in her early years and the eight albums made in her last year were done for one company, Mercury, which—much to its surprise, though not to Dinah's—achieved a top-10 crossover hit with her version of "What a Difference a Day Made" in 1959. The result was a siege of commercial records that remained steady sellers, while the jazz and blues sides that established and sustained her standing in the pantheon of singers were reissued fleetingly or not at all. Her vibrant career as a jukebox star in the late '40s and early '50s was largely forgotten or, worse, patronized: At the height of her fame, Mercury issued a compilation called *The Good Old Days*, picturing only a straw boater on the cover. It's been considerably more difficult to get a handle on her 20 years in the studios than on the careers of her very few peers, notably Smith, Holiday, Fitzgerald, and Vaughan.

Washington's loyalty to Mercury, however, is now paying off for her admirers. Under the guidance of Kiyoshi Koyama, one of the ablest archivists presently digging in the jazz vaults, PolyGram and Nippon have conspired to release her complete work for the label, a project that will be completed over two years with the release of 21 compact discs parsed into seven boxes. (Unfortunately for American consumers, the music will not be available on LP; the industry never intended CD technology to remain just another option.) The first two boxes have recently been issued, and they allow—no, force—all of us who pay lip service to the vagaries of legend to pay a more knowing homage based on the goods. Washington, as befits a performer who insisted on her right to sing without generic restrictions, was to become many things: the finest blues singer in the generations after Bessie Smith; an entrancingly original stylist on ballads; a bold and graceful embellisher of melody, and the jazz singer who most closely assimilated the brassy euphoria of Louis Armstrong's climactic flourishes; a pop star. *The Complete Dinah Washington on Mercury, Vol. 1 1946–1949* and *Vol. 2 1950–1952* goes beyond the obsession of completism. It's a labor of essential restoration. *

The figures alone bear daunting witness to the neglect of Washington's work. Of the 119 selections, 56 are new to the age of the LP, let alone CDs. Of those, 12 are alternate takes; 33—among them a few hits—were out only as singles; 11 were never issued at all. Although some material is simply abominable ("My Heart Cries for You," "That's Why a Woman Loves a Heel"), little of it is found in the rediscovered stuff, which offers several savory blues and ballad performances. The era under consideration is from Washington's apprenticeship, when the label had her tackling every fad and fancy of the day. She was compelled to cover songs made famous by the Andrews Sisters, Kay Starr, Billy Eckstine, Rosemary Clooney, the Four Aces, Bullmoose Jackson, Hank Williams, and many others. Some of those arrangements are stodgy, inept, tasteless, tactless. During and after the recording ban of 1948, she was choked by dreary vocal choirs.

In a way, this period mirrors the end of her career, when smoother but no less

---

*The production is exemplary. The crackling of old 78s is preferable to the lifelessness that results from the filtering techniques that plague much CD reprocessing. The liner notes by Leonard Feather and Dan Morgenstern are graceful and wise; James Kriegsmann's photographs are evocative. My only quibble is the absence of the 1943 Keynote session, now owned by Mercury. By way of compensation, though, there are snippets of conversation including the following dialogue (as prelude to "Cry Me a River" on *Vol. 6*) between the splendidly arch singer and a phlegmatic record producer:

"Do I sound like Julie London?"

"No, you sound like Dinah Washington."

"Would you like me to sound like Billie Holiday?"

"No, I'd like you to sound like Dinah Washington."

"I could sound like Spokane, Washington."

"I'd like you to sound like Dinah Washington."

suffocating choirs and dubious songs became the norm. A difference is that in the beginning, Mercury strove to enlarge her appeal among blacks; in the end, the company conceded what the singer had long insisted—that she could reach the white mainstream as well. But just as Dinah persisted in singing dynamic jazz and earthy blues when they were out of fashion, she steadfastly insisted on first-rate songs throughout her initial "singles" period. Every tediously arranged session almost guranteed that the next would be lean and efficient. Whether the date was promising or meretricious, Washington remained assertively and saltily her own woman. No singer ever approached song with a greater reserve of pluck. Even in the most dire circumstances, her powerful wit—shining from deep inside—mitigates all obstacles.

In optimum surroundings, another quality peeks through: a candid and teasing sexuality. Alberta Hunter, who once said, "They don't have blues singers now like they had then, except maybe Dinah Washington," considered Bessie Smith to be the greatest of all because even when she was "raucous and loud, she had a sort of a tear—no, not a tear, but there was a *misery* in what she did." Dinah, who came to resent the constant comparisons with Bessie, had a sort of laugh, a simmering ebullience, even when she sang self-pitying laments. Where Smith was sorrowful and Holiday disaffected, where Fitzgerald was girlish and Vaughan operatic, Dinah was gloriously carnal. She never got high-toned, unless it was with the kind of humor that lets you in on the joke. Her very cosmopolitanism was streetwise. At the height of her powers, from 1954 on, Washington's virtuosity was so completely at the service of her personality that its raiment all but disappeared. By then she had developed and perfected her most characteristic mannerism. It was a unique appoggiatura, an effect seemingly as natural to her as her stinging timbre—an upward glide pinned to or squeezed out of a note, usually at the end of a phrase. Like so many attributes of her style, this one suggests a trumpet: a brief gliss pressed with an extra dollop of vibrato (she was the ultimate mistress of vibrato, swelling and decaying neighboring syllables to maximize the expressive values of every word); an echo of the pitched note that sometimes states and sometimes merely suggests an overtone of a fifth or an octave.

By the mid-1950s, when she recorded a peerless series of vocal jazz albums (*Dinah Jams, After Hours with Miss D, Dinah!, In the Land of Hi-fi, The Swinging Miss D, Dinah Sings Fats Waller*) all the components of her style were in place, and she could successfully dare to outclimb the high-note trumpeters on "Lover, Come Back to Me," or outroister Waller on "Christopher Columbus." Yet listening to the earlier work, you realize how long it took her to consummate the ideal blend of technique and personality. Her timbre was enticing from the beginning, but full recognition of all that her voice could do, beyond the relatively obvious areas of range and dynamics, took time.

Consider the matter of that appoggiatura. You hear only its implications from time to time in the records of 1946 and 1947. Not until the 38th track, "Record

Ban Blues," probably recorded on the last day of 1947 and not released for 12 years (perhaps for fear of offending union boss James Petrillo, who demanded the ban and is named in the lyric), does it come fully into view. The highpoint of a good session with Cootie Williams's band, the song is simply the standard blues—complete with stop-time chorus—that Washington sang and recorded countless times. Maybe the daring lyric inspired her, or the apocalyptic fever of the coming ban (she would record only seven sides during the next 12 months). In any case, she is superbly loose and invigorating. The soon-to-be trademark gliss is heard on the words *boss* in the first chorus and *late* in the second. She does it once on the next song, "Resolution Blues," too, but you hardly hear it again until April 1951, on the ballad "I Won't Cry Anymore."

If Dinah's sound wasn't fully matured at 22, she was already a starkly distinctive performer. Indeed, if one considers all the singers who sounded like her or reflected her influence after she came to prominence—a list that includes Esther Phillips, Ruth Brown, Nancy Wilson, Etta Jones, Dodo Green, Dionne Warwick, Diana Ross—one is all the more conscious of how original her approach was. Washington always named Billie Holiday as her favorite singer, but aside from the shared inclination to phrase behind the beat, albeit to rather different effect, the influence is faint. A more fruitful search could undoubtedly be made in the vineyards of gospel. If Dinah was the Queen of the Blues (a title she held like a shield), she was a product of the church.

She was born Ruth Jones in Alabama, in 1924, and raised in Chicago, where her mother played piano at St. Luke's Baptist Church. After performing piano duets with her mom for the congregation, she became known as a local prodigy, and at 15 won a talent contest at the Regal Theater, singing "I Can't Face the Music." (Two versions of that song appear in the Mercury collection, each with an interpolation of Benny Carter's "Blues in My Heart"; the first was never issued, the second was released only as a single.) Neither the prize nor her growing infatuation with Billie Holiday pleased her devout parent.

The Jazz Singer is repeatedly filmed as a Jewish story, but it's really a black one. Few of the immigrant Jews who dominated songwriting in the Golden Age, and whose fathers were cantors and rabbis, experienced religious versus secular pressures anywhere near as profound as those facing not one but several generations of black musicians. (Artists as disparate as Ethel Waters, Hampton Hawes, Ray Charles, and David Murray have described those pressures. On one occasion, the basic plot of *The Jazz Singer* was actually filmed with an all-black cast, as a purported biography of W. C. Handy, called *St. Louis Blues* and starring Nat Cole.) To be sure, Ruth Jones was torn between the sacred and the profane—she sang secretly in nightclubs under adopted names, but finally took flight as the 16-year-old piano accompanist for a legendary figure in gospel, Sallie Martin. For two years she traveled the gospel circuit, working with the Rev. C. L. Franklin (Aretha's father), Mahalia Jackson, and Roberta Martin, who greatly inspired her. Dinah was a charter member of the first all-women gospel group, the Sallie

Martin Colored Ladies Quartet. Then she briefly married the first of many husbands (best estimate is nine, though no one seems to know for sure) and returned to the Chicago clubs.

An indication of the ease with which she returned to secular music can be gleaned from a story Tony Heilbut tells in *The Gospel Sound:* It seems that many years later, the highly successful Dinah mischievously suggested to an old friend, the then struggling gospel singer Deloris Barrett, that she moonlight in the more lucrative blues field. Heilbut goes on to quote Sallie Martin on her protégée's willfulness. "She could really sing," Martin recalled, "but, shoot, she'd catch the eye of some man and she'd be out the church before the minister finished off the doxology." Washington's experience on the gospel trail surely helped her to formulate an expressive use of melisma and scatlike humming—though Louis Armstrong, too, undoubtedly served as a prototype for those elements in her work. James Haskins cites another source of her style in his biography, *Queen of the Blues:* Bette Davis movies. Like Ethel Waters before her, Dinah was obsessed with proper diction and the possibilities of inflection. Her articulation, the luxuriant correctness of her vowels, the parlando with which she emphasizes meaning, are among the fundamental joys of her art. Her ability to lend credibility, sometimes underscored with sarcasm, to silly lyrics is another bond she has with Holiday.

Yet her jazz career languished for a while. Despite the triumph at the Regal, the enthusiasm of clubowners Joe Sherman and manager Joe Glaser, who landed her a job with Lionel Hampton (all three boasted of having changed Ruth Jones to Dinah Washington, though none could remember why), and the acceptance of audiences and critics, she remained in the twilight zone for years. Decca actually refused to let Hampton spotlight her on records, and he was careful not to let her overshadow his band in concert. The critic Leonard Feather changed all that by convincing the small Keynote label to record her with members of the Hampton band in a program of his own blues. Hampton was so impressed with her at the session that he sat in for two numbers and permitted his name to be used on the label. When "Salty Papa Blues" became a hit, Decca sued, and Hampton's name was removed from the label. But the bandleader now featured her on another Feather blues, the wacky "Blow Top." It was a hit, but she remained in recording limbo. A 1945 date for Apollo with a then nonstar band (Lucky Thompson, Milt Jackson, Charles Mingus) produced a dozen titles, mostly blues, but it wasn't until 1946, three years after the Keynote session, that she signed with Mercury and showed what she could do with a broader range of material.

Dinah began her Mercury contract with "Embraceable You" and "I Can't Get Started" and in the following years took a poke at every type of song making the rounds. In those days, a straight blues like "Baby Get Lost" (another Feather lyric) or "Long John Blues" (a fashionably double-entendre Washington original about a dentist with a soothing drill) could make the top of the rhythm and blues charts.

So she recorded dozens of blues—most of them with the same melody and stop-time climaxes, many in the key of C, though with varied tempos. She would remain a nonpareil blues singer until she died (for example, "The Blues Ain't Nothin' but a Woman Cryin' for Her Man," released by Roulette in 1963). Oddly enough, the only awkwardness to be found in her blues recordings is on the album she made of Bessie Smith songs, probably a consequence of the hokey arrangements, which patronize the material, and the pressures of the tribute. To trace her progress along the familiar 12-bar route is to confirm steady advancements in wit, nuance, and bravura. At a couple of magnificent sessions in 1952, she fulfilled all her early promise and intimated how much more would come. The diadem falls into her lap with her exquisite "Trouble in Mind" (supported by her husband, drummer Jimmy Cobb, and saxophonist Ben Webster). On "Mad About the Boy," she locates the soul within the whimsy of Noel Coward.

The pleasures she took in her reign as Queen can be adduced from two stories told by James Haskins. Once she inadvertently boarded a bus chartered for mentally retarded people and threw off the head count. The driver began to question the passengers. When he asked Washington who she was, she looked him in the eye and said, "I'm the Queen of the Blues." "Yes, you definitely belong here," he replied. During her tour of England, Dinah was cautioned not to say anything about the recently crowned queen. The first time she walked on stage, to a standing ovation, she announced, "Ladies and gentlemen, I'm happy to be here, but just remember, there's one heaven, one earth, and one Queen, and your Elizabeth is an impostor."

By that time, the press was covering her private and public behavior in lurid detail—all the marriages, the attempt on her life by a jealous woman, her temper tantrums on stage, her packing and firing a pistol, her outspoken and often hilarious comments to the press (Dinah's acerbic "blindfold tests" in *Down Beat* are classic), her principled refusal to appear on TV if she had to lip-synch. Then, at 35, she convinced Mercury to go whole hog in the production and promotion of "What a Difference a Day Made," which lyric she changed to the present tense. Floated by the arrangement's even triplets, she soared onto the pop charts. The label expected her to stay there, providing her with new motives for rebellion. Four years later, fighting a lifelong weight problem, she took too many diet pills while drinking, and it was all over. Neither the blues nor jazz has yet found a worthy heir.

(January 1988)

Divine

On May 1, 1984, Sarah Vaughan, one of the most sublime singers of this or any century, and Wynton Marsalis, the 22-year-old trumpet virtuoso who earlier this year won the perennially dubious (if in this instance unprecedented) Grammy award for recordings in both the jazz and classical music categories, joined with conductor John Williams to commence the 99th season of the Boston Pops. It was Vaughan's second appearance with the Pops (her first since 1976) and Marsalis's debut. Of considerably greater significance, it marked the first time the two guests performed with each other. During the past 40 years, the singer's luscious and incomparable voice has been entwined with the sounds of many great trumpet stars, including Freddie Webster, Dizzy Gillespie, Miles Davis, and Clifford Brown. Marsalis's jazz style is firmly rooted in their tradition. The two shared only a couple of numbers in Boston, but the results were festive and full of promise.

When Vaughan arrived in Boston, she had every reason to feel out of sorts. The week had been hectic and dispiriting, beginning with the news that Count Basie, her close friend and occasional performing partner, had succumbed to cancer. She attended the funeral in New York City after performing in Rochester, where, despite the presence of a noted music conservatory, she was greeted with an untuned and otherwise ailing piano that the producers agreed to replace only after adamant protest. Vaughan flew to Boston straight from the memorial service at the Abyssinian Baptist Church, still rankling at the rudeness of newspeople who pushed cameras and microphones into the faces of mourners and asked questions so idiotic it required some effort to maintain dignified silence. Then, hours after she checked into the Back Bay Hilton, a fire alarm went off. Her room was on the 25th floor, and she had to walk down 20 flights before she learned it was a mistake.

But at the next morning's rehearsal, Sarah Vaughan was effervescent—enlivened, as first-class artists usually are, by the prospect of working with other professionals. Although Marsalis's primary responsibility was in the Haydn Concerto in E flat for trumpet, he was thrilled at the chance to play a couple of numbers with Vaughan, whom he adores. She was impressed with him, too, especially after the rehearsal of "September Song," when he played, almost verbatim, Clifford Brown's solo from her classic 1954 recording of the Kurt Weill standard. Afterward, Wynton recalled the Vaughan-Brown album as one of the first to fire his interest in jazz. Of the Pops and its music director John Williams, Vaughan later observed, "They make it easy. Those musicians wouldn't be up there if they couldn't read, you know, and Williams is one of the best. I used to think all symphony conductors knew what they were doing. I know better now."

Rehearsal began at 10:30 a.m. for the Pops, and John Williams, now in his fifth year as conductor, was dressed in a black turtleneck and beige slacks. With characteristic evenhandedness, he led the orchestra through readings of Berlioz's "Rakoczy March," Copland's "An Outdoor Overture," a medley of themes from the Broadway musical *La Cage aux Folles*, the Artie Shaw arrangement of Porter's "Begin the Beguine" (which wasn't on the evening's program), Glenn Miller's "Sunrise Serenade," and "Swing, Swing, Swing," a derivative original that had recently made its debut. He alluded to an upcoming recording session by way of explaining to the musicians why there were so many swing pieces scheduled during the next few weeks.

"Measure 70, too loud, trumpets especially, as softly as possible . . . just be careful we don't rush 92 . . . woodwinds at 64, don't lose the end of the phrase, please . . . horns and brasses, please, at 135, we have a very odd sound." The rehearsal proceeded with the efficiency you'd expect from an ensemble that is famous, or infamous, for refusing to make distinctions between solid works and frivolous showpieces. During the Copland crescendos, where xylophone is voiced with the violins, Williams beat his left hand against his thigh for emphasis, and smiled a slightly crooked grin, his eyes popping in approval. During *La Cage*, a clichéd score performed at a businessman's bounce with lots of splashy cymbals, he warned, "If we can get beautiful pitch this kind of writing can sound quite good. If we don't have beautiful pitch, it's pretty awful." His own "Swing, Swing, Swing," which combines variations on the Benny Goodman record "Sing, Sing, Sing" with "Tiger Rag" chord changes and an episode for brass taken from Tadd Dameron's "Hot House" (all uncredited, of course), convinced the trumpeters and trombonists to woodshed in the moments before Marsalis arrived.

Although Haydn's trumpet concerto was the highlight of Marsalis's prize-winning album *Trumpet Concertos*, he hadn't played the piece through in concert since he was sixteen. He was sufficiently familiar with the score, though, to earn generous applause from the orchestra after each movement, despite a flub in the cadenza—at which point he shrugged and said, "I'll get it right tonight." Attired in gray slacks, a white shirt with sleeves rolled to the elbows, and sneakers, he glided through the second and third movements, reserving his strength for that evening's performance.

Orchestral cheers announced the arrival of La Vaughan, who sat at the piano as Wynton switched to cornet and rippled through his encore, "Carnival of Venice." Vaughan hugged Williams and Marsalis, and positioned herself on a

stool facing the orchestra as her trio (pianist George Gaffney, bassist Andy
Simpkins, drummer Harold Jones) set up. The first piece she called was Erroll
Garner's "Misty," in a version that Marty Paich had orchestrated for her. Wearing
large glasses, dark pants and shirt, a cream-colored rain hat, and high brown
boots, she swiveled slightly as she sang, saving her voice but singing with evident
feeling. Some performers give very little at a rehearsal, but Vaughan gets so
caught up in the sensation of singing that even when she seems intent on doing a
simple run-through, she ends up improvising and stretching her voice. She
concluded "Misty" on a sustained dark blue note, and ranged freely through the
melody of "Body and Soul," accompanied only by piano for the first 16 bars.
Marsalis returned for "September Song," and the singer concluded with her
celebrated version of "Send In the Clowns," complete with the dramatic finish
where she holds the word *my* longer than you can hold your breath and then
plummets into *career*. Orchestra members stomped their feet and applauded.

Boston is a city that vaunts tradition, and Opening Night at Pops is an annual
social event that brings out politicians and TV camera crews as well as charity-
conscious patrons who pay $20 to $150 a ticket. For the duration of the season,
the usual rows of seats in the orchestra section are replaced by tables and chairs at
which food and drink can be ordered. The concert was set for 8:00, but the room
started filling up two hours earlier, as people exchanged coupons for fancy boxed
dinners. The stage is also altered for the Pops, with a freshly painted red and gold
backdrop; on this night, nets filled with balloons dangle from strategic points on
the ceiling, and the usual concert etiquette is relaxed. Conversation and picture-
taking are tolerated, as is applause between movements.

While Williams led the "Rakoczy March," Vaughan was in great spirits.
Removing hair curlers in her dressing room, she exuberantly discussed recent
events in her remarkable career. Despite the tribulations of the past week, she was
thoroughly optimistic about the coming year. "I've just turned 60, and this is my
year," she said. She had just signed a contract with Quincy Jones's recording
company, accepted Barry Manilow's invitation to appear on his next album, and
agreed to collaborate on a project with the pope. Selections from John Paul II's
poetry have been translated into English and set to music; Vaughan will sing the
resulting songs in a production to be conducted by Lalo Schifrin. She has little
patience with critics who would have her perform exclusively in the jazz idiom,
especially one who a few days earlier reproached her for singing in concert with
soul singer James Ingram. "And it was great! He wrote that I needed James
Ingram like a fish needs a bicycle. As far as I'm concerned, I need everybody."
"Jones, Manilow, and the pope—the Holy Trinity," her road manager Larry
Clothier mused. "This is my year," she laughed.

Onstage, Marsalis, in white tie and wing collar, performed the Haydn effortlessly, although he still seemed a mite nervous on the cadenza. His triple tongu-
ing on the encore whipped the audience to a cheering ovation. After intermission, Vaughan swept on stage in a splendid gown—orange stripes, gold brocade,

and bangles. Though her set was only half an hour long, she made every minute count. After a buoyant "Just Friends" with the trio, she introduced the musicians and herself. Lately she's been identifying herself as Della Reese (before that it was Carmen McRae), but tonight she stuck out her chest and said, "I'm Dolly Parton." In addition to "Misty" and "Body and Soul," songs she's been identified with for more than 30 years, she did a lively trio rendition of "I Hadn't Anyone till You," with a stage joke coda in which the rhythm section finishes before she does. Marsalis returned to play obbligato for "September Song" and an incredibly fast "Autumn Leaves," on which she sang a wordless improvisation replete with substitute harmonies and dizzying arpeggios. "Send In the Clowns," in a somewhat less melodramatic rendition than usual, brought the audience to its feet.

Following the second intermission, Williams concluded the program, and a blue poster hanging by laundry pins from a cord running across the back of the stage announced the encores: first "When the Saints Go Marching In," in an overwrought arrangement that mixed gallumphing tuba, tailgate trombone smears, "High Society"-style clarinets, tambourine, and a whistle, and then "Stars and Stripes Forever," which caused an immense American flag and the balloons to descend. The audience rose and proceeded to burst all the balloons.

Next day Sarah Vaughan was off to another city for another concert, but Wynton Marsalis had a few hours before returning home to New York City. In a practice room in Symphony Hall, he relaxed at a piano and considered the performance. "I've been playing too much, every day, and that's a mistake. The phrasing was good on the Haydn, but my intonation was off. I thought I'd be nervous since I hadn't played it all the way through in so long, but I wasn't. I knew I could get the music across because I know every part and I love it. And Williams is real cool. But this is the last time I'm going to mix jazz and classical at a concert. It's too difficult—not on a musical level but on a technical one, and technical perfection is a part of me." Which made him think of Vaughan: "Sarah Vaughan is the greatest there ever was. She understands harmony and sings notes other singers don't sing. She sang something on the bridge to 'Autumn Leaves' [by way of demonstration, he played an angular, chromatic figure on the piano] I couldn't believe. I thought, 'Damn!' And she can really play piano. Last night after the performance she was playing Duke Ellington's 'Tonight I Shall Sleep,' putting in substitutions." Marsalis started to play the song: "Here's the pretty part. Ooh, I love that, that's a pretty chord."

(June 1984)

1924–1990

Sarah Vaughan gone. It doesn't seem possible—there were rumors for several months that she was ill, that she was recovering, that she was ill again. Somehow

I still expected to see her this summer, holding forth in a concert hall, introducing herself as Della Reese, mopping the sweat off her forehead, flexing good songs over four flaring octaves. I was sitting in a bar in Berlin when I saw an abridged version of the *Times* obit in the *International Herald Tribune,* and wished I was home again. A death in the family: the most glorious voice in American music stilled when the glory was still intact. I remembered the first time I reviewed her for the *Voice,* in 1974, absolutely thunderstruck. She was my opener in a wrap-up on the Newport–New York Jazz festival—a vain attempt to describe the way she stretched the bridge of "My Funny Valentine" into an arpeggio that began where her voice was a cello and ended where it became a flute. At that time, I had known a few of her records groove by groove—*No Count Sarah, Sarah* + 2, a couple of anthologies from the Continental and Columbia sessions—but seeing her, this great diva who alternated imperious arias with self-deprecating jokes and bebop gallops, was a revelation. So was the audience, which behaved like the gallery in a Baptist church, cheering and whooping her every virtuoso conceit. Sarah liked that. The one thing she couldn't abide was people clapping in time; she'd rearrange the marbles in their heads by adjusting the tempo so that they couldn't find the downbeat. When they stopped, embarrassed, not knowing where the two and four had disappeared to, she'd slip back into the original rhythm.

That night and for several years after, I assumed Sarah Vaughan had always been a concert artist with a loyal following. Much later I realized I had walked in on a new stage of her career, which began in part as an expression of contempt for the record industry. Almost from the beginning, in the mid-1940s, when she doubled piano with Earl Hines, palled around with Billy Eckstine, Charlie Parker, Dizzy Gillespie, and Tadd Dameron, and inherited Bernhardt's mantle as the Divine Sarah, she was poised for two careers—indomitable jazz genius, exquisite pop star. She sang "Lover Man" with Dizzy, made the charts with "Tenderly." After an apprenticeship at Continental and Musicraft, she signed with Columbia for five years, and though there were numerous conquests (including the 1950 "Mean to Me" session with Jimmy Jones, Budd Johnson, and Miles Davis), there was also "De Gas Pipe She's Leaking, Joe."

When she switched to Mercury in 1954, an affiliation that lasted more than a decade, notwithstanding a brief sojourn in the early '60s with Roulette, her presumed appeal to two audiences was underscored. For a while, jazz classics like *Swingin' Easy,* her most acclaimed album to date, were issued with the company's jazz logo, Emarcy, while pop classics like *Great Songs from Hit Shows* came out on the parent label. It was a ludicrous distinction. Vaughan was as creative mimicking the string orchestra on "Little Girl Blue" (the best version ever of that lovely Rodgers and Hart lament) as she was turning the phrase "and when your fortune's falling" into an ascending glide on "Pennies from Heaven" or reacting to Roy Haynes's bump on the line "I felt a bump" in "Polka Dots and Moonbeams." After a while, Mercury dispensed with Emarcy. By the mid-1960s, though, they were looking for middle-of-the-road hits; producers and song plug-gers were now less than enchanted by her spontaneity, her rapier reflexes, her astounding invention.

Vaughan complained that her producers were handing her lead sheets for new songs in the studio on the day they were to be recorded, depriving her of rehearsal time on the assumption that unfamiliarity would breed obeisance to the written score. They hadn't bargained on her resourcefulness (she could deconstruct a chord vocally as quickly as any instrumentalist) or her fierce pride. By 1966, she had had enough of songs like "Dominique's Discotheque" and attempts to mar-ket her as a middlebrow pop star. When her Mercury contract was up the following year, she turned her back on records for four years. She signed with Mainstream in the early '70s, reuniting with producer Bob Shad, who'd piloted most of the Emarcy dates, but she was onto something else now. Refusing to play supper clubs, she began to nurture a new following with concert tours. The last 16 years were really the most triumphant of her career, though inadequately documented in the studio. She bonded with audiences around the world—she didn't give a damn about hits.

The best evidence of her altered standing was the remarkable evolution of her longest-running encore, "Send In the Clowns." She had recorded it shortly after A *Little Night Music* opened, to negligible response. Then she worked the song into an encore routine: She'd coyly solicit requests, nod her head in patient solicitude as they were shouted back at her by the dozens, then announce, "I don't know how to tell you this, but I'm not gonna do any of those." Her pianist would limn a waltz, she'd intone the words, "Isn't it rich?" and the clock would stop for the next several minutes. When she built to the final cadenza—a characteristic joke that followed the phrase "losing my timing this year" and demanded impeccable timing—audiences roared. Within a couple of years, word was out, and people started responding to her invitation for requests by calling out "Send In the Clowns." By the mid-1980s, the whole audience was shouting it. The "I'm not going to do any of those" line didn't work any more. To exploit the phenomenon of a concert hit without a corresponding record, Pablo released a new version on which she was accompanied by Count Basie's band. Still, amazingly, after all those hundreds of renderings with her trio, La Vaughan passed away without leaving a representative recording of what had become her signature.

Sarah's independence was always a wonder to behold. Once in Boston, when she was performing with the Pops, I sat with her in her dressing room when a reporter arrived and blithely confided that she didn't know anything about jazz or Vaughan but hoped Vaughan would help get her through the interview. Sarah calmly, even graciously, showed her the door, saying, "Honey, I'm not going to be your teacher." Then she said to me, "Do you think they'd send someone out to interview Beverly Sills with a line like that?" She was proud of being a jazz singer, but she was contemptuous of those who wanted to limit her. Not all of the pop projects amounted to much (an album of Beatles songs was disastrous; one with lyrics by Pope John Paul II wasn't much better; and she never completed an album she was scheduled to record for the commercially slick Quincy Jones), but she reveled in the diverse challenges. Yet there were moments when her nerve failed her. Leontyne Price, her good friend, tried to convince Sarah to tour Europe with her, performing together onstage as they had informally. At first, she agreed; ultimately, she was intimidated.

It's hard to imagine Vaughan intimidated by anyone, though outside of music her life had its rocky places. Four marriages failed; she casually admitted her bad luck with men. She liked to work off her nervous energy by fast driving; she had a taste for coke; and for many years she smoked too much—lung cancer killed her at 66. Onstage, she could be quarrelsome if her requisite chair and glass of water weren't awaiting her, but I can't imagine her cowed by any performer. When reunited with the contemporaries with whom she helped create modern jazz— Dizzy, Eckstine—she appeared euphoric. Talent inspired her: Who can ever forget her soaring with Clifford Brown on "It's Crazy," a record later memorialized by Jack Kerouac? At the three-concert Vaughan festival George Wein produced in her honor in 1979, she requested that Eddie Jefferson and Betty Carter, whom she felt were underrated, be included. She allotted each a full set, and further boosted them by singing the girl's part on Jefferson's "Moody's Mood for Love" and inviting both of them to riff fours with her.

I worked up the nerve to introduce myself only after the *Village Voice*'s columnist Arthur Bell told me, "Sarah Vaughan loves you." "Really?" I asked, turning carmine. He went on to say that the previous night he and members of a disco group called the Village People attended her performance at the short-lived uptown club Grand Finale. After her set, they wanted to meet her, so Arthur pulled rank and marched them back to her dressing room. He knocked on the door. She asked, "Who is it?" He said, "The Village People." She said, "Come in, I love Gary Giddins."

Sometimes I'd visit her when she played the Blue Note, and though I never got over being shy in her presence, it was really no big deal—as long as you didn't expect her to entertain you, you were welcome. On every occasion, though, she would ultimately say something hilarious. Shortly after Basie died, she regaled the room with wicked impersonations of acid remarks that Eckstine, a lifelong pal since the days she sang with his big band, had made at the funeral to a veteran record producer. All three had dealt with him, and as far as Sarah was concerned, B's comments were sufficient revenge for everyone, including Basie. A few years later when I was drumming up support for the American Jazz Orchestra, I asked if I could add her name to the board of trustees. She said, "Now just don't expect me to sing at *every* concert." As it turned out, she didn't sing at any—we were always saving her for some rainy day.

It's often said (I've said it myself) that Sarah was indifferent to lyrics. But lately I've come to revise that blanket evaluation. When she liked a song's lyric, she embraced it—for example, her sexy rendition of "The Island" (on *Crazy and Mixed Up*, the one album she produced herself). More often her approach to lyrics was governed by her mischievous wit. She searched for apposite musical meanings. It's true that the big arpeggio in "My Funny Valentine" (on *Live in Japan*) has nothing to do with the song's meaning, but give her a line like "climb the highest peak" in "Cheek to Cheek" (on *No Count Sarah*) and you could be sure she'd reharmonize the cadence to do just that. I think her "Goodnight, Sweetheart," from a long unavailable Roulette album (*Sarah + 2*), is one of jazz's erotic benchmarks—she makes every vowel wink. In other instances, to be sure, she attacked the purely musical body of a song, and through repeated versions over decades worked her way to a final definition. Perhaps the ultimate example was "Body and Soul," the song with which she won the Apollo's ama-teur night contest at 18, later distilled into a continuously surprising chorus for *Swingin' Easy*, then recreated anew as a sublime duet with Ray Brown on *How Long Has This Been Going On?* There was so much more she ought to have tackled in the later years—from new versions of "The Lord's Prayer" and "If You Could See Me Now" to worthy opuses she never recorded at all. But as she blossomed in concert, records became tangential and fleeting. What a pity. What glory. Send in the clowns.

(April 1990)

PART III

PLAYERS

Satchmo's Nursery

Until recent surveys revealed that American school kids couldn't say which came first, the Civil War or Watergate, a handful of historical dates could be characterized as common knowledge. Many of us are programmed to recite not only the year Columbus sailed the ocean blue but that of the Battle of Hastings, and we will carry that information to the grave. Only one date in jazz has anything like ecumenical currency: Louis Armstrong's date of birth, July 4, 1900. That date resounds with a ring of poetic truth for the man who created the music of a new century and doubled as his nation's ambassador of goodwill. From the mid-1930s on, it was heavily featured in Armstrong's press packages and articles. How better to inaugurate an American myth than with a flag-waving birthday? Armstrong insisted his mother called him a "firecracker baby," ushered in amid roman candles and a couple of killings in the Battlefield district of New Orleans. Of course, some historians doubted him, citing the ignorance of many poor people when it came to birthdays. They figured the year was correct, but the month and day were chosen later—impoverished blacks in that era often chose July 4 or another holiday. Armstrong enjoyed no annual birthday celebrations as a child.

The point might have remained moot, except that in his 1983 biography, *Louis Armstrong: An American Genius*, James Lincoln Collier argued and convinced himself that Armstrong was born two years earlier. Other writers—including this one—subsequently took Collier's theory into account, though he built his case on evidence too flimsy even to be called circumstantial. He wrote, "There is not a single document to prove that Armstrong even existed until he was eighteen years old," and then adduced the 1898 birthday on the grounds that a couple of contemporaries *thought* Armstrong was older and because a 1918 draft form suggests that the registrar started to write July 4, 18——, then crossed out the 8 and wrote 1900. Collier leaps to the assumption that Armstrong shaved two years to avoid the draft during World War I, and that he was so dimwitted he started to give the true date, then suddenly remembered to give another. This makes no sense at all, even if—against all reason—you accept Collier's portrait of Armstrong as an obtuse, self-hating paranoiac. The Selective Service Act of 1917 drafted men between the ages of 21 and 30; when it was amended in September 1918, at which time Armstrong registered, the age was lowered to 18. Armstrong made himself only marginally less vulnerable by declaring himself 18 rather than 20. A far more likely reason the clerk wrote 18—— and then corrected himself is that he was in the habit of writing it. Since the majority of new draftees were 19 or 20, he would have been writing it all day.

In any case, earlier documents do exist, and they show that Armstrong altered his age for the same reason most adolescents do—to appear older, not younger. During the past year and a half, while researching Armstrong's life for a book and a film, I became obsessed with getting to the bottom of the birthday business. There were three leads to follow: birth, census, and baptismal records. The first, as expected, came to nothing, since the entrance of infant Louis was too insignificant for official notice. He was born in the poorest section of New Orleans, on a squalid block of ramshackle houses called Jane Alley, between Perdido and Gravier streets. His father, Willie, left at once; his mother, Mary or Mayann (as she was called), went to work in a nearby red-light district (not Storyville), leaving him in the care of his grandmother. Census records held out greater hope. They are available 70 years after they are taken, so those for 1900 and 1910 could be examined on microfilm at the New Orleans Public Library, a laborious process. I considered the strongest lead to be a statement in the first Armstrong biography, *Horn of Plenty*, written in 1947 by the Belgian Robert Goffin: "The next day little Louis was taken in his grandmother's arms to Sacred Heart Church to be christened."

Goffin's book is extremely problematic. It is rendered all but unreadable by platitudes and "colored" dialogue ("Dey gwine down tuh Congo Place"), * as well as countless misstatements, many of them quite ludicrous. Indeed, the very passage that mentions Louis's baptism is followed by a trek to the "Sunday aftehnoon" dancing at Congo Square, a ritual that had ceased half a century earlier. Moreover, Armstrong never mentioned Sacred Heart again, not even in his autobiographical writings, of which there is a great deal, most of it unpublished. Armstrong liked Goffin and sent him whole notebooks of recollections (as well as money) to help him with his book. Yet because Goffin is unreliable in so many obvious ways (he neglected to use some of the best material Armstrong sent him), he is dismissed out of hand. Goffin says, for example, that Armstrong's mother's name was Mary Albert. Collier, refusing to take that into consideration, prefers to speculate that her maiden name may have been Miles (*sic*), because she had a cousin named Isaac Myles.

During my two trips to New Orleans, several authorities on the city told me not to waste time at the Sacred Heart because it was a white church and not in

---

*Bilingual readers have informed me that Goffin and his English-speaking audience were ill served by an inept translation. Apparently Goffin himself didn't indulge in "colored" dialogue or as many platitudes.

the vicinity of Jane Alley. If Armstrong was baptized, they reasoned, the likely place was St. Catherine of Siena, a black church in the relevant section of Perdido Street. Realizing that it would take weeks to conduct a proper search, we hired an attorney to clear official channels when necessary, and Tad Jones, a historian of New Orleans, who co-authored *Up from the Cradle of Jazz*. Tad moved into the library at Loyola and began tracking census data into the appropriate neighborhood, street, and intersection. He soon found the census record for Jane Alley from the spring of 1900, which doesn't list either of Armstrong's parents, though it does list Mr. and Mrs. Isaac Myles and their children. This didn't mean much: If Armstrong was born in the late 1890s, his mother and he could have moved out by then. It did seem to confirm, however, that the pregnant Mary, who was raised in Boutee, a sugar cane community about 70 miles west of New Orleans, came to Jane Alley because she had relations there.

Working with the knowledge that Armstrong and his mother moved to Perdido and Liberty a few years later, Jones then found the census records for that area, taken on April 22 or 23, 1910. He found a family of three residing in a rooming house at 1303 Perdido—Thomas Lee, the 23-year-old "head" of the house, who gave his occupation as laborer on a schooner (Louis mentions him as one of several "stepfathers" in his 1954 memoir, *Satchmo: My Life in New Orleans*); Mary Albert, Lee's 25-year-old "companion," who gave her occupation as laundress; and Louis Armstrong, her eight-year-old son. We were stunned. Assuming Armstrong was born in the summer and would have turned nine in a couple of months, this meant that the year of his birth was 1901, something I never anticipated. For one thing, I had become convinced he was born in 1900 as he always maintained, or at least that he believed he was. He stuck to that date in all his writings as well as in picture captions in his scrapbooks (e.g., "This was in 1937, when I was 37 years old"). We tried to conceive a reason why Mary might have lied to the census taker, tried to imagine that the "8" was a "9," though the census taker's numerals were vivid. Beyond the entirely unexpected possibility that Louis was younger than he said, the 1910 census confirmed a number of other points: His mother's name was Albert, and they still lived near cousin Ike Myles, now a widower, and two of his sons, Aaron and Isaac Jr., just as Armstrong recalled in his 1954 memoir.

Having found one document that proved Louis Armstrong's existence before he was 18, we hoped for another. Not long after Jones came up empty at St. Catherine of Siena, he received a response to a letter he had written the archdiocese about church records. He was told that there was no reason Armstrong could not have been baptized at a white church. Finally, he made his way to the Sacred Heart of Jesus Church at 139 Lopez Street. The assistant pastor, the Reverend C. Richard Nowery, said yes, they were aware of a Louis Armstrong in their baptismal files, but it couldn't be *the* Louis Armstrong. Why? Because everyone knows that *the* Louis Armstrong was born on July 4, 1900—this one wasn't. Since the entire baptismal registry is alphabetized in a card catalogue, it didn't take long to pull Armstrong's entry. Louis Armstrong, the registry said in Latin, was the illegitimate black son of William Armstrong and Mary Albert, born on August 4, 1901, and baptized three weeks later on August 25. The baptismal entry and the 1910 census record backed each other up. Armstrong was, in fact, one year and one month younger than he claimed.

All the parts fit. Armstrong's memoir said he was raised by his Catholic grandmother, who worked in a white area. Willie had another wife and family in New Orleans, so it made sense to find that Louis was "illegitimus." The question remained—did Armstrong know his true birthdate? The 1910 census record certainly suggests that he knew the year, since his mother did. But he may not have known the month, except that it was in the summer. My grandmother was born in Poland in the late 1880s and never knew the year or month—only that it was in the dead of winter. After her children had children of their own, the family decided to give her a birthdate (December 30) so that we could celebrate it. Armstrong, who probably never stepped into the Sacred Heart of Jesus Church again, may have chosen July 4 during the period he spent in the colored Waif's Home, as other kids did. But why did he walk into a draft board at 17 and put himself into jeopardy by declaring himself a year older?

In 1918, Armstrong's career as a musician began to take off. Kid Ory invited him to replace King Oliver in his band at a Perdido Street saloon, and Fate Marable wanted to recruit him for an orchestra that made interstate tours on a Mississippi steamer. A year earlier, the United States Navy had shut down Storyville, the most notorious red-light district in New Orleans, and it is likely that officials were cracking down on the remaining dives. Cabaret owners may have had doubts about hiring a minor, and even if things remained loose in New Orleans, the same might not be true of places like Davenport, Iowa, where the steamboat docked. Perhaps the responsible Marable, or his boss, Captain Joseph Streckfus, required proof of age. It was also in 1918 that Armstrong married a young prostitute named Daisy. He may have needed proof for that, too. In any case, the one place a black 17-year-old could get "proof" he was 18 was the draft board. Nor did he put himself in much danger. The army wasn't drafting many young blacks at war's end, and armistice was declared only two months after Louis registered. Besides, as he admitted in his memoir, he took a job he detested, delivering coal from 7 a.m. to 5 p.m., to ensure his deferment. The false birthdate allowed him to embark on a career he was impatient to pursue. When the wily manager Joe Glaser took charge of his career, the date passed into legend.

(August 1988)

SIGNIFYING

Just as Civil War battles and the politics of Reconstruction are rehearsed cease-lessly by buffs and profs, the power plays between slave and master have also remained vestigially alive at the end of the 20th century, with this difference: that issue is secretly preserved, chiefly in popular songs handed down through generations increasingly deaf to their meaning. Subverted into neutralized meal for children (like much 19th-century American literature, for that matter), those songs, which once gladdened and even changed people's hearts, are now presumed to be opaque if not downright nonsensical. They are as invisible as many of the black bards who wrote so many of them. On the other hand, Stephen Foster, whose music embodied the widespread belief that former slaves spent the rest of their lives longing for the resumption of slavehood, remains a popular brand name, like Uncle Ben's and Aunt Jemima's.

One of the first songs I can remember learning well enough to sing was "Jimmy Cracked Corn" or "The Blue-Tail Fly" (its real name); not for 20 years or so did I realize it wasn't a nonsense song, a kids' song, but an expression of glee at a slaveowner's death. What makes the song chilling is that Massa isn't made out to be wicked; he isn't characterized at all, except as Massa—reason enough to crack corn in celebration of his demise. A blue-tail fly got him, as the singer details in a series of verses, each followed by the chorus of merriment ("Jimmy crack corn and I don't care/ My Massa's gone away"). We don't know for sure where he's gone until the end, when his epitaph is sung. The song was popular in minstrel shows of the 1840s and was handed down for 150 years, transformed into a campfire song for white middle-class kids. Perhaps "A Hard Rain's Gonna Fall" will be rediscovered in the next century as a cautionary ballad about the need to put on your galoshes.

These thoughts are prompted by a couple of reissues (volumes four and five of *The Mills Brothers Chronological*, on the British JSP label, distributed in the United States by Rounder Records), which collect the 11 sides recorded by the Mills Brothers and Louis Armstrong for Decca between 1937 and 1940. I had heard those performances at one time or another, but I'd never *heard* them. What most brought me up short were two numbers originally released together on one very successful 78 recorded at their first encounter—a politically dazzling response to the enforced pastoralism that became rife in the recording industry of the 1930s and continued into the early 1960s. I submit that in the long, irreverent history of black performers signifying attitudes that went over the heads of white audiences (for reasons Ralph Ellison plumbs in his great novel), this was one of the most ironic pop records ever released. The songs were James A. Bland's "Carry Me Back to Old Virginny" (1878) and Benjamin R. Hanby's "Darling Nellie Gray" (1856).

Part of the disc's power lies not only in the talents of the performers, but in how they were perceived by audiences. The Mills Brothers, the most enduringly successful male quartet in American pop music and one of the first black groups to win international acceptance, made the leap from tent shows to New York via a triumphant radio stint in Cincinnati in 1929. Soon they were touring the country, recording prolifically (teaming up with such white stars as Bing Crosby, the Boswell Sisters, and Al Jolson), and appearing in films and on network radio. With only one change in personnel (brother John Jr. died and was replaced by their father), they recorded a string of hits for 30 years, and then kept on as a trio for another 15, after John Sr. retired at age 74. Their biggest hit, the weirdly fetishist "Paper Doll," was the third biggest of the 1940s (after "White Christmas" and "Rudolph, the Red-Nosed Reindeer"), and was later beanballed in a noted essay by S. I. Hayakawa, once a respected semanticist. They had velvety voices, impeccable diction, dreamy harmonies, supple time, and—especially in their early, more jazz-oriented years—a remarkable gimmick. They imitated instruments (trumpet, trombone, sax, tuba) so well that they subtitled their act Four Boys and a Guitar to stress the cleverness of their mimicry. When they muted their vocal brass effects their riffs suggested the Ellington band. But straight as they were honest, they allowed their later work to be subsumed in a blandness that bespoke too many chic white nightclubs and hacked-out band arrangements.

Louis Armstrong, on the other hand, was always a renegade, even when he acceded to the same idiocies in material and setting. He could telegraph with a growl or a rolling of his eyes his independence, confidence, and security. If the Mills Brothers were heroes in the black community for their talent and success, Armstrong (whose music influenced theirs, as it did every black band and vocal group to come along in the '30s) was venerated for all that plus an indomitable will and irreverence. As the embodiment of jazz, he made jazz the embodiment of individual signifying; the singer, not the song, was what counted, or as Trummy Young used to chant, " 'Taint What You Do (It's the Way That You Do It)." There's no better example than the material Armstrong rendered with the brothers Mills.

By 1937, 72 years after the Civil War, songs of the 19th century had long since become a staple of recording sessions, not only because they appeared to tame black performers into a new kind of servility—singing proslave lyrics for liberal record producers on the grounds that they were true folk material—but because they were free, having escaped into public domain. One might reasonably assume that the lyrics of "Carry Me Back to Old Virginny" and "Darling Nellie Gray" had lost their bite if not their meaning, and indeed no one seems to have commented on the strangeness of black performers recording them, of black and white audiences buying them, of what Armstrong did with them. Though the lyrics of both songs are as explicit as those of "The Blue-Tail Fly," I haven't been able to find a single reference to them in the 59 subsequent years of pop and jazz commentary. This despite the fact that it was a major seller, putting the Mills Brothers back on the charts after a distraught three years during which John Jr. died. Its popularity contributed to the state of Virginia's decision to adopt "Carry Me Back to Old Virginny" as the official state song in 1940.

What kind of song is it? A nostalgic minstrel expression of mourning for the Old South, for Massa and the plantation. The melody is hauntingly beautiful, and the structure—32 bars, AABA—surprisingly modern. The Mills Brothers sing it exactly as written, including the line, "There's where this old darky's heart does long to go," and the stupefying release:

> There's where I labored so hard for dear ol' massa
> Day after day in the fields of yellow corn.
> No place on earth do I love more sincerely
> Then old Virginny, the state where I was born.

Armstrong, whose first entrance serves to introduce a scat figure that propels the piece immediately into double time, attacks the song with creative relish, and he makes a couple of seemingly casual changes in the offensive lines that make all the difference in the world. In the first case, he sings (twice, both times accommodating the loss of sibilance with a rhythmic adjustment), "There's where the [not 'this'] old darky's heart longs to go." In the release, he changes "dear ol' Massa" to "old master," carefully enunciating the consonants. (When Ray Charles recorded the song in 1960, he obviated the problem by changing the first line to "That's where this heart of mind yet longs to go," and omitted the release, replacing it with a new chorus about finding freedom in death). Perhaps Armstrong's most able signifying comes at the end of the first eight bars of his 32-bar solo, an unmistakable trumpet call—to freedom in life. If the flip side had been a similar piece or an ordinary ballad, the record would—despite Armstrong's saves—have limited meaning. But "Darling Nellie Gray" was one of the most powerful abolition songs of the 1850s; published only four years after *Uncle Tom's Cabin*, it is widely credited with changing people's minds on both sides of the Mason-Dixon Line.

Only 16 bars and five lines long, crooned with a scent of magnolia by the brothers, then swung with candid effervescence by Armstrong, it is a Kentucky slave's lament for his lover, sold or traded like a prize sow: "Oh my poor Nellie Gray/ They have taken you away." If the choice of material alone didn't counter the sentiment of the A side, the job was done by Armstrong's tender solo; utterly engaged vocal, made the more dramatic by syncopations (especially in the second of two surviving takes); caressing, virtuoso fills behind the quartet; interpolated remark before the close ("Now, boys, what do you know about this?"); second chorus alteration of the line "I'm sitting by the river and I'm weepin' all the day" to "I'm sitting by the river and I'm all in a shiver"; and extended scat cadenza.

The whole endeavor is heightened by the irony of authorship. The celebrated minstrel and tunesmith James Bland (he wrote "In the Evening by the Moonlight" and "Oh, Dem Golden Slippers" as well as the Virginia state song) was black. "Darling Nellie Gray" was composed by a white 22-year-old minister, Benjamin Hanby, to aid the abolitionists. His tune spurred heavy black sales of the record in the summer of 1937. Did anyone comment back then on the curiosities of that disc? It's difficult to know what contemporary black reviewers thought, since black newspapers have yet to be fully gleaned for the valuable anthologies they could undoubtedly produce. White critics, then as now, paid it no mind. Jazz critics hated the idea of Armstrong working with a silky pop group, which is one reason the sessions have been incompletely reissued in the United States, while that strange breed of folklorists who trekked into the Alabamy veldt in search of folk Negroes ignored city ones as ersatz. Yet most of the Armstrong-Mills material was uncommonly interesting—three Irving Berlin gems; a wry novelty about the WPA's impact on the Puritan work ethic ("Sit down and smoke while you joke, it's okay—the WPA"); Don Redman's gently lubricious "Cherry"; the scat-filled call to dancers, "Boog It," with its descriptive verse ("You do like shinin' a window/ But you ain't got no window/ So you just picture a window/ and Boog It!—slow and easy"); and, most pungent, Stephen Foster's outrageous and eternal "The Old Folks at Home."

They did the Foster song at the same session as the other minstrel tunes and coupled it with the turn-of-the-century ballad "In the Shade of the Old Apple Tree." With a few alterations, Armstrong could distance himself from "Carry Me Back"; with his natural élan, he could restore the emotion to "Darling Nellie." What in heaven's name could he do with Foster's recalcitrant song, in which free darkies sadly roam the dreary world, "longin' for the old plantation and for the old folks at home," except burlesque the hell out of it? No sooner does the quartet croon it straight than he suddenly turns the performance into a mock church service, entering like a deacon ("Now brothers!"), impaling every phrase on the precision of his caricature: "That's where *my* heart turns, *Yowsah!* . . . Know one thing? My heart am still *longin'* for the old plantation . . . Hallelujah, hallelujah . . . Oh, darkies!" He ends speaking, "Well, looka here, we are far away from home," and adds with devastating menace, "Yeah, man." Rasped with implacable finality, that phrase buries the song and the maudlin pastoralism that kept it alive, or should have. Few people, however, wanted to hear what old Deacon Satchmo was signifying. Yet here once again was evidence that as Pope wrote of Homer, Armstrong's art "is like a copious nursery which contains the seeds and first productions of every kind, out of which those who followed him have but selected some particular plants."

(May 1989)

King of the Savoy

The story of William Henry Webb, nicknamed Chick for his small size, seems to cry out for novelistic scope and nuance. His musical accomplishments were diverse: He was the first great drummer of the Swing Era, the leader of a fiercely competitive and innovative orchestra, a pacesetter for dancers during the golden age of ballroom dancing, and a nurturer of talent whose fabled generosity was rewarded when he discovered and groomed Ella Fitzgerald. But the nearly unconquerable King of the Savoy Ballroom was also a dwarfed hunchback, mangled by spinal tuberculosis, who lived most of his short life in pain and died within a year of his first major commercial success. He overcame staggering obstacles with a tenacity that awed other musicians, and he did it with élan, never asking for or requiring handicap points. He was as much adored by dancers as by musicians, and no one dared patronize him.

Chick Webb's story wouldn't exercise so powerful a spell if the contrast between his imposing reputation and atrophied frame didn't find a correlative in his music. He may well have been the first jazz drummer to convey complicated emotions, at least on records. Even today, despite half a century of virtuoso band drummers who surpassed and refined his technique, Webb's rattling breaks and solos are astonishing. Those who heard him live insist that records hid his genius, but there is nothing remotely like the feeling of a Webb break—a pealing explosion in which each stroke has the articulation of a gunshot. Fast and disciplined, he was attuned to his soloists and spurred them with flashing cymbals or emphatic shuffle rhythms. He orchestrated the components of his traps like an arranger, meshing the sound of his huge bass drum with bells, blocks, and rim shots, punctuating the airless rumble with choked swipes at two cymbals that swayed before him on gooseneck hangers. Writing in 1939, Charles Edward Smith observed: "Listening to [Webb's] drums, you got a sense of percussive build-up, to the blood as well as to the ear, but you also came to understand that a drummer was, after all, a musician playing tones." Webb didn't solo frequently, but when he did he was ferocious. At the Savoy, his drums were nailed to a movable stand; on tour, he often needed assistants to bolster them against his attack.

Unfortunately, there's no filmed record of Webb in action. His band appeared in a 1929 short, *After Seben*, but he's out of camera range. Numerous drummers who saw him, however, never forgot; they describe him in grandly romantic terms. Enthroned over his traps, which included a 28-inch bass drum with pedals built to accommodate his stunted legs, he is said to have conveyed a wry magnificence, dominating all the accoutrements with a winning lopsided smile, leaning into the hardware while hands and feet pumped rhythms and counterrhythms. Those who learned from him include Buddy Rich, Gene Krupa, Sid Catlett, Jo Jones, Dave Tough, Cozy Cole, and Panama Francis. Ronald Shannon Jackson says he studies Webb's records for inspiration. Krupa remarked, "When he really let go, you had a feeling that the entire atmosphere in the place was being charged. When he felt like it, he could down any of us."

Bandleaders also loved him, sometimes too well. Webb had an extraordinary ear for talent, and his band was raided in the years when he was known only in Harlem. Fletcher Henderson hired away trumpet players Bobby Stark and Cootie Williams, and Duke Ellington grabbed 20-year-old Johnny Hodges. Ellington later said that Webb came to him and offered Hodges because he "would be better in our band where he would have more freedom of expression," and played broker for Williams, who had left Webb for Henderson. Webb reportedly told Ellington, "He was with me for a while, but he's too much for me. Fletcher heard him and hired him but that style don't fit Fletcher's band . . . for you he'll be a bitch!"

If that sounds magnanimous even for the saintly Webb, it undoubtedly reflects his gratitude to Ellington for starting him as a bandleader in 1926—a position he accepted with some reluctance at first. Ellington later wrote that when he was in residence at the Kentucky Club, someone came in wanting to hire a band; the Maestro assembled a small group and dubbed Webb the leader. "As a drummer, Chick had his own ideas about what he wanted to do. Some musicians are dancers, and Chick was," recalled Ellington, who went on to elaborate the importance of the equation: "The reason why Chick Webb had such control, such command of his audiences at the Savoy Ballroom was because he was always in communication with the dancers and felt it the way they did. And that is probably the biggest reason why he could cut all the other bands that went in there."

All but one. Ten years after the Kentucky Club episode, Webb was the undisputed King of the Savoy, but in March 1937 he did battle with the Ellington band and was trounced. According to Teddy McRae, a Webb saxophonist and arranger, Webb saw Sonny Greer tuning his drums before the melee and said, "What is he tuning up for? I'm gonna kill him before he gets started. And he did." But his band was demolished. "I can't take it," Webb told trombonist Sandy Williams during a break, "this is the first time we've ever really been washed out." Webb and Williams recorded a few days later with several Ellington musicians (including Cootie Williams) as the Gotham Stompers; on "My Honey's Lovin' Arms," he showed how he might have sparked the Ellington rhythm section.

Webb's most celebrated battle came three months later, and it too was a rout, only this time Webb regained his crown. From 1931 on, Webb was admired by many white bandleaders—including Paul Whiteman—who knew they couldn't raid a black band. Benny Goodman got around that by appropriating the orchestrations of Webb's gifted saxophonist-violinist-arranger-composer Edgar Sampson, creator of several of the era's anthems. The early Goodman hits that didn't come from Fletcher Henderson's book came from Webb's, including "Don't Be That Way," "Stompin' at the Savoy," "Blue Lou," and "If Dreams Come True," all by Sampson. Goodman's appearance at the Savoy opposite Webb on May 11, 1937, was bound to be tense, especially since his drummer, Gene Krupa, was the most highly publicized percussionist in the country.

Helen Oakley Dance, who covered the event, reported that nearly 10,000 people showed up, half of whom were turned away at the door, causing a traffic tie-up that lasted all night. Mario Bauza, Webb's lead trumpeter, recalled the little man giving the band a pep talk—"Tonight we got to make history. Our future depends on tonight." The verdict rendered by the teeming crowd as well as representatives of *Down Beat* and *Metronome* was unanimously in Webb's favor. According to Dance, the climax came when Webb followed Goodman with one of Goodman's own hits, "Jam Session," and "blew the roof off the house." Earlier in the evening, Krupa had stood, facing Webb, and bowed down in respect.

Chick Webb's birthdate has been variously given as 1902, 1907, and 1909, but the last seems to be widely accepted now, which puts him in an increasingly long column of precocious jazz musicians who made themselves out to be older. He was born in Baltimore and raised by his grandfather, after his father and later his mother moved out. He is said to have started teaching himself drums at three, eventually arranging batteries of tin cans, pots, and stacks of magazines. At 11, he earned enough money as a newsboy to buy a set of traps, and was soon playing in the Jazzola Band on a riverboat on Chesapeake Bay, along with guitarist John Truehart. Three years later—when Webb was 15—the two arrived in New York, where the segregated band scene was dominated by Paul Whiteman and Fletcher Henderson. Webb convinced Tommy Benford to give him lessons and hustled for chances to play. Eventually Bobby Stark recommended him for a job with a group led by Edgar Dowell, and he began to earn a reputation. At first people made a point of coming to see him because of the way he looked. That began to change with the gig Eillington set up in 1926, which lasted five months. In Truehart, Stark, Hodges, and pianist Don Kirkpatrick, Webb had the nucleus of an important band. He soon added other musicians, including Mario Bauza and saxophonist Elmer Williams, and emerged as a tutor to drummers of both races who came to hear him in Harlem. Defensive about his band, he invited cutting competitions and invariably charmed his victims. Still, the Webb band was barely making it and remained unknown beyond a coterie of musicians.

Webb's luck began to change in 1931, when he was booked into downtown dance halls as well as the Savoy. He toured with *Hot Chocolates*, the show that made Louis Armstrong a star, and his band backed Armstrong when the great man resumed recording after his European tour of 1932. Webb's snare work is in evidence on "Hobo, You Can't Ride This Train," and his 11-piece band rips through the climactic riffs on "You'll Wish You'd Never Been Born," which opens with an enchanting Armstrong cadenza that anticipates his solo in "Laughin' Louie." By that time Webb had recorded a couple of sessions on his own. In 1929, he appeared on disc as the Jungle Band, hewing to the Henderson–Don Redman style on "Dog Bottom" but mining Ellington's shadowy terrain on "Jungle Mama." A session under his own name followed in 1931, around the time he began the first in a series of long residencies at the Savoy; on that date, he introduced Benny Carter's "Blues in My Heart" and a version of "Heebie Jeebies," with a benchmark trombone solo by Jimmy Harrison and a promising tenor sax solo by Elmer Williams.

During the next three years, Webb stubbornly refined his band and found an orchestral style of his own. By the time he recorded in January 1934, he had assembled a rigorous unit with efficient jazz soloists and some of the hottest arrangers of the day, especially Sampson, whose earliest contributions included "If Dreams Comes True," "Stompin' at the Savoy," and Webb's theme song, "Let's Get Together." Soon Webb hired Wayman Carver, the first jazz flutist and (aside from Albert Socarras, who was really a classical player) the only one of consequence for nearly 20 years. The unison sound of Carver's flute and Chauncy Haughton's clarinet, especially in Webb's small unit (Chick Webb and His Little Chicks), was startling. Neither man swung very hard, but they could project a daunting string of 16th notes with radiance, and they pointed up the diversity of Webb's band. By the time Benny Goodman kicked off the Swing Era with his triumph at the Palomar Ballroom in Los Angeles, in 1935, Webb had one of the most distinctive bands in New York—his arrangers included Van Alexander, Charlie Dixon, and Dick Vance. But like Henderson's, it couldn't break nationally. Webb and Henderson watched as their records caused small ripples, while cover versions by the Goodman orchestra caused tidal waves. Goodman even had his name added as composer. In the movie *The Benny Goodman Story*, you can watch Goodman compose Sampson's "Don't Be That Way."

Most of Webb's records were in the Henderson tradition, which massed reeds and brasses in antiphonal call-and-response. Yet the band's audacious attack, primed by Webb's prodding rhythms, rim-shot turnbacks, and explosive breaks, gave the arrangements a unique kick. In some of the band's best choruses, reeds and brasses collude like overlapping shadows. The band's stately, almost arhythmic side, as reflected in the Carver-Haughton passages, made for beguiling contrast. His soloists have been grievously underrated—among them trombonist Sandy Williams (spotlighted on "Organ Grinder's Swing"), trumpeters Stark, Bauza, and Taft Jordan (who came closer than most to capturing the Armstrong might), and saxophonists Sampson, Hilton Jefferson, Elmer Williams, and

Teddy McRae. With John Truehart and John Kirby, Webb had one of the better rhythm sections of the '30s ("That Rhythm Man" is a good example). In 1934, he finally discovered a musician who grabbed the public; unlike Hodges, Cootie, or Sampson, this one didn't get away.

In 1934, Ella Fitzgerald, 16 and recently orphaned, won a talent contest at the Apollo Theater trying to sing like Connee Boswell. Benny Carter heard her and told John Hammond, Fletcher Henderson, and others, who weren't interested. Webb agreed to give her a tryout and was hooked. He became her legal guardian, bought her clothing to perform in, and reorganized his band around the voice he predicted would be heard for decades. From the summer of 1935, she was featured on almost all his recording sessions and quickly attracted a following. The band began to tour, working some of the better hotels and picking up radio airtime. In 1938, Van Alexander orchestrated a novelty tune Fitzgerald had worked up from a nursery rhyme to entertain Webb during a hospital stay. "A Tisket, A Tasket," recorded in May and powered by Webb's offbeat accents, was one of the biggest hits of the decade—the biggest Ella, who had just turned 20, would ever have. Within months she was billed as "the first lady of swing." Lena Horne recently recalled, "A whole generation of us girl singers went looking for that yellow basket." Webb found himself a commercial property and, to the dismay of many of his supporters, made the band increasingly subordinate to his singer.

Helen Oakley Dance, who was hired as his publicist, has pointed out the painful irony in Webb's sudden celebrity. He had fought extraordinary odds for a decade to assemble a great band and now, just when swing was at the height of its popularity, he was playing it safe. Some thought he knew his time was running out and wanted to secure a foothold for Ella. In any case, the accusation wasn't entirely fair: Webb made many of his finest instrumental recordings during the Ella years, including Benny Carter's feature for drums, "Liza," "Harlem Congo," "Spinning the Web," and "Clap Hands! Here Comes Charlie." Some of his best work is heard on such peerless Fitzgerald sides as "Cryin' Mood," in which Webb seems to levitate the orchestra, "My Heart Belongs to Daddy," "Undecided," "Pack Up Your Sins and Go to the Devil," "Holiday in Harlem," "Shine," and "My Last Affair."

Almost from the time "A Tisket, A Tasket" topped the charts, Webb was in chronic pain; the tuberculosis worsened, and pleurisy developed. He was in and out of hospitals, and on at least two occasions he collapsed on the bandstand. He was in John Hopkins Hospital in Baltimore for a couple of days before the end came. According to Dance, he lifted himself from the pillows, said, "I'm sorry, but I gotta go," and was gone. If the 1909 birthdate holds, he was just 30 years old. Ella sang "My Buddy" at the funeral, and the pallbearers and honorary pallbearers included Fletcher Henderson, Benny Carter, Al Cooper, Duke Ellington, Gene Krupa, Cab Calloway, and Jimmie Lunceford. A couple of months later, Count Basie paid homage with a cover of "Clap Hands! Here

Comes Charlie." Fitzgerald returned Webb's loyalty by fronting the band for two more years, with Teddy McRae and Eddie Barefield as music directors, and then went out as a single. In 1947, a recreational center in Baltimore was named in his honor. Three years later, "A Tisket, A Tasket" was certified as a gold record.

(August 1988)

The Mirror of Swing

While memories are fresh, it won't do to consider Benny Goodman, who died in his sleep on the afternoon of June 13, 1986, at 77, exclusively as a jazz musician. The emotions conjured by his name are unique to those few who transcend the specifics of talent and come to represent an era. If he wasn't the king of a musical idiom called swing, he was surely king of the Swing Era, an agreeable focus for Yankee pride at a time when music counted not only for art, entertainment, and sedative, but as a balm with which to weather terrible storms. Goodman will be remembered for his contributions to jazz, which are manifold, and he occupies an impressive historical niche as the first musician to enjoy hugely successful careers in three discrete fields (jazz, pop, and classical). Yet in his time Goodman was also a blessed and seemingly eternal presence in media culture who, through an unofficial contract between artist and public, reflected the nation's new vision of itself in the arts—earthy, democratic, and homegrown, and at the same time refined, virtuosic, and international.

The enormous sense of loss that attended his death was animated in part by the realization that an age had passed, and not just a musical one. (Other Swing Era titans are still with us, including the great progenitor Benny Carter and the great crooner Frank Sinatra, who inadvertently helped supplant big bands in the public affection.) Goodman came to prominence when America was making major discoveries about the nature of its cultural life, and proved an exemplary figure for national preening. He was in all important respects distinctively American, purveying an undeniably American music with at least the tentative approval of academics and the Europhile upper crust, into whose circles he married. His connections put him in Carnegie Hall (a big deal in 1938) five years before Duke Ellington. The public took comfort in him, too. He was white, but not too white, which is to say Jewish, but not too Jewish; and serious, but not too serious, which is to say lighthearted, but sober. At the height of the Depression, he had perfect credentials for entertaining a suffering, guilt-ridden nation. Goodman was one of 12 siblings born to penniless Russian immigrants in Chicago. He received his first clarinet at 10, in 1919, and had a union card three years later.

Everyone knows this story, or a version of it. As the favorite fable of the 1930s, it was internalized by Depression-bred children who went on to dramatize it for

stage, screen, and radio countless times into the late 1950s, and occasionally ever
since. It's told of Berlin, Gershwin, and Jolson, and with appropriate variations in
ethnicity, of Armstrong, Crosby, Sinatra, Handy, Jim Thorpe, and Presley. Until
Vietnam and the civil rights era, it was standard grammer school indoctrination,
combining the American dream with melting pot diversity, cheerful tolerance,
and a ready willingness to brave new frontiers. If nations were judged by the lies
they told about themselves, this one just might guarantee salvation. Small wonder, then, that when an individual appears worthy of the crown, we bow our
heads in gratitude. With few exceptions, however, only performing artists and
athletes are able to pull this particular sword from the stone.

Few Americans have handled the role of cultural icon as well as Goodman.
For more than 50 years, he endured as one of the nation's favorite images of
itself. Several weeks before his death, a few musicians were sitting around trading
anecdotes about him, causing one to remark, "At any given time somebody
somewhere is telling a Benny Goodman story." Those stories are rarely kind,
usually having to do with his legendary cheapness, absentmindedness, mandarin
discipline, rudeness to musicians, and various eccentricities. But they never
dented his media image, nor were they meant to. Americans usually come to
resent the entertainers they've deified, yet Goodman remained virtually unblemished. Any real skeletons that may have resided in his closet rattled in peace. It
isn't hard to understand why. Everyone could feel good about Goodman. You
could send him anywhere, from Albert Hall to Moscow, and rest assured that he
would comport himself with quiet dignity and spread Americanism in a manner
the world would take to heart. Had he worn striped pants and a top hat, he could
not more naturally have embodied everything America wanted to believe about
its promise of tolerance and opportunity—those democratic underpinnings insufficiently embraced at home but glamorized for export to the rest of the world.

The *Time/Life* history of all things would have us believe that Goodman
helped the country unwind with a new and thrilling music, which is true only in
the sense that Columbus discovered America. The music wasn't new, and some
of the country had already unwound to it. Goodman, like Elvis 20 years later,
adapted black music for white tastes. He toned it down, cleaned it up. Unlike
Presley, he was willing to take risks with his celebrity. Perhaps he was so socially
unconscious, he didn't realize the implications of those risks. In any case, with
the politically astute critics John Hammond (his future brother-in-law) and
Helen Oakley spurring him on, Goodman hired Teddy Wilson virtually at the
moment he achieved commercial leverage. They first recorded together in the
summer of 1935, at two sessions produced by Hammond—the first in support of
Billie Holiday, the second the debut of the Benny Goodman Trio. A year later,
after the success of his big band, Goodman took Oakley's suggestion to take
Wilson on the road, and a bulwark of racism was fatally breached.

Goodman was proud of his musical origins, as witness his many tributes to
Fletcher Henderson, whose reputation was fading when Goodman and Ham-

mond conspired to revive it. Henderson's arrangements provided the original Goodman orchestra with a style, and remained Benny's favorite music to play (he especially loved Henderson's arrangement of "Somebody Loves Me") until the end of his life. Beyond the vagaries of race, however, Goodman's superb musicianship indemnified him as an honorable standard-bearer for the art suddenly thrust into his hands. He was, this above all, a nonpareil clarinetist; a bandleader who innovated chamber-sized ensembles; and the sponsor who introduced (again with the help of the ever-alert Hammond) numerous great players, arrangers, and singers.

With his unpretentious air and perpetually puzzled look, his amiable stage manner and nearly country-boy shyness, his strangely aristocratic inflections despite a tendency to mumble, and his unmistakable obsession with music/work, he was all that central casting could ask as the hero of the most celebrated parable in American music. The fabled night during which Goodman was transformed from mere musician to looming eminence is an elaborate morality play, involving the genesis of the Swing Era, the ascendancy of mass-market technology, the hero's conflicting feelings about race, and semi-rugged individualism. Goodman's rise is not unlike the touchingly grotesque 1930 Hollywood version of *Moby Dick* (starring John Barrymore and Joan Bennett), played out as a road story with a happy ending for an agreeably ambivalent Ahab.

Goodman was a 26-year-old fledgling bandleader when he embarked on a promotional cross-country tour in the summer of 1935. Despite six months of weekly appearances on the "Let's Dance" radio program, a library of arrangements by Fletcher Henderson, Edgar Sampson, Benny Carter, and others, and a band that included Bunny Berigan, Jess Stacy, and Gene Krupa, Goodman had cause for misgivings. Big band jazz was still far removed from the mainstream; talented jazz players of Goodman's generation were obliged to work in stuffy ballrooms, playing bland dance music and novelties to earn a living. Jazz was something you played after hours, or sneaked into arrangements as a condiment when no one was looking. Indeed, shortly before leaving New York, Goodman was fired from the Roosevelt Grill for not playing "sweet and low," as he later recalled. Reaction was no better on the road west, and after three dismal weeks at Elitch Gardens in Denver, where he was nearly fired for playing pieces that went on too long and for not offering waltzes, comedy, and funny hats (Kay Kyser was packing them in down the street, Goodman was drawing flies), his bookers suggested he cancel the ensuing engagements in California.

He refused. Tour's end was to be the Palomar Ballroom in Los Angeles. But first there was a Monday night in Oakland, and Goodman was astonished to find the place nearly filled; it reminded him that one reason he had been able to finance the tour was the report of interest in his records in California. Still, he knew the Palomar was a more imposing room, and, chastened by the experience in Denver, Goodman decided to open with stock arrangements and sugary ballads. He continued in that vein for an hour with no response, but by the second set he had made up his mind that if he was doomed to failure he would go down honorably. He called for the Henderson charts and counted off "Sugar Foot Stomp." The crowd roared with approval. He couldn't believe it. *This* was what they had come to hear, the good stuff. The young audience stopped dancing and pressed against the bandstand. On that night, August 21, 1935, the Swing Era was born, because on that night middle-class white kids said yes in thunder and hard currency. Goodman stayed at the Palomar for two months and then moved on to Chicago, his hometown, where he played six months at the Congress Hotel.

It's a good story, and variations on it have been told many times since with different protagonists. *The Buddy Holly Story* offered an almost verbatim reenactment, as the discouraged rock and roller opens a set with country favorites, before—pride of purpose coming to the fore—switching to rock and roll. Inherent in every retelling are two paradigmatic twists that first appear in the Goodman saga. First, the influence of technology: The mystery of California's enthusiasm was solved when Goodman and his booking agent, Willard Alexander, realized the impact of network radio. Through "Let's Dance," Goodman's music had been relayed around the country by 53 stations, with the necessary allowance for different time zones. In New York, he was heard from 10 p.m. until 1 a.m., playing the tame band arragements of the day. For the Los Angeles market, he had to perform two additional hours, beginning at the outset of prime time, 7 p.m., and finishing around midnight. To fill the larger time slot, he drew on the very jazz numbers that cost him his job at the Roosevelt Grill. He had no way of knowing he was nurturing an audience on the west coast with every Saturday night broadcast.

The second twist was racial. From the days of antebellum minstrel shows to the present, the point at which indigenous American music becomes pop culture is the point where white performers learn to mimic black ones. Many of Goodman's biggest hits were virtual duplications of records that Fletcher Henderson and Chick Webb had recorded months, even years, before. Ellington's band had been declaring "It Don't Mean a Thing if It Ain't Got That Swing" for three years before Goodman reached California, and territory bands had spread the sound of swing throughout the Midwest by 1930. Louis Armstrong's success on records opened the door for everyone. Even before that, the Original Dixieland Jazz Band, the first white band to popularize the New Orleans style, had caused a sensation in New York in 1917, helping to usher in the Jazz Age, with Paul Whiteman reigning as surrogate for the real thing. In one form or another, jazz had been skirting America's consciousness for nearly 20 years before Goodman's triumph.

Goodman himself learned jazz from those musicians, white and black (notably clarinetists Leon Rappolo and Jimmie Noone), who had left New Orleans for Chicago during the teens and early '20s. His borrowings have been held against him. But given the colonialist iniquities of the period—not least the network radio hookups that were closed to blacks—and the emotional prejudices directed at the very foundations of African-American music (the Puritanical distrust of heady rhythms, at least until they were distilled by white precision and decorum), it's no good blaming the symbol of racial favoritism for racism itself, especially when that symbol took an activist stand against it. As Milt Hinton recently observed, Goodman's contribution to dismantling the color barriers was "a daring, daring thing."

Yet by the mid-1960s, when race was a central issue in discussions about jazz, Goodman was often dismissed as though his stature in jazz was as spurious as that of Whiteman. The King of Swing hyperbole, an astoundingly effective public relations ploy in its day, had become an albatross, as did the invidious 1955 movie ("Here, Fletcher, hold my clarinet") *The Benny Goodman Story*, which, frequently broadcast, was a real source of embarrassment to him and did nothing to improve his reputation for insensitivity. The racial animus, matched by envy and personal resentment, not least in the ranks of musicians who had suffered under his withering stare (he was known as "the Ray" by bandsmen) or those who despaired at never getting the chance, resulted in a barrage of contentious carping.

Easy to understand why: In 1963, Goodman was still exhibited as the representative jazz artist for the home viewing and arts center audiences, while Ellington continued on the road playing one-nighters, composing and recording the most extensive body of music ever produced by an American. Musicians of John Coltrane's generation remained relatively unknown to the general public. As late as 1975, a leading classical music critic challenged me with the assertion that Goodman was a more important composer than Ellington. When I told him Goodman didn't compose at all, he was incredulous. Goodman himself had no trouble penetrating the delusions of reputation. I once asked him if he actually composed any of the several riff tunes for which he is co-credited. "Oh, maybe one or two, but I doubt it," he said.

Goodman, like all icons, was an easy target. In the '60s I heard a jazz musician acknowledge him as a great clarinetist who should stick to the classics since he couldn't really improvise, and a classical musician groan that Goodman had murdered Mozart but was a genius in jazz. Other forms of damning praise saluted him as a popularizer or as an ambassador. Even Bud Freeman, who presumably had no racial or high-versus-low-art axes to grind, put a weed in his bouquet. After describing Goodman, at 13, as having "the technique of a master and a beautiful sound to go with it," and recalling the "thrill" of working with him in 1928, he concluded, "I don't mean to imply that he's a creative player; but he certainly is a masterful player." I've heard people who ought to know better argue that Goodman never surpassed his early idol, Jimmie Noone, which is like saying that Louis Armstrong never surpassed King Oliver. In truth, Goodman's instrumental style is so much his own that you can recognize it almost immediately. His playing may ultimately have done more to sustain his reputation than his work as a bandleader. In the latter capacity, Goodman demonstrated an irreproachable taste in arrangers ("good taste in Negroes," one wag observed), but he offered little that was genuinely new until the 1940s, when he reformed his band to play the modernist music of Eddie Sauter and Mel Powell. As a clarinetist, he was his own man.

Goodman's victory at the Palomar meant that jazz would no longer be the property of the impassioned few. It now emerged from the underground jam sessions to engulf even the ballroom pioneers—the Whitemans and Pollacks and Reismans—who had tried to limit jazz to an occasional solo or effect. Following the examples of Henderson, Ellington, and Webb, Goodman played music that was jazz from start to finish. He upended the music business. Yet as a major white star, he had to pay the usual price; he was required to water down the original brew. On the surface, that meant recording nearly as many pop vocals as jazz instrumentals; the result was essentially popular music with jazz interpolations (or fusion, as it's known today). Even in this regard, he went his own way. In addition to his regular pop singers, including Martha Tilton and the talented Helen Forrest, he recorded with authentic jazz singers—Ella Fitzgerald, Jimmy Rushing, Maxine Sullivan, and others. The same little-known studio player who presided over Billie Holiday's first record in 1933 would launch Peggy Lee's career in 1941.

Goodman always kept his balance, refusing to allow his celebrity to dictate essential musical decisions. When he broke all records at New York's Paramount Theater in 1937, and faced the kind of shrieking adulation that was then new to American entertainment, he would sit placidly, waiting for the audience to finish its performance before he started his. By introducing trios, quartets, and other small groups in addition to the big band, he even made the fans sit still for chamber jazz. Yet subtler indications of musical dilution were felt, reflecting Goodman's stringent personality and insistence on precision. He often seemed more concerned with unison execution and projection than with the spirited abandon that typified not only the best black bands but his own early work as a sideman. Paradoxically, his rigidity was a primary reason for his success.

Goodman's soloists didn't compare with those in the Henderson orchestra, but his fastidious ensemble could sometimes get more value from a Henderson arrangement than Henderson's relatively unwieldy band did. If some of Goodman's records are anemic copies of Henderson's ("Wrappin' It Up," for instance), others ("Blue Skies," "Sometimes I'm Happy") are exemplary interpretations, which is undoubtedly one reason Henderson enjoyed writing for him. Despite his apprenticeship in hot jazz, Goodman had a preternatural understanding of what a mass audience would accept. Were the dancers discomfited by brutal tempos? Goodman simmered them down. He knew how to inject just the right touch of excitement into a performance.

Consider his hit version of Edgar Sampson's "Don't Be That Way," originally recorded by Chick Webb. Webb took the tempo way up and climaxed the performance with an explosive eight-bar drum solo. Goodman modified the tempo, streamlined the ensemble parts, introduced a famous fade-down in volume, and reduced the climax to a two-bar drum break by Gene Krupa that, because of its sudden intrusion, jolted the jitterbugs. (Coda: Years later, Krupa's formidable replacement, Dave Tough, completed a performance of "Don't Be That Way" with an extended break that awed everyone in the band but left the audience cold. He asked Goodman to play it again during the second show. This time he mimicked Krupa's relatively simple outburst, and the crowd cheered.)

Goodman was primarily a popularizer of big bands, but he was an innovator of small ones. The Benny Goodman Trio was conceived when Goodman heard Teddy Wilson play "Body and Soul" at a party given by Red Norvo. Shortly afterwards, in the summer of 1935, Goodman, Wilson, and Krupa recorded four sides for RCA. The combination of clarinet, piano, and drums was by no means new (Goodman had heard others, notably Jelly Roll Morton, use it during his adolescence), but Goodman greatly increased its flexibility and made it the foundation for several variations. A year later, in California, he was advised to visit a disreputable sailor's hangout called the Paradise Café to hear the entertainment—one Lionel Hampton. Goodman returned the next night with Wilson and Krupa to jam and had no trouble convincing Hampton to join them on the road.

The small groups were a popular draw at Goodman's shows, and although Wilson and Hampton were billed as special attractions rather than as members of the orchestra, their presence paved the way for integrated bands. Krupa went the distance when he left Goodman to start his own band and allowed his star soloist, Roy Eldridge, to sit in his trumpet section. (Integrated audiences came later.) The chamber groups also gave Goodman the opportunity to indulge himself as a clarinetist on wistful ballads ("The Man I Love," "Moonglow") and flashy stomps ("Runnin' Wild," "China Boy"), and rekindled the spark of his earlier playing. They gave him the chance to work with favorite musicians without regard to race. In the big band, Goodman's soloists tended to mimic the great stylists assembled by Henderson, especially Coleman Hawkins and Eldridge. Only Goodman himself bested his opposite number—Buster Bailey—in the Henderson band, though the arrangements tended to limit the size and scope of his solos. With the small group, which grew to a sextet ty 1939, he could stretch out in the company of the incomparable guitarist Charlie Christian, trumpeter Cootie Williams, whose temporary defection from Ellington wowed the musical community (Goodman also tried to snare, unsuccessfully, Johnny Hodges), and, on records, Count Basie. Before long, other bandleaders introduced chamber groups, including Webb, Ellington, Artie Shaw, Woody Herman, Tommy Dorsey, and Dizzy Gillespie.

If the combo recordings as a whole stand up better than those by the big band, which today suffer needlessly from the idiot obsession with reissuing complete works in chronological order, the generous playing time accorded the leader is a major reason. On the orchestra's pop sides, his clarinet is often the only solace: In the course of a conventional arrangement worsened by a dire vocal, Goodman's blistering clarinet flashes to the fore and creaky sentiments are momentarily banished. Goodman was a hot player whose adroit blues choruses distinguished him almost from the start during his days in Chicago. His command of every register enabled him to contrive a style of high drama and earthy swing. A student of the Chicago Symphony's Franz Schoep as well as of jazz clarinetists, he never allowed technique to vitiate the rhythmic charge of his music. Artie Shaw had a prettier tone, Barney Bigard a fatter one, but Goodman was unfeigned and lusty. He could growl with bemusement or ardor, according to mood, and when he really let go, leaning back on his chair, feet flailing the air, or hopping around on one leg, he could make anyone's heart beat a little faster. Goodman's rhythmic gait was unmistakable: His best solos combined cool legato, a fierce doubling up of notes, and the canny use of propulsive riffs.

He displayed some of those gifts as early as 1926, when he first recorded, still under the influence of Jimmie Noone. A year later, when Goodman was only 18, an English publisher brought out *Benny Goodman's 125 Jazz Breaks for the Saxophone and Clarinet*. Had he retired in 1935, he'd be remembered now for his rigorous solos on numerous records by Ted Lewis, Adrian Rollini, the Joe Venuti–Eddie Lang Orchestra, Red Nichols, the Charleston Chasers, and others. At his best, he was able to sustain a similar excitement all his life. Forty years after the kingdom of swing had been gentrified almost beyond recognition, he could still provoke the crowd's roar. Last summer, as an unbilled performer at a tribute to John Hammond, he provided the highlight of the Kool Jazz Festival. It was anything but a middle-aged jazz audience that cheered him on when he came out and played "Lady Be Good" with George Benson, and then—seated, both legs levitating—layered climax after climax on "Indiana." Up to that point, the young white-blues crowd had greeted every jazz performer with impatient demands for the man of the hour, blues guitarist Stevie Ray Vaughan. When Goodman finished, that same crowd was on its feet.

When my review of that concert appeared, Goodman's assistant told me the Old Man was pleased and surprised by it, since he'd gotten it into his head that I considered him outmoded. I have no idea why. How could anyone think that? Goodman kept his faith until the end. Ultimately, he mirrored not only a chapter in America's cultural history, but the spirit at the core of a music that can only be enfeebled when nostalgia gets between musician and audience. In 1975, I visited Goodman at his East Side apartment. He had been practicing Gounod's *Petite Symphony* when I arrived, and I asked him if he preferred improvising or playing written music. "Gee," he said, "I enjoy both. Listening to music is emotional. Sometimes you like something a lot, and another time you hate it. The whole goddam thing about jazz is emotional. I like to feel the excitement. If it doesn't come out as a wild endeavor—wild with restraint—it doesn't have it." Goodman had it in 1926, and he had it 60 years later. *

(June 1986)

*When I wrote "The Mirror of Swing," a couple of days after Benny Goodman died, I had heard many of the nasty Goodman stories making the rounds, but underestimated the depth of resentment. A few months later, John Lewis, Roberta Swann, and I produced an American Jazz Orchestra tribute to Goodman. More than two-thirds of the AJO had worked with Goodman at one time or other (an extraordinary statistic), and their recollections made the rehearsals memorably hilarious. Yet some stories were related with a naked hatred for what was described as the man's cruelty, cheapness, and vulgarity. Of course, virtually every one of them commenced with a statement of high regard for his musicianship. John Lewis, who does not traffic in gossip, mused one afternoon that throughout jazz history the most innovative and accomplished musicians on every instrument but one were black; his exception was the clarinet and Goodman.

My own limited experiences with Goodman were altogether positive. He graciously met with me in 1975, when I approached him for my own illumination, with no story or publication in mind; and he agreed immediately to lend his name and prestige to the initial board of advisers to the AJO. Still, Goodman was by all accounts a troubled and troubling man, which makes his untouchable status as a celebrity all the more remarkable. Despite the petty jealousies he exhibited and elicited, his private woes remained if not entirely private then confined to the grousing of musicians. I see no reason why they shouldn't be aired now. Yet it would be a shame if the contemporary thirst for pathographies (Joyce Carol Oates's sadly indispensable term) obfuscated Goodman's nearly impeccable public posture and the affection he inspired in the hearts of music lovers for more than half this century.

Ghost Stories

Larry Adler, the world's most ambitious virtuoso of the mouth organ (his preferred locution for harmonica), has likely passed through more cultural strata than any other living entertainer. His performing partners have included Duke Ellington, Django Reinhardt, and Dizzy Gillespie; Al Jolson, Eddie Cantor, and Ruth Etting; Andres Segovia, Isaac Stern, and Yehudi Menuhin; Jack Benny, Jimmy Durante, and Imogene Coca; and Fred Astaire, Ray Bolger, and the Nicholas Brothers. He's played vaudeville, concert halls, and jazz clubs. His touring act with dancer Paul Draper was one of the most successful of the 1940s. Darius Milhaud, Ralph Vaughan Williams, and Heitor Villa-Lobos composed music for him. Adler had achieved something only a handful of musicians in history can claim: He endowed a folk instrument with aesthetic clout.

Adler rescued the harmonica from a perennial Marine Band adolescence, dressed it in symphonic tails, integrated it into jazz ensembles and film scores, and enticed from it an unprecedented diversity of sounds and techniques, including seamless legato phrasing, trills, and contrapuntal harmonics. But despite his instrumental skill, the stigma of novelty is not easily expunged. No other musical noise has as many ready-made folk associations, from the bluesman's wail to the cowboy's lullaby, and few instruments so willingly give up a perfect tone—a moan, a cry, an evocation—to anyone's untutored exhalation.

Because most of us never got past that maiden tone, the instruments's landmarks—which include the whomping blues of the Chicago dynasty that extends from John Lee "Sonny Boy" Williamson to Junior Wells; the slapstick shenanigans of the Harmonicats; the cool, modernist reserve of Toots Thielemans; the ecstatic, dusty, yelping of Sonny Terry—tend to provoke skeptical wonder. No matter how commanding the performance, you never entirely forget that all that music is coming from a toy. The harmonica was invented by an Englishman named Sir Charles Wheatstone in 1829, but the whine that escapes its metallic reeds is the eternal sound of American nocturnes and American zip and American kitsch. The fact that most Americans no longer remember Adler can be traced to another seemingly indigenous phenomenon: the political witch hunts and blacklists that followed hard on the heels of World War II (nothing worse than a sore winner), grinding numerous careers under the wheels of regimented patriotism and personal betrayal.

Adler, who turned 65 in 1979, is himself quintessentially American in his pioneering arrogance, his improvisational know-how, his courage, persistence, and wily humor. At 14, he achieved the unique status of expulsion from the Peabody Conservatory of Music. His crime was to play "Yes, We Have No Bananas" instead of the Grieg he'd rehearsed. He was already sufficiently eclectic to count among his idols Heifetz, Rachmaninoff, Caruso, Armstrong, Ellington, and Jolson. That same year, he won first prize in a mouth organ contest, and set out from Baltimore, chromatic Hohner in hand, a talented musician with little music to play. During the next 40 years, Adler inspired or commissioned symphonic composers to write him a repertoire; he adapted numerous classical and popular anthems on his own, and learned to extrapolate handily enough to intrigue major figures in jazz. The adaptability that characterized his musical career fortified him during the House Un-American Activities Committee's reign of terror, when he found himself depicted, in his words, as "the greatest subversive, Communist, left-wing, agitating revolutionary character since Zinoviev tried to overthrow the British government, only I was doing the whole thing with a mouth organ."

Adler is a compact, energetic man who favors dark sports clothes and doesn't seem to have changed much in 20 years, except that he once combed his hair back and now combs it forward. He compares the mouth organ to the human voice in flexibility, and has strong opinions about his colleagues: "Toots Thieleman's jazz is far superior to mine—I get jealous as hell when I hear him play—but he's only got one sound. I admire Sonny Terry. He plays right out of his belly, I could never get those sounds. Stevie Wonder gets a good commercial sound, it's marvelous, but he has no variety at all. I don't think John Sebastian's very good, and Bob Dylan can't play for nuts. His sound is awful and his interpretation worse. I don't think any mouth organ player can get my variety. If they can play good jazz, they sure as hell can't play Bach. That's because I love every style of music with the sole exception of rock."

This variety is dryly exhibited at The Cookery, where music and anecdote are woven into 40-minute autobiographical montages. Interspersed with the music are stories and asides, related with the sing-song conversationalism and brevity of a master in the Jewish tradition of storytelling. Accompanied by pianist Hal Schaffer when he isn't accompanying himself, Adler plays a program of pop songs from the golden age, classical favorites (pop songs from another golden age), original selections from his film scores, and an occasional novelty, such as a medley of cowboy songs. When he hits a groove on the fast tempos—"Where or When," "On the Street Where You Live"—he achieves a rhythmic equanimity that is much like swing, though not quite the McCoy. On balance, he evinces a charming, Gallic, romanticism underscored by irony and drama.

The mouth organ lends itself to drama, with its startling dynamic range, and I find Adler most rewarding when he kvells his way through minor tempests, as on "Rhapsody in Blue," "Blues in the Night," "Malagueña," "Sophisticated Lady," "Am I Blue?" and "Bolero." He's been adding classical transcriptions to the sets in response to requests from the audience, but one selection that is a constant in his repertoire is Beethoven's Minuet in G, which he plays in C, employing counterpoint and double stops. In 1928, it was his ticket out of Baltimore. Adler had started out on piano at the conservatory but abandoned his studies in a fit of pique when his grandfather compared him unfavorably to a concertizing prodigy of the day. Four years later, he entered a mouth organ contest sponsored by the *Baltimore Sun*. While the other contestants trotted out pop ditties, Adler snared the judges with Beethoven.

He used the prize money to travel to New York, where he auditioned for Borrah Minevitch (who later apprenticed a couple of the Harmonicats) and received three words of advice: "Kid, you stink." Trekking despondently back to Penn Station, he eyed Rudy Vallee's name on a marquee, sneaked in, and wrangled a job for the evening. He flopped, but a subsequent evening with bandleader Paul Ash led to a 44-week contract with Paramount, traveling the country in what the English used to call Cine-Variety: "You'd be on the bill with a film, and the number of shows you did depended on how popular it was. In Mae West's heyday, I might find myself doing six shows a day, and you did the same goddam act, because once you rehearsed with the band you couldn't change. By the time you walked out for the fourth show, you hated it and were all tightened up. But it gave me the training to walk on and off a stage, not to be afraid of a cold audience—training you couldn't get today." Soon he was stooging for Dan Healey (Adler played mouth organ while two men wrestled a bear until the bear pulled someone's pants off) and Eddie Cantor. In Ziegfeld's 1931 *Smiles*, he worked with Fred Astaire and became famous enough to interest Hollywood.

Adler plays a lot of jazz at The Cookery, and hopes to record with jazz musicians while in New York. He can improvise cleverly and sympathetically, but as he once confessed, in a manner exemplifying what he calls Jewish gallows humor, "I am not now, nor have I ever been, a jazz musician." One evening, Mary Lou Williams came over from her gig down the block at the Knickerbocker and collaborated with him on "Caravan," commenting later, "He's a genius. He plays nice chords—usually they play corny chords. I think he could play the modern stuff if he worked on it." Adler's first encounter with a major jazz figure coincided with his first movie offer. He signed a contract to play "Sophisticated Lady" in the 1934 film *Many Happy Returns* for $300. The Guy Lombardo orchestra was hired to accompany him: "I refused. So they fired me and rehired me and fired me, and it went all the way to the head of the studio, William LeBaron, but I flatly refused to work with Lombardo. I said, 'You know who I like? I like Duke Ellington,' and LeBaron said, 'Well, I like Duke Ellington, too,

Larry, but you can't expect us to hire him to accompany you, he isn't even in California.' At 2 a.m., LeBaron called and said, 'Well, you little son of a bitch, we got Ellington.' "

Ellington was paid $5000 to back Adler's $300, but wasn't photographed or credited because Lombardo wasn't supposed to know about the switch. Subsequently, Adler's intractability resulted in "one of the greatest regrets" of his life. Ellington's manager, Irving Mills, offered him a contract to record 50 sides with Ellington at $25 each. Having read in *Variety* that Bing Crosby got a 5 percent royalty, Adler demanded the same. Mills told him what he could do with his royalties. "That same year, Duke and I were at the Grand Terrace in Chicago. Earl Hines, who had the band, called on us, and we got up to play 'Sophisticated Lady.' Afterwards, Duke brought me over to a table where a lady was sitting by herself. He said, 'Larry, I want you to meet Billie Holiday.' I put out my hand to say how-do-you-do and she said, 'Man, you don't play that fucking thing, you sing it.' Oh God, I can't tell you what it did to me."

Another encounter with a jazz legend followed in 1938, when Adler attended a concert by the Quintette du Hot Club in Paris. Charles Delaunay, the master of ceremonies, surprised Adler by introducing him and requesting he sit in for a number. "I stood up and said, 'It's very embarrassing but I haven't got a mouth organ.' And Django Reinhardt said, 'I've got one,' and pulled it out of his pocket." They hit it off so well that recording time was soon reserved at Columbia. Reinhardt's quintet accompanied him on four continuously reissued sides, including a coquettish "Body and Soul."

In 1934, at the start of his recording career, Adler scored one of his most enduring successes with a drastically abridged version of Ravel's "Bolero." When he performed it a year later at the Alhambra in Paris, a controversy ensued and Ravel requested him to play it in his home: "I played it in front of him, feeling like a shmuck. It was so embarrassing and he never moved a muscle. He just listened to me, and when I finished it, he said, 'You've cut it.' I said, 'Well, yes, I had to because I do a vaudeville act and you can't do just one number in a 12-minute act.' He said, 'You know Toscanini?' I said yes. He said, 'Toscanini doesn't cut it.' He was looking at me and I was looking at him and nothing was being said. So out of sheer desperation, I held up my record of 'Bolero' and said, 'Maestro, would you sign this for me?' He said he thought the record was a present for him, which amazed me, and I said, 'Sure, Maestro,' and left it with him.

"Three days later, I received a call from Jacques Lyon, who ran a record shop on the Champs Elysees. He said, 'Get over here at once. Maestro Ravel is in my shop and wants to see you.' I rushed over, and there was Ravel with a piece of paper bearing his signature. Then, in 1943, I did a concert with the Philadelphia Symphony and was asked to prepare an encore. I said what about 'Bolero,' and they said we'd have to pay a performing rights free, too expensive, think of something else. I said, 'Look, Ravel's publishers, Elkan, Vogel, are in Philadelphia. Maybe because I knew Ravel they'll give me a rate.' So I went over there, and Mr. Elkan came out and said, 'We know all about you, Mr. Adler.' Ravel had left in his will rights to me to play 'Bolero' without any performing fees. I could play it any way I liked, in boogie woogie tempo if I wanted."

European composers had been taking an interest in Adler since his 1934 tour of London. Cyril Scott was the first to write expressly for Adler; around the same time, George Gershwin authorized a mouth organ arrangement of "Rhapsody in Blue." When Darius Milhaud heard him play the "Rhapsody" in 1943, he offered to write him a suite. During the next decade, concertos were written for him by Ralph Vaughan Williams, Malcolm Arnold, and Arthur Benjamin, among a dozen others. Adler simultaneously honed his talents as a monologist under the tutelage of Jack Benny. They did USO tours together, and when Benny needed a 45-minute broadcast in Cairo, he assigned Adler to write it. He was at the pinnacle of his career in the '40s, touring as the guest soloist with philharmonic orchestras, or in a jaunty act with dancer Paul Draper that became a top box-office draw. Then the trouble began.

A certain amount of sentimentality attends Adler's engagement at The Cookery. His producer, Barney Josephson, created Café Society, the first integrated nightclub in the United States, which was shut down by the House Un-American Activities Committee. "What they wanted Barney to do was denounce his own brother," Adler says. "Walter Winchell wanted to make a deal with me—all I had to do was denounce Henry Wallace and Paul Draper." At times he grows weary of the reminiscing. "It's marvelous to see my old friends, but a lot of people who come to The Cookery are almost lachrymose about good old Larry and how brave he was. I do wish they'd let the subject alone."

Adler had been a member of numerous left-wing organizations when, in 1947, he joined the Committee for the First Amendment to protest the inquisition of the Hollywood writers known as the Unfriendly 19, later the Unfriendly 10. They charted planes to Washington, and all hell broke loose when they landed: "The press attacked us and Humphrey Bogart caved in in the most demeaning, debasing way, saying that he was duped, didn't realize what he was doing, but was sorry and knew the American people would allow him one mistake. And then Gene Kelly reneged, and Danny Kaye reneged, and Frank Sinatra reneged, and those of us who didn't stood out like carbuncles." During the next year, Adler and Draper filed a libel suit against Hester McCulloch, who had written that they should not be allowed to perform in Greenwich because money paid them went directly to Moscow. The Hearst press took up the cudgel, and soon the duo's signed contracts were canceled. A blacklist took effect, and in 1949, while touring London, Adler's wife convinced him to stay abroad until it blew over. It didn't.

At Isaac Stern's suggestion, Sol Hurok agreed to produce Adler in 1952 if the American Legion wouldn't picket. A concert at Town Hall sold out and received wildly favorable reviews, despite attempts to force him to cancel. Still, Hurok insisted that his board of directors would not let him continue the association. William Morris booked Adler in Las Vegas, but the legion stepped in and the contract was repudiated: "When I came back in 1952, I sat at Sardi's with Elia Kazan, John Garfield, Frank Loesser, Charles Lederer, and Abe Burrows, and we knew that Kazan had been subpoenaed by the Un-American Activities Committee, and Kazan said, 'I've got two million bucks in the bank and nobody's going to make me talk.' We thought, 'Good old Kazan.' Two days later, a quarter-page ad appears in the *New York Times*, signed by Kazan, in which he said that to keep silent was to play the Communist game. He went to Washington and gave a tremendous list of names, including Clifford Odets.

"The night Kazan went before the committee, I had dinner at Meyer Davis's house, and there was Odets. I said, 'Cliff, you must feel awful, having one of your best friends name you.' And Odets said, 'Larry, how do we know what kind of pressure he was under, who are we to judge?' I thought, this guy's a saint. I felt like a shmuck for even bringing it up. The next week, Odets went before the committee and named everybody, including Kazan. They'd made a deal—you name me and I'll name you.

"Abe Burrows called me to have lunch and said, 'Larry, you're about to give a recital at Town Hall. Why don't you make a public non-Communist statement and go down to Washington? What do you say? The main thing is to get back to work, we want you back playing your mouth organ.' I said, 'Abe, that's not for me.' He said, 'Larry, it makes it embarrassing for your friends. Your name comes up in conversations and I don't know what to say.' I said, 'I'll tell you what you say, say you don't know me.' He said, 'Come on, you're taking it the wrong way.' I didn't know that Abe was about to go before the committee and give names."

Adler returned to London, where the English director Henry Cornelius hired him to compose the score for his film *Genevieve* in 1953. Six weeks before it opened at the Sutton Theater, the producer was asked to submit a new set of credits omitting Adler's name. He complied. The music was nominated for an Academy Award, and when the nominations were read, Muir Matheson, who conducted Adler's music on the soundtrack, was named as composer. "About a year later, I saw the Mathesons and asked him why he accepted the nomination. He looked me straight in the eye and said, 'I thought I was being nominated simply for services to British music.' "

In 1959, Art D'Lugoff booked Adler for a triumphant homecoming engagement at the newly opened Village Gate, where he was accompanied by Ellis Larkins. Adler didn't learn until several years later that James Thurber, E. J. Kahn, and Kenneth Tynan had guaranteed D'Lugoff against any loss. His success at the Gate led to a TV appearance with Dizzy Gillespie and two pop/jazz recordings for Audiofidelity, with Larkins, Joe Benjamin, Paul Motian, and a badly undermiked Ruby Braff. Occasional tours and concerts in the United States followed.

Adler continued to live in London, where he is celebrated not only for his music but for his fanatical devotion to tennis and for his articles and book reviews in the *New Statesman*, the *Spectator*, *Punch*, the *Jewish Chronicle*, and the *Sunday Times*. As recently as 1965, Sol Hurok told Adler that a concert tour of America would be difficult to bring off because "concert committees are run by Republican ladies with long memories." Even Adler's instrument attests to those memories. He plays the Larry Adler Model of the Hohner Super Chromonica, which is sold all over the world—but not in the United States. Other memories, every bit as tenacious, asserted themselves one night at The Cookery. As Adler circled away from the mike in ritual prelude to his encore, a tall and gaunt Alger Hiss walked in. They embraced under Barney Josephson's benevolent gaze, and later toasted themselves for outlasting Walter Winchell and Dorothy Kilgallen and Joe McCarthy and other ghosts that not even the torrid lament of a mouth organ can lay to rest.

2.

Larry Adler is back in town, playing three weeks at the Ballroom. Last year, his repatriation took another step forward when the Peabody Conservatory, which expelled him some 55 years ago, asked him back and gave him an honorary degree. Coinciding with Adler's return was the appearance on the *Times* op-ed page of a strange study in eschatology by Richard Nixon, who insists that Whittaker Chambers, though dead, "was on the right side" even though Hiss "still lives." Adler himself is engaged in a more benevolent séance with the dead: He is at work playing duets with Gershwin, Youmans, and Rachmaninoff. His partner in metaphysics is an instrument so rare that most poeple are surprised to learn it exists at all. The Reproducing Piano was introduced in the 1920s as an acoustic miracle—the compact disc of pianolas. Unlike the well-known and fairly inexpensive player piano, an RP can replicate the dynamics of each note cut into a piano roll. Many great pianists of the era, including the young Horowitz, were importuned to cut rolls for it. But RPs were costlier than cars in those days, and the Depression, records, movies, and radio, soon erased them from the memory of all but a handful of collectors and antiquarians.

The Ballroom claims to have the only one on public display. Actually, its six-foot-six Knabe is the club's second RP. The first was sold to a private collector a couple of years ago. They ought to hang onto this one, an astonishing instrument capable of solo performances long after Adler returns to England. To inaugurate its acquisition, Adler was engaged to celebrate the 50th anniversary of the night he and Gershwin first played "Rhapsody in Blue." Although Gershwin cut several ordinary piano rolls in 1920, the "Rhapsody" was apparently the only piece he performed in 1925 for the Aeolian Company, which manufactured Duo-Art pianos and rolls.

Adler's duet with the composer is the highlight of his show, which in other respects changes nightly. As the lights go down, two spots come up: one on Adler and another on the keyboard. The performance is imperfect. The length of the piece is a strain on the mouth organist, and the roll is given to tempo shifts. Yet it is an eerie and wondrous thing to behold Gershwins' ghost at the keyboard. The depressed notes reflect his touch, force, tempo, and pedaling. Adler says that the corporeal Gershwin was a kinder accompanist than his piano roll, yet the exchanges between Adler and the machine have a spontaneous quality that is actually enhanced by the latter's temporal idiosyncrasies. They keep Adler on his toes.

"Rhapsody in Blue" itself seems deathless. It's been done just about every way short of didjeridoo and, despite decades of denigration, remains the most popular piece in American concert music. My own feelings about the various interpretations pivot on what seems to me the only perfect recording, that of Oscar Levant with Eugene Ormandy and the Philadelphia Orchestra. Only in that version, made for Columbia in the late 1940s, are all the parts in just proportion. Gershwin's Tin Pan Alley impulsiveness and Ferde Grofe's symphonic expansion meet on common ground, with no attempt to weigh down the driving melodies with anxious climaxes. Even Gershwin's 1927 recording, with Paul Whiteman's big band playing the original Grofe arrangement (no strings), sounds like a blueprint for Ormandy's cool amplitude.

Conductors less conversant with Broadway glitz usually offer portentous readings designed to make the "Rhapsody" sound more serious than intended. Toscanini's 1942 performance with the aptly named pianist Earl Wild opens with Benny Goodman handling the clarinet cadenza, but as soon as the orchestra, accompanied by hyperthyroid cymbals, enters you know the conductor wants your hair to stand on end. Gershwin didn't. Leonard Bernstein's crawling meditation is probably supposed to remind us that the piece has deep blues feelings. It doesn't. It has ordinary sevenths and minor thirds borrowed from the blues, but the music's charm is embodied in the rush of fragmented melodies, each perfunctorily resolved so that a new one can be introduced, until finally a grand Gershwin song is asserted for a big, weepy climax.

Gershwin's 1925 Duo-Art roll recreated the entire piece as a piano reduction, complete with "overdubbed" accompanying figures. In 1965, Movietone released it as a record, but the tempo was speeded up, and it sounded no more human than the usual player piano roll. About 10 years later, Columbia Records took that roll and covered all the holes that represented the overdubs, the notes that would be played by the orchestra. Then they hired Michael Tilson Thomas to conduct Grofé's dance band arrangement in tandem with an RP. The result was impressive technology, but the interpretation was less than convincing and occasionally off kilter. Adler also works with the edited roll, and while the collaboration might not travel as well on records, it has a stirring, agreeably sentimental impact in live performance. Gershwin seems to be there.

For other selections on opening night, Adler played Bizet's "L'Arlesienne Minuet" with Rachmaninoff, whom he had seen perform when he was five but had never worked with, and "Tea for Two" with the composer Vincent Youmans. For a savvy selection of standards, he was accompanied by the living Hubert "Tex" Arnold, and in the more relaxed ambience generated by those songs gave a better display of his powers as a discerning embellisher of melody. He made the verse to "My Funny Valentine" sound like a Rumanian folksong; improvised long, skittish variations on "Love Walked In"; and fired fierce, reedy salvos through the familiar territory of "I Got Rhythm."

The post-"Rhapsody" highlight of the evening was his reunion with the brilliantly inventive pianist Ellis Larkins, who, incidentally, graduated from Peabody. When Art D'Lugoff wrote Adler in London and asked him to play the Village Gate in 1959, Adler insisted that Larkins—whose duets with Ella Fitzgerald Adler had recently heard—be hired to play with him. They've worked together several times since. Larkins would be an ideal candidate to make some RP rolls, because his catlike touch is inimitable. He never plays the same thing twice, and his lilting time transforms Adler, who is flexible enough to swing when a natural swinger like Larkins spurs him to action. They played "Summertime," "How High the Moon," "Body and Soul," and "Where or When," and Adler's trilling high notes became increasingly bright and graceful as the night wore on.

(August 1979, January 1986)

The Wizard of Bop

Think of the Charlie Parker era, and you may think of dark glasses, gray pin-stripes, bebop jive, cool dudes, narcotics, and the lost glamor of an untouchable musical coterie. That's because the superficial aspects of the period became profoundly identified with a sensibility, hip but not yet beat, that attempted to transcend art. Think of the Charlie Parker era, and you also think of a music that was brazen with self-assurance, giddy with its own virtuosity, fierce to the point of arrogance, yet so nervously, tenderly vulnerable that its ballads were taken at tempos slow enough to seem nearly motionless, the melodies lagging way behind the beat, with rests as dramatically telling as the notes. As bop in its pure form evolved into subsequent styles of jazz, it lost some of its own shine, its authority and beauty. Considered frantic and wild in the parlous days of its birth, bop offers a heartening rigor for these parlous times. Small wonder that when an authentic apostle of Charlie Parker's dreamworld springs into view, the response mixes gratitude and confirmation. In the '70s, we witnessed the resurrections of Red Rodney, Dexter Gordon, and Art Pepper. Now we have the return of Frank Morgan.

Frank Morgan, who opened at the Village Vanguard on September 9 and is now visiting New York for the first time, is an alto saxophonist who participated in the Central Avenue days of West Coast jazz. Like the role for which his actor namesake is best remembered, the Wizard of Oz, he started down the yellow brick road and ended up in a land of glib delusions. Morgan first met Charlie Parker when he was a boy—his father, the guitarist Stanley Morgan, had known Parker in Kansas City, when the two men traveled with Harlan Leonard and His Rockets. He showed a precocious affinity for Parker's blues locutions and harmonic resourcefulness, and his career got off to a promising start. Before he turned 21, Morgan recorded with Teddy Charles and Kenny Clarke and cut an album of his own with Wardell Gray, Conte Candoli, and Carl Perkins. Before that, at 17, he was offered a chance to play New York, a trip delayed 35 years, most of which time Morgan was caught on the California penal system treadmill. "In retrospect," he says of the original offer, "I guess that's when I decided to fail. I knew enough about heroin to know that it was certain failure—that if anything would ensure failure, becoming a heroin addict would be it. I had full knowledge."

When we met last August in Los Angeles, Morgan had recently issued the second album of his comeback, *Lament* (Contemporary), and was finally enjoying the success that might have been his in 1955, when GNP issued *Frank Morgan* with a blurb anointing him as Parker's successor. Soft-spoken, candid, and disarmingly genial, he discussed his readiness, at long last, to enjoy the fruits of his talent. He had nearly 10 years to wrestle with the issue. In 1977, GNP reissued his first album and asked Leonard Feather to write the notes. Most people thought Morgan was dead, but Feather asked around and learned that he had been released from a rehabilitation center. He couldn't find him, though. A few days after he'd given up, the phone rang: "Leonard? This is Frank Morgan." During the next two years, Morgan participated as a sideman on records by Benny Powell and L. Subramaniam, but he wasn't ready for a career. Then on April 2, 1985 (Morgan remembers the dates of each entry and release), he completed a six-month prison sentence for a parole violation and learned that record producer Richard Bock was looking for him. Bock told him Fantasy Records was willing to sign him for an album on its Contemporary label. He recorded *Easy Living* that summer and cleaned himself once again of his habit. He even turned himself in to clear the slate. After serving another four months, he was ready.

Morgan's unlined face denies the often harrowing 53 years of his life. Perhaps the Ojibway blood on his father's side explains the strong cheekbones and the russet coloring. His face has a beaming, open quality and the glitter in his eyes counters the low volume and careful articulation of his voice. He has an immaculate presence, which was underscored by a white shirt patterned with lace. With his companion of many years, the artist Rosalinda Kolb, whom he credits with saving his life, he talked of his past; the subject often turned to Charlie Parker and the era that produced and destroyed so many musicians of his generation: "I was born in Minneapolis on December 23, 1933. We moved to Milwaukee when I was six and California when I was fourteen. My father had me playing guitar from the time I was two, but that changed when I was seven and he was playing with a band in Detroit. I joined him there for Easter vacation, and he took me to the Paradise Theater. At that time, several movie houses had stage shows, and this one happened to feature Jay McShann's band. Walter Brown was singing 'Hootie Blues,' and when Charlie Parker stood up to take his solo, it changed my whole life. I decided I wanted to be an alto saxophone player right then and there.

"I met Bird that day. My father talked to him about me playing the alto, and Bird suggested that they start me on clarinet. I thought Bird was going to pick out the horn for me, but he didn't show up. But Wardell Gray and Teddy Edwards, who were both playing alto then with Howard McGhee's band, did. They picked out a clarinet for me, and you know I was disappointed. I was a little mad with Bird, because I wanted to play saxophone. I didn't understand that he thought he was getting me off to a proper start. And it's perfectly true.

Just to get a sound out of the clarinet, a child has to develop greater control than you might ever get as a young saxophone player. It proved to be a blessing, insofar as I was able to develop a clarinet technique that has carried over into my saxophone playing."

Morgan lives in Topanga, but the two of us were in L.A. to work on a video documentary on Parker, for which I was to interview Morgan. As we got closer to the taping, he assembled his alto and warmed up with a blues. He remarked, "Bird once said to me that he believed in playing the blues on everything. I kind of questioned that, and he said that you could play with a kind of blues feeling on everything, no matter if it's a church hymn or a song. You could say he was playing the blues all the time, whether it was 'Parker's Mood' or 'April in Paris.' "

Morgan's alto sound is supple and lyrical in a way that recalls Benny Carter almost as much as Parker. His tone is fuller in the lower notes than on top, and it can be prim and dry, which makes his frequent use of pinched high notes to pace himself and increase tension all the more effective. In his current playing, such as his recent recordings of "Embraceable You" and "Until It's Time for You to Go," he sculpts notes, feeling his way into melodies—something you don't hear as much in the early work, with its exceedingly legato phrasing. His variations, which gently probe the chords, will shyly turn around phrases and then pick up steam with a double-time barrage. He constantly evokes Parker, but he also invokes a classic approach to the instrument itself: "Well, Charlie Parker's alto saxophone differed not greatly from Johnny Hodges or Benny Carter insofar as the approach to the horn. The harmonies that Bird played really made him different. I think his tone was as beautiful as Hodges or Carter. Bird played a little more forceful saxophone." He demonstrated the point by playing "Come Sunday," first in Hodges's style and then as he thought Parker might have played it, replete with progressive chords and asymmetrical phrasing.

When Frank Morgan and his family arrived on Central Avenue, the street was a glamorous hub of music and temptation: "We got to L.A. in the summer of 1947. My father opened a club called Casablanca, and all the heavy boppers played there and movie stars came over. Bird was revered by then—quoted by Hollywood, treated like a star. It was nothing to see Ginger Rogers or Ava Gardner or Gregory Peck or many of the very popular movie stars listening to him. Because he knew my father so well, he treated me almost like a son. He was very interested in helping me to play the saxophone and seeing that I only saw the right side of life. But it seemed almost socially acceptable to use drugs, as far as the people in and around music. I thought the heroin and the bebop and the whole lifestyle thing went together. I thought that one used heroin to play like Charlie Parker played. He was very disappointed when he found out I was using. I thought he would be extremely happy. I couldn't wait for Bird to get back to town when I turned 17 and started using, so that I could let him know that I was in the club—a member of the, you know, heroin addicts. It hurt him bad. He confided in me that people like me and Jackie McLean, and people all over the world, not just those that have been written about and recorded, but many young lives that were taken before they had the chance, hurt him because we didn't have the sense to just take the music and leave that part of his life to him. I think Bird took it to his grave with a great amount of sorrow. 'Can't you see what it's done to me?' he said. 'I mean, I thought you had sense enough to bypass that part of it.' He said, 'I was hoping that's what you would do, that maybe you were past the point where it was really dangerous.'

"Clearly, I wasn't. I don't think there was anything Bird could have done that would have stopped me from using. I chose to think that he was just trying to keep that good thing to himself. That's how stupid I was. And yet I knew that his addiction had a tremendous effect on his everyday existence. He didn't get a chance to practice as much as he would have liked, because having the habit is demanding. You must go where the drug tells you to go. You must find when it's available before you do anything else. I don't think one is going to sit down and practice eight or nine hours and say, well, I'll go score some heroin later on. It doesn't work like that. It's been my experience that when you wake up in the morning, the monkey is biting on the neck saying, feed me. And I don't mean feed me later. I don't mean feed me after you practice eight hours. I mean feed me now."

Parker died in 1955, shortly after Morgan completed his debut album. "When I first heard that Charlie Parker had died it was a Monday night, and I was on the bandstand at the California Club in Los Angeles. I was blessed enough to be working with Dexter Gordon and Wardell Gray. James Moody and Gene Ammons came to see us that night. Conte Candoli was there and Hampton Hawes, though I don't remember if he was playing piano. But we were all there at the California Club when we heard that Bird had died, and we took advantage of the fact to announce a long intermission. We proceeded—all except Moody and Candoli—to celebrate Bird's death by doing the very thing that killed him. That's the way we celebrated Bird's passing, to go out and do some junk. It would have been better if we'd realized it was time to stop. If Bird's passing could have made us say, none of us will use heroin from this point on, maybe Wardell wouldn't have died later that same year . . . and Gene Ammons . . ."

After that year, Morgan went underground. Yet except for periods in the Los Angeles County jail system, he never strayed too far from music. At most penal institutions, there were bands made up of inmates, and Morgan was greeted as a celebrity. He was constantly made gifts of mouthpieces, drugs, food, cigarettes. "The greatest big band I ever played with was in San Quentin. Art Pepper and I were co-leaders, and we were proud of that band. We had Jimmy Bunn, who still plays around California, and Frank Butler—he was the number three drummer, that's how many good musicians were already there. Some were known and some weren't, but they could play. We played every Saturday night for what they called a Warden's Tour, which showed paying visitors—at $17.50 a ticket— only the cleanest cell blocks and exercise yards. I noticed some people coming to the Warden's Tour repeatedly, and I realized they would take that tour just to hear the band, not to see the gas chamber. They'd heard Art was back in the pen and wanted to hear him."

In jail they felt like stars, an experience denied most of them on the outside, so it was comfortable going back in stir, where drugs were readily available and you didn't have to run around to find them. Morgan had a large room, which he was assigned to clean, where he was allowed to practice every day. The big band rehearsed daily. For the rest, he read books and played chess. One nonmusical celebrity he encountered was George Jackson, whose prison letters were published as *Soledad Brother* in 1970, a year before he was killed while attempting to escape. "George Jackson got someone off my back when I owed $600 for drugs and my mother hadn't sent the check. He was the toughest guy in the prison." According to Morgan, Jackson once defended himself against five guys with knives on a fifth-story galley walk. After he got through with the first four, the fifth jumped off the walk and pushed his pelvis around his neck. "If you were in trouble, you could say I'm marked and they would put you in protective custody, but that meant you'd be in it forever. They knew that I'd never do that. Jackson came over and asked who was bugging me. A short time later, the pusher came over to me and said, 'Man, I didn't know you were a friend of George, it's okay, forget the debt, here's some more dope."

Morgan committed small crimes, check forgeries, confidence games. He tried armed robbery once, with a toy gun that he was afraid to brandish because you could see the hole was made for BBs. When he pulled it out, the woman behind the counter laughed at him and said, "If you're hungry I'll give you a bag of doughnuts."

"That's what I got from my first and last robbery, a bag of doughnuts. A year later, she saw me backstage where I was playing and said, 'I knew you weren't a robber.' I said, 'Please don't turn me in.' She told me not to worry." He remembers more ruefully forcing his mother to deliver payments to keep him in dope. But that's done, and now he's home again.

"After two years in San Quentin, the Creator has given me the chance to play the music Charlie Parker made it possible for us to play. I don't want to play like Charlie Parker. I want to play as well. I want to play my own soul, which is what Bird told me I was doing all the time. He felt I might have taken some of his ideas, but he said, 'Listen, when it filters itself through your system, then it comes out you. It might have me going in, but it's you going out.' His music has had a tremendous effect on all of life. Even though he was a drug addict, his music spoke of many things, and it comes out so strongly—it's a very beautiful peaceful message in his music. That's why it's so alive. Now I'm playing it and people come to listen, and they really listen. I'm working with musicians like Cedar Walton, Buster Williams, and Billy Higgins. There have been offers from

Europe, but I haven't been able to get the change in parole status to do it. But I'm finally getting to New York, and I don't feel I have to fail anymore. It's like a beautiful dream. My life has changed so drastically, each day I have to question myself to make sure I'm not dreaming."*

(September 1986)

*Morgan eventually received his revised parole status and successfully played Europe, where he helped to introduce the gifted trumpet player Roy Hargrove, who was still a high school student at the time. He has made several well-received records, of which one of the best is A *Lovesome Thing* (Antilles), and in 1991 he and Rosalinda settled in Santa Fe. He performs regularly in clubs in New York and elsewhere and has earned a reputation for allowing other musicians down on their luck to sit in with his band at his expense.

Of Thad and Mel

In December of 1965, Thad Jones and Mel Lewis organized an 18-piece orchestra for an engagement at the Village Vanguard. It was a roaring success; within two months, they were permanently installed on Monday nights. The gig continued for 13 years, during which time they were the most constant conservators of new big band music in the United States. A highpoint was their triumphant tour of the Soviet Union. When Thad quit in 1978 and moved to Denmark (where he started a new family, a new band, and became a key contributor to the renowned Danish Radio Big Band), Mel was crushed, but he resolved to keep the band going. Greatly assisted by Bob Brookmeyer in the role of music director, he survived a couple of rough years and eventually brought the band to a new level of accomplishment. Thad and Mel each succumbed to cancer in the 1980s, but the orchestra they created continues to play Monday nights at the Vanguard. In February of 1991, on the occasion of its 25th anniversary, the band was officially renamed the Vanguard Jazz Orchestra. The pieces that follow—an interview with Thad, an obituary for Mel—focus on issues of jazz repertory and on what each man did before and after the collaboration; they are brought together here for auld lang syne.

GHOSTBUSTER

At the end of *The Glenn Miller Story*, June Allyson is comforted with the knowledge that, even though her husband has disappeared into the blue, his version of "Little Brown Jug" ("th-that s-SOUND" James Stewart was always looking for) will live on forever; they'll just get another conductor. In reality, which the film rarely touched upon, an interesting turn of events followed Miller's death. The orchestra regrouped under the leadership of Tex Beneke in 1946, but when Beneke, hardly a musical radical, attempted to assert himself and broaden the repertoire, the estate demanded he return its string of pearls. A decade later, partly spurred by the tremendous success of the movie, a purified Miller orchestra was reformed under the direction of Ray McKinley. Thus was born the most successful of the Swing Era's ghost bands—a phenomenon without precedent and, excepting other spectral bands from the same era (those of Jimmy and Tommy Dorsey, Guy Lombardo, Harry James), with no heirs, though perhaps a parallel can be drawn with Elvis impersonators. Ghost bands are held in low esteem by serious listeners. Even Stan Kenton, whose music could easily have bankrolled one, zapped the idea in his will. They perpetuate memories rather than concept, hits rather than invention.

Yet great musical ensembles ought to be able to survive their founders. In European music, they do. Zubin Mehta was no more hired by the New York Philharmonic to mimic Pierre Boulez than Boulez was hired to mimic Leonard Bernstein (though conservative board members may have wished he had). The ensemble is the instrument, and the conductor is expected to put his own imprint on it. Accomplished jazz ensembles, however, frequently get derailed by disputes of the sort between Tex Beneke and the Miller estate. A train won't travel without a strong engine; it will come apart with two engines pulling in opposite directions. Long before Miller, the Chick Webb and Jimmie Lunceford bands tried to continue after the deaths of their leaders and foundered under the batons of weaker deputies. Mingus Dynasty has similarly failed to measure up to its potential in the absence of a forceful leader. On the other hand, Rex Stewart organized a reunion of the Fletcher Henderson orchestra in the late '50s, and though that thrilling ensemble was short-lived (one concert, one record), it suggested—as have several subsequent adventures in jazz repertory—beguiling possibilities, some of which have been realized by the Ellington band as led by Duke's son Mercer.

A band that can play the work of our preeminent composer (*pace* and many happy returns, Mr. Copland) with authenticity and aplomb ought to have a permanent place in our cultural life, and the sheer immensity of the Ellington book precludes the necessity for expansion, though not for interpretation. The Count Basie band presents a different set of challenges. Its book is filled with hits or signature themes—from "One O'Clock Jump" to "Li'l Darlin' "—as well as dozens of enduring arrangements designed to spur improvisers. But long before Basie's death in 1984, the band had become more than the sum of its repertory. Basie had built himself a precision machine, probably the most purely and consistently virtuosic orchestra ever to evolve from traditional dance-band instrumentation. It boasts a peerless rhythm section built around the imperturbable guitarist Freddie Green; a brass section famed for immaculate unison shakes; a reed section that can spread like butter or hold ground like five redwoods; and an ability to dynamically interlock all parts that is the equal of any philharmonic. Never has jazz had as fine a ready-made ensemble to test the mettle of ambitious writers. Even if it commissions only works that fit the Basie mold, the possibilities are vast. Of course, the first problem was to find a leader who understands the Basie aesthetic and brings to it a complementary vision of his own. Several candidates were immediately apparent (Frank Foster, Ernie Wilkins, Eric Dixon, and more), but the choice of Thad Jones was a brainstorm.

Jones, a highly original trumpeter with impeccable bop-era credentials (Charles Mingus called him "Bartók with valves," and Miles Davis said, "I'd rather hear Thad Jones miss a note than hear Freddie Hubbard make 12"), is one of the few distinguished soloists of his generation who has spent most of his career in big bands. The middle brother in a renowned if rarely united triumvirate (Hank is older, Elvin younger) from Pontiac, Michigan, Thad devoted nine years to Basie's most popular orchestra (1954–63); two years to writing for and playing in the bands of Harry James, Thelonious Monk (or Hall Overton), Gerry Mulligan, and George Russell; and 13 years—as conductor and chief composer—to the Thad Jones–Mel Lewis Jazz Orchestra (1965–78). During the years with Mel, Thad's trumpet playing was habitually underrated, but there can be little doubt that as a writer he produced one of the most durable and influential bodies of work in that period, including a song, "A Child Is Born," that became the most ubiquitous new jazz standard of the 1970s. Then he moved to Denmark, where he became guest conductor with the Danish Radio Big Band as well as an associate of the Royal Danish Conservatory, and started a family.

Two summers ago, the late Willard Alexander, whose company has booked the Basie band since 1937, and Basie's stepson and executor of his estate, Aaron Woodward, asked Jones to take over. During a recent local appearance, he discussed his reaction: "I never really thought of myself leading or conducting the Count Basie Orchestra—that always seemed a rather sacred position that belonged to the Chief, Count Basie himself. But I always had the urge to play in the band, strictly as a sideman, just to get invoved once again with the music I had been so deeply involved with back in the '50s and early '60s. When Willard called, I thought for a while he was calling to tell me Basie was dead, that maybe I didn't know about it. But he came up with the idea, and I was stunned. He suggested I think it over and called me back a few days later. In the interim, my wife and I sat down and talked about what it would entail—the move back to America. She had lived in Denmark all her life, and we had a small son, and a house, a car—the whole schmeer. We both realized that wherever the job took me, that's where I would have to go. So we were in agreement, and when Willard called back I accepted. Aaron called about three weeks to a month later, and we talked for about an hour and found that we were both looking at the same thing the same way. So now we're living in Chicago."

Jones's first stint proved something of an apprenticeship for his present position, in that "all the members were involved in a very personal sense with the progress of the band. We all felt it was our band, and I think Basie was really proud of the attitude everybody had—it gave him a feeling of deep happiness to have people feel and care about what he loved so much. At rehearsals, there was input from all sources, but we all more or less agreed on definite ways of phrasing things—like those brass shakes, which developed out of the philosophy the musicians had about their playing and about how things should sound in a jazz context. It was just like an embellishment. And as writers we had several different sources to draw on—including Ellington's music and, in Lunceford's case, the arrangements of Sy Oliver and Lunceford's pianist, Eddie Wilcox. Today we can retain the Basie sound with some of the same people who were writing then. I sort of lean to people like Frank Foster and Frank Wess and Ernie Wilkins, because they've been intimately involved with the band for so long. Neal Hefti was an important contributor, of course, but I would say his primary importance was during that period—within the nine years I was with the band. But the Franks and Wilkins have been sending things in constantly. They've kept up with the progress of the band and know the changes that are taking place and have been growing themselves, so they're able to contribute and at the same time write the kind of music that takes the band forward."

The signature pieces will remain unchanged, as will the elliptical Basie piano punctuations: "That's a sort of stationary trademark that should always be there, an identifying feature. It gives form. I think the period I spent with Basie prepared me musically for the time I spent with Mel, when we had our band together. When I had first joined Basie, my ideas were fragmented. I didn't have a format, I just wrote ideas that would be scattered throughout a piece. Neal Hefti—I always give him credit for this—made me aware, in a very nice way [laughter], that maybe I should deal a little more with form. And then I noticed that the other writers all did the same thing! They had that form, and that's why their pieces were meaningful not only to the public but to themselves as writers. So I began to grow up musically, and I became very aware of the importance of ensemble—very aware. I think the same philosophy that existed then in my writing exists now—only I hope in a way that's more mature.

"You know, I've been listening to bands since I was old enough to listen to the radio. I was born in 1923, and that was the era of the radio, the crystal set, to be specific. And there was an awful lot of music aired—everything from washboard bands and hillbilly, which is what we called country and western, to Ellington. I used to spend my time listening to Ellington's broadcasts, and to Claude Hopkins, Jimmie Lunceford, Count Basie, Erskine Hawkins, and on Sundays to the Ford Symphony Orchestra conducted by Walter Poole in Detroit. Listening to all those programs really opened your head up; it caused you to create or sort out situations that might exist, that they were trying to tell you about. In other words, it created a lot of active imaginations, and you never became bored. We'd apply that same imagination to listening to records, always trying to find the story that the orchestra wanted to tell. We'd listen to a record, and each one would come up with his version. I started to play the trumpet when I was 14, because of listening to Louis Armstrong, and then my Uncle Bill gave me an old Conn. That was in 1937, and Louis Armstrong had such clarity—as though he were a giant up there telling everybody just what it was, telling it in a clear and happy voice. He was telling people that the trumpet isn't just an instrument that heralds the approach of something. It's a beautiful instrument. And when *he* played it, it was though he were speaking. He was telling people about music, and how much he loved it, and how much he wanted them to enjoy it, and to feel the beauty of it, and the *sound* that he got out of a trumpet was, well, you know. So I was really struck with it."

Not too long after that, Jones heard Dizzy Gillespie on the Lionel Hampton record "Hot Mallets" and memorized the solo. (He sang it for me.) But then Dizzy disappeared from the scene for a few years, or so it seemed. "I was wondering what happened to him, and I was in the army on an island called Guam, traveling with a GI show. There were about six of us, all in our tent preparing for the evening and listening to the radio, and all of a sudden Dizzy comes on playing 'Shaw Nuff' with Charlie Parker. And you know, I can't describe what went on in that tent. We went out of our minds! There was a good friend of mind, a saxophonist who lives out in California now, and he and I were rolling on the floor, man, so happy we were laughing. People must have thought we were crazy, because here's music playing and we're laughing, cracking up. It was so beautiful, but that was our reaction. It was the newness, and the impact of that sound, and the technique. It was something we were probably trying to articulate ourselves and just didn't know how. And Dizzy and Bird came along and did it. They spoke our minds. Later I used to have drinks with Bird at Beefsteak Charlie's on 50th Street, and he'd always start the conversation by saying, 'One day I'm gonna get a group with you and Hank and Elvin.' "

Although the Basie band tours more than 40 weeks a year, its recent performances in New York have only hinted at the band's dazzling new spirit; nor has it recorded, except to accompany the ineffable Manhattan Transfer. A concert in August with Sarah Vaughan in a Brooklyn bandshell at Old Boys High Field, however, showed how electrifying the band is. The new lead trumpeter is Byron Stripling, whom Jones describes as "fantastic—he has the range, he has the sound, and he has the moxie, and at 23 or 24 he's developing into a tremendous soloist." The redoubtable trumpeter John Coles is another new addition to the Basie brass section ("he's even more impressive *now*"). The rhythm section continues to play off the four-to-the-bar plunk of Freddie Green, and the reeds include veterans Eric Dixon, Danny Turner, and the formidable and strangely underrated Kenny Hing, whom Jones calls "one of the greatest improvisers I've ever heard." The book includes a flag-waving set-opener in "Strike Up the Band," with bruising brass punctuations and solos by Hing and drummer Dennis Mackrel; Ernie Wilkins's "Way Out Basie," featuring Turner, Coles, and the deferential, witty pianist Tee Carson; Mackrel's "And That's That," with the reeds sweeping through riddling eighth-note passages; a quartet number that features Jones's cornet (and his ironic approach to harmony); and a full-force "Jumpin' at the Woodside" that finishes with a riotous Hing-Dixon tenor battle.

A few weeks ago, the band appeared—without billing—at Manhattan Transfer's show at Radio City and played only one solo number, "April in Paris" (with Jones playing his patented "Pop Goes the Weasel" solo and exhorting Basie's patented "One more time"). Then the singers returned, pouring their usual quotient of vanilla sauce on day-old white bread—unable to swing with the swingingest band on earth. Vulgarizing a tradition in which Jon Hendricks (their newly adopted lyricist) and Basie played key roles, they indulge in sentimental cynicism that substitutes research for feeling and thought. It may have been sensible business to tag along with the Transfer, but I do find disturbing the confusion—evident in Brooklyn as well as at Radio City—over how to handle Thad Jones's role as frontman. His name was played down in both billings, and that's as much a mistake as playing down the name of the conductor of the New York Philharmonic. Jones is no ghost. Nor have we heard the fruits of new commissions, though it's probably too early to judge the ambitions of the conductor and the organization in that area. That the bloom is still on the rose no one can doubt. But the Basie band will sustain interest through many directorships only if each director is honored for the individual qualities he brings to this incomparable ensemble. In Jones it has a stellar leader whose entire career has prepared him to make the Basie band the great jazz orchestra of the day, with a larger reach and more flexible vision than was possible during Basie's last years. The alternative is just another ghost band, and ghosts always return to the graveyard—or should. *

(December 1985)

MEAN WHAT YOU SAY

It's a fact that when a jazz musician dies and his friends, family, and admirers congregate at a memorial service to tell stories and pay homage, the mood is invariably bright, upbeat, optimistic, droll. Music, which, in the manner of a traditional New Orleans sendoff, is a standard component at such gatherings, ensures a certain luster. But beyond that, there is a tendency to be comical, to recall illustrative anecdotes that are funny in the telling even if they weren't funny in the occurrence. The story that first comes to my mind about Mel Lewis, who died February 2 after waging one of the damndest fights against death I have ever seen, usually generated laughter in people who knew him—the kind of laughter that translates into, "Yes, that's Mel, that's him exactly"—but no one laughed when the incident took place. I tell it here at the risk of offending a Celebrated Academic Composer, but assume he will recognize my purpose.

Shortly after I helped organize the American Jazz Orchestra in 1985, we

---

*Thad's reunion with the Basie band was fleeting. Two months after we spoke, he returned to Copenhagen, exhausted by the one-night stands and distressed over differences about the band's future. In April he was diagnosed with cancer. He died four months later, on August 20, leaving unfinished two commissions from the Swedish National Symphony and the Danish Radio Band. Frank Foster was appointed leader of the Basie orchestra, a position he continues to occupy with energy and skill six years later.

agreed to perform a series of modern works commissioned expressly for the AJO, through ASCAP and Meet the Composers. In truth, we were feeling—at least I was—a bit cocksure about commissions. At our second concert, in the fall of 1986, we premiered a clarinet concerto by Bob Brookmeyer, commissioned through BMI. Everything about that event was idyllic; it seemed very easy to bring great music into the world. All you had to do was get someone to pay the freight, call a favorite composer, and wait for the masterpiece to land on your doorstep. The Brookmeyer concerto was played on an evening that we originally planned as a tribute to Benny Goodman, which became a memorial instead—and it was with that concert that Mel first joined the orchestra. Needless to say, we were honored to have him, and absolutely amazed when he committed himself to be our regular drummer. The next concert, the one for which the ASCAP pieces were commissioned, was problematic from the outset. Although the challenge to play new music was heady, in playing it we were failing our mandate, which was to keep jazz repertory alive. Each of four conductors was given a certain amount of rehearsal time. On this afternoon, I arrived at the Great Hall about half an hour after rehearsal had commenced. The solemnity hanging over the stage reminded me of a recalcitrant high school band—no one looked happy.

During a break, I walked out onstage through the back curtain, where the drums were set up, and asked Mel, "What's going on? Is everything okay?" Looking dour, impatient, he said, "It'll be fine. This music, look at this. Nobody can read it. I don't know. But it'll be fine, it'll be all right, it'll be okay. These guys can play anything. But it'll be fine. It'll be fine." He kept repeating it, like a mantra. Since it never occurred to me that it wouldn't be fine, I pressed him. "Remember how beautiful Brookmeyer's score was?"—he was referring not to the music, but to its legibility; the parts were immaculately written on standard manuscript paper. The parts handed out by the Celebrated Academic Composer looked like they had been scrawled by student copyists in a notebook. Mel continued, in a stage whisper that could have been heard down the block let alone 10 feet away where the CAC stood, suggesting he might have pocketed the fee intended for professional copyists. Then he added the coup de grace. "Look at this," he said, pointing to the score. "He's got a different time signature every measure. And you know something, it would sound exactly the same it if was written in four." By now I may have been turning green, because he resumed his mantra. "But it'll be all right. We'll play it and it'll be fine." The rehearsal resumed.

I went upstairs to the office for a few minutes, and as I returned, Loren Schoenberg, the orchestra manager, came whizzing out with the music under his arm. It was decided he was to take it to a photocopier to have enlargements made. During the break, everyone was grumbling. How can you play music when you're counting every measure? And why are we playing this music? I repeatedly heard words like *academic, pretentious, shit*. The CAC seemed a reasonable enough fellow, but he wasn't communicating; I was concerned about losing the loyalty of the musicians, who, after all, were not making AJO rehearsals for the bread. The rehearsal continued—18 pensive musicians and a singer, who was unimpressed with the lyrics she'd been handed, facing the professor. I don't remember what if anything in particular triggered it, but within minutes Mel threw his mallets across the stage and said in a remarkably evenhanded, reasonable voice, "You should have your balls cut off, handing music like that to musicians of this stature." It was breathtaking—at least no one seemed to be breathing. He continued for a while, repeating the business about the signature changes, until he was certain that the CAC, chagrined and looking it, got the idea. At which point Mel backtracked, assuring him that it would be all right, fine, okay, as long as he understood the level of musicianship he was confronting.

The CAC came over to Mel and apologized, blaming deadline difficulties in getting the parts made; defending, as he had every right to do, the integrity of the piece; asking for a rapprochement, which Mel immediately dispensed. It's important to remember that Mel was not the leader of the band. John Lewis was away, and so the guest conductors were de facto leaders. Mel was just the drummer. But he saw morale flagging and knew something had to be done. He had the authority—as a prominent bandleader in his own right—and the gumption to speak plainly on behalf of all the players. He changed the temperature of the rehearsal, restoring everyone's pride. Now they tackled the music as equal participants, and they played the hell out of it. Mel apologized to me for taking the initiative, pointing out that he was the only one who could. I thanked him, of course. It was a turning point for the orchestra, as well as for our friendship. He told me on the day it happened and on other occasions, "I didn't have anything to lose. What could happen to me?"

I hear those rhetorical questions a lot in my head, and they've given me courage over the years. I'm not sure it's possible to derive courage from the example of his bravery in fighting the cancer that killed him. You could only stand back in awe and hope you'd be as cool in the same situation. Mel liked to talk. He was as good a conversationalist as I ever expect to meet. He would go on and on—music, road stories, theories about anything and everything—and be riveting. The other day Nat Hentoff remarked that he ran into Mel on the street, not having seen him in years, and Mel started in as though resuming a recent phone chat. Roberta Swann, of Cooper Union and the AJO, often called to say, "I've just talked to Mel for two hours, and I feel elated." This was no less true when the subject turned to the terrible tragedy in his family (his daughter's suicide), or to his health. And he'd do it in a way that made you feel he was comforting you. At the memorial service at Riverside (a second one at St. Peter's soon followed), Pastor John Gensel noted, "Mel beat cancer by not giving in. He kept making plans." That's exactly right. He'd talk about radiation treatments as though they were an inconvenience, a challenge. The medics were going to zap those tumors and that was that. I believed him, in part because he retained for so long his beefy build, blond hair, imperturbable outlook, and astonishing skill.

After he collapsed at a rehearsal for the JVC Festival last summer, I went to see him at the Village Vanguard, and he said, matter-of-factly, that now they'd found a melanoma in his brain. But he wasn't giving an inch. They'd zap that, too, no question about it.

After 20 years on the job, I know full well that the primary perquisite of being a jazz critic in New York is that you often get to meet your idols; sometimes repeated encounters flower into friendship. The first time I heard Mel Lewis's music was in the summer of 1966, when I was about to matriculate as a college freshman and went to buy a portable phonograph. They only had one in stock of the model I wanted, and it was scuffed. To clinch the deal, the salesman offered me any two albums, and when he saw me trotting happily to the jazz section, he came over with a white jacket bearing the words Solid State and asked if I'd heard it. Under the label logo, in a more modest lettering, was the legend: *Thad Jones– Mel Lewis & The Jazz Orchestra*. The band had started up the previous December and was now playing every Monday night at the Village Vanguard, to much acclaim. I'd been anxious to hear it. "If you don't love it, bring it back," he said. I loved it. No less radiant than the ravishing ensemble passages were the snap and crackle of the snares, beautifully recorded by Sonny Lester's audiophile label, on Thad's "Once Around" and "Mean What You Say," and the savoir faire with which the drums signaled the turns in tempo and dynamics on Brookmeyer's capacious "ABC Blues." That album was followed by "comeback" collaborations with Joe Williams and Ruth Brown (her best album to date), the Vanguard recordings, and *Central Park North*, which used contemporary dance rhythms without sacrificing the bite of the orchestra or the elbow room always reserved for its superb soloists. There was also an irreproachable chamber session paced by Mel, on a new label, Milestone: *Mean What You Say*, by the Thad Jones/Pepper Adams Quintet.

The title was Thad's; the motto could have been Mel's. He always said what he meant and meant what he said. He was fiercely loyal, especially to his family of musicians. It was always "my band" and "my guys." Shortly after Thad left the country in 1978, I wrote a middling review of the new band, led by Mel with Brookmeyer as music director. I didn't know him then except to say hello, but he called and gently insisted, "You didn't hear my band at its best. You should come down to the Vanguard and hear what we can really do, not to write about it, but just so that you know." No critic ever received a more disarming invitation from a musician he'd just panned.

Last year, the AJO resolved to pay homage to Mel's band. It was John Lewis's idea—he greatly admired Mel's determination in keeping his orchestra alive. But Mel pointed out that it didn't make sense as we conceived it; we couldn't play his book as well as he could—better to mount a retrospective of music created around his drumming style during the years he worked with Stan Kenton, Terry Gibbs, and Gerry Mulligan, and close with a couple of Thad's pieces. Mulligan and John Carisi came down for rehearsals, and Mel was in heaven—once again playing their marvelous music, as well as classics by Bill Holman, Brookmeyer, Al Cohn, Med Flory, and Thad.

By that time he was thin and hairless. But the smile and the glint in his eyes were firmly in place. Throughout rehearsals, he insisted that I introduce the pieces. I'd look dubious and suggest that people would want to hear from him, and he'd say, "You know me and you know my music. I just want to sit with the band and play." But during the second set on the night of the concert, he walked to the mike and for 20 minutes talked about his life—from the beginnings as a teenage musician in Buffalo (as Melvin Sokoloff), through his mutual discovery with Tiny Kahn that the way to play for a big band is the way you would for a small one, through service with all the great orchestras and others not so great ("I had the pleasure of quitting that one"). He told of the exhilaration he got from accompanying great soloists, including those who moved him to tears—nor was he being sentimental or hyperbolic. In the context of a band, Mel was like the straight man in a comedy team who enjoys nothing more than his partner's wit. It's a cliché, but nonetheless true: Mel abides. Not just because his music does, but because his values, his honesty, his commitment, his integrity, his devotion to principles, his contempt for money, his belief in himself and his colleagues, his generosity—all of that has been assimilated by numerous associates. As Auden wrote of Yeats, he becomes his admirers.

(February 1990)

Juilliard Dropout
Makes Good

When Aldous Huxley visited Holland in the 1920s, he found a Cartesian paradise, a mirror world of geometric precision. "A tour in Holland is a tour through
the first books of Euclid," he wrote in *Along the Road*. You understand what he
means even before the plane touches ground, on first sight of the perfect plots of
greenery framed by waterways, the tiny box houses, the concentric canals of
Amsterdam. Holland is a country wrested from the ocean and preserved by an
awesome system of dikes—its cities and farms the conception of master planners
working with a clean slate.

Thus the Euclidian neatness that cheered Huxley triggers dread in those who
find Holland's existence shudderingly fragile, as though the dike might crack at
any moment and the low countries go the way of Atlantis. Poe's Dutch con artist,
Hans Phaal, took flight from its stolid bourgeois rationalists, and Camus's *The
Fall* saw postwar Amsterdam as "a dream" resembling the circles of hell. In *Two
Women*, by the contemporary Dutch novelist Harry Mulisch, the protagonist
drives out of Holland and muses, "Where morality changes to nature, I always
sense a seriousness in me which I don't feel in Holland. It rises up in me as the
earth rises up around me, it comes from deeper, harder, more elemental layers—
which in Amsterdam are covered over by a hundred meters of mud." It was in
Holland in 1984, at the North Sea Jazz Festival, that I fully realized the magnitude of Miles Davis's celebrity.

Produced in the enormous Congresgebouw complex in The Hague, North Sea
is one of the most acclaimed festivals in Europe, a musical carnival parsed into
26 areas on three floors. And behind the main building is the mammoth Tuin
Paviljoen, a canvas tent where the year's main attraction, Miles Davis, and
several other big draws would appear. When Paul Acket founded the festival in
1976, it drew an audience of 9000. Eight years later, 35,000 people swarmed
through, absorbing a catholic menu of music that lasted 12 hours on each of

three days. The *KLM* magazine on the plane coming over quoted Acket on the business of obtaining government funds: "The Ministry itself wants to have an influence and expects to have groups that nobody's interested in. We do have some non-commercial groups as well as big names, but the main aim of the Ministry seems to be to have groups with no public appeal at all." An American jazz lover could only find that attitude as startling as the landfills.

The roll call for the first two days of the '84 festival was no less comprehensive than the network of dikes, including a Dizzy Gillespie Septet with James Moody, Slide Hampton, and Kenny Barron; duets by Cecil Taylor and Steve Lacy; an edition of the Leaders with Arthur Blythe, Don Cherry , Chico Freeman, Hilton Ruiz, Cecil McBee, and Don Moye; B. B. King, Little Milton, Weather Report, Bireli Lagrene, Clarinet Summit, a J. J. Johnson Sextet, Benny Carter sitting in with the Dutch Ramblers, Mahavishnu Orchestra, Miriam Makeba, Carla Bley, the Dirty Dozen Brass Band, Abdullah Ibrahim, Billy Butterfield, Edward Kidd Jordan, a Mal Waldron quintet with Charlie Rouse and Woody Shaw, and several American high school and college orchestras. Our rationalist cousins made money, too.

Sunday's offerings started at 2 p.m., with the choice of a vocal group called Wall Street Crash, the Widespread Depression Orchestra (titles notwithstanding, there was no apparent theme here), a Philip Morris Dixieland event, and Miles Davis. All decisions should be so easy. Even at this most festive of festivals, Davis was the piece de resistance, receiving a reported $35,000 for one set. You could read about the reformation of the Prince of Darkness in *KLM*'s magazine, which ran an interview by Michael Zwerin: " 'I had to stop doing everything.' [Davis] paused for emphasis. 'Everything. Listen. I was snorting coke, right? Half an ounce a day, sometimes. I went out drinking brandy and beer all night, smoked four packs of cigarettes. Sleeping pills too. One day I woke up and couldn't use my right hand, couldn't straighten it out. Cicely panicked.' He is married to the actress Cicely Tyson, and together they form the royal couple of the contemporary Afro-American art world. . . . 'The only bad habit I got left now is sweets.' "

In the hugh circus tent euphemistically called the Garden Pavilion, some 6000 subjects wait restively for the last jazz icon, a man whose eminence finally rivals, and in some respects outstrips, his musical accomplishment. There is no room even to stand. The press section surges with photographers, writers, camp followers, and more photographers, bound in front by the stage, in back by the first row of seats, and on the remaining two sides by ropes that have them pinned at the waists and drooping over like sheaved wheat. Journalists in the know tell me that back at the Bel Air Hotel—which is all of 50 yards from the Pavilion—Davis's entourage is *disguising* him to fool fans they might encounter on the way.

At 2:00 sharp—true to form, the Dutch expect punctuality even at jazz concerts—the audience starts clapping in time. At 2:05 someone meekly apologizes for the late start and asks the photographers to sit so that paying customers will be able to see. "Okay, okay," they grouse, sliding tenuously to the ground.

Seconds later, Davis walks out, looking muscular and fit, though leaning on a black walking stick with a wolf's head (yes, very much like Larry Talbot's) peeking out from his right palm. Up jump the photographers, as those of us on the floor pull in our hands and legs, and those in chairs plead with them to stay down. Davis wears a white sailor's cap, large dark glasses, and a black leather jacket with billowing sleeves; when the jacket is peeled off after a couple of numbers, he reveals a red blouse with billowing sleeves. The opening piece is a riff played on sax (Bob Berg) and guitar (John Scofield); Davis spends his time at a bank of keyboards. But the second piece is a blues, and the pungent, uncharacteristically brawny trumpet solo is replete with rotund blasts aimed directly at the delighted audience. While Scofield solos, Davis plays trumpet and organ in unison. Every time he strolls near the apron, the photographers spring up like jack rabbits. People scream at them to sit, and one screams back, "I am doing my job! I am doing my job!"

In a short time those distractions are subsumed by the force of Davis's music, which is startling—not least because his set at the relatively anemic Kool Jazz Festival in New York just two weeks earlier had been listless and ersatz. Some objective distinctions should be noted: at Kool, Davis displayed a deafening level of volume—in Holland, the balance is roomy and clear; at Kool, the pieces meandered from one vamp to another—here each piece is clearly defined (blues and ballads), and Davis solos at greater length. Even his sound, which has steadily fattened since his comeback in 1981, after a six-year sabbatical, is more lustrous. The transitions he's been working on since the late '60s, to blend varied pieces into a seamless set, are skillful and to the point. Berg doesn't play much, and the synthesizer sounds of Robert Irving III are superfluous, but the band is energized by its lean, elemental rhythms, and Davis—prowling about, periodically waving his arms—keeps the change-ups fluent and interesting.

Davis plays a trumpet blues as slow and deliberate as "Star People," accompanied only by fugitive bass and percussion; he introduces written passages for tenor, guitar, and keyboard that bear the unmistakable stamp of Gil Evans; he paces Berg with stop-time trumpet blasts; he shadows Scofield with blistering keyboard chords. Hunched over, his trumpet bell parallel with the stage, he leads a winsome blues over a light bossa beat and into an emotional reading of Cyndi Lauper's song, "Time After Time" (the first notes are greeted with an ovation). With his canny feeling for restraint, he paints an abstract of the melody with sustained legato pitches. He concludes the 80-minute set with a fast rocker (the electric slap-bass solo recalls Milt Hinton) and a lusty version of "Jean Pierre." The audience rises to its feet as Davis claims his wolf's head stick and, haltingly, ambles off.

What to do now: the Chris Hinze Combination, Buddy Tate and the Texas Tenors, David Grisman, something called Loos, a reprise of Wall Street Crash? Not at all. Word is out that Miles is about to give a press conference. According to members of the European press corps, the notoriously elusive musician is a changed man and is giving interviews everywhere. It occurs to me, racing back to the Bel Air to kiss the holy ring, that I've never seen a jazz musician hold a press conference or heard of such a thing in all the years I've had a press card. After a credentials check that would have impressed anyone's secret service, I am admitted to a small, packed conference room filled with chairs. No one is sitting on the chairs—everyone is standing on them, in order to see the Prince over the shoulders of photographers. You wonder, How many Miles Davis pictures can they sell?

As expected, Davis is reasonably cordial, yet tart and brusque. Most questions are adoring or smug. Is your present band tight enough? "Didn't you hear it?" What do your drawings have to do with your music? "They don't have anything to do with the music." Why doesn't Berg play more? "Didn't he play enough for you?" (Someone shouts that he played too much.) When will you work with Gil Evans again? "I'd like to work with Gil, but Gil's too busy." Will you ever again work with contemporaries such as Sonny Rollins and Max Roach? "No!" An unctuous representative from his management, Blanc and Blanc, says, "Two more questions, Miles, then we go." Why do you play the Cyndi Lauper song? "I heard it on the radio and liked it." Why are your drawings on the covers of your records? "Columbia did that. They used them as a gimmick—threw a birthday party for me, where you could hear the record and see the pictures. It didn't mean anything." "Okay Miles," the toady from Blanc and Blanc says, "let's go." Bulbs roar obediently at his every departing step. Even Jane Austen's connoisseur of noblesse oblige, Mr. Collins, would have admired "such behavior in a person of rank—such affability and condescension!"

And not only on the illusory shores of Holland is Miles's fame enshrined at a level beyond that of any other jazz musician of his generation. If his celebrity has increased in direct proportion to his musical decline, as many would argue, the distortion in values can hardly be attributed exclusively to hype. No more could Louis Armstrong's ascension on the leaden wings of "Hello, Dolly!" be written off as a low-brow irony. The frothing photographers may be out for one of the few paydirt stories in jazz, but the kids who crowded the stage at Lincoln Center to press Davis's flesh and the slightly older crowd that squeezed into Tuin Paviljoen to scream its homages were responding to the immediacy of the moment. They have no attachments, sentimental or otherwise, to Davis's apprenticeship with Charlie Parker, or his quintets of the '50s and '60s, or his collaborations with Gil Evans. They like him now for what he is now.

What they recognize in Davis is a powerful center, a force of authority, who continues to produce concert music unlike that of anyone else. If his few disastrous records—*Agharta* (the ensemble has electrifying moments, but Davis sounds positively distraught), "The Man with the Horn," and "One Phone Call/ Street Scene" come to mind—suggest a cynical attitude toward fame and the meretriciousness of the recording business, Davis has sustained his musical mystique with florid and sometimes rapturous concert appearances. He can do what few musicians in history could do: With a few notes on the trumpet, he stills qualms, raises expectations, confuses issues, and hoodwinks the doubtful. It isn't that his sound is unique, though of course it is, but that it touches people in a place where they have to reach for metaphor to explain the effect. No brass player since Armstrong has been able to make such plenary claims on his audience as Davis.

From the time he arrived in New York in 1944, for the ostensible purpose of studying at the Juilliard School and the more urgent one of seeking out Charlie Parker and Dizzy Gillespie, Davis demonstrated his determination to speak a musical language of his own. He borrowed heavily from Freddie Webster (the languorous mid-register phrasing) and tried to mimic Gillespie's virtuosity, but as early as 1945, when he played a widely noted solo on Parker's "Now's the Time," he was clearly striving for a voice of his own. It would be balanced in the middle register, melodically piquant, harmonically bold. Armstrong came from dire poverty; Davis from the upper middle class. Armstrong learned the rudiments of the trumpet in a waif's home; Davis had keys to the academy. Yet each man discovered his metier in the blues; each established himself with the manifest destiny of his sound, whether it blazed or purred; and each transcended the era and style of his initial success. At 23, Davis turned away from his masters in modern jazz and organized the Capitol record sessions that were subsequently recognized as the "Birth of the Cool." Five years later, he turned away from what had become the paleface dominion of cool jazz and reestablished himself as a deeply expressive blues man with "Walkin' " and "Blue 'n' Boogie."

In 1957, Davis joined forces with Gil Evans—a guiding force at the "Cool" sessions who hadn't been able to find much work in jazz in the early '50s—for *Miles Ahead*, an extraordinarily ambitious suite of tunes that made full use of the long-playing album format, even to the point of employing transitional passages between selections. It was followed by the masterful *Porgy and Bess*, the more innovative *Sketches of Spain* (which virtually eschews conventional jazz rhythms), a television show, a concert (*Live at Carnegie Hall*), and a few aborted studio projects that produced tantalizing fragments. Evans once told me, "You know the records with Claude [Thornhill] and Miles were the only times I had the luxury of working with 11 brass or whatever I wanted." Sadly, the Davis sessions were recorded with inadequate rehearsal time, and the execution of Evans's difficult orchestrations was flawed. No matter: The music is sumptuous. Davis produced sounds that, according to Evans, were emotionally and physically painful for him, and those sounds helped define the emotional curve of modern jazz in that era. In 1960, Evans met the musician who most inspired him, Louis Armstrong, who told him he'd bought *Porgy and Bess* and suggested they make an album together. As Evans recalled, Armstrong joked, "You're not going to hand me any of those funny chords now," and, in a more serious vein, observed of Davis, "That boy reminded me of Buddy Bolden. Yes, he reminded me of Bolden."

During those same years, Davis launched the most celebrated band of the late '50s, with John Coltrane, Red Garland, Paul Chambers, Philly Joe Jones, and, in a later edition, Cannonball Adderley, Bill Evans, and Jimmy Cobb. With *Mile-stones* and *Kind of Blue*, which has been called the most influential jazz album ever made, he helped popularize modes or scales as an alternative to chordal improvisation. After a couple of transitional years, he triumphed again with one of the most astonishing quintets of the '60s, making stars of Wayne Shorter, Herbie Hancock, Ron Carter, and Tony Williams. While leading that band, he made incremental overtures to rock, album by album, before finally submitting to the tidewater with *Bitches Brew*—ultimately a minor effort, but his best-selling album to date, and one that launched a whole new movement. Though long-winded, ornate, and crotchety, *Bitches Brew* dwarfed most of the fusion bands and records born on its heels.

For all the transformations, subtle and broad, in Davis's music over the past four decades, one thread ties it all together and seems to make sense of his nearly reckless will to metamorphose. That thread is the surprisingly stable sound of his trumpet (unmistakable even when distorted by electronic masks), which rarely fails to produce insinuating drama with its steamy yet icy intonation, its healing blasts, its provocative lyricism and unsettling crablike runs that continue to crest fashion, fame, and the illusory geometry of a stable backbeat. The fact that he's been able to translate such drama into a personal myth is remarkable at a time when performance glamor has all but disappeared and is yet another reason to marvel at the man—the Prince, the Sorcerer—who walks on eggshells.

(August 1984)

THE DANISH CONNECTION

Miles Davis's new Columbia release, *Aura*, not to be confused with his tepid new Warners release, *Amandla*, is his most satisfying recorded work in years—at least since the 1983 *Star People*, with which it has some continuity. There's no surprise in that: *Aura* was recorded in early 1985. Thus its belated appearance, just in time to partake of the publicity surrounding the publication of *Miles: The Autobiography*, evinces no signs of renewal; but it does solve a puzzle in the Davis discography. *Aura* is not another compilation of live performances or studio outtakes, but a singular and ambitious suite by the Danish composer and trumpet player Palle Mikkelborg, who considers it one of his finest compositions. For his part, Miles, sounding rather like Holden Caulfield, says, in *Miles*, "I think it's a masterpiece, I really do." What's more, he blames Columbia's handling of it for his departure from the company.

In November 1984, Davis was given the Sonning Music Award, a Danish prize previously reserved for musicians in the, ahem, educated European tradition (prior recipients include Stravinsky, Messiaen, Bernstein, and Copland). In honor of the occasion, Mikkelborg was commissioned to provide a setting for

Davis to improvise on for a required minimum of five minutes; he adapted two chords from one of Messiaen's organ pieces, which so intrigued Davis that he played for nearly an hour and agreed to return to Denmark the following February to record Mikkelborg's music. A large Danish orchestra—more than 30 participants—was augmented for the sessions by percussionists Vince Wilburn (Davis's nephew) and Marilyn Mazur (who later joined his band) and guitarist John McLaughlin, who played so pivotal a role at the dawn of Davis's fusion conversion 20 years ago. Davis isn't precise about what happened next, but apparently Columbia withheld funds midway through the project, and Davis had to get an NEA grant to finish it. For five years it lay in the CBS vaults. Now that they have put it out, they've done something less than a fastidious job: insufficient information (no dates), incorrect banding of two movements ("Red" and "Green"), and the absence of any clue on the cover as to what this album is all about. You have to hunt the small print of the liner notes to find the odd credit: "All songs by Palle Mikkelborg."

It doubtless salves Davis's Promethean ego to have the cover to himself, and some justification can be adduced in the inspirational motive behind the work, not to mention the fact that the composer could never have gotten his music distributed here without the fronting of a celebrity soloist. Other than Gil Evans, Davis has refused to share his covers with anyone, and at least once he failed to credit even Evans in small print or large. For that matter, the Warners albums are essentially star vehicles for Davis engineered by Marcus Miller. That's the way it's done in America: In the '30s and '40s, composers and arrangers were the invisible men of big band music; before and after the Swing Era, name performers occasionally forced songwriters to share credits and royalties. Beyond that socially condoned blackmail, there is the competitive nature of showbiz itself, which favors the perception of solitary genius. I once asked Howlin' Wolf why he never listed the names of his musicians on his album jackets, and he retorted, "Why should I? They're my records." Still, throughout *Miles*, Davis rightly and often eloquently bemoans the lack of seriousness accorded jazz. Surely he can recognize that releasing the present album as "*Aura*: Miles Davis" is like putting out an album of piano concertos under the banner "*Emperor*: Mauricio Pollini," with inner sleeve acknowledgment of a conductor and orchestra and a tiny production credit reading "All songs by Beethoven."

In other words, although *Aura* is as much about Davis and his music as it is a vehicle for him, it is a long and complicated semi-serial suite that stands out among his recent recordings precisely because the setting focuses and underscores his strengths with formal compositional urgency. Mikkelborg's Nordic sentiment is like a slab of ice in the midnight sun, imbued with Ivesian fog and Messiaenic twitterings, and wholly congruent with Davis's electric and rhythmic seasonings, his contemplative vanity, and tenacious reveries. Davis's piquant sound humanizes the brew, but it's Mikkelborg's brew—Davis doesn't even appear in two of the ten movements.

The piece's overall structure is audacious, eclectic, and loose, yet it aligns the most durable modes and postures of Davis's post-1969 music, thus making a case for them while adding to the oeuvre. Occasionally, the composer adds sly references to earlier Davis periods, too, as when the orchestra's two-note riff echoes "So What" during "Blue," or when the Gil Evans connection to both soloist and composer is made manifest in the brass voicings of "Green," or when Thomas Clausen's piano and Niels-Henning Orsted Pedersen's bass (Miles is absent) recall in "Indigo" the complexity of rhythmic interaction that had peaked in Davis's last acoustic milestone, *Miles in the Sky*. For the most part, however, *Aura* is a bewitching affirmation of the deluge that followed his seemingly incidental discovery of the Fender Rhodes. Like the rousing and largely ignored *Tribute to Jack Johnson* in 1970, it smacks of the optimism that the initial jazz-rock alliance promised. That it proceeds from a Schoenbergian gimmick, a 10-note row corresponding to the letters spelling *Miles Davis*, shows how even-handed consolidations have become.

Mikkelborg is probably best known in this country for the rich orchestrations of his 1975 collaboration with Dexter Gordon, *More than You Know*, on Steeple-Chase. From 1964, when he was 23, he was associated with the Danish Radio Jazz Group and Big Band for more than a decade, often as leader. Highly regarded as a trumpet player, he worked with all the major visiting players and led various ensembles, including a trio with the talented Bill Evans–inspired Clausen and the phenomenal Niels-Henning. For a while he toured with a band that included the Norwegian guitarist Terje Rypdal, and it's impossible to listen to parts of *Aura* without thinking of Rypdal's ECM sessions and his glacial chords, hanging ominously in the wintry night. Inspired by Davis as a player and composer, he has fashioned for him a montage of backbeat rhythms and modes, held together by the signature row. Davis's wounded sound is contrasted with the full weight of an orchestra for the first time since he worked with Evans in the early '60s, and his response is kinetic and piping.

Davis's solos here haven't the level, mid-register, plaintive lyricism that practically invited lyrics, but they are animated by an unequivocal intensity, which keeps him leaping into the high end and chewing on the relentless rhythmic figures (tersely accentuated by Wilburn's electric drums) like a cat just let out of the house. Some of his finest moments are pockets of low pitches, but they are intermittent and brief—he skyrockets away from them soon enough. The "Intro" emerges from the ether as slowly as *Daphnis and Chloé*: McLaughlin states the serial theme and exchanges solos with Davis. In "White" Davis plays the most lyrical figure in the work, but almost immediately recedes from it for a strangely dejected overdubbed duet (a conversation with himself); the effect is not unlike the march-and-meditation of his and Evans's "Saeta." Davis doesn't play on "Yellow," an orchestral variation of "White," with key parts assigned to harp, oboe, and bells.

"Orange" and "Red" are among Davis's strongest performances of the '80s, the former a succession of coherent solos by McLaughlin and Davis, first muted and then open, punctuated by brief transitions, and the latter a torrid trumpet solo paced with characteristic deliberation over a fixed mode and nervy rhythmic vamp. "Red" is misbanded on the CD, clocking in at 9:52 instead of the correct 6:00; its second half, a shroud of synthesized chords that reverberate like Gregorian chant plus a Bo Stief bass solo, is really the first half of "Green." The second half of "Green" dazzles, as Davis actually responds to another soloist of comparable faculty, Niels-Henning, in a setting embellished by the wordless choir of a singer, Eva Thaysen, overdubbed 16 times. *Aura* loses some of its direction in the next three movements, though Davis plays with sunny élan in the reggae-buoyed "Blue," followed by another version of "Red," this one muted, and "Indigo," something of a non sequitur for piano and bass. The closing "Violet," a still-water blues, pulls it back on track, with McLaughlin filling in Davis's rests and both men soloing with patient finesse over a dense organ chord. As Davis records of the past decade go, *masterpiece* is probably not too strong a claim. As for Mikkelborg, *Aura* should recommend him to a wider audience, and to other soloists who long to hear themselves in settings of rich and frosty textures.

(November 1989)

IN HIS OWN WRITE

In his celebrated essay on Tolstoy, Isaiah Berlin invoked the maxim of a Greek poet: "The fox knows many things, but the hedgehog knows one big thing." Berlin hypothesized that the Russian novelist could not easily be labeled a pluralist fox or a monist hedgehog, because though he was by nature the former, he "believed in being" the latter. Miles Davis—who, at 63, offers himself as an autobiographer (*Miles*)—also eludes facile categorization, by repeatedly innovating, exhausting, and transforming the parameters of his musical style. But if I can borrow Berlin's analogy, Davis is the obverse of Tolstoy—a born hedgehog who believes in being a fox.

Foxlike, Davis has altered the context of his music to reflect the influence of manifold traditions and fashions—hot and cool, bop and funk, academic and streetcorner, blues and rock. His innovations in each idiom were so persuasive that four generations of musicians have followed his lead. Yet by the nature of his gift, Davis is also a hedgehog who knows one big thing: that individuality may subvert context but context ought never to vitiate individuality. As Davis's father—an outspoken dentist, landowner, gentleman farmer, and sheriff—advised him when he dropped out of the Juilliard School to play jazz, "You want to be your own man, have your own sound." Davis's sound is the unmistakable constant in his music, the true measure of his disposition, the ultimate payoff of an extremely personal approach to the trumpet. Whether he's echoing Charlie

Parker's circuitous improvisations, soloing in the matrix of Gil Evans's lush orchestrations, leading his brilliant quintets, or negotiating the bump and grind of 80's funk, Davis's siren call—plaintive, vulnerable, slashing—abides as one of the most seductive in the music of this century.

Yet Davis has never been just a musician; like Bernstein or Sinatra, he is a national phenomenon whose personal charisma has brought him to the attention of a wider public than his art ever could. Several wags noted that Davis hit a new peak in recognition when he was recently the subject of a scurrilous rumor in one of the supermarket tabloids. But even 30 years ago his records could be found in collections otherwise bereft of modern jazz. The subject of several lengthy studies (those of Jack Chambers and Ian Carr are best), his own book was eagerly awaited. The subtitle of his book ("The Autobiography") may suggest a Hollywood spinoff rather than a literary event, but Davis delivers the goods, at least most of them. Written with Quincy Troupe, a distinguished poet and editor, *Miles* is profusely detailed, exceedingly candid, and eminently readable.

In the absence of an explanation of their working methods, I assume *Miles* is an as-told-to—a peculiar genre in which the collaborator orders the facts without interpreting them. Troupe has elicited a wealth of psychological details that render Davis a convincingly narcissistic narrator. He emerges as admirable and enraging, cocksure and embittered, self-made and self-destroyed, a mass of contradictions, often lying cheek by jowl on the same page. The basic story is well known—beginning with how the child of a prosperous midwestern black family came to New York in 1944 at the age of 18 to study at Juilliard as a "smokescreen" for searching out Charlie Parker and Dizzy Gillespie, the leaders of the modern jazz movement. When an instructor at the conservatory told Davis's class that blacks played the blues because they were poor, the young man retorted, "I'm from East St. Louis and my father is rich . . . and I play the blues."

He found more valuable mentors at the jam sessions at Minton's, the after-hours club where "the cream of the crop of Harlem's black society" listened to the incubation of a new music ("in those days you didn't get too big to be sitting in"). So while he continued to examine the scores of Stravinsky, Berg, and Prokofiev and studied with members of the New York Philharmonic (oddly, he doesn't say who), he delivered himself into the hands of his own masters, "Professors Diz and Bird," as well as Freddie Webster, Thelonious Monk, Coleman Hawkins, and others. "If they smiled when you finished playing, than that meant your playing was good."

Davis's portrayal of Parker is the most complicated in the book, expressed in violent mood swings between veneration for his genius and generosity ("among the masters he was *the* master," "he treated me like a son") and contempt for his abuse of himself and everyone else, his fatal "greed" for stimulants of every description, which ended his life at 34. Davis's claim that "Bird didn't teach me much as far as music goes" is a touch of bravado contradicted by his own evidence. Semi-confident and impatient, he put himself on a dangerous deadline: "I had in my head that if I didn't make it as a musician by the time I was twenty-four, I was going to do something else . . . medicine." At age 24, in 1950, he completed the sessions that would usher in the cool jazz movement and triumphed professionally and personally (he fell in love with the French actress Juliet Greco) during a tour of Paris. It was too much too soon. Having resisted drugs throughout his tenure with Parker, he now returned to the United States and spent four years feeding "the monster" of heroin addiction.

Davis's fall is telegraphed in references to feeling unloved by his mother (his addiction served to reunite his divorced parents), and in several incidents of recklessness in his childhood, concerning fires and car wrecks that almost killed him. Yet, like Rilke gazing at "The Archaic Torso of Apollo," he realized the need to change his life, and, rather heroically, he did—finding inspiration in the contemporary torso of his friend and idol, Sugar Ray Robinson. He also took up boxing. From 1955 to 1959, Davis led one of the classic groups in American music, pioneered the long-playing album as a medium for sustained work rather than as a compilation of random pieces, and introduced a blend of pain and ecstasy into the language of the trumpet and of jazz, greatly enlarging its audience. He embodied a new presence in American culture. "All of a sudden, everybody seemed to want anger, coolness, hipness, and real clean, mean sophistication. Now the 'rebel' was in . . . not to mention that I was young and good looking and dressed well, too."

Davis organized his second great quintet in the mid-1960s, but by then jazz had taken a new turn, and many felt he had become passé, a complacent peacock. In fact, he created some of his most durable, original, and influential music in that period (one faction of the neoclassical movement in the '80s, led by Wynton Marsalis, is wed to it), but the criticism and the slow record sales hurt. When he recorded *Bitches Brew* in 1969, he stunned his admirers by instigating a fusion between jazz and rock. Although his music has changed as many times in the past 20 years as in the preceding two decades and produced several gems (from the incomparable jazz-rock of A *Tribute to Jack Johnson* to the agitated variations of *We Want Miles*), his detractors continue to see the entire phase as a cynical compromise with the marketplace. His huge popular success, blighted by illness, a car wreck, a return to drug addiction (cocaine this time), and the realization that "I didn't have anything else to say musically," imploded into a six-year retirement, a period of almost total seclusion. He has enjoyed many triumphs since his return in 1981, but the quality of his bands continued to decline. He stubbornly refuses to work with musicians of comparable faculty, and in *Miles* is at a loss to explain why.

Davis does not pretend that his fusion bands in any way rival the experience of playing with Parker and Gillespie or with John Coltrane and Philly Joe Jones (he says repeatedly that those where the musical highlights of his life), or in collaborations with Gil Evans, which, interestingly enough, he didn't fully appreciate until long after they were completed. Even the slackening in narrative energy in the last hundred pages suggests a correlative to his waning musical and personal health. Yet in attempting to justify his current situation he becomes incoherent, first blaming white critics—he forgets LeRoi Jones—for promoting the avant-grade, than blaming them for disparaging it. (Davis himself has always put it down.) What remains unviolated in his current bands is the supernal beauty of his trumpet. If the fox has become adrift in the kind of adulation measured by Grammy awards (which Davis disdains and covets), the hedgehog has remained true to his sights.

Miles, like its subject, is far from perfect. Much of the book seems unedited. The profusion of errors in the names of people and compositions is matched by annoying repetitions and misstatements, including a couple of howlers: Davis cannot mean that saxophonist Bud Freeman once played like Sonny Stitt (Von Freeman maybe?) or that Columbia Records paid him a guaranteed $300,000 per annum in the mid-1950s. Inconsistencies and odd lapses in voice (as when Davis occasionally refers to Louis Armstrong, whom he knew as Pops, as Satchmo) suggest the collision of subject and collaborator. Nor is Davis's candor entirely pleasant—his naming names of famous addicts, living and dead, borders on informing, and his contempt for women (notwithstanding the expected "I love women") is chilling. He admits to pimping to support his habit and to undermining the career of his wife, dancer Frances Taylor, out of jealousy; he sees Billy Eckstine slapping women around, admires him for it, and habitually does the same himself; he repeatedly harangues one of Charlie Parker's wives for being "ugly." In such instances, the Prince of Darkness myth is shattered by the Prince himself. Readers will be astonished to learn that as of 1946, Davis "still didn't even know how to curse." He learned, he learned. His constant use of profanity becomes blurrily tedious.

More distressing in a book of this kind is the insufficient analysis of his music. As a critic, Davis is remarkably conventional, holding to a line that is fairly standard in contemporary jazz criticism. I welcome his affirmation as well as his perspective (he is unfailingly right in evaluating his own music), but I had hoped to learn why Parker played tenor on both of the sessions he made under Davis's leadership; how the continuity between selections on *Miles Ahead* and the extended-theme arrangements of *Nefertiti* came about; why an old vocal by Bob Dorough that Davis disliked wound up on *Sorcerer;* why he permitted the release of poor albums spliced from concert leftovers (he never even mentions the notorious *Agharta*); what Gil Evans's contribution to *Filles de Kilimanjaro* was; and how the strangely Gothic 30-minute keyboard memorial to Ellington, "He Loved Him Madly," was conceived—to mention but a few puzzles in the Davis discography that remain puzzles.

Davis provides razorsharp if almost invariably unflattering and self-serving portraits of Bud Powell, Charles Mingus, Max Roach, Jackie McLean, Sonny Rollins, John Coltrane, Philly Joe Jones, Paul Chambers, Cannonball Adderley, Tony

Williams, Wayne Shorter, and others. On the other hand, Gil Evans, his "best friend" and foremost collaborator, is oddly elusive, and the wild, young Sonny Rollins he depicts is one-dimensional and at odds with everything else we know about him. He treats Bill Evans casually to the point of superciliousness ("a great little piano player"). He jumps to his own defense, reasonably enough, to assert that he and not Charlie Parker or Bill Evans wrote certain misattributed pieces, but he neglects entirely those many instances when he stands accused of claiming the tunes of others. As to the book's presentation, it has many fine photographs, though a few are insufficiently captioned, and an ambitiously conceived but incomplete index. It lacks even a rudimentary discography or list of works. For all its defects, *Miles* remains an extraordinarily colorful narrative, and it will be much quoted on all sides of the continuing Miles Davis controversy.*

(October 1989)

---

*According to Quincy Troupe, a comprehensive discography and bibliography were submitted as part of the original manuscript but jettisoned by the publisher, Simon and Schuster, to keep the price down. He says the publisher also injected errors and cut out 200 pages of text, including most of the musical material, which he and Davis hoped to publish in a subsequent volume. Troupe has publicly denounced his editor for the last chapter, an incoherent attempt at a summing-up. Apparently the chapter was concocted from deleted material and appended to the volume without his or Davis's participation or knowledge. As to Davis's involvement with the finished product, it must be noted that when asked to comment on a particular passage during a segment of "60 Minutes," Davis said he hadn't gotten that far yet. Miles Davis died on September 28, 1991 at age sixty-five.

Giant Walks the Earth

Don't ever shrink from the belief that you have to prove yourself every minute, because you do, and probably it's a healthy thing . . . one of those natural things you can only get from yourself.

Sonny Rollins, 1976

ALONE AT LAST

Sonny Rollins, the world's greatest living saxophonist, performed alone in the Museum of Modern Art's Sculpture Garden on July 19, 1985. In the estimation of one police officer, he drew about 2500 people to 54th Street, about half of whom were able to get into the free concert. Among the many tunes Rollins did not play, and in some cases did not play many times, were "To a Wild Rose," "Autumn Nocturne," "Love in Bloom," "I Can't Get Started," "Open the Door, Richard," "Shortnin' Bread," "Should I," "Peter and the Wolf," "Frankie and Johnny," "It's Raining," "St. Thomas," and "There's No Place like Home." That is, he quoted fragments, shards, often just a couple of notes from those and other melodies—a few of which cropped up in every selection—but never got farther than allusion. Each piece, then, excepting an encore of Coleman Hawkins's "Stuffy," consisted of shambling riffs that momentarily blossomed into familiar cantabile and then skulked back into additional, deliberated riffs.

Skulk is the wrong word for an artist as forthright as Rollins. His concerts are psychodramas precisely because he gives so much of himself so transparently. He can give the audience what it wants, or thinks it wants; he can play to the gallery; he can dazzle the musicians in the house; he can be romantic or funny or thrilling or analytical or euphoric. Indeed, he has been all of those things—but only, to cite the title of his worst record, when that's the way he feels. On this lovely night, before an ecstatic audience, the way he felt was apparently discursive. And also, my guess is, nervous. Looking now at those song titles, an olio so omnifarious no one but Rollins could stir it up, one may begin to decipher an autobiographical subtext that touches upon children's ditties, signature themes of his early idols, pop hits, originals, semi-classics—even an observation to explain the evening: "I Can't Get Started." The performance may have been disappointing, but it was never dull. As the pianist and critic Amy Duncan noted, "It was like an entire evening of foreplay."

The event was one of the most eagerly awaited in jazz history. Rollins has been promising a solo concert for 30 years, though never explicitly. When interviewers asked him whether he would ever do one, he'd say something like, "Well, that's something to think about." Yet the fact that people often asked suggests how logical it always seemed. The idea of a solo recital by a wind player has long been implicit in jazz itself; even before Louis Armstrong's startling "West End Blues" cadenza, there were the two-bar breaks that climaxed New Orleans jazz. Every jazz musician practicing alone has experienced the elation of self-generating rhythms. In 1948, Hawkins recorded "Picasso," an unaccompanied abstraction of "Body and Soul," and a decade later Rollins recorded his own solo versions of "Body and Soul" and "It Could Happen to You." Moreover, Rollins regularly appeared with just drums and bass, sometimes for no discernible purpose other than companionship or to spell him when he paused; the rhythms all came from Rollins. His legendary cadenzas, which could fall anywhere, were often the highlights of his sets—like traditional two-bar breaks elaborated into expansive fanfares, suspending the music and the listener until he brought in the band for a chord of resolution. Several Rollins cadenzas have been captured on records—the Impulse "Three Little Words" and the Milestone "Autumn Nocturne" are outstanding—and they whet the appetite for more. The logical extension of more is a solo concert or record.

I don't recall any demands for unaccompanied wind recitals in the '60s by Rollins or anyone else. But in the '70s, when everyone was doing it, usually for financial rather than musical reasons, Rollins loomed as the one musician fated to take up the challenge. His solo solos were different than those of Shorter or Shepp, Braxton or Brown, Hemphill or Lake or Murray or Bluiett. When Rollins played by himself he wasn't any more arcane than when he played with a rhythm section. Since he stuck by familiar melodies and seemed to swing even harder to compensate for his solitude, his solos sustained a sense of exhilaration. Yet Rollins defied his fate, though not entirely. His unaccompanied improvisations were highlights of the Milestone Jazzstars tour; he confused the hell out of Johnny Carson's audience by playing a 10-minute solo one night when Bill Cosby was the host; he regularly inserted solo pieces or lengthy cadenzas in his concert and nightclub sets. Such moments were cherished almost as much for their rarity as their tension, especially since his recordings were so uneven.

So here we are in 1985, when the fashion for solo sax has long since passed, and Rollins announces that he will give his last solo recital ever at the Museum of Modern Art, and it will be recorded. His *last* recital! The press release neglected to add that it was also his first. Well, you could cut the anticipation with a knife. At 8:10, he stepped before the reverent audience and hunkered into what I naively described in my notes as a "long cadenza." "To a Wild Rose" wafted by. "Autumn Nocturne" made a pass. "Mr. P. C." appeared, and as Rollins noticed the Henry Moore couple behind him he played at them for a while. A car horn blasted from the street, and he responded with "Pop Goes the Weasel." But it was all cadenza, no theme. During the second piece, he harmonized with the sounds of a police siren, quoted a couple of songs, and hinted at a calypso rhythm— which aroused everyone's attention with the promise of concerted swing. But it was just a tease. Give him room, you thought, he'll get there. Dressed in white pants and sneakers and a striped polo shirt, he bowed rhythmically from the waist without bending his knees, nudging short, blustery riffs—always imposing, wielding his tenor at times like a pickax.

By the third and fourth pieces, it was obvious that he couldn't get certain tunes out of his head, though he didn't want to play more than fragments of them. Nor was he interested in swinging, per se. There was no doubling or halving of tempo, no sustained groove, no rebounding accents: just a determined effort to locate himself in a music that seemed continuously to elude him. The Charlie Parker vamp on "Bird of Paradise" set up an intense gambit that might have taken off but segued instead into "Frankie and Johnny," then "No Place like Home," which he indulged for nearly a chorus, then big band licks, then "To a Wild Rose," then "It's raining it's pouring the old man is snoring," then "Love in Bloom." At least once during each piece he interrupted the music to declaim "thankyouthankyouthankyou" or "gottagogottagogottago," which may be his way of keeping those pieces off the record. Then, incredibly, he did go.

In a few minutes, however, he returned and began to dally with "I Can't Get Started." Now it will happen, you thought, easing back and waiting for the throbbing to begin. But if you blinked, you opened your eyes on "St. Thomas," and if you applauded that anthem you drowned out two others he tested and rejected. At this point I believe I heard him mutter, "What can I do now?" He jumped back into the fray, stomping in place, hinting at a calypso, returning to wooden riffs, biting off and spitting out "Fly Me to the Moon," "Alfie," "Mr. P. C.", "To a Wild Rose." He found countless figures that lent themselves to chromatic modulation, up and down, down and up, and he never relieved the tautness of his bow. "Thankyouladiesandgentlemen gottagogottagogottago." But at this point he didn't want to go any more than the audience wanted him to. The amazing thing about Rollins is that even when he's off he's on. He kept starting up again as though he'd find what he was looking for this time for sure. And had he continued searching until dawn, I suspect a good part of the audience would have remained no less vigilant. Finally, however, he made his last foray and, prompted by audience time-clapping, played a few hot choruses of "Stuffy"—now strolling, now stomping in place. Then something incredible happened. Rodin's Balzac, who had looked skittish throughout, flung away his cloak, jumped off his pedestal, and began leaping into the air. It took the efforts of several MOMA attendants to wrestle him to the ground and subdue him with tranquilizers. Asked to comment, Rollins remarked, "Thankyouthankyouthankyou."

(August 1985)

DANCING, ROMANCING, CHANTING

Who is that subtly dexterous hand-drummer keeping up phrase for phrase, shadowlike, with Sonny Rollins's opening cadenza on his new recording of "Dancing in the Dark?" Of course, it's Rollins himself, and no, he wasn't overdubbed. The castanet effect results from a tight recording that picks up the tenor's clicking keys and thumping pads as he plays. As an example of microphone technique that turns presumed extra musical sounds into music, it recalls records Ben Webster made for Verve in the 1950s, which captured and reified his gusty breathing as an integral part of his tonal production. With Webster, the issue was embouchure; with Rollins, rhythm. That kind of gilded fallout is less pronounced in concert where the eye undercuts the ear. Heard live the percussive clicking of Rollins's keys is merely another offshoot of the man's imposing presence and force. He carries the tenor up and down the stage like a bagpipe, musical phrases filing out in the naturalness of his breathing. His virtuosity is daunting not least because it bespeaks absolute intellectual control. I mean, imagine writing one perfect sentence on top of another without hesitation, let alone revision.

I suppose it's fortunate that Rollins fails just often enough to prove how extraordinary the successes are. Otherwise, we might dismiss him as a warlock and not take to heart the standards he sets. One indication of how unique his place is among living jazz musicians is the disappointment invariably sounded by critics and fans at every performance that is less than a five-alarm blaze. With equal severity did people respond to Ellington and Armstrong concerts: Genius was never enough, it had to be genius at the apex of self-renewal. At Town Hall last week, Rollins played with a vivacity and amplitude so far beyond the ken of most musicians that it might shame the most apprehensive among them into another line of work. During intermission, the audience was brimming with his contagious energy. Perhaps because the second set was less propulsive than the first, the final verdict was a knowing shrug: It wasn't the best we've ever heard him. What a position to be in. No wonder Armstrong took to opening every set with "Indiana"; having started out on Mount Olympus in the '20s, there was no way he could continue to please the expectations of mere mortals 30 years later. Better to please himself.

In fact, the concert did have moments of revelation—the kind that almost always follow on the heels of a new album, when Rollins hits the road to show that the studio recording was just a warm-up and, oh, look at me now. One highlight was his new ballad, "Promise," delivered with an unaffected and graceful attack, the arpeggios bubbling upward like champagne, the afterbeats nodding in crosscurrents of supple wit. "Promise" is a relative dead spot on his album, *Dancing in the Dark*, in which the melodic pull of the pretty piece keeps him in check beyond the theme statement. "O.T.Y.O.G.," which helps light up the record, was even more jubilant as the opener at Town Hall. The piece is parsed in 16-bar passages, with a change in rhythm between the first and second 8-bar units, so that at first Rollins retards the beat and then leaps on top of it. Good as the recorded version is, it hardly prepared one for the surging double-time, thematic hammering, loopy quotations, and sustained notes—especially at the blistering close—of the live one. On the other hand, the live "Duke of Iron," Rollins's latest calypso, was a throwaway; his six-chorus solo on the album is incomparable lyric swing, at once boisterous and lucid.

Significantly, the concert's highlights did not plug the new record: an unidentified waltz with a Dameronian cast, in which Rollins eschewed harmony for an intense davening in riffs; an exquisite "Autumn Nocturne" with a jocular cadenza that married "St. Thomas," "Swanee River," and "Doin' What Comes Naturally"; a relatively brief but heavily thematic "G-Man"; and, the encore, his "Theme from Alfie," delivered with fly munificence, including an exchange of fours that allowed drummer Al Foster to shine. In contrast to those pieces, the record is an exercise in controlled lyricism—a deft chaser after last year's exhaustingly brilliant *G-Man*. My first impression was—surprise!—disappointment. But the disc has grown on me steadily. The reverse side of Rollins's euphoria in the past decade has been a cloying melodicism that inhibits his improvisation. Gone with the sardonic probing of his early playing is the kind of introspection that allowed him to flay open a ballad, taking from it what appealed to him and then fleshing it out with his own variations or fleeing for parts unknown. Strong melodies now exert a powerful gravity that he can dispel only with the kind of pyrotechnics that defuse the song's appeal.

The Mann-Weill hit "Just Once" doesn't have much appeal, and perhaps Rollins recorded it in the hope of finding another "Isn't She Lovely." He wrings from it a convincing, bluesy, after-hours paraphrase that climaxes in a few seconds of fierce reed-biting. But though you wish he'd squeal his way beyond the tune's locus, he complacently lets it fade out. More irksome is "I'll String Along with You," because it has the promise of a perfect vehicle; yet it's roped to a contrived dance beat vamp, and though Rollins begins his solo with a singing riff, he quickly collapses back into the melody, never finding his own. The bulk of the album is fairly marvelous. After the cadenza on "Dancing in the Dark," Rollins seems intent on deconstructing the superb ever-climbing Arthur Schwartz melody, poking around without milking it. He establishes a peace between the song and his own diction of stark, energizing riffs, doubling the time and sharing it with drummer Marvin Smith, who anticipates his every move. Consequently, the fade-out is a drag. In addition to "O.Y.T.O.G.," "Promise," and the irresistible "Duke of Iron," there is a beguiling original called "Allison," a 52-bar construction in which two 8-bar segments are followed by a 10-bar segment (twice). Rollins improvises a neat countermelody and then trades fours with Smith for a chorus. On the CD, there's an alternate take of "Allison," in which the rhythm vamp is absent, the theme statement is foreshortened by half, and the tenor solo cuts far closer to the bone. If *G-Man* was an invocation to the gods, *Dancing in the Dark* is a gentleman caller's bouquet of roses. Even the respective cover photos tell you that.

(May 1988)

BIGGER THAN LIFE

Let me begin with a ludicrous, indefensible statement: Sonny Rollins is the most commanding musician alive. It's a ridiculous thing to say; my credibility is shot. Avoid further embarrassment by turning the page. Still, if you were at Carnegie Hall on May 19, you know, or at least suspect, I'm right. He confirmed two things we've known for a while that nonetheless demand annual confirmation. First, he has an unchallengeable monopoly on those musical emotions characterized by jubilance or euphoria. Second, he no longer plays tenor saxophone in any conventional sense; the horn is an appendage of the man, like a surgically implanted amplifier. Charles Mingus once said something to the effect that if Charlie Parker were thinking of a woman while playing, you could tell the color of her hair and eyes. With Rollins, you can count the fillings in her teeth.

Of course, his thoughts hardly seem that mundane. John Coltrane was considered a spiritual musician because of the chanting grandeur with which he drove home a brittle religiosity. Rollins's spirituality is a good deal earthier, but no less profound. Nearing 60 (this, too, is ludicrous, but biographical sources insist), he summons forth a contagious energy that must either transform you or leave you ashamed of your inability to rise to its challenge. "Don't worry, be happy," is not his song—"sing hallelujah, be ecstatic" comes closer to the mark. Shameless as ever, the man who once resurrected "Toot, Toot, Tootsie," "I'm an Old Cowhand," "There's No Business like Show Business," and "To a Wild Rose," has now reclaimed the "Tennessee Waltz." Over march rhythms. With an interpolation of the Alphonse Picou clarinet lick from "High Society." Daring you to get sentimental or titter or turn away from the light.

Rollins possesses you with his own possession, getting inside you to restore recollections of the first time you ever realized music was bigger than life. When I was a kid I felt the small hairs on the back of my neck rise during an impetuous performance of the harpsichord cadenza in the fifth Brandenburg Concerto; later that year, I heard Louis Armstrong's 1928 "Basin Street Blues," where the trumpet emerges from the fog, taking on shape and weight with every bar, and I had to stop the album to breathe awhile before I could go to the next cut. In restoring for me a sense of wonder and passion, Rollins reminds me why music is worth living for, and defines the distinction between musicians who play music and musicians who are music. Think of Armstrong or Coleman Hawkins or Bud Powell at their most assured, of Gilels playing Beethoven or Schnabel playing Schubert or

Casals Bach, and if that isn't enough name-dropping, think of Rollins himself, the sound and substance of his phrases riding roughshod beyond bar lines and notes to the place where meaning and feeling are all, and doing it with a fractious wit that ambushes every conceit with deliberated surprise. You think you know how that headlong arpeggio is going to resolve, but somehow it travels four more measures to another place altogether. He honks repeatedly for eight bars and imparts a different nuance to every blast. He overtakes his own electrifying dance turns with cresting waves of notes, then lands nimbly on his feet ready to meet the next self-generated wave.

I've compared Rollins to Louis Armstrong before, and I find the comparison increasingly unavoidable, if for no other reason than that Armstrong developed a sound on the trumpet so personal and consequently inimitable that it made all other trumpets sound relatively dim. Rollins's sound is Gargantua come to life. It's so capacious you could step into its palm and never see all the fingers; the result of a three-decade search, this is the sound he strove for through all those experiments in timbre, when he masked the core virility of his tone with edgy, cold, gritty, congenial, winking appliqués—never quite satisfied with any of them for long, never quite dispelling the suspicion that his truest timbre was the rounded, noble bebopping clarity he perfected in the mid-1950s. Among his predecessors on the tenor, Ben Webster alone comes to mind as someone who perfected one sound in his youth, then developed another that transcended the instrument. Mottled as the acoustics in Carnegie are, Rollins's timbre burnished the place. At no point did he lose his footing or inspiration; or if he did, he was prescient enough to cut the piece off before anyone knew about it. Who else can keep you upright all night, and who else can sustain his unsurmountable level of energy for the exclusive expression of well-being?

Who but Rollins would invite Branford Marsalis as his "special guest soloist" and leave him pacing the stage looking for a way to make himself useful? Having confessed to the *New York Times* his expectation of serving Rollins as a "sacrificial lamb," Marsalis can't have been too surprised that the spit was fired and turning when he arrived. But *sacrificial* is the key word here. If he hadn't arrived, Rollins might have played a relatively routine set, something more akin to what he plays on records. During the second half, Rollins allowed Marsalis a ballad of his own, "Embraceable You"—his sound, played into a mike (whereas the wily Rollins uses a pickup in the bell of his horn), melted before the hall's cruel indifference. When Rollins later introduced "Tenor Madness," you anticipated the title's mandate, but they didn't even trade fours. Rollins's real partner was his heavily featured drummer, Al Foster, the only musician onstage who could spell him without collapsing the tension. Marsalis didn't disgrace himself; indeed, he was charming in his self-effacement, finding utility at one point by announcing the Knicks score. He simply played tenor, while Rollins was the thunder on Mount Sinai—a difference that not even the most intoxicated Sting fan could miss. (To be sure, Marsalis may have earned something of a comeuppance for permitting a

five-page bio, perhaps the longest ever, in the *Stagebill*; it included the astonishing claim that he "is the first soloist [to his brother Delfeayo's "knowledge"] whose
contributions to music *openly* display the multifarious qualities of all major
saxophone stylists in the jazz idiom, in addition to his own." If Rollins happened
to read that, he may have been doubly inspired.)

I have had occasion to criticize some of Rollins's rhythm sections, but that,
too, is an area fully mastered. After more then a quarter-century, Bob Cranshaw
can breathe the right bass lines, and he falls into rigorous lockstep with Foster.
Mark Soskin, who miscalculated several years back with a dreary attempt at
fusion, remains an effective, fluent soloist who can sustain those few gaps the
leader leaves, and guitarist Jerome Harris proved on "Tennessee Waltz" to have a
sense of humor equal to his sense of economy. Clifton Anderson, whose trombone is like a one-man brass section to beef up ensembles, has so little to do that
when he finally gets a chance to blow, you're surprised at how cagey and coherent he can be.

The program was diverse, as usual: the calypso "Duke of Iron" (Rollins rigor),
followed by "East of the Sun" (Rollins lucidity), "The Tennessee Waltz" (Rollins
transcendence), "Three Little Words" (hold the phone), "O.T.Y.O.G." (Rollins
merriment, complete with "Happy Birthday," "I Dream of Jeannie," and "In a
Country Garden"), "Don't Stop the Carnival" (Rollins rapture), a three-minute
unaccompanied cadenza that ended with the barest nod to "Here's That Rainy
Day" (Rollins spellbinding), and farewell glimpses of "Tenor Madness" and
"Strode Rode." He brought the capacity audience to its feet three times, most
dramatically after "Three Little Words," which was the highlight of the concert,
if not the millennium. This is one piece he has recorded brilliantly in the studio
(see *Sonny Rollins on Impulse!*), though even that masterpiece might seem an
hors d'oeuvre compared to the impulsive fireworks at Carnegie. After a paraphrase of the you-are-a-dope melody (thank you, Red Skelton), he drew in gusts
of air and exhaled a Niagara of sustained lyricism—tensile phrases bounding in
an effusive song, wrought with visionary exuberance. I leave you with two
thoughts: (1) Like all great black musicians, Rollins is not a member of the
National Academy of Arts and Letters, unlike, say, John Cage, and (2) like all
great Sonny Rollins concerts, this one wasn't recorded.

(June 1989)

YESTERDAY, TODAY, AND TOMORROW

Well. . . .

He walks out, blinding red shirt hanging loose over black ascot and pants,
followed by Bob Cranshaw, Al Foster, Mark Soskin, and Clifton Anderson, and
the audience, primed with hair-trigger adulation, roars. He says, "Thank you,"

and the audience, which had just quieted down, goes crazy, because it is a very good sign when he talks, and besides, everyone seems to recognize that of all the places one could be on April 13 at 8, Carnegie Hall is, biblically speaking, the chosen venue. He introduces the band and announces "a little standard, 'Long Ago and Far Away,' " which he preps with a short cadenza. Bang!—he's off. Chorus after chorus after chorus after chorus, never leaving the melody far behind, but playing catch-up with the time, so that a furious effusion of arpeggios will suddenly, after seven bars of free-fall, swoop into an eighth bar downbeat. Foster monitors every second—still, those arpeggios are like extended press rolls. They lift you up, and you don't know when you're going to touch down. He does it several times, retard and catch up, retard and catch up, and every time he hits the ground, people applaud in gratitude. Soskin's keyboards are miked too high (every chord crunches), but the tenor sax is splendidly imaged; you can hear all the nuances, the chortling double-time figures, the countless ways of paraphrasing the key melody, which he returns to at the top of every chorus. By keeping the melody in focus, he can sustain interest in a solo for hours. He nervily caps it off with a shave-and-a-haircut, by way of setting up fours with Foster's drums. So far, tour de force. Then a new calypso with old New Orleans changes gets underway via solos by Cranshaw on bass guitar, Soskin on two keyboards, and Anderson on trombone, but they are as interludes, breathing spaces, before the leader returns swinging with a serpentine vivacity, snakehips stuff, all patterned on riffs. When he plays there is a hot chill in the air, and when he doesn't it's all pretty mortal. "Now," he says by way of bringing out trumpeter Roy Hargrove, who is barely into his 20s, "the young man we've been hearing so much about." With Anderson off to the right and the master standing by the piano, Hargrove begins his solo feature, "Once in a While." Of course, this is madness. You don't debut with a slow ballad while the Lord Sonny Rollins stands 12 feet away from you, politely staring. You come out blowing, and then, after the blood has left your eyes, you take your solo bow, and even then you might want to avoid a slow ballad. Unless you are very, very sure. Hargrove is. The night turns out to be a major coming-out party, though his triumph gets off to a tentative start: His opening phrases are so legato that the rhythm section can't quite figure out where and how deep to cut a backbeat. But as the theme chorus continues, he lets more brass into his sound and pushes the rhythm; by the time he is out of the tune's gravity (Foster is like a chef with brushes), he makes it clear to those who might have expected another Wynton or Terence or even the somewhat inhibited Roy of his first solo album, that his strongest suit is unbridled wailing. The response is so exuberant, Hargrove blushes. Yet, to paraphrase a composer whose music Rollins recorded in the '50s, we ain't heard nothing yet. The next piece is Charlie Parker's "Big Foot." For emphasis, I repeat: The next piece is Charlie Parker's "Big Foot." My gosh. Let me not spend time on the ebullient tenor solo, which passed the baton to Hargrove by means of a quote from "Sentimental Journey," or the trumpet solo, a rip-roaring case of Brownie *reditus*, or the trombone solo by the much underrated Anderson, who eschews riff patterns in favor of complicated expansions of melodic ideas (who has he been listening to?) devised with rapid slide-work, and get to the heart of the matter, the fours. My hair stands straight up. In fact, a couple of minutes into this episode, which is exclusively a tenor-trumpet thing, the whole audience looks like Al Pacino in *Godfather III*. Astonishingly, the master has largely dispensed with the throatiness of his modern sound. The reach-back also extends to content, such as steely orchestra riffs that he stretches over the bar lines, so that the exchange quickly becomes dialogue or call-and-response. Hargrove echoes some of Rollins's calls before they are fully laid out. No preening here, just rampaging trumpet in the tradition of Brown, Dorham, and the young Howard McGhee. Unlike just about every other young guest Rollins has feted at these annual rites of initiation, he holds his own. Soon they are down to twos, then ones—you know, the kind of thing you usually have to turn to Gene Norman Presents records to hear anymore. This is why the blues were invented, to straighten your hair. Three-quarters through the first set, the benign mob of an audience rises. The closer is a new piece written by Rollins in honor of "Young Roy"; the eight-bar ditty repeated with a four-bar extension embodies the only indication thus far of the great man's normative '90s style.

That style seems likely to return to the shadows at the outset of the second set, when Cranshaw brings out—to tumultuous applause—a real honest-to-God doghouse bass, reportedly at the insistence of Jim Hall. As everyone knows, more than 30 years ago, Rollins—to protest the expulsion of the Dodgers, whose great pitcher, Don Newk, was so named after his resemblance to Rollins, known in his youth as Newcombe—retired from music and played exclusively in the Lincoln Tunnel, dodging cars while using his horn to catch coins tossed by exasperated if empathic drivers, or something like that. He returned to form in 1961 with a much celebrated quartet, including Hall and Cranshaw (drummers were caught in a revolving door), and a much-publicized contract with RCA, which produced six records that didn't sell as well as expected but quickly earned the status of world-renowned classics. (In the U.S., those classics are either O.P. or pointlessly reconfigured for CD and lacking all composer credits.) So here they are, nearly 30 years later, Rollins in a white-fringed black jacket that might have seen service on the cover of *Way Out West*; Hall, in a suede vest; and the ageless Cranshaw, holding his instrument like a woman instead of a log. The air is now charged in a completely different way. If Rollins is the master of sustained elation, good for what ails you, Hall is the master of space and economy, good for mental push-ups. The guitarist's graceful lyricism and especially his harmonies—the unexpected phrase-ending, the chord that goes just left of where you anticipated—charts a new landscape, and Rollins fills it with *his old sound*. He hasn't lost it—here it is, just as you remembered. Cranshaw, contrary to rumors that he can't play stand-up anymore, hasn't lost it either: He plucks and sometimes strums lovely lyric lines, fleet and easy. On "Without a Song," Rollins and Hall share the theme, followed by the latter's spare variations; both of them comp a written figure during the bass solo. When Rollins hits the bridge (so to speak) in his solo, Foster starts pressing, Hall strumming, and Cranshaw plucking, until they buoy him on waves of rhythm, which he crests into a cadenza followed by an extended coda by the quartet. Hall's feature (Rollins, seated at the piano, listens intently), "With a Song in My Heart," is introduced with oblique harmonies and then springs forth into melody, like the sun darting through clouds. He and Cranshaw achieve semi-counterpoint in the last chorus, closing with eight bars of parallel chords. Rollins returns for "Where Are You?" and "The Bridge." The chief virtue of the first is the tenor cadenza midway, and the set of chords Hall lays out to bring Rollins and the ensemble together again; the second starts with beaming energy, Hall strumming up tension behind a heated tenor invention, but dissipates during a long and subtle drum solo. This music is so much more cerebral than what we've come to expect from Rollins that, notwithstanding the pleasures of the harbor (so to speak), the night is ripe for another blast of growly post-1960s fury. Back comes the ensemble (and the bass guitar) for "The Everywhere Calypso," on which the master revs himself up, banking riffs into small cathedrals and imparting the expected rush. Before anyone else has time to comment, he spins into "St. Thomas," and now Carnegie shakes once more. Hargrove is biting off high notes and shooting them at the chandelier, and for his turn, Rollins is dancing and bowing; just when you think Hall is going to get his say, master turns to prodigy and starts the fours going. They converse in rapture, and the piece turns out to have more false endings than *Gone with the Wind*. The ensemble is looking at Rollins for a cue, but after the fours, he starts a new solo and then another, until finally he strolls to the apron and barks a huge implacable Beethovenlike finish. They leave, but four or five minutes of shouting, stomping, whistling, cheering (no way is this audience dispersing without an encore) brings them back. "Thank you, ladies and gentlemen," he says, which from him is like a benediction. "Tenor Madness": Hargrove goes for it, with Rollins clapping in time through the whole performance, and Hall, after a spare survey of blues territory, follows suit. But the leader isn't giving much on this—a couple of choruses of fours with Foster and out. Then he looks out at the crowd, and walks away from the ensemble. Digging deep—his classic sound intact once more—he limns a ballad cadenza that slowly, evenly, brilliantly shapes up as another blast from Charlie Parker's past, "This Is Always." Such a poet!

It was an old-time concert, or so it seemed, because they don't happen like this very often—the mixture of excitement, subtlety, and surprise; of unembarrassed rapprochement with the past and a major debut for tomorrow. The audience played an important role, too: It crossed not only the lines of race and gender but of age, as graying beboppers from the '40s cheered side by side with kids—including one group who told me they attended 1989's Rollins concert to see guest Branford Marsalis, whom they knew from his Sting tour, and discovered this god whom they had known by name only. Was it recorded? No, at least not officially. Is Rollins a member of the Academy of Arts and Letters yet? Of course not: It's easier to mourn the days when giants walked the earth than to face up to the giants in your path.

There are no words.

(April 1991)

Dizzy like a Fox

The first time I heard modern jazz live was on a triple bill at the Village Gate in Greenwich Village, in late 1964 or early 1965. I was 16, and though I had heard several kinds of jazz on records and television, the only kind I had seen in concert was the traditional New Orleans brand, during a trip to that city. We arrived—a friend, his father, and me—at the Gate early enough to get a good table, and the show unfolded: the Gerry Mulligan Quartet (with, if memory serves, Jim Hall on guitar), comedian Dick Gregory, and the Dizzy Gillespie Quintet. I have long since come to revere Mulligan's music, but on that night its glazed sonorities glanced off my ignorance; my initial response to Mulligan's lucid cool was of trying to climb a glass wall, and neither the 19th-century classics nor rock and roll nor Dixieland nor the blues—my musical education to date—had prepared me for it. Gregory was funny, but I recall only one line of his routine, something about his parents instructing him not to eat in the bathroom, and his rejoinder that the family toothbrushes resided in the bathroom all day long.

The Gillespie band was something else—and my recollection of his performance is remarkably vivid after more than 25 years. With his first number, the temperature of the room went way up. Yet I didn't really "get it" any more than I did Mulligan. Sidney Bechet observed, "You got to be in the sun to feel the sun. It's that way with music, too." What brought me in out of the shade were the comic routines that ensued. Dizzy announced he would introduce the members of the band, and introduced them to each other. The joke itself was not nearly as funny as the context in which it was so expertly delivered. I had somehow come to believe that modern jazz was a fairly arcane discipline, witty if you knew the language, but essentially serious. Gillespie's humor, not unlike P.D.Q. Bach's, had an unabashed slapstick quality. During a number with a Latin beat, he embraced saxophonist James Moody for a rhumba. He also danced on his own, wriggling his hips. His announcements, double takes, articulation, and posture were as farcical as they were unexpected. Because of them, the music was no longer intimidating.

At that time, I knew nothing about Gillespie's reputation as a wag and a ham. But listening to him, I learned something about the calming effect of humor. As

I leaned forward to share in his lunacy, I became more receptive to the music itself. He played a piece called "And Then She Danced," plugging the forthcoming record it would appear on, *Jambo Caribe*. I purchased it as soon as it came out. Released on Limelight, a label famous for elaborate gatefold covers, the album also compounded the music with jokey asides and terrible puns in several pages of liner notes. The package confirmed for me the sense of having discovered a new universe of irreverence and caprice.

In the last 25 years, I have seen Dizzy Gillespie introduce the members of his band to each other countless times; I've seen him shimmy and fool with language and play congas and tell some member of the audience, convulsed with laughter, to shaddup; and though I half expect to become impatient with the comic relief, I never do. The main reason is that he is so good at it—few performers are. Another reason is that the comedy never vitiates the deep sobriety and wicked intelligence of his music. Gillespie is an American paradox: a quintessentially critical and innovative artist who plays, often superbly, the clown. Of musicians of his stature, only Louis Armstrong and Fats Waller were his equal at walking the tightrope from jazz complexity to inspired silliness and back. Yet Armstrong and Waller played a relatively accessible music. Gillespie is a fearsome modernist—the man who, with Charlie Parker, invented jazz modernism in part to repudiate the very entertainment values that were thought to have dimmed the music's power during the commercially extravagant Swing Era.

In 1990, the year Gillespie turned 73, he was heaped with homages, including a Kennedy Center Honor and several tribute concerts (one of which—a retrospective of his 1949 big band—I produced with John Lewis and the American Jazz Orchestra). Yet when so many honors, deserved as they are, alight on the head of a man of 73, they tend to shore up his historical importance instead of celebrating the miracle of his ongoing resourcefulness. This is especially true when the individual is an indisputably historic figure. Shortly after John Birks Gillespie left his birthplace of Cheraw, South Carolina, and began playing professionally in Philadelphia and New York, he earned his famous moniker for antics onstage and off. One bandleader is said to have observed of the new name, "Sure he's dizzy . . . like a fox." The dizziness did not detract from his innovations then, nor should it undermine our appreciation of his brilliance now.

From the time he joined Cab Calloway's band in 1939, Gillespie plunged into every aspect of music, as soloist, composer, and arranger. After encountering Charlie Parker ("the other half of my heartbeat") in Kansas City, presiding over after-hours jam sessions in Harlem (where the new jazz, later dubbed "bebop" by a cynical press, was incubated), and serving as music director of the transitional Billy Eckstine Orchestra, he emerged as the most public representative of a new style in American music. Yet as a serious artist who functioned as an entertainer, he was hard to pin down. At a time when black artists insisted on the dignified presentation of their work, Gillespie remained as true to his secondary calling as an irrepressible cut-up as he did to his primary calling as a musical radical. And he has continued to do so for more than 50 years. Let it be remembered that the man who initiated the vogue in berets ("hot water bottles," Louis Armstrong called them), goatees, and dark glasses; who claims to play a trumpet with a 45-degree bell because someone sat on his original instrument and bent it out of shape; who is so renowned for his puffed-up cheeks that medical science has conferred a name, Gillespie's Pouches, on the condition, is also the man who recorded what is generally conceded to be the first modern jazz improvisation and who remains one of the marvels of 20th-century music.

That first recorded incursion by modern jazz is found on an otherwise negligible 1942 performance by the Les Hite band. The song, "Jersey Bounce," was introduced by Tiny Bradshaw and recorded by Earl Hines in 1941, turned into a number one hit by Benny Goodman in March 1942, and soon covered by several other bands, including those of Jimmy Dorsey, Shep Fields, Red Norvo, and Jan Savitt. Hite's version undoubtedly had the lowest sales of them all, but it has the surest place in history because of a 16-bar solo by a then little known trumpeter with a disarming nickname. The Hite performance consists of three choruses infused with uneventful solos, in the idiom of the day, on tenor sax, piano, and guitar. After the second chorus, a four-measure transition sets the stage for Gillespie's improvisation.

Gillespie's solo has become one of those defining musical moments when it seems as though a window has opened onto the future. Earlier examples include the surprising fluency of Louis Armstrong's performance of the trio strain on King Oliver's 1923 record "Chimes Blues," or Bix Beiderbecke's sublime eight-bar episode on Paul Whiteman's otherwise leaden "Love Nest." The distinction between Gillespie's solo and the music that precedes and follows it in the Hite performance can suffice as a primitive but unmistakable example of what modern jazz offered in pyrotechnical expressiveness and thoroughgoing originality. Gillespie's solo begins with a spare melodic figure whose first two notes are separated from the rest by a dramatic pause (measures 1 and 2); his second phrase (measures 3 and 4) expands that initial idea with triplets, breaching the orchestra's plodding 4/4 time while suggesting an almost detached authority. His third figure, a dazzling, frenetic arpeggio, begins with high notes and continues uninterrupted for four measures (through measure 8), ending precisely on the first beat of the ninth measure. The second half of his solo is a more stately version of the first half, conveying something of Gillespie's sense of symmetrical form.

Yet "Jersey Bounce," no less than Armstrong's interpretation of written material on "Chimes Blues," represents Gillespie in embryo. The full force of his trumpet playing and of his matured conception was revealed in the mid-1940s, in dozens of performances that constitute the most innovative body of trumpet playing since early Armstrong. Gillespie himself, it should be noted, has always insisted that there is a trinity of formative players, adding the name of his idol, Roy Eldridge, to Armstrong's and his own. Gillespie calls the luminous trumpet star who arose in the 1930s "the Messiah of our generation," and some of his own early solos are unembarrassed imitations of Eldridge. Unlike Parker, who, until recent excavations turned up revealing private recordings, was unrepresented by apprentice performances and so seemed to have been born fully formed, Gillespie developed his mature style during seven years in recording studios. Eldridge enjoyed recounting that his first impression of Gillespie's solo on the Lionel Hampton record "Hot Mallets" was that he was hearing his own playing. Even so, because of the recording ban demanded by the American Federation of Musicians between 1942 and 1944, the final steps in his maturation process took place in relative privacy. Few jazz fans were prepared for the explosive Gillespie-Parker discs that appeared at the end of World War II.

In 1945, Gillespie recorded several tunes for Guild that, along with Charlie Parker's initial Savoy session a few months later, set the standards for the new music. The following year, he signed with RCA and made plans to organize a full orchestra. At his third big band session he recorded "Manteca," one of the most important records ever made in the United States. With justifiable immodesty, Gillespie told an interviewer for the recent PBS documentary series "Routes to Rhythm," "It was similar to a nuclear weapon when it burst on the scene. They'd never seen a marriage of Cuban music and American music like that before." If "Manteca" had done nothing but demonstrate that such a marriage was possible, its impact on Latin music and jazz would still be incalculable. In a sense, the salsa movement of the 1970s was born with the release of that performance, recorded on December 22, 1947. The oddest thing about the original "Manteca" is how little Gillespie's trumpet is featured. Yet in two eight-bar statements, he offers a comprehensive foundation for modern jazz, while pointing to a direction in jazz improvisation—the use of modes instead of chords—that wouldn't be popularly assimilated for more than a decade, when Miles Davis began employing modes on such recordings as *Milestones* and *Kind of Blue*.

Practically every moment in this performance, which is a breath longer than three minutes, rewards close scrutiny. But before we look too closely, perhaps I should note the obvious: The key virtue of "Manteca," which made it an instant classic and assures it lasting admiration, lies less in the details than in the overall luster of the total work. Few of the elements in "Manteca" were genuinely new in 1947. Bass vamps, modal improvisation, layered rhythms, tritones, and other aspects of Gillespie's performance predate jazz history. Gillespie himself had made earlier attempts at fusing Afro-Cuban rhythms and jazz, including "A Night in Tunisia," possibly his most famous composition (though it uses a relatively conventional approach to rhythm and harmony), and "Cubana Be/Cubana Bop," his collaboration with the composer/theorist George Russell and the Cuban drummer Chano Pozo, a two-part work recorded eight days before "Manteca" that was actually more advanced in its use of the same elements. "Manteca," however, had the requisite emotional and intellectual allure to successfully effect a Cuban-American fusion.

The origin of "Manteca" is well known. Gillespie became interested in Cuban music in 1939, shortly after the veteran Cuban-born big band trumpeter Mario Bauza encouraged Cab Calloway to hire him. When Dizzy started his own big band, he asked Bauza to recommend a Cuban percussionist, and was thus introduced to Chano Pozo, a 31-year-old immigrant already famous in Havana as an entertainer, composer, and brawler. Pozo spoke little English, but he had no trouble communicating musically with Gillespie, who was uncommonly receptive to his ideas. While touring California, Pozo came to him with an idea for a new piece. It would begin with three simultaneous rhythms. First, a B-flat-7 bass vamp—not the usual four-beat bass walk that was then universal in jazz, but a singular melodic-rhythmic figure. *

Then (at measure 7 of the 1947 recording) the saxophones enter with another vamp, a simple B-flat octave stretch.

Finally (at measure 13), the trombones enter with a third B-flat-7 melodic-rhythmic figure.

As Gillespie tells the story, he wrote out the three riff figures and realized he didn't have a finished piece of music. Missing was a bold harmonic interlude that would play off the rhythms and give the piece variety. He devised a 16-bar bridge, a harmonic oasis that dramatized Pozo's vamps by providing contrast and furnishing a compelling basis for improvisation. Gillespie gave the various parts to his gifted staff arranger, Gil Fuller, who fleshed out the big band orchestration. "Manteca" had its premiere at Carnegie Hall on September 29, 1947, and was an immediate success. Since the birth of jazz, nearly half a century before, musicians had attempted to fuse it with Latin rhythms and forms. Jelly Roll Morton, the exemplary New Orleans composer, advised, "If you can't manage to put

---

*The transcriptions used here are by Jon Schapiro, whose insights into jazz musicology were invaluable in helping me make sense of the stories they tell.

tinges of Spanish in your tunes, you will never be able to get the right seasoning, I call it, for jazz." Louis Armstrong recorded "The Peanut Vendor," and numerous bandleaders from north and south of the Gulf, including such popular entertainers as Paul Whiteman and Xavier Cugat, attempted to blend the musical cultures. One reason "Manteca" was so successful is that it didn't disguise or vitiate its dual patrimony. The jazz and Cuban aspects—opulent harmonies, passionate rhythms—exist side by side with equal integrity.

As heard on the 1947 recording, the performance unfolds as follows. The introduction consists of the three vamps (measures 1 through 14) and an eight-measure Gillespie improvisation in the same mixolydian mode as the rhythmic figures—played in the key of B-flat-7 in concert, but written in C-7 for trumpet.

In these eight measures, which connect Pozo's vamps to the interlude that sets up the actual melody, Gillespie provides a dazzling if seemingly offhanded display of virtuosity. His earlier piece "A Night in Tunisia" included a stunning four-bar break (in which the entire ensemble except for the soloist drops out) between the written theme and the improvisation. Gillespie's first appearance on "Manteca" isn't a break; the ensemble continues to simmer while he plays so that soloist and ensemble carom into the interlude together. Yet it functions similarly to a break, providing transition while raising to a fevered pitch the excitement generated by the vamps (and heightened by the vocal shout, "Manteca! Manteca!"). One thing that distinguishes Gillespie from the great trumpeters who preceded him is his ability to think coherently at breakneck tempos. These eight measures last only 10 seconds, sustaining from first note to last the headlong rush required to cap the intro and set up the next episode. Yet the statement glows with a relaxed logic and wit.

Gillespie's first two notes are enticing. By beginning on the first beat of the measure with a quarter note, G, he underscores the rhythmic feeling of the performance (the saxes and trombones also enter with first-beat quarter notes);

the following leap to E provides a rather colloquial two-note set-up for the subsequent chromatic run down, via a characteristic triplet, to the E one octave below, before dropping to a B-flat in a tritone, or flat fifth—the notorious interval that provided one of bebop's lines of harmonic demarcation (traditionalist Eddie Condon famously wisecracked, "The boppers flat their fifths, we drink ours") before it became accepted as a blue note scarcely more provocative than a minor third. The long rest is a masterstroke of symmetrical balance, and a lull before the torrent of quadruplets and quintuplets that advance unabated until the sustained high A (the sixth of the C-7 scale and another favorite Gillespie interval) and the bluesy finish. He ends with the shrewd clang of a flat ninth, consistent with the clashing return of the ensemble.

After a six-measure interlude (two measures by the winds, four by the rhythm section), we hear the theme proper. Now the piece becomes a fairly orthodox jazz performance, notwithstanding the marvelous rumbling of Chano Pozo's conga drums. The stout rhythms of the melody represent a perfect rapprochement between the Cuban influence and jazz riffs, but they are molded into the standard 32-bar AABA pop song format, except that the bridge (the B in AABA) is 16 measures long instead of the usual 8. The A parts employ commonplace "rhythm" changes (so named because of their codification in the song "I Got Rhythm"), while the bridge is an original pattern by Gillespie built on a progression of dominant seventh chords. In this chorus, the reeds play the first half of the bridge and Gillespie plays the second. The gorgeous, entreating quality of his sound might cause a modern listener to wonder at the accusations of "thin tone" that plagued Gillespie for much of his career. His volatile style demanded a relatively sleek sound, and though some of Gillespie's disciples developed fatter or more personalized approaches to timbre (Fats Navarro or Miles Davis, respectively), Gillespie's intonation was unfailingly vigorous and evocative, if never plush or indulgent.

After another rhythmic interlude, this one of 10 measures, the second and last chorus of the theme is played, beginning with a 16-bar tenor saxophone solo by Big Nick Nicholas. Though robust and generally convincing, this solo contains, for me, the only flaw in the recording. Nicholas begins its second half by paraphrasing Rodgers and Hart's "Blue Moon." The practice of quoting other songs in the course of improvisation has a long and honorable history in jazz; Gillespie's youthful solo on "Hot Mallets" begins with a highly effective reference to Irving Berlin's "Cheek to Cheek." Yet perhaps because everything else in "Manteca" bubbles with creativity, the "Blue Moon" quotation seems conspicuously retrograde. Perhaps, too, the familiarity of the harmonies in this section warrants an especially inventive response.* The return of Gillespie's bridge is

---

*The business of quoting has been a source of controversy. Some people find the practice clever or witty, and in many contexts it surely is. But quotations can also suggest laziness—a reliance on familiar melody patterns when the soloist is bereft of ideas. While recording with the American Jazz

thus all the more welcome. This time, the first half is played by the brasses; Gillespie's half is a canny variation on the written material.

Bridge

He begins on F, pushing it an octave to high F. The fact that F in the key of B-flat-7 is a major fifth may remind the listener that the introduction also began with a major fifth (G in the key of C-7). What follows is a headier version of the written material, made increasingly dynamic by three well-placed triplets—the first of which (measure 11) comes on the heels of a rapid B-flat/G turn. He then paces himself with beautifully articulated eighth notes (measures 13 through 15), leading to the highlight of the passage—the crucial last measure. Measure 16 displays, in summary form, the harmonic changes bebop brought to jazz. It's also pure Dizzy Gillespie, exemplifying the kind of ideas that inspired generations of trumpeters. The indicated chord is G-7, but Gillespie plays a tritone substitution, suggesting a D-flat-7 chord instead. The centerpiece of the measure is the D-flat, which he anticipates with a flat-ninth, A-flat, and resolves with his final notes, B and C. Today, that conceit plays as an appealing touch of spice; in the 1940s, it epitomized a way of playing that was vilified as bombastic, divisive, and worse. In this measure, we stand at the door through which Gillespie, Parker, Thelonious Monk, Miles Davis, George Russell, and others brought modern harmonic ideas to jazz. Beyond that, "Manteca" allows us to glimpse the coming affinity with world rhythms and scalar improvisation. *

Orchestra, Benny Carter stopped a take when a soloist slipped a fleeting reference to a standard into his solo. "Please don't play other people's music when you're playing my music," he said, eliciting surprise and comment. Carter's admonishment encouraged every member of the orchestra to think creatively rather than reflexively in their improvisations. The result was a deliberate approach to solos, which related all the more cogently to the music at hand.

*Chano Pozo, an unsung hero in bringing together the musics of the Americas, came to a terrible end a year after "Manteca" was recorded. He got into a brawl over a woman and got the best of his rival. The next day, December 2, 1948, he was standing at a jukebox in a Harlem bar, listening to "Manteca," when the man entered and fatally shot him. Many Cuban percussionists succeeded him in Gillespie's bands, but none had quite the impact of Pozo, who, stripped to the waist, his body oiled, electrified audiences with his dramatic solos on congas. Other than "Manteca," his best-known composition is the jazz standard "Tin Tin Deo." In later years, Gillespie himself became a deft performer on conga drums.

On the occasion of Gillespie's 60th birthday, in 1977, I wrote an essay celebrating him as proof "that the cocky irreverence at the heart of all musical movements can be sustained beyond the initial burst of inspiration." Now, as Dizzy approaches his 74th birthday and I am too advanced in age to think of 60 as the other side of mortality, my youthful admiration has hardened into devotion. Mind you, I know him just well enough to be able to state categorically that he isn't a saint. This seems important to say, because when American artists get old, especially if they are women or black, the arts establishment is exceedingly quick to patronize them as harmless old duffers. I have seen interviewers rage with disappointment at the discovery that Gillespie is a complicated and moody man, not the cute teddy bear or clown they wish him to be—as if a clown could have created Gillespie's body of work. He understands all too well the assumptions people bring to him and to his art, and he is capable of exploiting them for what little they are worth. People who expect only a chuckle are likely to get just that, or nothing at all. Those who take his full measure, on the other hand, may be bowled over by his candor and cunning.

Dizzy's savvy extends to his music as well, of course, in more ways than are immediately evident. If the joking never gets in his way, it may help him to get what he wants. In 1974, he was set to record an album of duets with Oscar Peterson, whose facile virtuosity can be overwhelming. From the first rehearsal, Gillespie complained of having been ill and suffering from a sore lip. He never let up on his infirmity. When the tapes started rolling, Peterson, determined to be supportive, held back to follow Gillespie's lead. Dizzy, of course, was in imperial shape. The ensuing battle of wits remains one of the remarkable recordings of the '70s, but it was little noted by those concerned exclusively with the latest musical innovations. Gillespie has always described himself as less a revolutionary than one of several leaders in a long and focused tradition. Yet by the '70s, and indeed much earlier, his status as elder statesman and celebrity was held against him.

Gillespie once told me that there is a level beyond which no black man can rise in the United States, and illustrated the idea by describing the apprehensive look he gets whenever he walks into a hotel lobby. In the moment before the clerk recognizes him, he is invariably greeted with a glance of suspicion reserved for blacks. Gillespie has traveled all over the country registering that look, which in the space of a second changes from "What does he want?" to "Oh my goodness, it's Dizzy Gillespie!" The secondary response, of course, is accorded his celebrity, not his genius. The irony of his career is that as his fame increased, the critical regard for his current work declined, not because of a falling-off in his music but because of the first law of cultural revolutions: The radical who doesn't continue to fan the flames of revolt will soon be consigned to the limbo of "living legend." At the age of 30, Gillespie had changed jazz and was confronted with the prospect of earning a living. Had he burned himself out in his prime, like Charlie Parker, Gillespie would have joined the ranks of the jazz saints.

Instead, he endured. As audiences grew more enamored of younger players who, building on his foundation, pushed the music to new frontiers, Gillespie remained faithful to his muse. Notwithstanding occasional misfires, Gillespie has produced extraordinary performances during every stage of his career. Albums from the '50s and '60s as varied as *Sonny Side Up*, *Gillespiana*, *For Musicians Only*, *On the French Riviera*, and *Something Old, Something New* are increasingly viewed as classics. In recent years, often with the help of his most stalwart disciple, Jon Faddis, he has organized unexpectedly ambitious bands, big and small (including one with saxophonist Sam Rivers). Yet probably no performance of recent years was quite as startling as his 1989 concert in Paris, with drummer Max Roach. The sheer physical effort of sustaining a 90-minute recital of duets is unprecedented for a jazz brass player of his age. But that is nothing compared with the ingenuity he displays. At moments, Roach seems bent on tripping him up, but Gillespie responds with unfailing assurance. We have become accustomed to Gillespie's pacing himself in his shows. Usually, he will play one prominent solo early on, then feature the other musicians, storing up sufficient energy for another fine performance toward the end of the set. In Paris, he enjoyed—and we enjoy—a state of grace.

One of the most beguiling selections is "Salt Peanuts," not least because that redoubtable warhorse has been traversed by him on hundreds of occasions since he first recorded it, with Parker, in 1945. If the basic chorus structure is routine (it's based on "rhythm" changes), the piece in its entirety is made far more interesting by Gillespie's use of interludes and transitional passages, a technique favored by Duke Ellington. On the original recording there are transitions composed of two-, four-, six-, and eight-bar units. The most effective is a 10-bar episode, consisting of a six-measure written passage played by the ensemble and a four-measure break improvised by Gillespie, leading directly into his 32-bar solo. This device has the effect of a springboard, and as such recalls the break with which Louis Armstrong launched his own solo on the 1928 recording "Muggles." Gillespie's solo is played entirely on the chord changes, as would be expected.

The 1989 version is another story. Gillespie's tone, which became richer and more bluesily expressive in the '60s, has now suffered the decay of age, and one doesn't expect to hear the old radiance. Yet he compensates with a looseness and ingenuity that ought to endear him to leading lights of the avant-garde; the lessons of modality, as sampled in "Manteca," have not been lost on him. After the introduction by Roach and a theme chorus with the two-bar vocal riff "salt PEA-nuts, salt PEA-nuts," Gillespie plays the written six-measure interlude and the four-bar break, leading into his solo of two choruses. The transcription (written in G but played in concert F) begins with the break, which occurs 97 seconds into the performance.

The tempo is formidable—Gillespie and Roach play 64 measures in about 46 seconds. Since the interplay between trumpet and drums is unfettered by the presence of harmonic instruments such as bass or piano, neither musician is

BREAK (1:37)
1 FIRST CHORUS
6
11
17
21
24
30 SECOND CHORUS
36
41
48
52
58

obliged to count a resolute four beats per measure. Although Roach sustains the quarter-note beat, his responses to Gillespie's two- and four-measure phrases are fluid. If the outline of the chorus is clearly audible, the time is indefinite. At this speed (every second represents about five and a half beats), it would almost have to be. The assurance of accurately landing on the first beat of each measure is slim. As a result, the music sustains an avid, unpredictable quality as they race over the terrain. And yet how fantastically casual Gillespie is in ordering his ideas. A constant pleasure of his solo is the way he staggers the rhythm—using triplets to suggest the imposition of a slower meter in measures 5 through 7 (as though he were thinking in half-time); or adamantly accenting the F-sharps in measures 21 through 24 (implying a three-against-two rhythm and calling to mind a kind of phrasing associated with the avant-garde trumpet player Don Cherry); or riding the series of 10 Gs (in measures 58 through 60) before shooting up to a high F-sharp.

Harmonically, the piece is far more advanced than the 1945 recording, yet it's also more elemental. On the progressive side, though Gillespie plays on the chords in the bridge sections, he develops most of his ideas in the A sections by playing in G and ignoring the changes. In measures 9 through 12, for example, he fastens on two notes, B-flat and C, that are related to the G-scale but not to the chords. In the 12th measure, the only other note (D-flat) is our old friend, the once forbidding flat-fifth. Because of that D-flat, and Gillespie's phrasing, the 12th measure is perhaps the bluesiest in the chorus. Another savory moment is the series of ascending fourths and thirds in measures 41 through 44. Yet the scalar approach also encourages a more basic limning of blues tonality, embodied in the solo's constant motif—the varied grouping of three notes: tonic, minor-third, and fourth (G, B-flat, C). As Gillespie became more adept at playing the blues in the 1950s, his penchant for fourths became more apparent; he used this gambit to open his "After Hours" solo on the 1957 *Sonny Side Up* album. On the 1989 "Salt Peanuts," he plays the motif four times between measures 9 and 14, and at the end of the second chorus.

What I most admire about this solo, this concert recording, this man, is the self-assured authority with which he braves the turf. We are endlessly familiar with artists in every field of music, serious or popular, who are saddled with hits or encores they are expected to play at virtually every appearance. How rare it is to find a mature artist surveying one of the benchmarks of his youth and turning it into a startling test of his skills. Yet because Gillespie persists in having fun with his mastery, there will be those who never hear the verve and determination that animate his gallant refusal to give up the hunt for something fresh and expressive. At the time he turned 60, Gillespie told me he had thought playing the trumpet would get easier over time, but that it got harder—not because his lip was showing wear, but because he had exhausted so many ideas he once used to explore. Jazz has no corners for hiding. Gillespie can spell himself with comedy and other diversions, but in the heat of improvisation he is served only by the truth.

(July 1991)

PART IV

WRITERS

Hard-boiled

JAMES M. CAIN RINGS AGAIN

James M. Cain was a caustic writer of newspaper editorials who published his first novel at 42 and his 18th at 84, a year before his death. In the 1930s, his short, squalid thrillers made him as famous as Hemingway. More purple than noir, they creaked with ludicrous plot contrivances and panting dialogue, but how the pages crackled! From the first sentence, pitching you headlong behind the headlines of tabloid murders, to the last irony, which sounded a note more in keeping with Puritan tribunals than the requisites of hard-boiled realism, Cain drummed his trashy American fairy tales with relentless drive. By 1950, however, his tempo enfeebled not least by literary ambition, audiences abandoned him for fresher sleaze. His once enthusiastic critics were silent, his later books ignored. Cain and his bestsellers were treated as relics of the Depression, often bracketed with lesser monuments of the hard-boiled school (detective and proletariat divisions). His lingering admirers resorted to indirection in praising him, hoisting the flags of existentialism and sociology. Still, as Benny Goodman once remarked begrudgingly of rock and roll, Cain held on.

The trashier aspects of Cain's work are so glaring that his virtues are sometimes noted with sheepish enthusiasm. Even the most eloquent explicators of his peculiar art—notably David Madden, Joyce Carol Oates, and Ross Macdonald—were caught in an uphill battle against the kind of revulsion privately expressed by Raymond Chandler, who called Cain "a Proust in greasy overalls, a dirty little boy with a piece of chalk and a board fence and nobody looking" and consigned him to "the offal of literature." Yet a handful of Cain's novels are successfully reprinted every decade or so, and the biggest groundswell in 30 years has taken shape in the period since his death in 1977. Vintage has reprinted six of his best-known books: *The Postman Always Rings Twice* (1934), *Double Indemnity* (1936), *Serenade* (1937), *Mildred Pierce* (1941), *Love's Lovely Counterfeit* (1942), and *The Butterfly* (1947). Gregg Press, a reprint house in Boston, has collected in one volume, called *Hard Cain*, his three least-known books, originally published as paperback originals by Avon in that company's salad days: *Sinful Woman* (1947), *Jealous Woman* (1950), and *The Root of His Evil* (1951).

What's more, there is Cain's much touted rediscovery by Hollywood, where he labored for years as a scriptwriter and consultant, though not on the many adaptations of his own books. As of 1973, his writings had fostered at least 14 films: three of *Postman* (*Le Dernier Tournant* in France and *Ossessione* in Italy, as well as the famous Hollywood version); two of *Double Indemnity* (one for TV); one of *Serenade*, bowdlerized beyond recognition; three of an unpublished magazine story, "The Modern Cinderella," with interpolated scenes from *Serenade* (first as *When Tomorrow Comes*, then twice as *Interlude*); one of *The Embezzler* (as *Money and the Woman*); two of *Career in C Major* (as *Wife, Husband, and Friend* and *Everybody Does It*); and one each of *Mildred Pierce* and—the only novel written with a movie sale in mind—*Love's Lovely Counterfeit* (as *Slightly Scarlet*). The movie studios passed on his later books, but now Cain is all over the lot again. The fourth *Postman*, which subverts the novel's intentions at every turn, is out, and *Butterfly* is due later in the year. *Past All Dishonor* (1946) is slated for a TV adaptation, while *Galatea* (1935) has been optioned for a first film version and *Serenade* for a second. Even *Mildred Pierce* is under consideration, though the celebrated Michael Curtiz film has apparently daunted all comers.

It can't be merely Cain's rotgut lubricity that keeps his reputation bobbing along the surface when far scrubbier, up-to-the-minute sensationalists exhaust their time on the bestseller lists and sink without a trace. By contemporary standards, Cain was a prude who tweaked Hemingway for using four-letter words and considered vulgarity an "affectation." In the disarming introduction to his first omnibus, *Three of a Kind*, he distinguished between aiming for passion and hitting lust, "which isn't pretty or even interesting." Cain's defensiveness—lust is a pretty good word to describe the gasping amorality of his infantile outlaws—may have stemmed from his upbringing as the son of a college president, and his training as the protégé of H. L. Mencken and Walter Lippmann, who convinced Alfred Knopf to publish *Postman*. It was also a reaction against being, in his words, "the most mis-read, mis-reviewed, and misunderstood novelist now writing." Lust is pervasive in his work, in a variety of guises that flout the literary schools to which, kicking and struggling, he is usually condemned.

If Cain was a tough-guy writer, he was also the first American novelist to explore bisexuality (*Serenade*) and incest (*The Butterfly*); and the first to assert the connection between motiveless violence and sentimental religiosity (*Postman*), which, especially in his later works, assumes a born-again arrogance. Unlike Hammett and Chandler, Cain did not dispatch saints to patrol mean streets. He was mesmerized by evil. It animates his raunchiest images—Frank making the blood spurt from Cora's lips, for example, or Kady daring her father to lick the milk off hers. His theme was the ugliness that underlies American dreams, which he found more arbitrary and consequently more terrifying than Ragged Dick's desire for riches or Jay Gatsby's for social standing. Cain saw the American dream as a childish demand for gratification at any cost, accompanied by a haunted craving for moral retribution. He is often considered a chronicler of California's lower depths, but he documented those dreams in all the classes of a classbound society, from the poverty of Appalachia (*The Butterfly*) and Mexico (*Serenade*), up through the lower (*Postman*), middle (*Mildred*), and upper (*Double Indemnity*) strata of California, to the filthy rich in New York (*Career in C Major*). In each instance, a wish is granted, a futile delusion realized, and, as Dr. Johnson put it, "fate wings with every wish the afflicted dart."

Cain examined the variety of human wishes in stories that might be classified, giving the terms some slack, as tragedies or comedies. In the tragedies (including *Postman*, *Double Indemnity*, *Past All Dishonor*, and *The Butterfly*), the narrative is a hasty confession, scrawled in the final moments before certain death; hell is a yawning pit waiting to engulf the narrators, and there is no possibility of escape. In the comedies, which can be further subdivided as dark (*Mildred Pierce*, *Galatea*) and light (*Career in C Major*, *Sinful Woman*, *Rainbow's End*), the central characters are ultimately forgiven their sins and permitted to survive and perhaps prosper. Cain thought himself a funny man. Oddly, his most doom-laden stories have sly moments that border on comic madness, while his comedies, though often amusing, are invariably undermined by mawkish, disingenuous conclusions. When Cain doesn't call for the hangman, he retreats into sentiment and formula.

In his most celebrated triumph, *The Postman Always Rings Twice*, the Cain mannerisms are sharpened to a steely glint. Frank, a 24-year-old drifter, wanders into a diner run by Nick, an old patriotic Greek who amuses himself by singing, and his disenchanted wife, Cora. "I kissed her," Frank recalls. "It was like being in church." Cora is disgusted by Nick—particularly his greasiness, a hazard of running a diner. She convinces Frank to help her kill him, although Frank already possesses her and bears no animosity to her husband. At Nick's funeral, Frank chokes up. "Singing those hymns will do it every time, and especially when it's about a guy you like as well as I liked the Greek," he says, prefiguring by 30 years a similar and widely noted comment credited to Perry Smith in Truman Capote's *In Cold Blood* ("I thought he was a very nice gentleman . . . right up to the time I cut his throat").

By that time, Frank has convinced himself that the murder was somehow fated, out of his hands, and therefore condoned. He thinks a lot about God: Kissing Cora is a churchly experience; meeting Katz, the cynical Jewish lawyer who gets them off, is as if "the sweet chariot had swung low and was going to pick me up." When their love sours, Cora insists "God is laughing at us," and when, at her insistence, Frank takes her to the ocean to prove he has no intention of killing her, he feels as if "all the devilment, and meanness, and shiftlessness, and no-account stuff in my life had been pressed out and washed off, and I was all ready to start out with her again clean." Waiting to be electrocuted for the accident in which Cora has been killed, Frank solicits the readers' prayers. Like

Ruth Snyder, whose murder case inspired the novel, Frank is neither bitter nor afraid.

Frank doesn't believe in psychology ("to hell with the subconscious," he says), but Cain does. His moral retribution dramas are fueled by a guilt proportionate to what Freud characterized as the supreme crime of patricide. Frank kills an industrious older man for his wife, as does *Double Indemnity*'s Walter Neff, who has even less of a motive. Neff makes a good living and doesn't love his fatal femme, Phyllis Nurdlinger. In both instances, the husband is a domineering papa-bear who stands in the way, and the decision to kill him is embarked upon as a game of wits. Herbert Marcuse identified the consequences of patricide as destruction of "the life of the group by the removal of the authority which (although in terror) had preserved the group; and, at the same time, this removal promises a society without the father—that is, without suppression and domination." The murderous infants have their playtime, but in the end meekly court their own destruction. Phyllis, ghoulishly made up like the dead Jocasta, and Walter end up feeding themselves to sharks.

Time is everything in Cain's first-person narratives, especially when the first person is facing death. Non-Freudians all, Cain's puppets have no inclination to explain or justify themselves, only to tell how they got trapped. Plot is fate, and Cain will not have his victims worrying about motivation at the expense of terse, candid, apparently guileless accounts that carry the implicit warning: Here but for fortune, reader, goes you. Yet he does allow them the latitude to break out of their rapid-fire narratives for dissertations on whatever it is, besides killing, they do well. Only in the area of good old American know-how do these zombies become almost human, even proud; their skills, however mundane, are hard-won and consequently relished. By laboring, they temporarily keep hold of themselves and of reality. Like Hemingway with his fishing and bullfighting tips, Cain passes along pointers on selling insurance, cooking an iguana, dieting, running a restaurant, uprooting trees, distilling liquor, and, most of all, singing.

Cain's mother was an opera singer, and Cain longed to sing as well. He settled for using opera as the backdrop to a few of his novels and making song his standard metaphor for the powers of art. Singing doesn't save anyone, but it briefly bestows magical properties: Nick's last bellow echoes back from the canyon at his murderers after he's dead. Song is a destructive weapon in *Career in C Major*, *Mildred Pierce*, and, especially, *Serenade*, a study in obsession through an opera glass darkly and Cain's most resonant novel. John Howard Sharpe, an American drifter in Mexico, encounters an Indian whore, Juana, who recognizes in him an irreducible kernel of self-loathing. Sharpe's dirty secret is an occasional partiality for other men. Bi-sex has destroyed his career as an operatic leading man. Cain is a good deal more judicious on the subject than Norman Mailer is in *The Deer Park*, where bisexuality is emblematic of Evil. Cain offers Sharpe's homosexual bent as less an affliction in itself than a rack on which to test the limits of his doubts and weaknesses—an intriguing position for a tough-guy novelist.

With Juana's help, Sharpe returns to New York and quickly recovers his stature as an opera star. But once again he falls under the spell of his homosexual mentor, Winston. (A troubling development for movieland: In the 1956 film, Sharpe's malign lover was played by Joan Fontaine.) Juana kills Winston and flees with Sharpe back to Mexico, where they successfully assume new identities. Naturally, the postman rings again. To assert his masculinity in a moment of impotent rage, Sharpe sings, thereby revealing his identity and alerting the police, who promptly kill poor Juana. Throughout *Serenade*, a preposterous sea captain (and would-be music critic) aids Sharpe at every turn. Edmund Wilson scoffed at what he considered an absurd deus ex machina, but Joyce Carol Oates encouragingly dubbed the wise old salt Prospero. In any case, the captain is an amiable reminder of Cain's impatience with the machinations of realism. His talent lay elsewhere. Cain's single-minded, symbol-laden narratives churned melodrama into myth, hysterical yet strangely reasonable, unreal but true.

Oates and others have argued that Cain promises no "religious salvation," that his antiheroes are not "metaphysically inclined." Yet Sharpe, like most of the others, is convinced that through confession he has received absolution "and some kind of gray peace came over me." Cain may have discerned the American facility for God through his study of the Ruth Snyder case. The last words of Snyder's accomplice, Judd Gray, were, "I am ready to go, I have nothing to fear." Perhaps what's most terrifying about Cain's outcasts is their self-righteous certainty. Cainland is out of whack with any objective moral system, but it isn't really oppressive—it's bleak and balmy, but not forlorn. God is there if no one else is.

Sometimes Cainland is almost slapstick funny. *Career in C Major* (1940) is an underrated comical view of the opera world glimpsed in *Serenade*. This time singing replaces the sword in a sadistic duel of the sexes, and it is used to wound instead of kill. In a plot as senseless as most librettos, an engineer becomes a professional opera singer with no prior knowledge of music. Cain hones his mockery with such relish, you go along for the ride. But as invariably occurs in his nonlethal romps, the momentum and bitchy ingenuity are betrayed in a last-chapter reversal; here the most formidable virago to filter through an opera lover's imagination since James Huneker's Easter (in *Painted Veils*) becomes a tame and obedient spouse. Singing also reverberates throughout *Mildred Pierce*, which Cain narrated from a woman's point of view. Though it has many splendid scenes, the novel is a rather one-sided chess game in which the diabolical daughter, Veda, finds countless ways to make Mildred's life unbearable, until Cain brings it to an arbitrary end by sending the brat out of town. For the movie, a murder ensues so that Veda can get her just desserts—such was the morality of the Production Code.

In 1942, Cain published his dreadful gangster saga with a neat title, *Love's Lovely Counterfeit*, a lamentable spin-off from Hammett's *Red Harvest* and Burnett's *Little Caesar*, the reigning champs in that genre. A college-educated hoodlum betrays the domineering mob boss when he's forced to work on his day off and takes over the gang. The novel bombed, and Cain—evidently as tired and cynical as that book—announced his intention to write "tales of a little wider implication." After a three-year silence, he produced his diffuse historical novel, *Past All Dishonor*, set in the Virginia mining towns he knew from his boyhood.

Its successor, *The Butterfly*, recaptured the tremor and pace of Cain's early work and gave a new wrinkle to his Oedipal obsession. The maddeningly unpredictable mountain girl, Kady Tyler, who is salacious, innocent, loyal, or treacherous from one page to the next, is determined to seduce her father, Jess. He'd like to help her out, but being a righteous Bible-thumping innocent he demurs until he discovers that Kady isn't really his daughter—a piece of information he withholds from her. Under Kady's spell, Jess stoops to lust, bootlegging, deceit, and murder. But it isn't for those foibles, nor for his insufferable hubris, that he has to be punished. It's because he interferes in her plans to marry the town prince that Kady orchestrates his execution. *The Butterfly* is more affecting than its predecessors, because Jess resents his fate; his meticulous account (he's killed mid-sentence) is as much a rationalization as a confession. He knows he's in hell, but can't quite comprehend the events that brought him so low.

The Butterfly was Cain's last major success, though five more novels quickly followed, including the three Avons, each of which he worked up from an earlier idea. *Sinful Woman*, a play he couldn't get produced, was altered into a novel of the same name, a frequently funny poke at Hollywood, complete with a language-mangling Hungarian producer (perfect role for Akim Tamiroff), dialogue redolent of medium-level Preston Sturges, and a cast of oddballs who act the way movies have taught them to act. Once again Cain undermines his own mischief with a cynical finish that's hokier than the B-movies he thought he was satirizing. Yet inspired lunacy prevails when the sheriff tries to blackmail the star of his favorite film because she is morally unworthy to play movietown's favorite martyred nurse: "You used [Edith Cavell's] name and said her words and died her death and for two hours you were nothing but a common trollop. . . . *The Glory of Edith Cavell* goes back in the can and it stays there," he sobs.

Galatea (1953) is easily Cain's most bizarre story, an all but incomprehensible variation on *Postman*, in which the sentimental flashes of religion experienced by Frank and Cora now assume a protective fervor. This time the drifter, Duke, is a good guy—an all-purpose handyman whose unlikely punishment for a stick-up (Depression-bred writers, in the manner of Victor Hugo, often depict thieves as good guys) is indentured servitude on a farm. The farm's patriarch, Val, is a smarmy social climber who tries to kill his young wife, Holly, by overfeeding her. She's sufficiently obese to qualify for a sideshow. Duke puts Holly on a diet, carving a ravishing beauty out of all the lard. They plan to run away, but Val intervenes and is killed trying to kill them. The lovers are arrested for murder. A lot of information, much of it grossly irrelevant, is introduced at the trial, but only one fact matters. Maryland is haunted by the ghost of John Wilkes Booth, which inhabits a black cat with a bell around its neck and is visible only to the wicked. No one believes Duke is innocent until he mentions—after the jury has been sequestered—that Val fired at some cat. At this point, the attorney brings together the hands of Duke and his Galatea and asks them to pray. The prayers get through to the jurors, who acquit them, and the happy couple move to Nevada where they start a fat farm.

Cain was 61 when he wrote *Galatea*, and nine years passed before he brought out his moderately entertaining historical novel, *Mignon* (1962). Set in New Orleans at the close of the Civil War, it's the best of his later books. Cain's Mignon, foxy and doomed, was presumably named but not patterned after the androgynous heroine of Ambroise Thomas's opera. She's one of two women who are alternately pursued or in pursuit of the shifty young hero, Bill Cresap, as they get caught up in the transport of "hoodooed" cotton. Cain's prose is fast and wasteless; the sex is steamy if mostly interruptus; and the laborious research is discernible on every page—clothing, decor, colors, business practices, army protocol, details about the manufacture of Cuban cigars, and the doings in Nicaragua (William Walker is described as "a homonculus") are all duly noted. Yet *Mignon* is finally just a costume drama, with telegraphed plot turns and lips that go mash in the night—a tough-guy's version of Daphne du Maurier.

The Magician's Wife followed in 1965, and then, after another decade, Cain summoned the energy for two final testaments, *Rainbow's End* (1975) and *The Institute* (1976), of which the former is more characteristic. Like his early work, it was fueled by newspaper headlines (the D. B. Cooper skyjacking), but merely as a backdrop for another joust with unrequited incest. The skyjacker's corpse and the money he ransomed fall right into the front yard of a Li'l Abner type who is forever kicking Mammy Yokum out of his bed. At long last, Cain delivered himself of an authentic dirty-old-man yarn, replete with sorry attempts at humor grounded in constant references to round fannies and heaving cleavage. Yet the moral purview of *Galatea* is extended: The money is a jinx on them that stole it, and a blessing from heaven on the goodhearted hero, his mom, and his buoyant Daisy Mae.

In chronicling an arc that begins with the idle acceptance of Depression despair and ends with the kind of moral imperviousness that made Vietnam possible, Cain traced America's increasing conviction that God is on her side. In step with his country's myths, his own myths floundered. In *Galatea* and *Rainbow's End*, dreams come true and the stouthearted live happily ever after. Cain achieved his flabby optimism at the cost of the corrosive humor and skeptical newspaperman's eye that had made his early work austere and vital; all that remained was the leer. He once said his favorite stories were Cinderella and Pandora, solid analogies for an age that woke up from an opulent ball to find broken pumpkin shells and mice. In the early years, Cain probed more than most of his contemporaries the foul dreams of a discouraged America, and he executed his stories with tabloid gusto and pitiless irony. The use of Augustinian confessions and avenging twists of fate enhanced his rhythmic velocity. Yet they are not the source of Cain's immediacy, nor do they suggest the nature of his originality (before Cain, Faulkner used the postman gambit to punish Popeye in *Sanctuary*). What keeps Cain shuddery and compelling is the unadorned vitality of his craftsmanship, which topples you into the lower depths without set-up or preface; the blank menace in his tone; and his intrepid willingness to pursue murderous scamps to the far side of guilt and retribution. Foul dreams being what they are, even trash has its dominion. In that realm where the surveillance of a greasy Proust is valuable, no one squats more imposingly than James M. Cain.

(April 1981)

CITIZEN CAIN

Thumbing through some back numbers of *Esquire* recently, I came across (in the September 1961 issue) James M. Cain's last published short story, "The Visitor." In recycling material from one of his earliest stories, "The Baby in the Icebox," and an even earlier newspaper editorial, it brings to Cain's long and extremely uneven career a touch of unexpected symmetry. The story has never been re-printed, and Roy Hoopes hardly mentions it in his extensively researched new biography, *Cain: The Biography of James M. Cain*. Yet this tale of a man's obsessional confrontation with an escaped circus tiger mirrors Cain's own obsession with numerous novels and plays he hadn't the talent to bring off. Its whimsical final image, as the man turns into a media buffoon rubbing noses with the tiger on TV, would seem to indicate Cain's ambivalence about the immense notoriety he achieved with his string of bestsellers in the 1930s.

Cain may prove to be an indelible part of America's literary history. As Hoopes demonstrates, the popular success of his first novel, *The Postman Always Rings Twice*, was unprecedented in the annals of publishing. It established Cain, a 42-year-old newspaperman known for his mocking wit, as a tough, terse chronicler of the seamy underside of the Depression. His reputation grew over the next 12 years with the publication of the magazine serial "Double Indemnity" and the novels *Serenade, Mildred Pierce*, and *Past All Dishonor*. Great claims were made for the economy of his prose, the accuracy of his dialogue, the Aristotelian cohesiveness of his plots. Gertrude Atherton wrote of *Postman*, "There are several disgusting scenes and the characters are scum, but that book is a work of art." Hemingway's enemies used Cain to jab at Papa (who was, in fact, Cain's junior by seven years), and even Edmund Wilson reluctantly conferred upon him the mark of a potential Olympian. Then it all vanished—the talent and the adulation. He continued to write as doggedly as ever, but much of his later work is so stupendously inane that it tends to cast retroactive doubts upon the integrity of his Depression novels. If his publishers thought *Galatea* and *Rainbow's End* signaled a return to his old form, one can't help but wonder about the five novels they rejected.

Perhaps Cain's most innovative touch was his grasp of a born-again conviction that escorts his attractive young barbarians into hell. Their capriciousness and ennui strike a modern note—they choose evil as relief from boredom. Cain himself still crops up in writing seminars as a model for hard-boiled storytelling. The first sentence of *Postman*—"They threw me off the hay truck about noon"— is probably the best-known example of an *in media res* lead in contemporary fiction. The momentum that makes his books "unlaydownable," in Franklin Pierce Adams's phrase, remains unrivaled. If the monomaniacal preoccupations of his misbegotten tramps occasionally seem laughable, Cain's elliptical character studies, jet-propelled plots, attention to unlikely details, and zealous fatalism give his tabloid fictions a depth and emotional weight that certify them as literature.

Hoopes's biography is not entirely successful. It is overlong, unimaginative, tenuous in its too infrequent attempts at critical evaluation, and not without errors. Yet even amid the current bonanza of literary biographies, it is impressive, not because Cain's life was the stuff of fiery gossip—as were the lives of Porter, Camus, or Lowell—but because, by contemporary standards, he was dismayingly normal. He occasionally drank too much, but he was not an alcoholic; he married four times, but he was no satyr; he could be mean, but not vengeful, self-serving but not pretentious; he was not homosexual; he enjoyed triumphant success and endured grim failure, but he never stopped writing five hours a day until his death in 1977 at 85. Hoopes generates unexpected suspense: How, you wonder, will he sustain a 688-page narrative with a character who does nothing but write and who refuses, in the face of every temptation, to succumb to either block or nervous breakdown? What could be duller, other than biographies of Isaac Asimov and Joyce Carol Oates?

But Cain's life isn't dull at all. He wrote in provocative circumstances among provocative people, and he had a genius for making things more difficult than necessary. He was born in Annapolis, Maryland, in 1892. His father was a college president and his mother an erstwhile opera singer. Although he affected a tough-guy image all his life (perhaps because his rumpled, homely face looked like something out of *Black Mask*, but more likely because it was a way of preserving ties with his beloved newspaper world while living in effete Hollywood), Cain prided himself on the perfect diction and manners that won him a job with Walter Lippmann on the *New York World*. He resolved to have a writing career only after he realized he hadn't the talent to pursue his only other passion, opera. Success as a journalist came quickly. While serving in World War I, he edited the *Lorraine Cross* (his regiment's newspaper) and was involved in a calamitous expedition that became the basis for his celebrated war story, "The Taking of Montfaucon," published in 1929 in Mencken's *American Mercury*. In the early 1920s, he attracted attention with the editorials he wrote first for Mencken and then for Lippmann, and with articles in the *Atlantic Monthy* and the *Nation*. His 1923 report in the *Nation*, "West Virginia: A Mine-Field Melodrama," exhibits a command of descriptive writing that he rarely displayed in his novels, until *Past All Dishonor*. He wrote the first of several unsuccessful plays (apparently, Cain's knack for dialogue worked only in fiction), briefly served as managing editor of the *New Yorker*, collected a volume of his *American Mercury* pieces, and embarked on what would become a 17-year stint as an ineffectual Hollywood scriptwriter before Alfred Knopf reluctantly published his first novel.

Cain's reaction to fame and fortune was curious. Despite pleas from editors for more of the same, he constantly wrote his agent with suggestions for books and articles about kids, food, and other unlikely subjects that he believed were his true métier. One hot idea was "a sort of neighborhood series, with an eight-year-old boy, his squirrel, his eight-year-old lady friend, his mother who wins diving contests, his father who teaches Greek." Another was a story about the War of 1812, called "Beauty, Booty, and Blood." Somehow, he continued to write the books for which posterity cherishes him, though, like Hammett, whose response to success was a 25-year block, he didn't always perceive their true merit. Cain's most Byzantine and, I think, best novel, *Serenade*, is a pioneering and sympathetic study of an opera singer's battle with homosexual impulses so destructive to his sense of identity that they destroy his life and art. Here, as elsewhere, Cain wrote better than he knew. We learn from Hoopes that he thought he was making a brief against the debilitating effects of a dreadful perversion. Similarly, he thought *Mildred Pierce*, his suburban inquiry into the lives of an ambitious mom and her thankless daughter, was really about what happens when a Philistine parent produces an artistic child.

In 1948, having embarked on a thriving fourth marriage (to opera singer Florence Macbeth), Cain decided to abandon Hollywood for a full-time career as a novelist. He also made the disastrous decision to move back to Maryland. Hoopes has few clues to his reason, but Cain had good cause to be frustrated with California. After he attempted to organize a writer's union, he was labeled a Commie and the screenwriting jobs petered out. Perhaps his wife encouraged the move. In any case, at 56, he was finally ready to commit himself to doing nothing but writing books. He never wrote another good one. Convinced after the huge success of *Past All Dishonor* that his vocation lay in historical fiction, he set out on grueling research trips. No sooner had one novel been rejected than he was working on another. Believing now that commerical acclaim was the only excuse for writing, he was forever trying to anticipate the public's fancy, but by the late 1940s, he had completely lost contact with his public.

Much of Hoopes's research is based on Cain's unpublished memoirs and on numerous letters that are admiringly referred to so often that I expect we'll get a volume of them soon enough.* But Cain ultimately evades his biographer, who

---

*We haven't yet, though in 1985 Hoopes edited the illuminating *60 Years of Journalism* by James M. Cain (Bowling Green).

fails to answer the question posed in his preface: "What was wrong with being James M. Cain?" A long literary biography that declines to take responsibility for putting the writer's work in perspective is bound to compromise its presumed mandate. Since Hoopes refuses to discuss what the novels might mean, he is unable to relate them to the life, though they surely unravel more secrets than Cain's self-conscious memoirs. When Hoopes wants to comment on a novel, *The Magician's Wife*, for example, he does so intelligently, yet a few pages later he's content to treat *Rainbow's End* (a revealingly bad novel) with bland quotations from contemporary reviews. His arbitrariness is at times exasperating, as when he refers to an editorial as Cain's "greatest moment," or speaks of the ruthlessness of "the best article he ever wrote," but fails to account for his enchantment.

Cain's business life is confusing. Though we are reminded continuously that Cain's books were selling in the millions, he was always strapped for cash. On the basis of Hoopes's evidence, Milton Friedman would have a hard time figuring out his finances. Also slighted is the intriguing fact that Cain did his best work when he was married to his second wife, Elina Tyszecka. The Hollywood account is inaccurate on a few minor points. Hoopes refers to Cain's work on a script by Daniel Mainwaring based on Jacques Tourneur's *Out of the Past*, and to his subsequent collaboration on a script based on Geoffrey Holmes's *Build My Gallows High*, which became *Johnny O'Clock*. Actually, Tourneur directed *Out of the Past*, which was adapted from *Build My Gallows High*; Geoffrey Holmes was Mainwaring's pseudonym. Milton Holmes wrote *Johnny O'Clock*, another film altogether. Nor does Hoopes appear to be aware that Cain briefly worked on a Chekhov adaptation for Douglas Sirk, or that when Sirk directed the first version of *Interlude*, it was assumed at Universal that the original source was *Serenade*. This is significant because when the *Interlude* story was originally filmed (under the title of another Cain property, *When Tomorrow Comes*), Cain unsuccessfully sued on the grounds that a key scene had been plagiarized from *Serenade*.

Hoopes has nonetheless written an absorbing account of an ordinary man with an unusual talent he could only intermittently control. A streak of guilt runs through the life as it does the work. Cain may have excelled at writing about the lower depths because some part of him thought that's where he belonged. He refused even the mildest perquisites of fame in his later years, insisting that writing was his job and passion but not his genius. This self-appraisal, if true, would not be altogether fair, of course—he did have 14 extraordinary years (1934–48) in the fiction business. If the Muse who punctured his balloon at the pinnacle of his glory remains impervious, the image of the largely forgotten Cain, ailing yet undaunted, pounding out one unpublishable work after another, is curiously inspiring.

(March 1983)

PULP AND CIRCUMSTANCE

Two weeks before he attempted to shoot himself (he fired but missed), Raymond Chandler wrote to his publisher, "All us tough guys are hopeless sentimentalists at heart." The letters, stories, and essays collected in *Selected Letters of Raymond Chandler*, edited by Frank MacShane, *The Baby in the Icebox* by James M. Cain, edited by Roy Hoopes, and *Self-Portrait: Ceaselessly into the Past* by Ross Macdonald, edited by Ralph S. Sipper, each of which could be subtitled "The Making of a Writer," show how sentimental, sad, decent, and finally tough some of them were. The paradoxes are constant.

Celebrated for their mastery of the vernacular, these novelists are inordinately defensive about their high marks in textbook literacy—Cain with his "perfect diction," Chandler with his Latin and Greek education, Macdonald with his thesis on Coleridge. Like the Mariner himself, they buttonhole all who will listen with news of their seriousness, of their lofty literary standards and high moral purpose. Not quite hard-boiled at the center, they rail against supercilious critics who relegate them to the very genres they once enthusiastically embraced. They turn, in their off-hours, from the cities and city dwellers immortalized in their fiction to an imagined, untroubled past where such books couldn't exist. Cain traumatized his career with historical novels he was unable to bring off; Chandler saw himself as a misplaced curmudgeon who might have palled around with the young Max Beerbohm; and Macdonald, haunted by the theme of vague origins, relives five times in his short, makeshift memoir the pleasure of Pearl White serials. Perhaps the paradoxes aren't all that surprising. All three were concerned with restoring the tragic mask to urban fiction, and in modern times tragedy is frequently less a matter of the big fall than of the long goodbye.

Chandler's letters are of far greater interest than Cain's apprentice work or Macdonald's autobiographical droppings. It was predicted decades ago that technology would obliterate letter writing (if technology doesn't, the post office may), but in the past 15 years, an avalanche of published letters has unveiled much of the finest correspondence in American belles lettres. Nor have the best collections come from the expected titans. Whereas Faulkner's letters are businesslike, Hemingway's affected and mean, and Wilson's given to an impersonal noblesse oblige, those of Aldous Huxley, John Steinbeck, Flannery O'Connor, and now Chandler display patience, candor, craftsmanship, and some of the same tonal resonance that animates their best fiction. I didn't expect many surprises from Chandler's letters, since I assumed the best of them had been plundered by Dorothy Gardiner and Katherine Sorley Walker for their much consulted anthology, *Raymond Chandler Speaking*. It turns out they omitted numerous gems and bowdlerized some they included.

Reading Chandler's correspondence put me in mind of Lionel Trilling's comment on Santayana's: "One doesn't have to read very far . . . to become aware that it might be very hard to like this man." Chandler is testy, waspish, and, like every other writer of stature, occasionally self-serving. He attacks *Harper's* in a personal letter to the editor of the *Atlantic*, and praises James Gould Cozzens (whom one might expect him to deplore) in letters to the powerful agent who was Cozzens's wife. He makes arrogant generalizations about everyone—Jews, blacks, Irish, homosexuals, Catholics—and then insists that his outspokenness is healthy and his perceptions absolutely correct. He's a loner, a sad case.

Chandler published his first novel at 51, married a woman 18 years his senior, and drank himself unconscious. He made money and earned international recognition, but money and fame were never enough, and in the end he felt trapped by the genre he couldn't quite transform. He refused to let the Mystery Guild distribute his books, because "if people call my book just another mystery I can't help it, but by God I'm not going to do the calling myself." Yet he realized "that the better you write a mystery, the more clearly you demonstrate that the mystery is not really worth writing." It comforted him to think that he didn't take himself seriously, but of course he did, and he knew precisely how good he was. Of John Dickson Carr, one of his many critics decimated in the letters, he writes, "He knows I can not only handle [the English language] in any style but that I am helping to make it." He took himself more seriously than was warranted in his last years, when he summed up: "I might be the best writer in this country, and with two exceptions I very likely am, but I'm still a mystery writer."

Except for two letters to magazine editors in 1937, the collected correspondence begins two years later with the publication of *The Big Sleep*. Fame brought him bulky mailbags, and he encouraged everyone to write. John Hersey asks if he'd like to do an article for a magazine, and Chandler writes back a 500-word no. Requests for autobiographical information (about Chandler or Marlowe) invariably net generous responses, always imbued with a dozen discursive opinions. He becomes so attached to a woman who writes from Australia that he wakes up thinking of her, although they've never met. And when he finds a photograph of the *Atlantic*'s Charles Morton in the magazine, he writes a hilarious commentary on Morton's face, reminding the recipient that for all the intimacy of their energetic letters they've never met either. Chandler's capacity for friendship blossomed at the typewriter. He may not be likable, but he is irresistible—incisive, funny, diabolical, unyielding, brainy, discerning.

Chandler spent much of his time reading novels by his contemporaries/rivals and writing long letters detailing their shortcomings. His epitaph for Hemingway is "Here Lies a Man Who Was Bloody Good in Bed. Too Bad He's Alone Here." Yet he's impressively sensitive to what Hemingway gambled in *Across the River and into the Trees*: "That's the difference between a champ and a knife thrower. The champ may have lost his stuff temporarily or permanently, he can't be sure. But when he can no longer throw the high hard one, he throws his heart instead. He throws something. He doesn't just walk off the mound and weep." He admires Hammett and thinks Macdonald may amount to something if he shuffles off his overworked similes, but he detests Cain and Graham Greene. He roughs up any number of critics (George Jean Nathan is "that fading wit and tired needlepoint worker"), but none with the gusto he reserves for Edmund Wilson. Of *Memoirs of Hecate County*, he writes, "The book is indecent enough, of course, and exactly in the most offensive way—without passion, like a phallus made of dough." He sees through Eugene O'Neill's putative realism: "O'Neill is the sort of man who could spend a year in flophouses, researching flophouses, and write a play about flophouses that would be no more real than a play by a man who had never been in a flophouse, but had only read about them." Yet he is compassionate and definitive in a one-page evaluation of Somerset Maugham: "He has an accurate and fearless appraisal of his own gifts, the greatest of which is not literary at all, but is rather the neat and inexorable perception of character and motive which belongs to the great judge or the great diplomat."

Like all collections of literary letters, this one is filled with technical stuff about publishing: Chandler's particular peeves were paperback royalties and plagiarism. But there is also a liberal dose of commentary on the movie business, alternately bemused and depressed (and only partly transmuted into his Hollywood novel, *The Little Sister*). In early 1948, he wrote with impassioned contempt of Hollywood's caving in to HUAC, suggesting what the moguls should have told Parnell Thomas: "Congress hasn't legislated anything that would cause . . . present or future membership in the Communist party to be a crime, and until it does we propose to treat them just as exactly [sic] as we treat anyone else." He continues, "You know what would happen if the producers had the guts to say a thing like that? They would start making good pictures, because that takes guts, too. Very much the same kind of guts."

In his last years, Chandler wrote several moving and quite beautiful love letters, though all were written after his wife's death. When she was alive, Cissy barely figured in his correspondence, and one gets little sense overall of his domestic life. But her death, after nearly 30 years of marriage, triggered Chandler's suicide attempt and opened an emotional stream that engenders a completely different character in the subsequent letters: "And late at night I would lie on the eight-foot couch reading because I knew that round midnight she would come quietly in and that she would want a cup of tea, but would never ask for it. I always had to talk her into it. But I had to be there, since if I had been asleep, she wouldn't have wakened me, and wouldn't have had her tea. Do you think I regret any of this? I'm proud of it. It was the supreme time of my life." His last letter contains an epitaph for Marlowe that might have served as the book's epigraph. It ends, "I see him always in a lonely street, in lonely rooms, puzzled but never quite defeated."

Chandler's biographer, Frank MacShane, has done an imperfect job of editing the letters. The collection is marred by a few inexplicable omissions of enlightening letters that appeared in *Raymond Chandler Speaking*, as well as elisions in those he uses. For example, in reprinting one famous letter (of April 19, 1951), he omits this sentence: "I should say [Marlowe's] attitude toward women is that of any reasonably vigorous and healthy man who does not happen to be married and probably should have been long since." MacShane never explains his omissions and is annoyingly parsimonious with footnotes overall. Few readers will know that the story discussed in the letter of October 17, 1939, is "I'll Be Waiting," or fathom why Chandler wanted to title *Farewell My Lovely, 'Zounds, He Dies*. These are lamentable failings in a collection that fully justifies the editor's high regard for his subject.

By contrast, the Cain and Macdonald volumes must be considered hors d'oeuvres rather than main courses. Cain's biographer, Roy Hoopes, argues in his introduction that Cain was primarily a short story writer, but his anthology doesn't bear him out. The first third of *The Baby in the Icebox* is a sampling of newspaper and magazine sketches that plainly reveal how the Cain style evolved. "Dreamland" would have garnered an A in a high school writing class, though the first sentence is better than that—pure Cain, plummeting you into the action—and he keeps you reading despite the abominable sweetness of the tale. "Gold Letters Hand Painted" is a funny anecdote about the vanity of adolescent boys. "The Hero" is a wicked send-up of small town bureaucracies. A few pieces suggest Cain might have become a third-rate O'Henry, but the subsequent short stories find him evolving into his own man.

"Pastorale" is a gruesome comedy with antecedents in Washington Irving and Mark Twain that works despite the ungainly dialect. In his breakthrough story, "The Baby in the Icebox," Cain replaced the Long Island "brungs" and "fittens" with the less stylized, simpler speech patterns of California, and his economy and irony come together in an unmistakable harbinger of his short novels. "Dead Man" is a beautifully rendered crime story sullied by Depression morality (if the cops don't catch you, your conscience will). The ironies are often oppressive and the sentimentality is rampant (in "Joy Ride," a 23-year-old con joins the French Foreign Legion to make up for a life of minor crimes), but the psychological perceptions are often acute, and Cain can make you turn the page even when you know better. The best example of his ability to snooker the reader is the novel that rounds out the volume, *The Embezzler*. Cain was sharpest when charting sexual undercurrents, and much of the intrigue in this small-town melodrama (a gorgeous, saintly wife loses her husband to a crazy, frumpy femme fatale) rings true—until the denouement. Suddenly, tension gives way to melodrama, as the pieces of the puzzle are mutilated into fitting the wrong holes, and happiness obtains despite implacable odds. Cops turn into nurses and bankers into Santas. Cain started ringing the right bells when he began thinking less like MGM and more like pre-Code Warners.

Cain and Chandler were big on femmes fatales, but no more so than Ross Macdonald, whose California is peopled with Medeas disguised as suburban matrons. Asked why, he tells an interviewer, "I regard woman as having, essentially, been victimized. In nearly every case the women in my books who commit murder have been victims." The rest of *Self-Portrait* isn't much more revealing. Consisting of 21 brief essays (including the valuable studies previously published as *On Crime Writing*), it's a too often vague and prissy rummage through the writer's soul, hardly a worthy summa for the most polished and prolific of the hard-boiled novelists. Macdonald has some interesting things to say about his chosen genre, his peers, the relationship between his past and the particular wrinkle he brought to detective fiction with *The Galton Case* (the first of his many novels in which ancient crimes come back to haunt innocent children), but he is not a lively anecdotist. He doesn't even explain basics—like why he chose to writer under an alias. His recollections are weighed down by a lachrymose nostalgia, reminiscent of Ray Bradbury, and deadened by repetition. The same phrase pops up in essay after essay, a circumstance which, coupled with certain inconsistencies, makes me wonder if he really supervised the paste and scissoring. On page 100, he writes, Hammett's prose "could say almost anything but often chose not to." Ten pages later, he remonstrates, "Hammett's prose is not quite a prose that can say anything, as Chandler overenthusiastically claimed it could."

Macdonald's novels, perhaps even more than those of Hammett and Chandler, are better the second time around, when you are no longer drawn by the question of whodunit and can take a closer look at the accretion of details, geographical and psychological, that make his intricate little horror stories persuasive. He's not as witty or offhanded as they are, but he was the best of the three at airtight plotting. When you know the identity of the killer and the long-buried secret that set off the action, you're in a more advantageous position to admire the astuteness of his characterizations and the integrity with which he plays the genre's compulsory shell game. That writerly adroitness is only sporadically apparent in *Self-Portrait*. None of the hard-boiled writers bother with autobiography, and it looks as if Macdonald won't either. Possibly he wrote good letters.*

(November 1981)

GLITZED OUT

I don't know why the Boys in the Back Room, as Edmund Wilson called the raunchy realists of the '30s, flourished in California. But as the century draws

---

*Ross Macdonald, whose real name was Kenneth Millar, died in 1983, at which time it became public knowledge that he had been suffering for three years from Alzheimer's disease. Obviously, he had little involvement in the preparation of his last book, and I regret the tone (which now strikes me as supercilious) of some of my remarks. If Macdonald wrote good letters, they have not been collected. Far more alarming is the unavailability of many of his 24 novels—this despite the increasing critical favor in which they are deservedly held.

to a close, the three most widely admired hard-boiled detective chroniclers—
Hammett, Chandler, and Macdonald—as well as the more expansive Cain,
remain those who spent time in the sun and did their best work there. You
wonder why New York, which has pretty mean streets of its own, hasn't done as
well in the mythology racket. Mickey Spillane sold more books than the west-
erners combined, but he wrote them so badly only TV wants to claim him.
Cornell Woolrich might have done the job as the East Coast's Cain, but he was
a recluse, and his New York is a state of mind, atmospheric but insufficiently
specific to qualify as a determining agent. In recent years, Lawrence Block has
written an entertaining series about an unlicensed alcoholic detective named
Matthew Scudder; he has his thumb on the city's pulse, and Scudder's a likable
sort, but the novels are formulaic and flyweight. The only great New York
series, the only one on a par with those of the Californians, is the one Chester
Himes wrote between 1957 and 1969.

Himes turned to the genre in his late forties, while living in Paris. He had been
writing impressively for a dozen years, beginning with two irreplaceable novels
that should have ensured him a devoted coterie, *If He Hollers Let Him Go* and
especially *Lonely Crusade*. But Himes chose his subjects carefully, locating racism of equal virulence in industry and labor, and looked hard at the concealed
friction between blacks and Jews. To his everlasting credit, he alienated the very
readers a black postwar novelist was expected to accommodate. His eight or more
genre novels (they remain so little known that not even a reliable checklist is
available) about two violent police detectives, Coffin Ed Johnson and Grave-
digger Jones, are wittier by far (frequently—e.g., *All Shot Up*—to the point of
slapstick) than their western counterparts. The plotting is first-rate, and the city is
alive on every page.

Himes knows exactly why Harlem has become an isolated fief, a stomping
ground for whites too corrupt for downtown (e.g., the pederast in *The Real Cool
Killers*), but he doesn't exonerate its denizens. His Harlem is a Bedlam of numbers
runners, transvestites, preachers, gangsters, Muslims, druggies, whores, and the
good citizens. He conjures every inch of its topography, from the abandoned
warehouses to Strivers' Row, and he relishes the fact that it's the one community in
Manhattan where roses grow publicly and untrammeled. But having confined his
locale to 110th Street and above, he has been insufficiently valued—despite the
popular movie adapted from *Cotton Comes to Harlem*—as a conscientious, satiri-
cal, unapologetic, and fiercely entertaining chronicler of New York's demimonde
before, during, and after the civil rights era.

Himes's fringe position is made ironic by the advent of Elmore Leonard as the
apotheosis of the '80s urban crime novelist. Crack has so changed the surface of
crime that a modern westerner who wanted to grab the mantle of Hammett et al.
would probably have to be black or Hispanic to probe a terrain that's become all
too familiar from network news. Everything else seems passé. So along comes
Leonard, who focuses on the racially charged inner cities of Detroit and Miami,

and gives us the latest fashion in barbarians—professional, conscienceless killers who don't talk too good or think too hard. Leonard isn't a mystery writer (Himes mined that convention as expertly as the Californians). Cainlike, he does his best work looking up from the lower depths. He's perfected a formula that's been growing sub rosa in the crime field since the late '40s, in the paperback originals of Jim Thompson, Charles Willeford, and others.

Like Cain's savages (or even such predecessors as the narrator of "The Tell-Tale Heart"), the sheriff in Thompson's *The Killer Inside Me* and the art critic in Willeford's *The Burnt Orange Heresy* disarm the reader with what appear to be reasonable complaints. After you've identified with them, the logic of their pathologies becomes suffocating. Leonard is a better craftsman than they, but very often a lesser artist, opposing his sociopaths with good guys who invariably bring order in the end, sweeping the scum off the page and out of mind. Leonard's villains are so scarifying, you turn the page as an act of retaliation, hungry for redress. He turns you into a vicarious avenger, but he doesn't encourage you to identify with the anarchy of the soul that makes Thompson more troubling. He's imaginative, but slick, and because he distinguishes good from evil as decisively as Spillane, but without the facism, he's the ideal pop crime writer of the day. Starved for sex and violence rendered with brutality and snappy dialogue, we race to the trough.

Leonard is a genre veteran who started out with westerns and then switched to the city; he was a paperback writer waiting for the sanction of an intellectual. In the late-1960s, Eudora Welty did the trick for Ross Macdonald (in a review in the *New York Times*), and how delighted we were to discover a sensitive detective who knew almost as many metaphors for ennui as he did scary broads with murderous or incestuous pasts. In 1984, Leonard's arrival was signaled with the publication of *La Brava*, an irony-laced guide to the underbelly of Miami and one of his best fictions. He didn't need a Welty; the book was praised everywhere—intellectuals stumbled over each other making facile comparisons or writing blurbs and introductions to compilations of his earlier work. The stage was set for *Glitz*, his 19th novel, to be a huge commercial hit.

But how good is it? Once again Leonard has engineered a thriller that delivers beefy characterizations, macho competence, bimbos aplenty, and stomach-turning violence, all at a whizzing velocity. Yet it seems almost rote after *La Brava*, which moved the *New York Times* to calibrate his talent: "Leonard gives us as much serious fun per word as anyone around." The *Christian Science Monitor* was moved to formulate a biblical assessment: "Leonard knows that providing entertainment is the novelist's first commandment." All told, the reviewers—according to the heavy-breathing jacket copy on *Glitz*—compared him to Dickens, George V. Higgins, Macdonald, Hammett, Dostoevsky, Chandler, and Balzac. What book critics won't do for a little amusement! In any case, *Glitz* is not "Elmore Leonard's best"; stylish mannerisms that amused in one book are now wooden and self-conscious.

What Leonard does well he does very well. His supporting characters, though often stock types (especially the women), are splendidly drawn, and he never loses sight of them. A scene as funny as the one that introduces a former Miss Oklahoma named LaDonna, who has a phobia about Italian restaurants because she's afraid of accidentally getting shot in one, virtually ensures her return to the narrative. (Dickens!) Leonard's sense of place suggests the scrutiny of a careful researcher. His portrait of Atlantic City as a rotting resort festering with mobsters, done over in plastic glitz to attract busloads of tourists who come to have fun but never smile, is ornate and convincing, as is his Puerto Rican scenery—decaying barrios, the mainstem, rain forests. (Balzac!) He has an uncanny capacity, reminiscent of the more perverse if less sophisticated Jim Thompson, to get into the skull of utterly monstrous psychos who can rationalize every extreme of antisocial behavior, even necrophilia. (Dostoevsky!)

Leonard's empathy for villains is frightening—they are more energetic, determined, and colorful than his heroes, who tend to be rather sentimental (a far cry from Hammett or Chandler, whose errant knights always get the best parts). Leonard's freaks scare the hell out of you in *La Brava*. They even walk away with the better movies based on his stories—*The Tall T*, *3:10 to Yuma*, *Mr. Majestyk*. Yet the scumbag villian in *Glitz*, the killer-rapist-necrophiliac Teddy Magyk, so outclasses the hero cop, Vincent Mora, in eliciting the novelist's best conceits that the story's moral equilibrium is fatally skewed. Even the suspense mechanism is sometimes derailed by Mora's slowness in recognizing facts long since handed over to the reader. For a veteran Miami-based cop, he's incredibly naive about the 20-year-old prostitute who takes a job as a casino "hostess." When she falls 18 floors from a high-rise balcony, clad only in panties in which an envelope with his name and address is tucked, he requires a hundred pages to learn what the reader already knows, and probably could have guessed if the novelist hadn't already spilled the beans.

Leonard's dialogue usually sizzles. Yet the very gimmicks that seem startlingly right in moderation wear thin when they're applied to every character. His favorite tricks include sentences that start in the middle ("You asking me for?" means, "What are you asking me for?"); sentences without conjunctions ("You two're the perfect combination I ever saw one"); strangely misspelled words ("homasexyul"); and—worst of all—pointlessly parsed phrases ("that's all you got a do"). Instead of racing along with the repartee, you begin to wonder how the pronunciation of "want a argue" differs from "wanta argue," and whether either is as accurate as "wanna argue?"

Leonard's classiest technique is the way he shifts the point of view between major and minor, active and passive characters. The opening scenes with Teddy and a cab driver are riveting because you don't yet know which of them will dictate the action. Leonard effortlessly inhabits the perceptions of every soul he brings onstage. (Gogol!) But as the loose ends of the mystery are tied up, the story suddenly switches to a *Dirty Harry* mode—the scales of justice are balanced in favor of the bad guys, so what's an honest cop to do? The spirited supporting players fade away, the inevitable confrontation is set up, and the unsurprising conclusion is all ashes to the taste. (Byron!) Since the evidence suggests that Leonard's true gift is for penetrating the workday delirium of crazed megalomaniacs (Shakespeare!), perhaps his most impressive bid for seriousness will come with a story set entirely in the muck. The hell with sexy heroes and movie sales.

(February 1985, rev. February 1990)

The Jilting of
Katherine Anne Porter

Ever since Johnson published his *Prefaces* and Boswell his *Johnson*, literary biography has been a progressively bullish market, though I sometimes wonder who but other writers or would-be writers, low-minded ones at that, read them. I read them with relish. Nothing is quite so comforting, so inspirational, as the perusal of a great writer's life—a life, typically, in which sloth and privation, bad marriages and alcohol, rejection and missed deadlines, paranoia and bitterness, and guilt, guilt, and more guilt are overcome and transformed into art. As Katherine Anne Porter once asked, "But who wants to read about success? It is the early struggle which makes a good story." Porter's long life provides exemplary material, full to bursting with all the elements that make the genre so therapeutic for less talented malingerers.

Like E. M. Forster, whom she much admired, Porter survived nine decades and was unproductive—as far as fiction goes—for most of them. They had one excuse in common: Forster liked men and so did Porter. But whereas the predilection in Forster's case was punishable by imprisonment, in Porter's it meant merely a constant intrusion on her time. She could not write when in love or in wedlock. Unlike Forster, she was a late bloomer; her first story was published at 33, by which age Forster was close to packing it in. Each was painstakingly autobiographical, and each managed to shroud his or her private life in secrecy. To this day, for example, few people know the identity of the man Porter married in her mid-teens (one J. H. Koontz), though she stayed married to him for nine years, longer than to anyone else. * A few years ago, Forster was honored with an exemplary life, efficient and eloquent, by P. N. Furbank. Porter, dead not quite a year, hasn't been as lucky. The first attempt to put the facts of her life in order has just arrived, and while her admirers may find it vaguely useful, it raises more questions about the integrity of the biographer than it resolves mysteries surrounding his subject.

*Koontz's identity and the details of the marriage were actually revealed a year after this essay was written, in Joan Givner's comprehensive biography, *Katherine Ann Porter: A Life*.

Enrique Hank Lopez first interviewed Porter in 1964 for an article that ran in *Dialogos*, a Mexican magazine, and *Harper's*. A year or so later, he says, Porter selected him as her biographer, insisting he publish his work after her death. To these conditions he readily agreed, advising her that he would also interview others and thereby transcend the limitations of an "approved" biography. Somewhere along the way that lofty ambition waned, as witness his warning that the finished book presents Porter's world "as seen through her eyes," and his disingenuous title, *Conversations with Katherine Anne Porter: Refugee from Indian Creek* (Little, Brown). Yet Lopez hasn't simply edited and reproduced conversations, allowing Porter to speak for herself. On the surface, he seems to have written a conventional biography of a contemporary writer, for which, naturally, he interviewed his subject, but for which, quite unnaturally, he interviewed no one else. Closer scrutiny, however, reveals his primary source to be *The Collected Essays and Occasional Writings of Katherine Anne Porter*, which he has freely and comprehensively pilfered. I say *pilfered* with regret, but advisedly. His book constantly raises the question: Can a biographer plagiarize his biographee?

The odor of plagiarism would be slightly less noxious but for that problematic title. In the preface, Lopez quotes Porter, "I'm telling you things I've never told anyone—not even to myself," and goes on to comment that by the time "Miss Porter suffered a physical setback . . . I had already acquired far more information than I had ever hoped for." Is it then unreasonable for the reader to assume that when Lopez is recounting a story, colored with quotations from Porter, those quotations, unless otherwise identified, come from their conversations? Usually they do not, as readers of *The Collected Essays* will soon realize. Readers who are not intimately familiar with Porter's published work will find it impossible to know when Lopez is drawing on privileged information and when he is simply appropriating her own writing—there are few footnotes and no scholarly apparatus. Considering how frequently he relies on her published memoirs, we can assume that large areas of her life never came up at their dinner-table chats, and that Lopez had little, if any, access to her unpublished journals and letters.

Thus Lopez has filled whole episodes of his biography simply by paraphrasing his subject's own work. To pick one glaring example, an extensive account (pp. 83–90) of Porter's first experience with bullfighting is drawn exclusively from the recollections she published in 1955 as "St. Augustine and the Bullfight," an essay to which Lopez never alludes until page 274. The reader is led to assume that the first-person interjections come from his conversations; they come from her essay, as do many of his descriptions. Lopez describes a bull,

> blindfolded in one eye, disemboweling the defenseless horse with one vicious sweep of his sharp horns while the picador feebly pretended to stave him off. The horse staggered in his own entrails as Miss Porter flinched back and covered her eyes, whereupon Shelly grabbed her wrists and pulled her hands down to her knees as inconspicuously as he could. And when she shut her eyes and turned her face . . .

No private conversation was necessary. As Porter wrote in 1955, the bull rushed forward,

> blindfolded in one eye and standing at the proper angle for the convenience of his horns, the picador making only the smallest pretense of staving him off, and disemboweled the horse with one sweep of his head. The horse trod in his own guts. . . . I sat back and covered my eyes. Shelly very deliberately and inconspicuously as he could took both my wrists and held my hands down on my knees. I shut my eyes and turned my face . . .

Lopez, curiously enough, earns his keep as a trial lawyer. He undoubtedly believes that a biographer has proprietary rights to his subject's words. Yet the absence of source references in a book that purports to be based on exclusive material is damning. Occasionally, when he does identify a source, he does so in a conniving manner. Thus he makes reference to Porter's defense of Ezra Pound's Bollinger Prize in a letter to the *Saturday Review*—one of the flintiest letters since Dr. Johnson laid into Lord Chesterfield—but neglects to point out that all of his information on the episode, including the series of events by which she was inducted into the Society of Fellows, was drawn entirely from that letter. Similarly, his account of Porter's house-buying adventure in Saratoga Springs (pp. 239–41) is taken from her essay "A House of My Own"; he mentions the piece, but refrains from revealing it as his exclusive source. Lopez writes:

> They slogged through deep drifts of snow to look at a huge ugly Victorian house large enough for a boarding school, later inspecting a desolate crumbling shack where leaves and snow had drifted through broken windows and were piled in corners of the living room. After each wild-goose chase she would patiently . . .

Porter wrote:

> We slogged through snow to our knees to inspect Victorian Gothic edifices big enough to house a boarding school. We crept into desolate little shacks where snow and leaves were piled in the corners of the living room. Between each wild-goose chase, I repeatedly, patiently . . .

Lopez, having happened on a new approach to biography based on the tedious task of altering pronouns, forges right ahead:

> . . . a hen pheasant suddenly flew past them, lightly brushing the radiator cap of his car and losing a few breast feathers. Asking him to stop she hurriedly got out and picked up the feathers off the ground and stashed them in her handbag, solemnly explaining that they might bring her luck.

Porter wrote:

> . . . a hen pheasant flew up and struck lightly against the radiator cap and lost a few breast-feathers. With desperate superstition I got out and picked them up and put them in my handbag, saying they might bring me luck.

All Lopez has added to the episode is the word "solemnly," which I take to be a bit presumptuous since he obviously never broached the subject with Porter. More interesting is his omission of the phrase "with desperate superstition." Earlier in his book, in one of three passages introduced with italics, as if to signpost a scoop, he reports a fascinating visit: While they were discussing Porter's interest in the occult, who should drop in but Flannery O'Connor's ghost. "In all her published work," he declares, with a masculine wink, "there was nothing to indicate that this distinctly feminine side of Katherine Anne Porter ever existed."

His other "scoops" concern Hart Crane and Hermann Goering, and although the material is striking and well told, the author will have to forgive the reader's well-earned suspicions, especially if the reader has read John Unterecker's biography of Crane. The story, briefly, is that Porter housed Crane and his homosexual lovers, found him his own place when that situation proved intolerable, and fought with him so bitterly one evening that they never spoke again in the remaining year before he committed suicide. When Lopez read Porter a letter in which Crane expressed his anger toward her, she wept, and he did not pursue the issue. Strangely enough, the business about Goering is more amusing. After a dinner party at which she attempted to show him that, historically, it was bad luck to mistreat Jews, he took her dancing and tried to kiss her goodnight; it will come as no surprise to learn that she rebuffed the monster.

The central problem facing a biographer of Katherine Anne Porter lies not in discovering how her work reflects her life, since she left a bevy of explicit clues on that issue, but what occupied her life when she wasn't working, which was much of the time. Porter, after all, is rivaled only by Henry Roth, Ralph Ellison, and J. D. Salinger among American writers who have earned enduring reputations with a very small body of work. It was once common to believe that she "disciplined herself by prolific writing but only occasional publication," as observed in an editor's note in the Modern Library edition of *Flowering Judas*. One imagined her arduously rewriting every story into perfection. But she scotched that notion herself, first in the introduction to *The Days Before*, a volume of nonfiction subsumed by *The Collected Essays*, in which she wrote of writing her stories "in one draft, and if short enough, in one sitting." In subsequent interviews, she came up with astonishing figures: "Pale Horse, Pale Rider" in nine days; "Noon Wine" and "Old Mortality" seven days apiece; "Flowering Judas" five hours—no rewriting. It's a relief to learn that "Maria Concepción" required 16 drafts. In 1962, critics were pleased to think of her having devoted 20 years to *Ship of Fools*. But Lopez makes it clear that she worked sporadically; the intrusion of others and her recurring writer's block forced her to abandon the project, sometimes in mid-sentence, for months at a time.

Lopez provides a persuasively agonizing portrait of a stubbornly talented woman who moved 50 times in as many years—in one hand, a suitcase full of clothing; in the other, a suitcase full of frayed, unfinished manuscripts. Porter didn't earn money at writing until she was 72, and enjoyed security only during doomed marriages (her third and last to a man 27 years her junior), when she couldn't bring herself to write at all. The holes in her story, as Lopez tells it, are gaping, and errors are frequent. Take the business about her grandmothers, who play such a powerful role in her fiction. At one point, Lopez admits confusion because Porter merged "her maternal and paternal grandmothers . . . into one person," yet he's more confused than the facts require. Robert Penn Warren, in the *Twentieth-Century Views* volume devoted to Porter, said she was raised chiefly by the paternal grandmother, Catherine, who died in 1901. Warren may have been mistaken, but Lopez muddies the issue without even acknowledging Warren's statement. The rest of her family doesn't fare much better. The birthdate of her father is 10 years off; her siblings are mentioned only in passing.

As the errors and omissions proliferate, you begin to wonder what Lopez and Porter did discuss, and how closely he read her work. On page 8, he reports an anecdote from "The Old Order" that actually comes from "Portrait: Old South"; he says there really was a Mme. Blanchard (as in "Magic"), although as Porter wrote in the *Village Voice* in 1956 her name was Branchard; on page 129, he says she won a Guggenheim to write a biography of Cotton Mather, but on page 193, he says it was to write fiction; he says *Ship of Fools* is 160,000 words, which is close to 50,000 words short; he captions a photograph with the information that she collapsed in Michigan in 1954, when the text proper has her spending 1954 in Belgium; he self-righteously quotes Glenway Wescott as having written, "One of the revolutionaries wrote a song about her, 'La Pelerina'," chiding Wescott for misspelling "La Peregrina," when Wescott, in *Images of Truth*, actually referred to the song "La Norteña." These are not the sort of errors that can be explained away with the warning "There were, as one might expect, certain contradictions in what she told me," especially when he refuses to signpost those contradictions, and when the reader can never be sure just what she did tell him.

Lopez's account of Porter's minimal involvement in the Sacco-Vanzetti protests, which she reported in her last book, *The Never-Ending Wrong*, confutes Porter's book in several details, but since he never acknowledges her book, he never notes the discrepancies. His strangest lapse concerns the last 15 years of her life. After the extraordinary success of *Ship of Fools* and *The Collected Stories*, Porter settled into a comfortable house in Washington, D.C. Lopez portrays her sitting cross-legged on the basement floor surrounded by unfinished manuscripts and consumed by guilt over work never done, wasted time. Like Queequeg, she eventually orders a coffin and prepares for the grave. Well, actually, this was not an entirely unproductive period for her. She finally completed and published her Sacco-Vanzetti memoir at 87: For a writer whose output consisted of little more than three collections of stories, a novel, and a volume of essays, a new book would seem to be something of an event. She also collected her essays, published *A Christmas Story* with paintings by Ben Shahn, and furnished *Ladies' Home Journal* with a new (more likely old, but in any case previously unpublished) short story, "The Spivvleton Mystery."* Lopez also neglects to mention *Katherine Anne Porter's French Song Book* from 1933 or the teleplays ("Noon Wine" and "The Jilting of Granny Weatherall") and movie (*Ship of Fools*) made from her work. His bibliography of secondary sources, though extensive, also has surprising omissions, notably M. M. Liberman's critical essays and the Waldrip-Bauer bibliography.

It may be that we are in for a rash of Porter volumes that will all but swamp the landmarks of her career, at least in bulk. Her will prohibits the publication of her letters, but we know how adaptable the injunctions of dead writers are. Hemingway made similar admonishments, but whereas great claims were never made for his correspondence, Porter's letters have been privately praised for decades. Westcott called her "an incomparable letter writer," and there are particularly tantalizing reports about her exchanges with Josephine Herbst.** Then there are the reportedly copious journals, which will doubtless demand a volume, and the unfinished biography of Cotton Mather, and possibly even unknown sketches of fiction, all stored at the University of Maryland—a supplementary library to the radiantly chiseled stories and especially the short novels ("Old Mortality," "Noon Wine," "Pale Horse, Pale Rider," "Holiday"), a form she did more to sustain than any American writer since Melville. The hard, unflinching, reverberating bravery of that work demands a suitably reliable, imaginative biography.

(August 1981)

ADDENDUM: Aside from a favorable citation in the *New Yorker, Conversations with Katherine Anne Porter* was little noted in the press before or after this article appeared. At the *Voice*, we expected a slight clamor—at least a rebuttal from Lopez (the *Voice* lawyer insisted I ask him for a statement, but when I traced him to Mexico, where he was vacationing, he refused to take my call), not to mention other reviews and discussions. Instead, a silence settled over the book. The *New York Times*, which usually leaps at publishing controversies, declined to review it at all. In a letter to the *Voice*, Porter's nephew, Paul Porter, enumerated additional examples of Lopez's misinformation and hinted, perhaps more than intended ("parasitically sucked" is a bit extravagant when you recall that Lopez did interview K.A.P. for a couple of legitimate pieces that appeared when she was alive), at the bitterness between the would-be biographer and his subject.

After commending my discussion of a "shoddy and slapdash book," and noting a similar review by "Porter's longtime friend Eleanor Clark (although with Clark for

---

*Givner points out that "The Spivvelton Story" was written in the late 1920s and astutely rejected by Malcolm Cowley. Forty years later, her stock was so high that its belated publication won her an award from the Mystery Writers of America.

**Letters of Katherine Anne Porter, edited by Isabel Bayley, and covering only her "working years," 1930–63, was published in 1990.

a friend, one might welcome enemies as a rescue party)," Porter gave half a dozen examples of errors, which he insisted could "fill several pages." He continued: "On page 307, Lopez writes, 'Shortly before her death, while bedridden at the Johns Hopkins Hospital, she stared at an old friend through eyes clouded by glaucoma. . . .' In fact, she lived three and a half years after leaving Johns Hopkins; and she did not have glaucoma. . . .

"And just who *was* that old friend? It certainly wasn't Lopez; she had sent him packing more than a decade before, completely disabused of any illusions she might have had about his motives and abilities. She protested that he was not to write anything about her then or ever, and as late as 1976 she was talking to her lawyer about preventing Lopez from using the material he had so parasitically sucked from her brain. . . .

"Happily, we can look forward to a solidly researched, reliable biography next year when Joan Givner's book, written at Katherine Anne Porter's request, will be published by Simon and Schuster. Also Gary Giddins is wrong (and I'm sure he will be pleased to know it) when he says that Porter's will prohibits the publication of her letters. It does not, and they will be published in good time, along with her notebooks and journals.

"Incidentally, I wonder if Mr. Giddins, in alluding to plagiarism, was aware that Enrique Hang Lopez was sued in 1979 by Joseph C. Goulden for using material from Goulden's *The Superlawyers* in *The Harvard Mystique*."

I did not know about the lawsuit and haven't learned how it was settled. My information concerning the letters came from "Ole Woman River" in Porter's *Collected Essays*: ". . . my will provides that no letter of mine to anyone at all shall ever be published or shown in any collection." I guess she changed her mind.

Vlad the Impaler

Bad teachers are all alike; every good teacher is enchanting in his or her own way.

All was confidence in the Nabokov house—house, as Nabokov might have pointed out (viz. his reading of Tolstoy), being interchangeable with home, household, and classroom. How bracing it must have been for students at Wellesley and Cornell in the '40s and '50s to file into that house, where opinions were as grand and tenacious as royalty, and behold his affair with literature. A good teacher is a good actor, and Nabokov clearly understood the importance of entrances, exists, and postures. He knew that a just mixture of resonant profundities and mordant asides was indispensable, that well-fortified arrogance was irresistible. The publication of two volumes culled from his university lessons—last year's *Lectures on Literature* and this year's *Lectures on Russian Literature*—discloses evidence of extraordinary teaching skills and corroborates the avid testimony of grateful pupils. Nabokov was part pedant, endlessly annoyed by the barbarisms of cavalier translators, and part moralist, ever willing to excoriate the sentimentalists and Philistines likely to bamboozle his innocent stud-ets. But he was chiefly a celebrant, who kept his classes spellbound with lengthy readings from his own improved (we have his word for it) translations, capped with poetic flourishes about the "wonderland of great books." Too bad Harcourt couldn't include a little cassette of Nabokov reading.

The *Lectures* are, for the most part, makeshift essays assembled by Fredson Bowers from Nabokov's typewritten fragments, handwritten notes, and marginal annotations. They confirm the emigré Prof's stature as a good and close reader, an amiable, incisive, and witty guide—a literary Baedeker. In what can be thoroughly enjoyed as postgraduate refresher courses, Nabokov prompts you to relive novels you've read—albeit through his demandingly tubular vision—and gets you hastening to those you never tackled. Much of the *Lectures* consists of long, quoted passages punctuated by teacher's comments. Nabokov's ability to get to the nub of the matter in a canny sentence or two has the effect of good brandy after a perfectly digested meal: "The weather does not exist in [Dostoevski's] world, so it does not matter how people dress. Dostoevski characterizes his people through situation, through ethical matters, their psychological reactions, their inside ripples"; "the worst of Turgenev was thoroughly expressed in Gorki's works and Turgenev's best (in the way of Russian landscape) was beautifully developed by Chekhov"; "[Tolstoy] is the only writer I know of whose watch keeps time with the numberless watches of his readers"; "Chekhov's books are sad books for humorous people; that is, only a reader with a sense of humor can really appreciate his sadness."

The new collection's pungent opening and closing essays, "Russian Writers, Censors, and Readers" and "Philistines and Philistinism," are filled with mots, including an assertion underscored by the intervening chapters as well as his previously published lectures on European fiction: "Of all the characters that a great artist creates, his readers are the best." Yet perhaps the qualities that made Nabokov a mesmerizing teacher also account for the narrowness that hobbles his criticism. The distinction between teacher and critic is unavoidable, since the publication of his college discourses confers upon them the stature of criticism. The *Lectures* will not enhance Nabokov's reputation for balanced appraisals or impartiality. Ever the lepidopterist, he impales the beautiful and the damned with equal precision, scrutinizing details from an impervious vista. Yet like God, whom he so intractably resembled, Nabokov could breathe life into his specimens. Even those he dismisses are illuminated.

Nabokov's primary contribution to literary criticism was probably his abhorrence of Freud. With singlehanded tenacity, he put the brakes on a kind of interpretive symbol-mongering that produced numerous travesties, from such deservedly forgotten fossils as Fredric Wertham's *The World Within* (a shrink straps great stories to his couch) to Laurence Olivier's creepy *Hamlet* and Leslie Fiedler's homoerotic backwoodsmen. Anticipating Susan Sontag's plea for an erotics of art while avoiding the clannish presumptions of the New Critics, he approached fiction on its own terms. He took detailed notes of biographical and historical relevance, but he based his judgment on the words. His lecture on "Metamorphosis," for example, is a useful corrective to prevalent exegeses, providing a satisfying and imaginative reading without recourse to arcane symbols and algebraic transliterations. By tending closely to the surfaces of his favorite writers—Kafka, Flaubert, Joyce, Gogol, Tolstoy, Chekhov—he penetrated the innermost secrets of their sorcery. Perhaps because he spent his extracurricular hours conjuring his own fictions, Nabokov played sorcerer's apprentice only for writers with whom he identified.

The Impaler could do away with Freud because he trusted great writers— enchanters—to give the reader everything necessary to facilitate an understanding of a character's actions and motives. The enchanter is the writer who invents a whole world, who makes the reader smell, hear, and see. What Nabokov admired in Turgenev ("the first Russian writer to notice the effect of broken sunlight or the special combination of shade and light upon the appearance of people") has little to do with Turgenev's ideas or the ideas of his characters. Nabokov is fascinated by the way people in *Fathers and Sons* talk to each other, by the sexual undercurrent, and by the delineation of character through conversation. He has nothing to say about the novel's concern with individualism, the theme of principles versus sensations. In reading favorite passages, Nabokov takes time out to upbraid the novelist for his ignorance of natural history or to coo over a particularly ingenious conceit. He isn't dazzled by Turgenev, as he is by Gogol and Tolstoy: When Bazarov shoots Pavel in the leg and binds the wound, Nabokov remonstrates, "Actually Bazarov would have behaved still more nobly if he had coolly discharged his pistol in the air." But in perusing structural niceties at the expense of thematic imperatives, he fails to show why *Fathers and Sons* is "one of the most brilliant novels of the 19th century."

Nabokov's discomfort with ideas, his refusal to bend his own aesthetic needs to the visions of a different kind of writer, is most manifest in his inability to comprehend, or admit his comprehension of, the significance of Dostoevski and Thomas Mann. That same condescension is apparent in his waspish attitude toward certain fictional types. Since the merest whiff of Philistinism sends his nose into the clouds, Nabokov refuses to acknowledge Kafka's affection for the Samsas, or Flaubert's for Emma, or Gogol's for Chichikov. He knows monsters when he sees them, and he skewers the buggers as though he were making shishkabob of Lenin and Stalin. Inevitably, the lectures on Russian lit are notched with a political edge. The Bolsheviks didn't destroy his literary wonderland until 1917, but totalitarian proclivities had been lurking in the wings for a century, producing a "strange double purgatory"—censors on the right, propagandists on the left. Gogol, Turgenev, and Dostoevski were hounded and punished; the first two chose to live their later years abroad. Nabokov's politics are predictably moralistic and absolute, sometimes to the detriment of his critical view. The most extreme example is his take on Dostoevski, in whose Christian sentimentality Nabokov hears the nascent thundering of the Reds.

Convincing as Nabokov is when he condemns Dostoevski's technical waywardness, grotesque plots, xenophobia, and middlebrow redemptions, the real worm gnawing in his craw is the dubious class of people Dostoevski wrote about: "We can hardly accept as human reactions those of a raving lunatic or a character just come out of a madhouse"; "It is questionable whether one can really discuss the aspects of 'realism' or of 'human experience' when considering an author whose gallery of characters consists almost exclusively of neurotics and lunatics"; "Raskolnikov is a neurotic, hence the effect that any philosophy can have upon a neurotic does not help to discredit that philosophy." This from the man who gave us Humbert Humbert and Charles Kinbote! You get the feeling that those neurotics would have been more in keeping with Nabokov's aesthetics had Dostoevski been able to show us how they dressed, saddled their horses, and ate. The Impaler, who in *Lolita* wrote comically of a "passion for tantalization," misses the intimacy, the quotidian detail, that underscores the visionary fastidiousness of Flaubert and Tolstoy. Psychological acuity is not enough. You wonder if in debunking Freud he didn't toss out the "inside ripples" with the interpretive quackery.

How revealing that Nabokov traces Dostoevski's neurotics to the influence of Europe (he mentions Eugene Sue, as if the nexus might settle the issue of Dostoevski's true worth once and for all), without noting the lineage of wounded bowmen in his own tradition, beginning with Lermontov's Pechorin in a novel (*A Hero of Our Time*) best known to American readers through Nabokov's own translation. Nabokov's assault is crafty: He "regrets" not having an ear for Dostoevski's prophetic tongue, and dutifully notes passages that reveal "caustic humor," "ingenious devices," and "well-written scenes." But he's out for blood. You'd never know from his retelling of *Notes from the Underground* that the whore, Liza, abandons the narrator in the final comic debacle, or from his summary of *The Idiot* that Mishkin's Christianity leads to disaster instead of salvation. (He is unchallengeable, however, lampooning the idiocy of *The Idiot*'s plot.) Concerning *Karamazov*, he needles Dostoevski for some of the same cunning he admires in Gogol, and never comes close to drawing a bead on the novel.

Nabokov's survey of Gogol no longer seems as provocative as it did in 1944, when it first appeared, since hardly anyone still teaches Gogol as a realist (thus did the Impaler help salvage Gogol for American readers). *Lectures on Russian Literature* includes most of chapter 3 and all of chapters 4 and 5 from his book *Nikolai Gogol*, but the selection is haphazard. It begins with a reference to "social *poshlust*" but omits Nabokov's amusing digression on the meaning of that "one pitiless word"—in brief, a "beautifully timeless" and comprehensive tackiness. A definition is provided a hundred pages later, in the chapter on Dostoevski. Also, it seems senseless to include Nabokov's extensive meditation on Gogol's evangelistic craziness (the reason he couldn't bring off the second part of *Dead Souls*), when his analysis of *The Inspector General*, which is omitted, is more to the point.

Nabokov's trenchant approach to Chichikov is considerably less rounded than Gogol's, and is another instance of the teacher subsuming the critic. Criticism is in itself a kind of fiction, a variation on the original, but Nabokov's creative reading stops short of posing, let alone answering, the major questions. As far as he is concerned, Chichikov deals in dead souls because he is the devil (actually "a soap bubble blown by the devil"), and the whys and wherefores of Gogol's intentions are ignored, though his metaphorical fancies are generously enumerated. If Chichikov is terrifyingly nondescript yet utterly amoral, he is also riotously comic. Nabokov sees the vaudeville but not the Hardyesque (as in Oliver) aspect of Chichikov's bungling misanthropy. He nearly suffers the vapors in his admiration for Gogol's ironic masterstroke at the end of "The Overcoat." Orating from the teacher's podium rather than interpreting from the critic's study, he inflates it with gas: "The man who prefers the monsters of the deep to the sunshades on the beach, will find in 'The Overcoat' shadows linking our state of existence to those other states and modes which we dimly apprehend in our rare moments of irrational perception." Not a sentence Nabokov would have cherished in the work of, say, his pen pal Edmund Wilson.

The Impaler is dazzling on Tolstoy and Chekhov, especially Tolstoy. That chapter was intended for a book and worked over in the comfort of his study. His multilayered investigation of *Anna Karenin* ("rhymes with rainin' " and the final *a* should never have been tacked on by translators) is a virtuoso appreciation of technique, plot, characters, and rhetoric. Footnotes include a few entertainingly self-serving deletions made by Nabokov from the original draft, and the fact that they were deleted confirms the impression that he was truly humbled by Tolstoy. Amid these redwoods, he is warm, diffident, and uncharacteristically forgiving. Tolstoy's emotionalism respecting marriage and agriculture is unfortunate but acceptable. "Unsatisfactory scenes" are indicated, but Nabokov is too transfixed by Tolstoy's powers of observation to vent spleen. "Tolstoy never misses a gesture," he sighs, describing the moment when Kitty puts on her rings after bathing the baby.

Nearly breathless with enthusiasm, he includes an appreciation of Tolstoy's timing (complete with dates and meal times); structures ("the synchronization of seven major lives"); physical and verbal gestures that are emblematic of characters; a rundown of the dramatis personae; and a fascinating compendium of annotations to the translation by Constance Garnett, whose work he abominates. Surprisingly, he also dabbles in sticky bilingual puns. To note that the repetition of *dom* (Russian for house or home) tolls "for doomed family life," or that Ilyich "is pronounced ill-itch—the ills and itches of mortal life," may have mnemonic value (good teacher), but misconstrues Tolstoy's intentions (not so good critic). Most of what he says about "The Death of Ivan Ilyich" is what you'd expect in an undergraduate course, though its heaven-sent tone is a tonic. When Nabokov was transported, he transported his students.

The chapter on Chekhov consists mostly of avuncular tours through "The Lady with the Little Dog" (*sic*) and "In the Ravine," and once again Nabokov is benevolent and inspired: "The variety of [Chekhov's] moods, the flicker of his charming wit, the deeply artistic economy of characterization, the vivid detail, and the fade-out of human life—all the peculiar Chekhovian features—are enhanced by being suffused and surrounded by faintly iridescent verbal haziness." Nabokov in love, or even content, may emit a dolorous haze himself, but he scrupulously develops and proves his points. Yet even here in the russet mist of Chekhov, he spies the serpent in the woods. For just as totalitarianism slobbered in the wings of the mid-19th century, bedeviling Gogol and Dostoevski with Christian panaceas, so it now looms behind Chekhov in the sociological art of Gorki. "As a creative artist," Nabokov writes, "Gorki is of little importance. But as a colorful phenomenon in the social structure of Russia he is not without interest." The color is red: Nabokov sees Lenin under the bed, and prepares to clear out—though not before a final assault on Philistines and corrupt translators, for whom he has many a constructive hint.

Earlier in this collection, Nabokov issues a challenge: "In reading exam papers written by misled students of both sexes, about this or that author, I have often come across such phrases . . . as 'his style is simple' or 'his style is clear and simple' or 'his style is quite beautiful and simple.' But remember that 'simplicity' is buncombe. No major writer is simple. The *Saturday Evening Post* is simple. Journalese is simple. Upton Lewis is simple. Mom is simple. Digests are simple. Damnation is simple. But Tolstoys and Melvilles are not simple." For 20 or so years, Nabokov endeavored to deliver the misled up from buncombe. The trip was more often than not inspired and audacious, but, critically speaking, it was occasionally simple.

(November 1981)

A Face in the Crowd

The Torch in My Ear, the second volume in Elias Canetti's extraordinary autobiography, is leavened with gossipy portraits of writers and artists in 1920s Berlin. Yet it can hold only marginal interest for those readers unfamiliar with the accomplishments of Canetti himself. This sagacious and honorable man has published relatively few titles in 50 years, but as with other models of literary diligence (in this he bears comparison with Proust and Joyce), his books are of a piece. Almost every chapter of the autobiography presumes intimacy with the two masterworks, the novel *Auto-da-Fé* and the treatise *Crowds and Power,* in which Canetti attempted to exhibit and diagnose the disorders of a world bent on self-immolation. As a third pinnacle, the still incomplete memoirs (640 pages covering his first 26 years) sharpen and enrich the vision of the first two while embodying Canetti's conviction that the "public and the private can no longer be separated." Until about 15 years ago, the private Canetti was a cipher even in Europe. His recent books give the writer parity with his writings.

As a novelist, philosopher, playwright, and autobiographer, Canetti, the intransigent witness, offers no moral codes, utopian dreams, or escape hatches for "our monstrous century." The only code to which he adheres absolutely—a writer's code—is to stand in undaunted opposition to his time. In the sequence of fragments called "He," Kafka identified the great man as one who did more harm to his contemporaries than they to him. Canetti isolates precisely that animus in the writer's mission; paying tribute to Herman Broch (in *The Conscience of Words*), he warns against the writer's temptation to "simply freeze or silently resign himself. He has to kick and scream like an infant; but no milk of the world, not even from the kindest breast, may quench his opposition and lull him to sleep." He restates his ambition in one of the aphorisms collected in *The Human Province:* "To find the path through the labyrinth of one's own time without giving in to one's own time, and without jumping out." In his autobiographical works, Canetti demonstrates a third way—after the novel and the treatise—of not jumping out, a third angle from which to ponder a lifetime's obsession with paranoia and power, individuals and crowds, death and God, the self and the world. Writing with the Flaubertian relish he admires in Kafka ("nothing is trivial so long as it is right"), he reinvents himself as a literary character, rigorously mining memory for clues to the riddle of Elias Canetti.

Born in Bulgaria in 1905 to a comfortable Sephardic family, the Canetti of *The Tongue Set Free* (his first volume of memoirs) is a prodigious and arrogant child, though easily terrified—of gypsies, wolves, the height of his high chair, the intrigues of his haughty bourgeois family, and more. The word *terror* recurs like a drumbeat throughout the book. He is given to violence (at five he tries to ax his cousin), jealousy (his rivalry for his mother becomes increasingly neurotic in adolescence), and unstoppable curiosity, especially regarding languages. Canetti grew up speaking first Ladino (the Sephardic equivalent of Yiddish) and Bulgarian, and later English, French, German, and Swiss German. To escape the tyranny of the paternal grandfather, Canetti's family moved to England in 1911; but shortly after arriving, his father died under mysterious circumstances. (Canetti, who employs several novelistic devices, handles the tragedy with an unseemly dispatch that recalls E. M. Foster's disposal of Gerald in *The Longest Journey*.) The grieving widow moved the family to Vienna, enthusiastically assuming her husband's role in educating Elias. During a momentous stopover in Lausanne, she forced him to learn German (the language of his vocation): "I was reborn under my mother's influence to the German language, and the spasm of that birth produced the passion tying me to both, the langauge and my mother." At the same time, Canetti's inability to accept his father's death petrified into the implacable hatred of death that remains one of the most peculiar and vigorous aspects of his thinking.

Canetti's emotional and intellectual involvement with his mother is the central drama of his youth. At first she encouraged his prodigality; later she turned against what she perceived as an ineffectual bookishness. But she never treated him like a child, and the testing and badgering she subjected him to is alternately inspiriting and harrowing to observe—Canetti recalls in exhausting detail the extremes of dependency and distrust that warped their relationship. At 11, frenzied with the very paranoia he later analyzed as the source of malignant power, he appointed himself the rival of any potential suitor for his mother's attention, reasoning "it was she who gave me this right to her, she attached herself so close to me in her loneliness because she knew no one who was her equal." Frau Canetti had her revenge five years later when they lived in Zurich and their intellectual intimacies had reached a peak. Ridiculing the high-minded interests she'd helped to instill in him, she forced him to leave his bookish paradise for inflationary Frankfurt (*The Tongue Set Free* closes with the 16-year-old Canetti once again "filled with terror"). Moreover, she stultified his awareness of sex—which is conspicuously absent from the autobiography—and warred with the woman Canetti eventually married.

In 1929, Canetti received his doctorate in chemistry at the University of Vienna and began supporting himself by translating two Upton Sinclair novels. Two years later, at 26, he wrote one of the monuments of 20th-century fiction, *Auto-da-Fé*. Before the novel was published, however, he made his literary debut in 1932 with a play, *Hochzeit* (*The Wedding*), a sardonic comedy that reflects his preoccupation with sudden disruptions—in this instance, the collapse of a building during an orgiastic wedding. Though shrewdly demonstrating Canetti's ear for mimicry, bolstered under the influence of Karl Kraus and inspired by Büchner's *Wozzeck* and the caricatures of George Grosz, the play wasn't staged until 1965. (In 1934, still months before the publication of *Auto-da-Fé*, Canetti completed a second play, *Komedie de Eitelkeit* [*Comedy of Vanity*], which opposes the fascism of "we" against the chaos of "I," and burlesques Nazi book burning by depicting a society in which mirrors and photographs are banished. It went unpublished until 1950.) By the mid-1930s, Canetti had been marked by a series of events—inflation, panic, fires, crowds—that fixed the obsessions of his adult life, and are in large part the subject of *The Torch in My Ear*. His fidelity to the study of crowd behavior, sparked by his metamorphosis during a political demonstration, represents one of the most stubborn devotions in contemporary scholarship. Canetti resolved to produce nothing less than a phenomenology of crowds so comprehensive that it would rival and even counter Freud's investigation of the ego.

His novel, completed in one year and published in 1935 as *Die Blendung* (*The Blinding*), was originally planned as one of eight, each a study of an obsessive paranoiac. Though acclaimed by Thomas Mann and others, it had a short shelf life; the Nazis invaded Austria in 1938, and Canetti, after a year in France, relocated to London, where the historian C. V. Wedgewood prepared the forceful translation called *Auto-da-Fé*. For the next 10 years, Canetti applied himself to an awesome regimen of reading, and in 1948, he embarked on the 11-year trial of writing *Masse und Macht* (*Crowds and Power*), first published in 1960. During that siege, he produced only one play, *Die Befristeten* (*Life-Terms*), which postulates a world in which every citizen knows the age at which he or she will die; written in 1952 and produced four years later in England, the most corrosive of Canetti's comedies argues that those who acquiesce to the inevitability of death also surrender their freedom. Canetti's plays have rarely been performed in German, let alone in translation. Thus at 60, Canetti enjoyed a lofty reputation based almost exclusively on two books. His subsequent work can be read as an attempt to integrate the writer into the vision, to demonstrate that "the representative writer of this age" can personally exemplify the virtues—diligence, detachment, scholarship, realism, ideation—that make grace possible in an insane world.

In *Auto-da-Fé*, Canetti puts into the mouth of Confucius a wry prediction of his own fate: "At fifteen my inclination was to learning, at thirty I was fixed in that path, at forty I had no more doubts—but only when I was sixty were my ears opened." Actually, Canetti's ears have always been exceptional; the success of the novel is greatly dependent on the hermetic virtuosity with which he isolates and dissects each character. At once vicious and uproarious, the novel sets four vile paranoiacs at relentless cross-purposes, skewering logic with slapstick fanaticism, blind to any reality but their own. A rapacious housekeeper protected by the carapace of a blue skirt, a Jewish hunchback dwarf who dreams of coming to

America to become the world's champion chess player, and a murderous and incestuous caretaker who thinks of himself as a pillar of law and order separately conspire to part the asthenic sinologist Peter Kein from his banknotes. Kein, an inflexible scholar who depends on memory rather than genius and who carries the contents of his massive library in his head, is the one character who abjures power. But he also abjures reality, preferring blindness ("What I do not perceive, does not exist," he crows with twisted Cartesian certitude), petrifaction, and, finally, self-immolation. The only "crowd" he can hope to mobilize in his defense is his library, which he democratizes—over the protests of German philosophers (Kein literally converses with all his books)—by turning the spines to the walls. This measure, he reasons, "will deprive the piratical but uneducated enemy of the means to measure us one against the others." The novel's three sections—"A Head Without a World" (Kein in his library), "Headless World" (Kein exiled to the city's underground), and "The World in the Head" (Kein consumed)—are hallucinatory refutations of Kant's critiques of pure reason, practical reason, and judgment. Indeed, Canetti originally called the novel *Kant Catches Fire* until Herman Broch convinced him to change the sinologist's name.

Auto-da-Fé opens with as devious a first page as can be found in any novel, a gentle dialogue between Kein and a young boy. It is the only dialogue in the book in which two individuals genuinely communicate. Seduced by that breezy prelude, the reader is soon bogged down in a fastidiously detailed nightmare. The minutiae of lunatic delusions are explored with the patient banality of, say, the stone-sucking ritual in Beckett's *Molloy* or the hilarious digressions in Thurber and White's *Is Sex Necessary?* Never have murder, incest, thievery, arson, and suicide been dramatized at so gruelingly dilatory a tempo. In this book, all crowds are ominous and easily aroused, not least the police, whose "uniforms cover a multitude of action, permitted to others only when the police are not there." With a gift for mimicry worthy of Gogol (a primary influence, whom Canetti later described as having thrown himself into the fire by turning against his characters instead of the outer world when he abandoned *Dead Souls*), Canetti swoops into the heads of numerous passing characters, uncovering monsters and fools. Charting with a terrifying literalness what Suzanne Langer called the logic of consciousness, Canetti drives neck-deep into the quicksand of paranoia. His steadfast theme is the fascism of the soul, the tendency of the human mind to fortify itself with aggressive power plays. Only Kein's brother, a psychiatrist who strangely prefigures R. D. Laing, can pierce the delusions, but his late entry in the novel serves ultimately to hasten Kein's auto-da-fé. In *Crowds and Power*, Canetti suggests that even inert objects—raindrops, coins, books—can form crowds. Kein's ineluctable crowd is fire, a fate he accepts with hysterical laughter. Canetti writes in *Crowds and Power* that laughter represents superiority at a moment of powerlessness.

For Canetti, powerlessness is an attribute, a state of grace. In his ingenious if highly speculative discussion of Kafka's letters to Felice (*Kafka's Other Trial*), he expresses admiration for Kafka's refusal to marry. Marriage would only distract him from his labor, solidify his place in the world, and void the "possibility of ever becoming so small as to be able to vanish." Better to side with humiliation, shunning all the trappings of power. Canetti's analysis probably makes too little of Kafka's involvement with Grete Bloch, Felice's friend and intermediary who later claimed to have borne Kafka's child, and the misogynistic tone is surely more Canetti than Kafka. Yet it was his identification with Kafka's rejection of power in favor of literature that spurred Canetti in the labor with which he attempted to grab "this century by the throat." *Crowds and Power*, a strenuously exhilarating inquiry into power and death, manifested Canetti's conviction that to be the representative writer of his time, he would have to extend Kafka's understanding of power another step. Kafka dramatized the impossibility of escape, but he died a decade before the Nazification of paranoia—before the industrialization of death. Canetti recognized his own literary fate as that of witness to the age in which human beings finally achieved the massive systematic disposal of life envisioned by Brueghel in *The Triumph of Death*.

For all the sexlessness of his books, Canetti is never more animated than when depicting the carnal attraction between individual and crowd. Having lost himself in a crowd (the bloody assault on Vienna's poor in 1934), he can never forget the headiness of the experience. The carnality of his description of the Vienna riot in *The Torch in My Ear* suggests a germinal sexual encounter (and, in fact, supplants the expected account of his first sexual experience) and is consistent with his established approach to crowd phenomena. As detractors of *Crowds and Power* invariably point out, Vico, Marx, and Freud are missing from its extensive bibliography. Canetti, the erstwhile chemist, prefers a biological, zoological, and mythological approach, aiming for a framework that transcends historicism. A true phenomenologist, he trusts evolution more than he does psychology. Reasoning that it settles nothing to isolate mankind's madness in Nazi Germany, he locates its impetus—the yearning for power—in the very mitosis and cellular colonization from which life derives. Canetti, who continues to write in German "because I am Jewish," is nonetheless determined to correlate the horrors of his time (horrors, as he insists in "Realism and New Reality," that have permanently altered the nature of literary thinking) to the horrors destined for an organism thwarted by death.

Canetti rages against death, refuses to accept it. He demands for himself longevity (he'll settle for a century) and would coolly accept immortality. The judicious, drudgelike industry embodied by his career substantiates his expectation of a long life. Death is pernicious not merely because it mocks the acquisition of knowledge, but because it is the source of paranoia. "The moment of survival is the moment of power," he writes; the passion to survive is itself dangerous. For Canetti, who so admires powerlessness, yet covets the ultimate power of victory over death, life is a puzzle that wisdom can justify but not even God can decipher. In *The Human Province*, he surmises, "There can be no creator, simply because his grief at the fate of his creation would be inconceivable and unendurable." He further conjures a "God who keeps his creation secret. 'And lo, it was not good.' "

Crowds and Power employs banality as the springboard for insightful connections, the commonplace as the key to biological imperatives. His reference to the Holocaust is characteristic. Hitler, though his shadow darkens every page, makes only a brief appearance, as Canetti relates the final solution to inflation. He argues that as the reliability of the coin is undermined, so too is the regard in which the populace holds itself, creating "a dynamic process of humiliation." Germans, feeling devalued as a crowd, needed another and more worthless crowd against which to measure themselves. Hitler handed them the Jews, who doubly served his purpose: They were seemingly on good terms with money, and as a wandering crowd with only a mythic homeland (next year in Jerusalem), they could be purged as parasites on the German economy. "In its treatment of the Jews, National Socialism repeated the process of inflation with great precision. First they were attacked as wicked and dangerous, as enemies; then they were more and more depreciated; then, there not being enough in Germany itself, those in the conquered territories were gathered in; and finally they were treated literally as vermin, to be destroyed with impunity by the million." The establishment of Israel gave Jews a new corporeality, marking the end of Exodus and the beginning of a "closed crowd," susceptible to the manifestations of nationalistic power-seeking illustrated by recent history.

Since the publication of *Crowds and Power*, Canetti has written several shorter books that encircle the major works like satellites. Taken together, they underscore the new, less isolated stage in Canetti's career. The critic, by definition, is a humanist, an advocate; he can't be entirely opposed to his time. In the essays and the autobiography, Canetti's scorn is allayed as he pays meticulous, reverent homage to the teachers, writers, painters, and acquaintances who helped shape his thinking. After 30 years as a man in the shadows (Susan Sontag identifies him as the prototype for the philosopher Mischa Fox in Iris Murdoch's *The Flight from the Enchanter*, "a figure whose audacity and effortless superiority are an enigma to his intimate friends"), Canetti now bounds into daylight. "I wish that some men would also record the leaps in their lives," he writes in *The Human Province*. "It seems that the leaps belong to *all* people; anyone can easily take whatever pertains to oneself."

In 1967, he published *The Voices of Marrakesh*, an illuminating, artful journal in which life's stubborn hold against death is observed at the lower depths; the voices of storytellers, beggars, and hucksters whirl around Canetti's eager ears. The essay on Kafka's letters followed two years later. (Two editions of *Kafka's Other Trial* are available in English: Schocken's has the advantage of footnote references to the letters; *The Conscience of Words* includes a later translation.) *The Human Province*, a bewildering 1973 collection of jottings and aphorisms from 30 years of his journals, is by turns insightful and innocuous, offering clues to Canetti as well as notes for *Crowds and Power*, *Marrakesh*, *Earwitness*, and some of the essays. The frequently hilarious *Earwitness*, published in 1974, is hardly a work of fiction, but it marks the sole reemergence of the satirist who engineered *Auto-da-Fé*: In brief accounts that combine deft mimicry and hyperbolic fantasy, Canetti describes 50 "types," producing a cautionary bestiary of not-quite-imaginary beings. The superb essays collected in 1976 as *The Conscience of Words* include homages to Broch and Kraus as well as Kafka, addenda to *Crowds and Power* (notably an analysis of Nazi architecture prompted by Albert Speer's memoirs), and a revealing account of the genesis of *Auto-da-Fé*. Its autobiographical revelations complement those in *The Tongue Set Free* (1979) and *The Torch in My Ear* (1980).

Beginning with his expulsion from Zurich at 16, and concluding with the completion but not the publication of *Auto-da-Fé* at 26, *The Torch in My Ear* details the making of a writer, or more precisely the making of a writer's obsessions. Its relationship to the twin masterworks is explicit, but not entirely consistent: although Canetti carefully signposts the revelations that put him on the trail of crowd psychology, he resists drawing connections between the events of his life and the plot and symbology of *Auto-da-Fe*. Nevertheless, part of the pleasure to be had in this sometimes perversely detailed memoir is coming across bits of cloth that eventually became the fabric of the novel. Canetti eloquently describes his reactions to pertinent paintings by Brueghel, Grunewald, Michelangelo, and Rembrandt. He furnishes splendid portraits of a lecherous, malevolent dwarf; of his saintly younger brother, after whom the psychiatrist in the novel is named; of a full-skirted landlady who sneaks into Canetti's bedroom at night and licks the portraits of her dead husband. In an essay on Tolstoy, Canetti audaciously compared the novelist's marriage with that of his invented sinologist. But until *The Torch in My Ear*, one could only speculate as to what degree *Auto-da-Fé* was grounded in the reality of boyhood observations.

Canetti's adolescence wasn't all fires, inflation, madness, and violent crowds. Several remarkable people took over from his mother in furthering his education. Canetti grew to worship Karl Kraus, the editor and sole writer of the polemical journal *Die Fackel* (*The Torch*). Constant attendance at Kraus's histrionic lectures helped Canetti develop his gift for parody and mimicry, though Kraus's political activism was beyond Canetti's grasp. During a brief stay in Berlin, the young writer came to admire Grosz (though the artist's lechery at a party offended him), hate Brecht (not unusual, but as a lover of Aristophanes, Canetti is unconvincing in his dismissal of *Threepenny Opera*), and worship the owlish perceptiveness of Isaac Babel. The most haunting people in the second installment of Canetti's life, however, are his mother, with whom he is locked in a struggle less paralyzing but no less burdened than that of Kafka with his father, and Veza, an intelligent and mysterious woman whom Canetti later married. Unhappily, Frau Canetti and Veza disappear from the narrative before those relationships are in any way resolved. He never mentions his marriage, or the response of either woman to his novel (indications of the mother's astonishment can be found in *The Tongue Set Free*). Not only is this volume less tidy than its predecessor, it is oddly elusive in tracking the writing of *Auto-da-Fé*, and omits several relevant facts that appear in *The Conscience of Words*.

The Torch in My Ear is filled with minutely observed recollections of incidental figures and scenes. The reader can, for example, chart (with Professor Nabokov's exactitude) the seating arrangement at dinner in a boardinghouse. The main point of the passage is to depict political bickering in postwar Frankfurt, something he might have accomplished in half the space. But the Flaubertian zeal to get things right tells us something important about Canetti. In this and similar passages concerning teachers and schoolmates, he exhibits his generosity, his humanist ability to really hear what people say. "With Kafka," he wrote in *The Human Province*, "something new came into the world, a more precise feeling for its dubiousness, a feeling, however, that is coupled not with hatred, but with respect for life." As with so many of Canetti's tributes, the words rebound to the author. Nowhere is his respect for life more manifest than in these incidental and often delightful vignettes.

Still another of Canetti's tributes suggests something of the steady, knowing arc of his life's work—the one in *Crowds and Power* to Stendahl, whose early influence made Canetti "stick to clarity." The 1981 Nobel Prize in Literature has secured Canetti an international audience, but in the '50s, when his novel was little read and his life consumed by a 20-year project, he must have identified with Stendahl, who "was concerned to write for a few . . . certain that in a hundred years he would be read by many." He concludes: "But whoever opens Stendahl will find him and also everything which surrounded him; and he finds it *here*, in this life. Thus the dead offer themselves as food to the living; their immortality profits them." And thus the dauntless, persevering earwitness Canetti holds death to a stalemate, anchoring his time and himself in books that sustain literature as a vocation of courage and principle.*

(October 1982)

*Since this essay appeared, Canetti's plays have been published in the United States by Performing Arts Journal Publications, in two volumes: *Comedy of Vanity and Life-Terms* (1982) and *The Wedding* (1986). Volume three of the autobiography, *The Play of the Eyes*, appeared in German in 1985 and in English a year later. This surprisingly brisk installment continues Canetti's odyssey through the death in 1937 of his mother, who does not otherwise appear. Veza, too, is elusive, alas—a mere sounding board for Canetti's continuing education. Yet the genesis of his early plays and the fading glory of Vienna's intellectual life is vividly portrayed. Profiles, alternately contentious and poetic, abound, including those of Robert Musil, Herman Broch, Alma Mahler, Alban Berg, Emil Ludwig, and, briefly, Joyce, who after hearing Canetti read from *The Comedy of Vanity* (the play in which mirrors are confiscated) remarked gruffly, "I shave with a straight razor and no mirror," and left. The one unequivocally "good man" is the inscrutable Dr. Sonne, who earns Canetti's admiration by lacking purpose. Unlike Canetti's writer friends, made testy by the strain of competition, Sonne disdains ambition and power—he's as close as we get to a Canetti hero. The fourth volume of memoirs will presumably touch on Canetti's nose, ready to catch the stench of the blitz if not the ovens. As of 1991, however, the only addition to the corpus is *The Secret Heart of the Clock*, a medley of aphorisms and meditations that continues the logbooks of *The Human Province*.

Scat Song

Last time around, in his "autobiographical collage" *Palm Sunday,* Kurt Vonnegut rated his books one against another on a scale of A+ to D. This is not an acceptable form of literary criticism;* all the same I'm tempted to write *"Deadeye Dick:* B−" and break for lunch. The reason is simply that Vonnegut's 14 books, of which 10 are novels, are so similar in style, outlook, tone, and characterization that they seem to constitute a genre. A Kurt Vonnegut, like a P. G. Wodehouse or an Alfred Hitchcock, is a fairly dependable product, entertaining, bankable, and entirely sui generis. The reader who discovers him through his current offering may be as goggle-eyed with pleasure as I was after coming across *Cat's Cradle* 19 years ago, but the reader who has followed Vonnegut's travail from the science fiction racks to the black humorists' clique to the Spokesman for Youth lectern to the mainstream may find a letter grade adequate information.

Like many of his novels, *Deadeye Dick* is a case history from the holocaust, though this time Vonnegut gives us his smallest and most painless holocaust to date. Having destroyed the world in *Cat's Cradle* and the United States in *Slapstick,* he now localizes his devastation in Midland City, Ohio—a provincial town not unlike the one in which Vonnegut was raised, which is accidentally depopulated by a neutron bomb. The narrator, Rudy Waltz, who shares Vonnegut's diction and several biographical details (including a father who built the family home and lost the family fortune), can easily identify with murderous accidents. At the age of 12, he celebrated Mother's Day by firing a rifle into the air; the bullet landed several blocks away, between the eyes of pregnant Eloise Metzger, who was vacuuming at the time. Nicknamed Deadeye Dick, Rudy became the town pariah and an affectless servant to his misfit parents, who have been rendered bankrupt by Mr. Metzger's lawsuits.

Yet Rudy has his moments. Like Vonnegut, he writes a terrible play—about the search for Shangri-La—that is produced in New York City. It flops there but is more appreciated at a Midland City revival, which, not so incidentally, stars the once beautiful, now Methedrine-addicted Celia Hoover, whose husband, Dwayne, went haywire in Vonnegut's 1973 novel, *Breakfast of Champions.*

*At least it wasn't until the appearance, in 1990, of the magazine *Entertainment Weekly.*

What's more, Rudy ends up in better shape than the witnesses to previous Vonnegut holocausts. The novelist sentenced a guilty bystander in Nazi Germany to suicide in *Mother Night* and an innocent bystander at the firebombing of Dresden to exile in *Slaughterhouse-Five*. He gives Rudy, an accomplished cook, his own hotel in Haiti, where he lives with his much-divorced brother, Feliz (formerly the president of NBC), and Hippolyte Paul De Mille, a Haitian who can raise the dead. There he whips up delicacies like banana soup and polka-dot brownies.

So here we have all the ingredients for a whimsically pessimistic meditation on the lunacies of contemporary life, with sharply focused assaults on parents who tyrannize their children, doctors who prescribe nerve-decaying drugs, expatriates who search for Shangri-La everywhere but home (surrender Dorothy), and a gun culture predicated on the assumption that life is cheap. Yet *Deadeye Dick* is stilted in comparison with Vonnegut's A and A+ work—*Cat's Cradle, Mother Night*, and *Slaughterhouse-Five*. His voice, that dispassionate croon that pretends to misanthropy while somehow intimating affection for even the most pathetic of his characters, has soured. It's as though his anger has bullied his wit at the expense of his imagination. The misanthropy is no longer pretended. Vonnegut's final sentences have a ring of desperation and the inconsequence of a non sequitur: "You want to know something? We are still in the Dark Ages. The Dark Ages—they haven't ended yet." On the one hand, Rudy Waltz's story lacks the momentum, the drive, the invention to justify Vonnegut's contempt; on the other, the Dark Ages seem positively sunny compared with a world capable of imagining, let along building, a neutron bomb.

Ray Bradbury, whose stock has fallen as low as his output, wrote a better neutron bomb story nearly 30 years before anyone ever heard of the thing; it's called "There Will Come Soft Rains," and it describes a house that survives its occupants, although not for long. Vonnegut appears stymied by this bomb that kills people but leaves their property undamaged. In his preface, he writes that a real neutron bomb—unliked his "fantasy borrowed from enthusiasts for a Third World War"—would cause far more "suffering and damage than I have described." What excuse, other than exhaustion, can explain the decision to mute that reality? For a joke? It's a thin joke. In *Cat's Cradle*, Vonnegut introduced Ice-Nine, which destroyed the world by freezing all its water and freed him to play God with the comic buoyancy of a writer who has out-imagined science. The neutron bomb, however, may be beyond the imagination of most humans, because it is real. Vonnegut can do little more than state its existence and wryly describe an episode in which Rudy and company wander through lifeless Midland City, now under martial law. Rather than animating the novel, the bomb is merely inserted—a howdy-do from the world of current events.

Small wonder that Rudy thinks of people as "undifferentiated wisps of nothingness." They aren't born, and they don't die; rather, their peepholes are opened and closed. This bit of information is found on the first page, and though it may sound like an awfully cute conceit, it's actually handled well. The first page ends with the phrase "Blah blah blah," and I suspect Vonnegut enjoyed imagining how his readers would tremble with the apprehension that those words—like the catch phrases "So it goes" and "Hi ho" from earlier novels—would appear every page or so. They never appear again, but there are other catch phrases, judiciously interpolated, like "Imagine that" or "Think of that"; in addition, Rudy passes time by scat singing, so there are occasional "skeedy wahs" and "foodly yahs."

At his best, Vonnegut is a masterly stylist, much in the way Count Basie is a masterly stylist—economic, droll, rhythmic. Consequently, some people think they have no style. But try and imitate them—it can't be done. *Deadeye Dick* has its share of well-turned phrases ("festive inhumanity") and jokes: "It is virtually impossible to harm a Timex watch. For some reason, the less you pay for a watch, the surer you can be that it will never stop"; "you can claim a piece of land which has been inhabited for tens of thousands of years, if only you will repeat this mantra endlessly: 'We discovered it, we discovered it, we discovered it.' " There are several amusing set pieces, notably a plane ride with the founder of the Mildred Barry Cultural Arts Center, and a few dramatically compelling playlets that make you wonder how Rudy's real play (or, for that matter, Vonnegut's real play, *Happy Birthday, Wanda June*) could have turned out so awful.

Still, some of the familiar mannerisms are intrusive and betray bad comic timing. There must be two dozen sentences that position a climactic phrase after a colon (i.e., "The words were these: Deadeye Dick"), and in almost every instance the colon strains the humor. Expected yowls fall flat, ironies fail to resonate. Rudy's father palled around with Hitler when they were both art students, but little is made of it. A couple of Italian immigrants (the Maritimo brothers) promise to be major characters, but never come alive. Random observations—pro capital punishment, anti modern art—and unmodulated spleen conspire to rob Vonnegut's voice of its usual disenchanted wisdom. He is frequently capricious: Celia Hoover's son is shown in her thrall on one page; on the next, he's grown into a "notorious homosexual." So much for him. But then, nobody's children come to any good in *Deadeye Dick*.

Vonnegut is ambivalent about the Midwest of his youth. The little house—complete with white picket fence and all modern appliances—given to Rudy and his mother by the Maritimos is invariably described as a "shitbox," but notwithstanding its radioactive mantelpiece (which kills Mrs. Waltz before the neutron bomb has a chance to), it's the kind of shitbox many people would kill for. Reading *Deadeye Dick*, it's hard to understand what motivates Vonnegut's undying nostalgia for "the American Middle West of my youth." Yet he turns the horrific barn of a house in which Rudy grows up into the town's very own Mount Fuji. This happens when the Maritimos replace the structure's cupola, from which Rudy fired his fateful shot, with a large white cone. Thus Midland City itself aspires to Shangri-La; in fact, now that the original inhabitants have been vaporized, the government is thinking of turning it into a refugee center. But nostalgic or not, Vonnegut is unlikely to join those refugees. More probably, he'll turn up in Port-au-Prince, Haiti, eating Rudy Waltz's spuma di cioccolata. For him, the rest is "Foodly yah, foodly yah. Zang reepa dop. Faaaaaaaaaaa!"

(November 1982)

ADDENDUM: As an undergraduate, I had the pleasure of meeting Vonnegut, who was then an instructor in the writing program at Iowa City; not having published *Slaughterhouse-Five*, he was little known beyond a cult, of which I, a passionate admirer of *Cat's Cradle* and *Mother Night*, was a member. Resentful of the science fiction label imposed on him, he observed of Edmund Wilson (after 25 years, this may not be exact), "He's the kind of critic who thinks anyone who knows how to use a screwdriver or fix a refrigerator writes science fiction." Of course, anyone who can fix a refrigerator probably does. Let it be noted of Vonnegut, however, that, in the tradition of Mary Shelley and H. G. Wells, he has proved to be a sci-fi prophet of corrosive accuracy. His propagandist Campbell, in *Mother Night*, is now writing for the *New York Times* under the byline William Safire. In a 1991 column, the erstwhile author of Spiro Agnew's alliterative attacks on his betters reproached the victim of a sexual assault at Senator Kennedy's Palm Beach compound on the grounds that she did not have the good breeding to know, "drinking all night and going to a man's house at 3:30 a.m. places one in what used to be called an occasion of sin." Here is *Mother Night* with a vengeance.

Similarly, the accidental shooting in *Deadeye Dick*, which seemed whimsical in 1982, was no smirking matter a few years later. In an editorial on March 18, 1990, the *Times* observed, "There's a touch of spring in the air in New York City and something else, too: stray bullets. One day last week, one struck Amy Rosen while she ate her lunch in Central Park. That evening, another struck Loretta Rivera as she walked home from a pizza parlor in Brooklyn. Dr. Rosen, luckily, survived her chest wound. Ms. Rivera dies on a street so riddled by shootouts that none of her neighbors expressed surprise. Police call the victims in bystander shootings 'mushrooms'—they pop up unexpectedly and stop a bullet for someone else. Loved ones describe them differently. They say the dead were nice people 'in the wrong place at the wrong time.' . . . The blossoming of bystander shootings is a recent phenomenon. Only since last year have New York City police felt a need to monitor its growth. But judging by news reports, stray bullets ended the lives of an estimated 30 New Yorkers in 1989, more than twice the 1988 number and seven times the number killed in 1985."

And so on. It is difficult, nay, impossible to believe that a policeman and not a distinguished American quasi-science-fiction writer came up with the term "mushrooms." Indeed, the whole style is Vonnegut's—the growth metaphors ("blossoming" is outstanding), as well as the see-Spot-run tone of resolute insouciance ("One day," "nice people"), which continues through to the kicker: "Too many guns in a tight space; too many bullets in the air." Perhaps critics have become impatient with Vonnegut because they are sick of living in his nightmare. Wake up, people!

Yet not even Vonnegut himself is immune to the haplessness that inevitably descends on his characters. Once again the setting was the *New York Times*. In the Book Review section of December 9, 1990, he reviewed a new edition of Robert A. Heinlein's *Stranger in a Strange Land*, to which a whopping 60,000 words (about 150 pages) had been restored. Busy fellow that he is, he didn't feel obliged to actually read the volume he agreed to evaluate. Nothing unusual about that. What was unusual was Vonnegut's ingenuous willingness to admit his oversight, sort of, thereby increasing the perquisites of fame.

Vonnegut begins by recounting a dinner party in London, including the identity of the host and the hotel to which he later retired. Table chat concerned the best novel ever written—a book review cue if he ever heard one, for no one mentioned Heinlein's novel, not even Vonnegut. "An enormous number of readers have found this book a brilliant mind-bender," he notes, declining to tell us whether it bent his mind as well. He continues to clear his throat for several more paragraphs, reflecting on the "social prejudices" and "snobbery" used against Heinlein and his ilk, which includes Voltaire and Swift. Finally, with only a few lines left, he gets to the book itself; after noting that the excised 60,000 words "are at last taking their rightful place in the body of world literature," he offers, in the tone of Elliot Rosewater, this judgment: "Is the story much improved by the restored passages? I leave it to someone else to compare the two versions line by line." It is difficult, nay, impossible to believe that the disingenuously insouciant phrase "line by line" wasn't added by a *Times* editorialist.

Zuckerman Strikes Back

When last encountered, in *Zuckerman Unbound* (1981), the literary lion Nathan Zuckerman was cruising incognito through Newark like Frank Sinatra, another of New Jersey's native sons, nestled securely behind an armed chauffeur, "his lyrical feeling for the neighborhood" used up, his childhood synagogue now an African Methodist Episcopal Church. Rich, notorious, pestered by literary fame and acrimony, Zuckerman was still reeling from the unexpected success of *Carnovsky*, his sensational 1969 account of "a budding soul . . . bedeviled by onanism in Jewish New Jersey." Carnovsky's family was widely assumed to be Zuckerman's own, for which dishonor he received his dying father's curse. *Zuckerman Unbound* was assumed by many to embody Zuckerman's farewell to his past and Philip Roth's farewell to his alter ego. We now find that one or the other couldn't let go: Zuckerman is back, his adventures in affliction expanded to a proper trilogy.

As *The Anatomy Lesson* demonstrates, Nathan's problems were just beginning. During the four years that followed *Carnovsky*, his self-esteem withered under repeated assaults until he no longer knew if his talent was still intact. His mother's death left him mourning their unfinished business; his brother blamed him for both parents' deaths and stopped speaking to him; a hugely respected critic—once a supporter—published a savage attack, legitimizing middlebrow accusations that had been leveled against him earlier. On the occasion of Zuckerman's first published story, the grandiose Judge Wapter wrote him a preposterous letter. "Can you honestly say that there is anything in your short story that would not warm the heart of a Julius Streicher or a Joseph Goebbels?" the distinguished judge asked (in the trilogy's first volume, *The Ghost Writer*, 1979). The distinguished critic is none too sure.

Add to this a confluence of psychosomatic ailments that have altered Nathan's calling to that of full-time patient. When he isn't visiting doctors, poring over volumes of anatomy, or imbibing pills, liquor, and grass to kill the undiagnosed pain, he is reduced (not unlike David Kepesh in *The Breast*) to an immobile mass of libidinous nerve endings stretched out on a mat, a passive offering to the four women who take turns squatting over his face and groin. After four such years of inactivity, however, Nathan takes action. He decides, at 40, to go for the road not taken, and flies to his alma mater, the University of Chicago, with the intention of entering medical school. The feminists who branded him a misogynist ("Those girls meant business—wanted blood") will soon find in him a gynecological savior; the Jews who reviled him for anti-Semitic self-hatred will applaud his rehabilitation—he will be the Nathan Leopold of bestsellers. It's the kind of pipe dream you might expect from Zuckerman, who once imagined himself trumping Judge Wapter by winning the hand of Anne Frank.

So broad an outline tells very little about the substance and richness—the satiric bravura—of *The Anatomy Lesson*, but it brings up a couple of preliminary matters that have become almost inescapable in discussing the gripes of Roth. Can the book stand alone without reference to, first, Roth's other work, and, second, Roth himself? The answer in the first instance is a defiant no, in the second a qualified yes. Those who resent Roth for demanding of his readers as much devotion as, say, John Jakes demands of his will derive little pleasure from the latest installment. Indeed, early readers of *The Anatomy Lesson* have already echoed those reviewers of *Zuckerman Unbound* who were piqued by Roth's presumption of familiarity with his previous novels. They generally claim to be impatient for Roth to get to his Big Novel (but not another great American novel), and will continue to miss the impressive scope, let alone the inspired japery, of the Zuckerman trilogy until, bound between one set of hard covers, it assumes the bulk and binding of a Big Novel.

The Anatomy Lesson isn't necessarily dependent on the earlier novels for plot elements; it can be read—if not fully savored—on its own. But the trilogy gains irony and gravity from the manifold ways in which the three volumes interlock. In *Zuckerman Unbound*, Roth's alter ego was virtually Walter Brennaned out of the action, as the best and funniest role went to a supporting character, the former TV quiz kid Alvin Pepler. Nathan's plight paled by comparison. *The Anatomy Lesson* redeems and gives perspective to its predecessor, confirming themes only sketched the first and second times around, clarifying Roth's ambivalence about Zuckerman.

For all the exuberance of his wise-guy wit, Roth is a deeply moral writer, and the Zuckerman trilogy approaches the decorous imperatives of an exemplary novel. Nathan was made, transformed, undone, and revived by literature, and our interest in him is as much sustained by the lessons he seems to learn (but, in fact, incompletely grasps) as by Roth's comic brilliance. Many critics of *Portnoy's Complaint* asked whether Roth was any smarter than his protagonist. No one can mistake the derision—though it is naggingly undermined by stubborn and mischievous autobiographical tidbits—in Roth's portrait of Zuckerman. When we take leave of him, Nathan is an outpatient in a Chicago hospital in 1973; he follows the interns on their nocturnal patrols, "as though he still believed that he could unchain himself from a future as a man apart and escape the corpus that was his." Of course Roth knows better.

In 1974, a year after he was presumably cured, if we can find any concrete logic in Roth's shadowplay, Zuckerman made his literary debut, not as a writer but as the alter ego of Roth's earlier alter ego, the novelist Peter Tarnopol, in the best and probably the most neglected of Roth's previous fictions, *My Life as a Man*. In that hair-raising account of a beastly marriage, Zuckerman is the means by which Tarnopol confronts his own past; Tarnopol, too, "may not be well suited for the notoriety that attends the publication of an unabashed and unexpurgated history of one's erotic endeavors." He compensates with "useful fictions" about one Nathan Zuckerman.

To be sure, this is a slightly different Zuckerman, one with an older brother, a dentist named Sherman (instead of a younger brother named Henry, also a dentist) and a father who owns a shoe store (instead of a father who is a chiropodist). Both Nathans, though, were born in 1933, attended college at 16, and avidly read Thomas Wolfe. Moreover, the Tarnopol-Zuckerman relationship occasionally makes you wonder who's pulling whose strings. Like Zuckerman, Tarnopol has to learn "what a past is." He confesses he "is beginning to seem as imaginary as my Zuckermans." Five years later, Zuckerman starred in *The Ghost Writer*, a variation on James's "The Author of Beltraffio" and a first-person account of his formative years that, in its Jamesian nuance and propriety, is presumably closer to Zuckerman's style than the third person kvetching of *Zuckerman Unbound* and *The Anatomy Lesson*.

Make what you will of Zuckerman's various manifestations, but suffice it to say that, minimally, familiarity with *Portnoy's Complaint*, *My Life as a Man*, and the trilogy is necessary to relish Roth's gamesmanship on the subject of how literature acts on American readers and writers. It might be argued that too much depends on the reader's memories of Alex Portnoy or at least on the furor over his complaint. The trilogy never tells us what kind of writer Zuckerman is, and all it gives us of the contents of *Carnovsky* are a few clues that make it indistinguishable from *Portnoy's*—this in a work that filibusters, page after page, for a novelist's right to be presumed innocent of autobiography, for an imaginative process that transforms facts into something else. If you don't know Portnoy, you can barely imagine Carnovsky, and if you don't recall the impact *Portnoy's/Carnovsky* had in 1969 (there's been nothing like it since), you are entitled to feel impatient with the entire conceit.

Yet partly, and only partly, because Portnoy *is* so well remembered, Roth gets away with it. André Breton warned Luis Buñuel in 1955 that "it's no longer possible to scandalize anybody." Yet Portnoy's sticky palm did the trick, providing Roth with a nearly unique vantage point from which to study, in his aggressively anecdotal style, the upshots and pratfalls of literary endeavor. One might wish that his probing had been even more autobiographical, since Roth's response to his sudden notoriety was more creative if less calamitous than Zuckerman's: The rapid publication of three diverse and extremely uneven books, culminating in *The Great American Novel* (surely the most tiresome indulgence by an important American writer in the decade preceding Norman Mailer's incomparably chuckleheaded *Ancient Evenings*), is more interesting than writer's block. He might have explored how Zuckerman graduated from onanism to Nixon, mammary metamorphosis, and baseball. He might have explored the dangers of disappearing into the looking glass.

In any case, the Portnoy experience prepared him for a new subject, an expansion of his corpus. Roth's stunning return to form with *My Life as a Man* (he's been on a roll ever since) established, among other signs of a dazzling increase in powers, his willingness to aim at a particular kind of reader—one who shares with Roth a nearly collegiate enthusiasm for literature's gods and ghosts. He strikes a special chord with the peculiarly American—even peculiarly Jewish American—first-generation intellectuals, who, like Roth, discovered literature in school, used it to rebel against their bourgeois backgrounds, and were left to ponder its political and medicinal uses. This business about writing for a discrete audience strikes a tonic chord in *The Anatomy Lesson*.

In a 1969 interview (reprinted in *Reading Myself and Others*), Roth said that he didn't write for an "audience . . . if you mean by an audience a particular readership which can be described in terms of its education, politics, religion, or even by its literary tone." The much respected critic Irving Howe concluded his widely noted denunciation of Roth on this imperial note: "Flaubert once said that a writer must choose between an audience and readers. Evidently Roth has made his choice." It's difficult to tell from "Philip Roth Reconsidered" (reprinted in Howe's *The Critical Point*) exactly which audience Howe had in mind, though it's obviously not one that he covets. Yet it surely isn't one that will be untroubled by frequent and sometimes arcane references throughout *The Anatomy Lesson* to George Herbert, Mann, Chekhov, Beckett, Kafka, and a dozen other real writers, not to mention a fictitious one, Milton Appel, who published a diatribe similar (if not identical) to Howe's about Nathan Zuckerman.

Which brings us further into Roth's house of mirrors, for clearly he does have an audience in mind, a well-read one where his own literary history and enthusiasms are concerned. Milton Appel is the subject of some of the most riotous writing Roth has done. Appel isn't an onstage participant, like Alvin Pepler, but rather a source for the narrator's manic improvisations, like Kafka in *The Professor of Desire* and Anne Frank in *The Ghost Writer*. Appel is always in the wings— his only dialogue is heard over the phone, during which conversation he sounds "wearyingly intelligent," as Wilfred Sheed once said of Howe. Otherwise, we know him by what he writes or by what Zuckerman chooses to tell us about what he writes. He is the critic as ogre, a comfort to the Philistines and a probable source of Zuckerman's mysterious pain.

Is Appel Howe? Appel was born in 1918, wrote studies of Camus, Koestler, and Dreiser, and attacked Zuckerman in *Inquiry* (editor: Mortimer Horowitz) in 1973. Howe was born in 1920, wrote studies of Anderson, Orwell, and Faulkner, and attacked Roth in *Commentary* (editor: Norman Podhoretz) in 1972. Clearly, there's no connection. Well, maybe a little. For one thing, they look alike:

"round-faced, bespectacled, tallish, balding." For others, they taught at some of the same schools, worked for *Partisan Review*, published similar essays, and have identical reputations. Also, Appel used exactly the same words to first praise Zuckerman's *Higher Education* and later denigrate it along with *Carnovsky* as Howe employed to praise Roth's *Goodbye, Columbus* and later demolish it along with *Portnoy's Complaint*.

As fictional invention, Appel is an inspired foil. Nathan rails at him with an occasionally fatuous dialectic, branding him as one of those aesthetes who are suddenly sympathetic to "the ghetto world of their traditional fathers now that the traditional fathers are filed for safekeeping in Beth Moses Memorial Park. When they were alive they wanted to strangle the immigrant bastards to death because they dared to think they could actually be of consequence without ever having read Proust past *Swann's Way*." He rings a jarringly false note here—how many immigrant fathers read *Swann's Way?*—but accurately reflects Nathan's own vanity on the matter of education. Earlier in the book, Nathan recalls that when his parents failed to respond with proper awe to their son's encounter with Thomas Mann, he muttered to himself, "Sorry it wasn't Sam Levinson."

Appel and Zuckerman represent two generations of apostasy from the Jewish bourgeoisie (which differs little from any other bourgeoisie); both feel less pride in their own bookishness than shame at their parents' lack of it. Nathan is outraged at Appel's hypocrisy as an intellectual mandarin who suddenly pretends solidarity with the Catskills culture that is the butt of Zuckerman's satire. But he's also plain wounded by the devastating attack from a writer he once admired. When dialect fails him, he settles for expletives ("fucking regressive nut!") that spur his anger into the ultimate vengeance—a fullblown fantasy made real. Traveling to and around Chicago, Nathan identifies himself as Milton Appel ("A-p-p-e-l. Accent on the second syllable. *Je m'appelle* Appel"), while masquerading as a flamboyantly crude pornographer, the editor of *Lickety Split* and proprietor of a swingers' club called "Milton's Millennia."

Undoubtedly, Zuckerman has been learning something about the consequences of literature. Diminished in his obsession and pain to a blathering Beckettian mouth while prostate on his mat before a harem of willing mother-substitutes, Nathan finds himself turning into his fictional stand-in Carnovsky, "smothered with mothers and shouting at Jews." He blames his "whammied" muscles on Appel's "Jewish evil eye," and when he finally confronts Appel on the phone, Nathan sounds disconcertingly like a Jewish father defending himself against the superiority of his overeducated son: "My shitty books are cast in concrete, you make judicious reappraisals. I'm a 'case,' I have a 'career,' you have a calling. Oh, I'll tell you your calling—President of the Rabbinical Society for the Suppression of Laughter in the Interest of Loftier Values!" Nathan is furious at Appel for attributing to him "the rebellious outcry of a claustrophobic fourteen-year-old boy [Carnovsky]," but when his impotent rage is exacerbated by a plea from Appel on behalf of Isreal, he's tempted to repeat what Carnovsky/

Portnoy shouted at 14—that the world can take its concern for the good of the Jews and shove it. Roth, anticipating his readers, has Nathan demonstrate restraint, thereby proving "to himself if to no one else the difference between character and author."

Zuckerman's revenge—his intricate, "burning" improvisation on the idea of Appel as porn tycoon—is a splendidly deranged metaphor for the practical uses of art. Roth's revenge, on the other hand, raises questions of propriety. He has waited 10 years to respond to Howe, and for all the textual validity of his conceit, there is blood on the page. Previous literary feuds on the order of the Sinclair Lewis–Bernard De Voto and Edmund Wilson–Vladimir Nabokov exchanges were relative models of decorum. Because Roth has scrupulously adhered to verifiable facts regarding Appel's attacks and positions (they are unmistakably Howe's), the reader must wonder how much of the less easily verified information also relates to Howe. Zuckerman is especially and justifiably repulsed by a letter Appel wrote to an intermediary, and never intended for Zuckerman to read. Are we to assume that Howe, too, wrote such a letter? On a more mundane level, Zuckerman, in trying to find something to use against Appel, hears of problems concerning his daughter. Does Howe have a daughter? One can insist that such questions are irrelevant, but because they are unavoidable, *The Anatomy Lesson* is tainted with a buzz of cheap gossip in which the reader is fully implicated.

Even in the age of the true-life novel, Roth would appear to be treading on precarious ground. But, of course, Kafka-disciple that he is, he begs for the critical abuse he earns. It's the wise-guy in him, laughing all the way through the gauntlet, comforted by the knowledge that he is offending all the wrong people for all the right reasons—fulfilling the admonishment of his favorite "sit-down comic," Kafka, to do more harm to society than it does to you. Still, in many respects he is quite fair to Appel. Howe's essay doesn't stand up against *Portnoy's Complaint* because it fails to comprehend its intentions or appreciate its comic extravagance. (Zuckerman is astonished that Appel didn't think *Carnovsky* was funny.) But Howe does real damage to *Goodbye, Columbus* when he argues that "even a philistine character has certain rights, if not as a philistine then at least as a character in whose 'reality' we are being asked to believe." Zuckerman never invokes sentences like that in Appel's essay, concentrating instead on more easily refutable passages (all with parallels in Howe) concerning Zuckerman's motives and the charges of anti-Semitism. Yet he seems to agree with Appel's negative reassessment of the early fiction when he whines, "My first stories you can't forget."

Evidence that Roth has long since become too good a novelist to cheat a character (Philistine or critic) of his integrity is vaunted when Appel is finally heard from, in a phone call. He is sufficiently convincing and sensible to enfeeble Zuckerman's rage and turn it back on him. Nathan is riddled with doubt: "What if twenty years of writing has just been so much helplessness before a compulsion—submission to a lowly, inconsequential compulsion that I've dignified with all my principles, a compulsion probably not all that different from what made my mother clean the house for five hours every day?" And not all that different from Portnoy's complaint? Who would have foreseen the shifty and prolific Philip Roth as the poet of literary terrors, the bard of block?

For most of *The Anatomy Lesson*, Roth's narrative hand is wonderfully sure, his comic timing worthy of the Ritz brothers, with whom Zuckerman compares himself, his voice unencumbered by the typographical screaming of *Portnoy's Complaint*. Not since Henry Miller has anyone learned to be as funny and compassionate and brutal and plaintive in the space of a paragraph. Juggling elegiac passages with broad lampoon, Roth frequently keeps the reader off balance. A heartfelt meditation on his mother, set in her Miami apartment immediately after her death, is suddenly interrupted with a maid out of "Amos 'n' Andy," who fulfills *her* obsession by cleaning Mrs. Zuckerman's closets. A nostalgic meeting with the elderly Dr. Kotler, for whom *Carnovsky* provoked pleasant memories of the Newark he loved, is followed by a tryst with Gloria, the wife of Nathan's accountant, who arrives with "nippleless bra, crotchless panties, Polaroid camera, vibrating dildo, K-Y jelly, Gucci blindfold, a length of braided velvet rope—for a treat, on his birthday, a gram of cocaine. 'Times have changed,' said Zuckerman, 'since all you needed was a condom.' "

The impersonation of Appel as pornographer is nasty and hilarious. Nathan reinvents *Inquiry*'s editor, Mortimer Horowitz—"he's not very deep, but he's a sweet sort of schmuck"—first as someone who's idea of making it is to achieve 15 orgasms in 14 hours at Milton's Millennia, and second as an impotent checker champion, "always sitting there looking at his board. 'King Me.' " He accosts a formal gentile businessman with facts about sex statistics ("semen production is up in America by at least two hundred percent"), and bullies an implacable woman chauffeur into defending herself and humanity against his lubricious tirade. There are dead pages in these final episodes (some things haven't changed: Roth grows finicky when he tries to write about the Midwest). A long conversation with the school chum Zuckerman hopes will get him into medical school is laborious, though leavened by Nathan's hapless attempts to seem sober while under the throttle of Percodan, and his climactic assault on the friend's father is unconvincing. The chauffeur subdues Nathan after he turns on the father, putting him in hospital, where he emerges from unconsciousness feeling nothing but the inside of his mouth—"The mysterious stillness, the miles of silence, the tongue creeping conradianly on toward Kurtz. I am the Marlow of my mouth."

Thus constricted, Nathan considers the books he knows, the books he's written, the doubt that "is a half a writer's life. Two-thirds. Nine-tenths. Another day, another doubt. The only thing I never doubted was the doubt." The literary baggage, another instance of the encroaching past, is an inalienable part of his suffering corpus—notes from that cloying underground, the library. Zuckerman spends *The Anatomy Lesson* hiding from his talent—as a patient, as a fake-Appel, and as an AWOL writer trying to enlist in the University of Chicago. Like

Tarnopol in *My Life as a Man*, he can insist that literature got him into this mess and will have to get him out. But his only hope is to face up to his fate, his obsession. Kvetching is salvation. As A. J. Heschel, a writer decidedly not in Zuckerman's pantheon, once wrote, "Only those who have not tasted the terror of life, only those who claim that it is a pleasure to live and that more and only pleasure is in store for the generations to come, can deny the essential necessity of asking: Wherefore? For whose sake?"

Roth is frequently accused of having turned his back on Judaic culture, and, to be sure, there is nothing in his writing to suggest much interest in the covenant with Moses. Howe was right to point out the spuriousness of "Eli, the Fanatic" 's conversion. But Judaic culture in the United States is largely the secular world in which American Jews find themselves presently living. Far from turning his back on it, Roth has given a texture and shape to that experience unmatched in the work of his contemporaries. Far from ignoring his birthright, he celebrates its cultural resonance in his diction and themes. In refusing to demand special dispensation for Jews, he's been able to engender a howl that is quintessentially American, though infused with a Jewish accent and vitality. His irreverent energy has always conveyed the promise of a writer who might make sense of insensible times. Because he writes with a firm hand on the literary and personal tillers of the past and delineates the spleen of urban isolation with a steadier mixture of exuberance and intelligence than anyone else around, Roth is in the enviable position, at 50, of being promising still.

(November 1983)

Senses and Sensibility

Eudora Welty is a master of what jazz musicians call stop-time. In music, the phrase refers to those episodes when the rhythm section lays out for one or more beats per measure, thereby seeming to make time stand still while focusing greater attention on the improvising soloist. In Welty's writing, narrative time is syncopated to allow for the accretion of metaphorical details that draw attention to the storyteller's delicious command of her craft. The effect is not simply to underscore her cleverness or to compound with gnomic symbols the already mythic dimensions of her stories, but to bring us deeper into the tale. Like Conrad, she wants to make us see, and hear and taste and smell and feel. The "exacerbation of poeticism" that Diana Trilling, writing in the 1940s, found so objectionable in her early fiction is in large degree the lifeblood of Welty's writing.

Even some of Welty's admirers, captivated by the acid wit of her dialogue, have questioned the frequency of her metaphors. Yet no one acquainted with the steadfast independence of her work could have been surprised when it culminated in a novel, *Losing Battles*, told almost exclusively with metaphors and conversation. "Then a house appeared on its ridge, like an old man's silver watch pulled once more out of its pocket." Welcome to Weltyland, peopled with neighborly eccentrics and gnarled, dislocated souls; voiced in disarming monologues and easy gossip; filtered through fable and fancy by an imagination painstakingly attuned to time, place, and character. Here are the petty horrors and calamitous jokes that keep life in a state of awful suspense.

In her provident and amazingly popular memoir, *One Writer's Beginnings*, which originated in three lectures delivered at Harvard in 1983, Welty reminds us time and again that her primary gift is love, the love that animates and guides the leap into fiction. Attentive from her earliest years to every kind of story, she acquired "the turn of mind, the nature of temperament, of a privileged observer; and owing to the way I became so, it turned out that I became the loving kind." Only her 1963 story, "Where Is the Voice Coming From?" written in response to the murder of Medgar Evers, was fueled by anger, she says, and even there, "I don't believe that my anger showed me anything about human character that my sympathy and rapport never had."

It may fuel a deception to speak too much about Eudora Welty and love, now that she is 75 and so widely honored that even this slim university press volume is fixed high on the bestseller list. The danger is that she will be misprized as simply a grand old lady—the kind of subversion of reputation from which Mark Twain almost didn't recover. Love, in Welty, ultimately means comprehension, a means of breaking through the paralyzing isolation that she finds epidemic. There has never been anything easy or reassuring in her vision, and she emerges even in this memoir as a disinterested if penetrating and compassionate observer. *One Writer's Beginnings*, though humming with candid sentiment, is never sentimental. The stunning craftsmanship, here as in her best fiction, is inseparable from the points she wishes to make. The eye is cool, the ear is flawless.

The book has three parts, "Listening," "Learning to See," and "Finding a Voice," measuring—not unlike the first page of Joyce's *Portrait of the Artist as a Young Man*—the child's budding senses, and only then the surrounding world. The first section offers few commonplace facts (names, occupations); it is rather a rubato exploration of her awakening powers of observation and imagination. Welty's memories, like her stories, are filled with music—indeed, her memoir begins epigrammatically with a vignette of her parents whistling a duet. The house her father built in Jackson, Mississippi, in which she has lived all her life, is filled with the music of clocks (he loved gadgets), her mother's songs, and a victrola with a tone arm that "gave off a metallic smell like human sweat, from all the hot needles that were fed it."

During summer trips to her grandparents in West Virginia and Ohio, she discovered that her outgoing uncles on her mother's side kept banjos at the ready and sang in perfect unison, while the more contemplative relatives on her father's side retained an unplayed organ ("I chilled my finger by touching a key") and a music box, which made a sound so strangely distant that it "might even have been the sound going through the rooms and up and down the stairs of our house in Jackson at night while all of us were here in Ohio, too far from home even to hear the clock striking from the downstairs hall." At the populous Mississippi State College for Women, she notes, only the music students found a way to be really alone, through solitary practice.

This, of course, is the Welty we've known from the earliest stories, her senses flaring excitedly with every stimulus. Her memory is unfailingly tactile. She recalls traveling with her father on a train, and drinking from his collapsible cup: "The taste of silver could almost be relied on to shock your teeth." She details the porter's preparations at bedtime, and recaptures the moments before sleep: "When you lay enclosed and enwrapped, your head on a pillow parallel to the track, the rhythm of the rail clicks pressed closer to your body as if it might be your heart beating, but the sound of the engine seemed to come from farther away than when it carried you in daylight." Welty's heart does a lot of hard beating, and this jittery, characteristic responsiveness to sight and sound might wear thin if it weren't guided by her consuming interest in documenting the development of her uncommon reportorial powers, and if it weren't leavened with vivid and frequently hilarious portraits of the people around her. Here is her imperious grade school principal:

> Miss Duling dressed as plainly as a Pilgrim on a Thanksgiving poster we made in the schoolroom, in a longish black-and-white checked gingham dress, a bright thick wool sweater the red of a railroad lantern—she'd knitted it herself—black stockings and her narrow elegant feet in black hightop shoes with heels you could hear coming, rhythmical as a parade drum down the hall. . . . With a swing of her bell that took her whole right arm and shoulder, she rang it, militant and impartial, from the head of the front steps of Davis School when it was time for us all to line up, girls on one side, boys on the other. We were to march past her into the school building, while the fourth grader she nabbed played time on the piano, mostly to a tune we could have skipped to, but we didn't skip into Davis School.

The most satisfying portraits are of her immensely likable parents—her optimistic father, staring resolutely into the future while holding on to fragile mementos of his sorrow-filled childhood, and her brave, stern mother, who once ran into a burning house to preserve a collected Dickens, and who instructed the local librarian that nine-year-old Eudora could read any book, "children or adult," except *Elsie Dinsmore*. "Later she explained to me that she'd made this rule because Elsie the heroine, being made by her father to practice too long and hard at the piano, fainted and fell off the piano stool. 'You're too impressionable, dear,' she told me. 'You'd read that and the very first thing you'd do, you'd fall off the piano stool.' " Miss Welty's detractors should especially relish this joke. (Her memoir fails to note a Weltylike coincidence: the two literary shades whose priggish heroines haunted her mother's generation—Martha Finley, Elsie's creator, and Augusta Evans, after whose Edna Earl the narrator of *The Ponder Heart* is named—both died within months of Eudora's birth.) Her parents were imbued with the pioneering spirit, inherited from *their* parents. Perhaps Eudora's dreamy hold on the family's history, which was rooted east and north of Mississippi, helped free her from the defensiveness prevalent among true regionalists; perhaps it helps explain the tonic chord of alienation throughout her work.

If "Learning to See," a radiant account of a summer's trip to her grandparents, focuses Eudora's senses in regard to the past, the final chapter is a resolute attempt to understand her entry into writing. It begins, in the manner of *Delta Wedding*, with a train trip, although unlike the observant nine-year-old in that novel, Eudora is traveling to college, where she will write humorous pieces for the school paper. She realizes now that "it was not until I began to write, as I seriously did only when I reached my twenties, that I found the world out there revealing, because . . . *memory* had become attached to seeing, love had added itself to discovery, and because I recognized in my own continuing longing to keep going, the need I carried inside myself to know—the apprehension, first, and then the passion, to connect myself to it."

Carefully sewed into that sentence are words that invoke two of her models,

Conrad and Forster, as well as a notion from *The Optimist's Daughter:* "Memory lived not in initial possession but in the freed hands, pardoned and freed, and in the heart that can empty but fill again, in the patterns restored by dreams." One begins to understand better how, through the process of connecting, she etched an indelible gallery of characters that made the familiar grotesque and the grotesque credible. Yet like the autobiographical essays in *The Eye of the Story,* these musings, though they suggest new trails into her work and are far more intimate than anything else she's done, never really penetrate her wall of privacy. One of Welty's special talents is juggling the specific and the elliptical with such easy grace that the reader is willing to maintain a respectful distance. You don't feel cheated the way you do with Lillian Hellman's doled-out anecdotes, though Welty has far less to say about her professional life. Who ever thought she would tell this much?

Before *Losing Battles* appeared in 1970, Welty was considered very much a writer of the 1940s, a decade she fairly dominated with the rapid publication of three story collections and two novels. In 1954 and 1955, she published the dazzling comic monologue *The Ponder Heart* and the stories in *The Bride of the Innisfallen.* Then the long silence, 15 years, broken in quick succession by the appearance of her two richest and most accomplished novels, *Losing Battles* and *The Optimist's Daughter;* a photographic collection, and the assembled essays. Her concerns and her strategies have been, for all their outward variety, remarkably constant, but the later works—especially *The Optimist's Daughter,* which can be read as her *Howard's End,* her tracking of the loss of the old south and the rude displacements of the new—are more socially conscious (you would not know from the '40s books that a war was going on). This may account in part for the numerous prizes she has finally garnered. Prizes, however, are insufficient tribute to one of the last and best of our unblinking classicists. As Welty wrote of Ford Madox Ford, "a larger response is also due." She was quite specific: "There are many who believe as this reader does that the response of love is the true and the right one."

(May 1984)

Appendectomy

Edmund Wilson ridiculed the grinds at the Modern Language Association who read books backwards to catch typographical errors and produce "definitive" texts encumbered with welters of footnotes. I agree that the novelist's or poet's page ought to remain unblemished by academic midrash; anyone who has had the experience of slogging through a critical edition of, say, *Paradise Lost*, in which every line is keyed to an annotation, knows how easily the poetry is washed away in exegesis. Still, at a time when alternative versions of modern works appear more frequently than Mesozoic fossils, the casual publication of "New, Corrected" editions fills me with apprehension. Let the paid clerks who think Huck Finn's opening remark is ".erofeb ereht neeb I" do the investigative proofing. Better them than innocently curious readers who, in the absence of scholarly apparati, are forced to compare new edition with old, word by word, for the mild thrill of detecting a long-lost hyphen or an unsuspected indentation. But let them distinguish between proofing and reversing, and let them not shield their more impertinent decisions behind the authority of academia. Textual accuracy is no longer the exclusive concern of specialists.

Sensible editors and executors of literary estates can usually be counted on to distinguish between what a writer wanted published and what he stuck in a drawer; no one could possibly confuse Mr. Eliot's *The Waste Land* with Mrs. Eliot's Facsimile Edition, so it's pleasing to have both. But what are we to make of editor Philip Young's boast that his reinstatement of passages that Hemingway scrupulously excised from the Nick Adams stories represents a narrative improvement?*

---

*The posthumous disposition of Ernest Hemingway's work has become increasingly bizarre. In 1986, Scribner's assigned an editor to manufacture a pop novel from the reportedly unwieldy, unpublished manuscript of his novel *The Garden of Eden*. Nowhere is the editor identified, though the reader is assured that nothing was added other than transitions—in short, an unidentified person made unidentified additions as well as voluminous cuts to a Hemingway manuscript. From a commercial vantage, this detestable betrayal was a coup—the book became a bestseller. Five years later, the work as Hemingway wrote it remains suppressed by the publisher. In 1987, *The Complete Short Stories of Ernest Hemingway* was issued in what is loftily subtitled "The Finca Vigia Edition." Far from complete this collection presents the stories in illogical order, omits—as did the 1938 edition—the original book titles (no small part of Hemingway's prowess, and in the instance of *In Our Time* rather essential), and retains typographical errors from that edition of half a century ago.

Readers can no longer shop for *Sister Carrie*, *The Red Badge of Courage*, *Sanctuary*, or *Ulysses* without having to choose between widely varying editions. The lesson of this annoying circumstance is not that writers ought to burn their first drafts, since obviously they cannot depend on spouses and editors to do so (though the instant revisions facilitated by word processors may do it for them), but that literary excavations ought to be presented more rationally than has lately been the case. It seems, for example, inexcusable of Avon to publish Henry Binder's annotated restoration of the prepublication version of *Red Badge* as "THE ONLY COMPLETE EDITION OF THE FAMOUS AMERICAN CLASSIC"; their edition is not a classic, and previous ones were not incomplete. It is equally inexcusable for the Library of America to produce a 1379-page Crane omnibus that rudely dismisses Binder's work as useless; an additional five pages of "notes" would have sufficed to include the newly published chapter 12 and the noteworthy alterations in the much-revised final chapter—which are of greater interest and literary value than much of what the LOA edition does include.

The most widely publicized restoration is the three-volume "Critical and Syntoptic Edition" of *Ulysses* (published by Garland). Since the international Joyce lobby would never stand for the naked revelation of some 5000 changes in this century's most worshipfully analyzed literary work, the editors have covered their tracks in bibliolatrous hieroglyphics more devilish than anything in, say, *Finnegans Wake*. The changes I have perused are merely felicitous, but I've found them by balancing the new version on one knee and a standard edition on the other—not by deciphering the footnotes. *

Taking quite the opposite tack, Random House offers as the latest in a series of revamped, rediscovered, and reclaimed volumes of Faulkner a new edition of *The Sound and the Fury* that makes "every effort" to conform to "Faulkner's 'final intentions' for the novel." The pages are unsullied by footnotes. But a brief "Editor's Note" in the back, followed by two tables of sample corrections (one from the first edition, one from the carbon typescript), will not allay the reader's suspicion that some arbitrary decisions have been made. Far more disquieting is an outlandish violation of the novelist's "final intentions" as regards the Appendix he added in 1946, which is now deleted. As a result, this "New, Corrected Edition"—which arrives just in time to extend the novel's copyright another 28 years—is more an addendum to, than a replacement for, the standard text.

The mystery of the missing Appendix is strange indeed, and I can imagine only

---

*Random House subsequently published the revised *Ulysses*, edited by Hans Walter Gabler, as the standard one-volume edition, displacing the "reset edition" of 1961, with its three page-sized section-opening letters, indented dialogue, and, we are now told, 5000 errors. By that time, however, Joyceans had begun the task of second-guessing Gabler, and soon mounted a protest that is still being argued five years later. Many scholars insist that the 1961 edition is closer to Joyce's original intentions! Random House, after the usual bout of stonewalling, blinked: A committee was enjoined to decide which *Ulysses* is closest to the author's original intentions. Meanwhile, the 1961 edition is now back on bookstore shelves, side by side with Gabler's.

two excuses: Either the publisher blundered, and will soon make amends with a corrected corrected edition, or the publisher drew the draconian conclusion that the novel was complete as offered by Cape & Smith in 1929, and Faulkner had no business making subsequent changes. That argument would be more usefully employed in defending a decision *not* to publish stories, fragments, early drafts, and various emendations that Random House and other publishers, quite properly, I think, market in Faulkner's absence (not just uncollected stories and letters, but discarded manuscripts, first drafts, and movie treatments).

Just to keep the record straight, there is no shortage of proof that Faulkner considered the Appendix an essential part of the book he claimed to "love the most." He wrote it after Malcolm Cowley requested material for *The Portable Faulkner* in 1945; according to Cowley, Faulkner remarked of the finished genealogy, "I should have done this when I wrote the book." The following year Random House prepared to reprint *The Sound and the Fury* in the Modern Library. Faulkner wrote the new senior editor, Robert N. Linscott, "When you reprint *The Sound and the Fury*, I have a new section to go with it. I should have written this new section when I wrote the book itself. . . . When you read it, you will see how it is the key to the whole book, and after reading it, the 4 sections as they stand now fall into clarity and place."

At first, Faulkner wanted the Appendix to be the first section, but shortly before publication he realized it should come last. Every subsequent edition published during his life and after included the Appendix, and since the novel was not widely read before the Modern Library reprint, one can safely assume that anyone born after 1930 knows the novel's last lines to be, "Dilsey. They endured." In appending that informative and witty section, Faulkner was amplifying the novel along the lines of its original creation. He never tired of explaining how Quentin's narrative was written because he realized Benjy's was insufficient, how Jason's was added because the first two sections still hadn't done the job, and so on. "And when I got done," he told a class at West Point, in 1962, "it still wasn't finished, and so twenty years later I wrote an appendix to it, tried to tell that story." On this score, Faulkner's final intentions are unambiguous: The "new, corrected" edition is unfinished.

An unsigned editor's note, presumably written by Noel Polk, who is elsewhere credited with having directed the project of preparing a new text, skirts details about how the corrections were made: "There is not enough space here to provide a complete textual apparatus for this novel," he writes, though such brashness merely proves that the Faulkner lobby hasn't the sway of the Joyce lobby, which sees that enough space is made. In any case, Polk compared the holograph manuscript, the carbon typescript, and the Cape & Smith first edition; yet the paucity of information surrounding the original publication made it "impossible to reconstruct in all cases exactly what [Faulkner's] 'final intentions' were." My first response is, why do they keep putting quotation marks around "final intentions"? My second is, how dare they call guesswork, however educated, "corrections."

Polk and company are intrepid, however. When in doubt, they reproduce the carbon typescript—though a reader might reasonably surmise that Faulkner himself made changes on the galleys, a habit that is universal among writers. The reader might also surmise that if Faulkner saw the need for major changes, he would have made them in later years. As we've seen, he did make one (the Appendix), and he sought to make another for a special edition: He wanted to substitute different color inks for the italics that signify shifts in time and perspective, an expensive project that can never be realized because the crayon-colored manuscript he gave Bennett Cerf was lost. The reader's doubts may also be kindled by the "highly selective" tables of "significant variations." Table B (variations *from* the carbon typescript) could have been dispensed with altogether, space being at such a premium, since these changes were long ago standardized in all editions of *The Sound and the Fury*. Only the 34 alterations listed in Table A (and some that aren't listed but should have been) are newsworthy.

And lo, the most significant corrections actually clarify passages that once seemed impenetrable; others are relatively slight but appropriate; still others render passages more obscure than they were. Perhaps the most elucidative change comes nearly a third into the idiot Benjy's narrative. The standard version of the paragraph reads:

> "I told you mother was crying." Quentin said. Versh took me up and opened the door onto the back porch. We went out and Versh closed the door black. I could smell Versh and feel him. "You all be quiet, now. We're not going up stairs yet. Mr. Jason said for you to come right up stairs. He said to mind me. I'm not going to mind you. But he said for all of us to. Didn't he, Quentin." I could feel Versh's head. I could hear us. "Didn't he, Versh. Yes, that's right. Then I say for us to go out doors a while. Come on." Versh opened the door and we went out.

One thing we know about Benjy is that he records conversation accurately: He hears Dilsey say "liberry," but he says "library"—whether he knows they are one and the same is another story. The passage I've quoted is troublesome because Benjy never masks the dialogue of two or more characters as that of a single character, yet no one person could have made the statements set off in the second or third sets of quotation marks. In the corrected version, those marks are removed and the final "that's" becomes "that." Now, we can easily hear an argument among Versh ("Yes, that right"), Caddy, and Jason. Dramatized, it would play like this:

> Versh: You all be quiet now.
> Caddy: We're not going up stairs yet.
> Versh: Mr Jason said for you to come right up stairs.
> Caddy: He said to mind me.
> Jason: I'm not going to mind you.
> Caddy: But he said for all of us to. Didn't he, Quentin. Didn't he, Versh.
> Versh: Yes, that right.
> Caddy: Then I say for us to go out doors a while. Come on.

Other revealing alterations restore dropped words or lines. Jason's inexplicable affront to Caddy in the graveyard—"We don't even know you with him and Quentin"—should read, "We don't even know your name. You'd be better off if you were down there with him and Quentin." When, in the same section (Jason's, the novel's part 3), Dilsey laments the need for "a man can put de fear of God into dese here triflin young niggers," Frony, in the corrected text, sensibly replies, "Rev'un Shegog kin do dat," instead of repeating "Rev'un Shegog gwine preach today," which she had said a few lines earlier. In Quentin's section (the novel's second part), we find that Caddy "told Jason and Versh" why Uncle Maury didn't work (instead of "Caddy told Jason Versh said that the reason . . ."), and in case anyone failed to understand Quentin's abdominal complaint—"my insides would move, sitting still"—we now have the additional phrase "My bowels moved for thee." Perhaps this last line was removed from the first edition for reasons of propriety; perhaps two references to getting a "dope" or "shot" were changed to getting a "coca-cola" for the same reason. The question remains, who made those changes—how do we know Faulkner didn't?

We know that Faulkner's agent, Ben Wasson, made some "additions to the script," but Faulkner (in an impatient letter to Wasson, in 1929) claimed to have "effaced the 2 or 3 you make." Some of the changes made from the typescript to the first edition, and now changed back, smack of editorial attempts to subvert Faulkner's obscurity. Again, whether they were made in defiance of auctorial intentions or with Faulkner's consent, we don't know—and if Polk and company know, they don't say. So: The first-time reader will no longer recognize by the second sentence of Quentin's narrative that it *is* Quentin's narrative, since in the corrected edition his name has been deleted from the phrase "when Father gave it to me he said, Quentin, I give you the mausoleum of all hope and desire." The revised rhythms sound right, though, and so do the rhythms that result from other deletions of phrases that were evidently inserted to help the reader.

In other instances, the editor corrected what he considered to be typographical errors. Perhaps Faulkner did mean for his New England urchins to refer to the Unitarian steeple as "unitarial," as they do in the new edition, and the revised reading of water "healing" instead of "heading" out to sea seems likely since Faulkner uses that conceit elsewhere in the novel. But on what authority are we to accept the image of Negroes struggling up the "shaling levee" instead of the "shading levee?" Most of the remaining alterations relate to Faulkner's style of punctuation and typography: Apostrophes have been added to two-syllable contractions for consistency, but remain absent from dont, cant, and aint; Luster and T.P. now say "les" instead of "let's"; two of Quentin's interior dialogues are no longer indented; spaces have been added between italicized and Roman phrases when they run together without punctuation.

The editors may have had compelling reasons for making all those changes; the reader is entitled to know what they are. That's the way it is with classics, culture, democracy. We have here the spectacle of literature bullied by academic fiat—in short, a covert operation. A middle road might easily be paved between the arcane bibliotics that disfigure the revised *Ulysses* and the bluff reticence with which the corrected *The Sound and The Fury* is offered. The changes in the latter are not that extensive: An afterword of five or six pages, outlining the editing process and setting forth the essential arguments, plus about three double-column pages listing all the changes made from the Cape & Smith edition, would suffice to satisfy the reader's need to know what the editor knew and when he knew it.

The absence of the 20-page Appendix is a more pressing issue. Without it, this edition should be shunned by the academics who play so large a role is sustaining Faulkner's readership. The postgraduate reader would do better to photocopy Table A than invest in what amounts to an incomplete volume; those who obtain it for their first encounter with Faulkner's masterpiece will have to consult an earlier version or Cowley's *The Portable Faulkner* to read "the key to the whole book."*

When I accepted the "new, corrected edition" of *The Sound and the Fury* for review, I did not expect to write exclusively about textual problems. Having been ambushed by those issues, I want to comment briefly on the widespread impression—brought home to me in recent weeks by friends who say they have tried and failed to tackle the novel—that Faulkner's masterpiece is unyieldingly difficult. Reading it for the first time in 10 years, I was especially moved by how essential a role memory plays in it—for Faulkner, for the characters, for the reader. Before he began writing, Faulkner made preliminary notes on the order

---

*Almost exactly one year after the "corrected" version of *The Sound and the Fury* appeared, Noel Polk published *An Editorial Handbook to William Faulkner's The Sound and the Fury* (Garland, 1985)—neatly reversing the order of events in the debut of the "corrected" *Ulysses*. After reading my essay, Professor Polk was kind enough to send me an advance proof of the manuscript, in the hope that it would clarify questions I raised. It does; but it also underscores his admitted guesswork in deciding who made what typescript changes and under what circumstances. He candidly refers to "complex choices, most of which could as easily—and as correctly—be made by flipping a coin as by hours of editorial anguish, and many of which are of no consequence whatsoever." As I said in my review, most of the major changes advance Faulkner's meaning; if the justifications in the *Handbook* don't allay all doubt, they demonstrate Professor Polk's care and consistency.

On the subject of the Appendix, he is less convincing. After presenting all the evidence that would warrant its conclusion, he dismisses Faulkner's instructions on the grounds that they were issued during a period of depression and bitterness. Polk concedes that the Appendix is a "superlative piece," but argues that it ought to be considered a separate work, and that it diminishes "the rare white heat of the 1929 text, with its deliberately controlled revelation and concealment of the Compson family history, and its carefully contrived ambiguities: all seriously compromised if the reader approaches them from the vantage of the Appendix." But in fact, nothing is compromised if the reader discovers the Appendix where Faulkner planted it, at the end of the novel, nor is its impact significantly altered if the reader is forced to search it out in a volume (i.e., *The Portable Faulkner*) other than the one for which the author intended it. All textual arguments, however, are dwarfed by the fact that Faulkner's intentions were nullified on the grounds of amateur psychology. In this case, editorial anguish was supplanted by critical caprice. The Appendix is missing from the 1991 Vintage paperback edition; it remains to be seen what the Library of America will do.

and dates of key events in the dissolution of the Compsons. When he set about composing *The Sound and the Fury,* he reconstructed those events but skewed them in time, beginning with the innocent recollections of an idiot who has little sense of chronological time; continuing with the emotional agitations of the suicidal Quentin, who is bedeviled by a watch, and the tyrannical Jason; and concluding with an objective accounting, later amplified in the Appendix, a genealogy that places the Compsons in historical perspective, stretching from the 17th-century Indian Ikkemotubbe ("Doom"), who bestowed the Compson land, to Caddy ("Doomed and knew it"), who disappeared when the Nazis overran Paris. Many early readers agreed with Clifton Fadiman's assessment that the novel was "a psychological jigsaw puzzle."

During my first readings, I spent so much time struggling to figure out the puzzle—the plot, the voices, the symbols—that only the constraining, claustrophobic drive of the narrative sustained my determination. Coming to it now, with the story in mind, I am moved less by its linguistic sorcery than its resonant humanity. For one example, Faulkner allows us a more intimate look than perhaps any other white writer at the quotidian texture of white and black interaction, as well as a compelling glimpse at the cabin life of black sharecroppers and a nearly visionary regard for the evangelical power of black preachers, embodied by the Reverend Shegog. For another, because Benjy is not merely an idiot, but an eternal child for whom time does not progress but rather circulates, he presents a candid and comprehensive view of childhood's vulnerability, with which the reader, hesitant though he may be, is invited to identify. It would be presumptuous to say of any imaginative work that it reveals itself only on second or third encounter. Yet although Faulkner was only 30 when he completed the manuscript, *The Sound and the Fury*'s resonance undoubtedly increases when the reader's stock of memories is capacious enough to bind its many revelations. One returns to the novel's Mississippi and Harvard Square, so vivid in recollection, observing actions and statements with an engagement that only recollection can warrant, knowing and assenting—as with any great tragedy—to its inexorable outcome, overwhelmed by its scope and anger and sorrow and nobility.

(November 1984)

Fathers and Son

Until you understand a writer's ignorance, presume yourself igno-
rant of his understanding.

Coleridge

CRITICS

If you are a critic, nothing is harder to criticize than the critics who influenced you most. The eager predilection with which you originally monitored their thinking takes on a familial strain. They, in effect, have opened your eyes, shown you where to look, raised you to your feet, and given you a shove. You, in time, pay them back by cataloguing their limitations and failings. The situation may be Oedipal, but it isn't necessarily unjust, at least if you're discreet about it. A critic is in part the sum of the critics he admires (and perhaps also of those he loathes), and he's bound to consider their blunders as well as their triumphs in nourishing his own ambition. You know you can never be as good as Coleridge; still, you aim to be better.

I opened the revised edition of Martin Williams's *The Jazz Tradition* with trepidation because here my familial ties are thickest, and I'd better admit them at the outset. Several years before the original edition appeared in 1970, I had practically memorized the contents of many of its essays when they were published in the *Evergreen Review*. Smitten by jazz shortly before the world succumbed to the Beatles, I needed a tutor. The jazz journals, then as now, were wanting, but since at no time in the short, noisy, and incredibly prolific history of jazz criticism was there a more formidable array of talent than in the early 1960s, a few trustworthy guides were easily found. I immediately responded to two, Williams and Dan Morgenstern, and soon warmed up to a third, Whitney Balliett. (I am also eternally in debt to Leonard Feather, whose *The New Encyclopedia of Jazz* I enfolded as a bible; but years would pass before I knew him as a critic, and not exclusively as an encyclopedist.) Rereading them now is not unlike perusing a family photo album—hardly a fair, responsible basis for reviewing them. Still, I'm pleased to affirm that my admiration for these three writers—my numerous disagreements notwithstanding—isn't merely steadfast, but rejuvenated.

Dan Morgenstern (successively an editor at *Metronome*, *Jazz*, and *Down Beat*, and now director of the Institute of Jazz Studies at Rutgers), with his encyclopedic knowledge and boundless advocacy, is the great generalist. He is reportedly and at long last compiling an anthology of his best work. Whitney Balliett, a consistently stylish *New Yorker* writer for more than 25 years, regularly collects his essays; *Jelly Roll, Jabbo, and Fats* is his 11th volume since 1959. He can be trenchant and damning, but his most enlightening pieces are multilayered profiles, chiefly of musicians associated with styles that antedate bop. As a novice, I found the enthusiasms of both men contagious, but unless they were reviewing records (a Morgenstern forte, a Balliett weakness), they didn't provide much in the way of hands-on experience. That is, even when they told you what to listen to, they rarely told you how.

For that you turned to Martin Williams, a born pedagogue who seemed obsessed with locating masterpieces, pinpointing their significance, and demonstrating precisely what made them tick. He wrote in an unadorned style, authoritative and concise, with a minimum of local color and personal asides. His every sentence resonated with earnestness. His surface theme was the diverse accomplishment of jazz music; simmering below the surface was his impatience with American intellectuals who condescended to American art. Williams's work has been so influential on critics of my generation—he remains a frequent topic of conversation, even though he ceased to function as a critic more than 10 years ago, when he joined the Division of Performing Arts at the Smithsonian Institution—that it may be difficult to realize how innovative he appeared in those years.

Williams's innovations had as much to do with his perspective on jazz as with his method of reporting. As co-editor, with Nat Hentoff, of the finest jazz magazine ever published in the United States, the *Jazz Review* (November 1958–January 1961), he made an evenhanded, discriminating case for a jazz tradition that superseded the music's various styles and schools. This sounds commonplace now, and, to be sure, Williams wasn't alone even then. But most jazz critics were partisans of the music they grew up with: Swing critics thought bebop was silly, bebop critics labeled the avant-garde antijazz, and avant-garde critics considered everybody else reactionary. (A Marxist critic once accused Williams of hypocrisy because he championed Ornette Coleman yet also voted for Jack Teagarden in a critics' poll.) The *Jazz Review* was a magnet for pangenerationalist critics, including the young Morgenstern, as well as musicians who were encouraged to write criticism, among them Gunther Schuller, Cannonball Adderly, Dick Katz, Bill Crow, Cecil Taylor, and Zita Carno.

Williams saw the development of jazz as a mutually beneficial dialogue between its composers (Morton, Ellington, Monk) and improvisers (Armstrong, Parker, Coleman). Of course, he allowed that each of these musicians was both, but he was specifically concerned with the way formalists expanded on the discoveries made by improvisers and, in turn, spurred the improvisers of the subsequent generation. This kind of listening made his essays especially arresting:

For example, he traced the bass figure of John Lewis's "Django" to King Oliver's "Snag It," catalogued the origins of Count Basie's riffs, and located the genesis of Miles Davis's style in Louis Armstrong (the received wisdom at the time connected Davis to Bix Beiderbecke). More important than those informational gems, however, was the way Williams's propensity for form shaped his approach to criticism.

Music criticism is faced with the impossible task of conveying the critic's experience of the abstract. There are basically two approaches—metaphorical (Balliett is the best example) and textual. Those inclined toward the latter usually attempt to share their enthusiasms by zeroing in on specific musical passages, though they have to avoid notation and most musicological jargon, at least in the mainstream press. Popular criticism and musicology are very different disciplines, and though I've heard Williams complain of the "amateur" status of most jazz critics, himself included, a professional knowledge of music is no guarantee of perceptive listening, as witness numerous *Down Beat* Blindfold Tests, or musicologist Frank Tirro's notorious *Jazz: A History*, or even the sainted Gunther Schuller's dismissal of post-1930 Armstrong in *Early Jazz* (an issue Williams redresses in *The Jazz Tradition*). How, then, does the journalist-critic bring the general reader into the musical work? One touching solution was introduced by the indefatigable B. H. Haggin, in *Music for the Man Who Enjoys Hamlet*; included in every copy of the book was a four-inch cardboard ruler with which the reader was expected to locate the musical passage under discussion by measuring, say, 1.6 inches beyond the first groove of a record. Since the book came out in 1944, all of Haggin's laborious measuring was made obsolete four years later when the 78 rpm record was replaced by the LP. Most recently, the German critic Ekkehard Jost has written essays that require of his readers the use of a stopwatch.

Williams required only that his readers be able to hear a numeric 4/4 pulse and count measures—a difficult task for some, as I've learned from teaching. As almost every major jazz performance recorded before 1960 was based on the 12-bar blues or the 32-bar pop song, Williams wrote a series of short analyses, collected in 1966 as *Where's the Melody?*, that explained those forms and how to hear them. I know of no more avuncular advice in all criticism than this: "So, count off a chorus of Sidney Bechet's 'Blue Horizon': 1 2 3 4, 2 2 3 4, 3 2 3 4 . . . and so on, up through 12 2 3 4. I realize this sounds mechanical and, perhaps, even a little difficult. But with a little practice, it isn't very difficult, and for some people the rewards in listening can be quite worth the trouble." Indeed. With a little counting under your belt, you soon began to think of a jazz performance as a succession of choruses, and when Williams alerted you to something interesting in the third release of the second chorus, you knew just how to find it.

By demonstrating how to listen and what to listen for, Williams removed some of the sentimentality and mysticism that had attached themselves to improvisation. Yet he retained his appreciation for the magic. Here he writes of King Oliver: "He had dignity, a dignity which allowed him to speak uncompromisingly, unapologetically of the deepest sorrow and anguish and the most sublime joy and communal jubilation." Here, in three sentences, is most of what you need to know about Louis Armstrong: "His genius is such than he can apparently take any piece, add a note here, leave out a note there, condense or displace this melodic phrase a bit, rush this cadence, delay that one, alter another one slightly, and transform it into sublime melody, and pure gold. He can turn something merely pretty into something truly beautiful and something deeply delightful. Conscious taste has little to do with such transformations; they are products of an intuitive genius, and of the kind of choice where reason cannot intrude."

Those lines are from *The Jazz Tradition*, Williams's most compressed and important book, though not his most readable (that distinction probably belongs to *Jazz Masters of New Orleans*). It contains chapters on 21 major figures, five of them (Oliver, Bechet, Art Tatum, Sarah Vaughan, and Charles Mingus) written for the revised edition. Most of these essays should be read with the relevant records at hand. When Williams dissects "Dead Man Blues" into its component choruses, or outlines the thematic development of Sonny Rollins's "Blues for Philly Joe," or enticingly refers to "the marvelous 'mistake' between bars 127 and 142 in which [Ornette] Coleman enters 'early' and turns the beat around," you want to be able to hear what he's talking about. Williams's essays stand up handsomely as critical surveys (the new one on Art Tatum is among the best, incidentally), but they are ultimately a kind of commentary on the recorded evidence, essential to the novice, provocative for the experienced listener.

When I first encountered a few of them in the *Evergreen Review*, I would go from text to music and back trying to appreciate Williams's distinctions, blithely unconcerned about the relative importance of a Morton or a Coleman, but willing to accept on faith Williams's conviction that attention must be paid them all. Twenty years later, I expected to whiz through this book (I made the mistake of taking it along on a vacation), and found it as frustrating as ever to read without a stereo at hand. Williams always binds his opinions to specifics. Are Tatum's embellishments on "All the Things You Are" really "pompous and vulgar"? Not to my mind, but there was only one way to find out.

The overall scheme of *The Jazz Tradition* underscores another Williams theme that has come to seem commonplace—the idea that the most fundamental changes in the evolution of jazz have been rhythmic. He writes, "Dizzy Gillespie has said that when he is improvising he thinks of a rhythmic figure or pattern and then of the notes to go with it, and I am sure than any important jazz musician from any style or period would give us a similar statement." In the absence of other such statements, Williams provides his own, sometimes with eloquent concision ("Jo Jones discovered he could play the *flow* of the rhythm and not its demarcation"), and they provide a subtext and *idée fixee*.

The general approach Williams takes to each artist is likely to be taken for granted, too, I suppose. After all, what could be more natural than a brief discourse that attempts to put into perspective the achievement of a particular musician? Countless thousands of such essays have been written about writers, actors, painters, filmmakers, and composers of "serious music" (my favorite euphemism: all that condescension, girded with racial and class biases, filtered into a term of polite cultural approbation). But damn few about jazz musicians. Williams's model seems to have been the French critic and composer André Hodier, whose *Jazz: Its Evolution and Essence* (1956) set new standards for the discipline of jazz criticism. Other European critics, notably England's Max Harrison, have done similar work. Yet the American jazz press, infinitesimal thing that it is, as well as mainstream newspapers and magazines—which still regard jazz as too arcane to treat critically, *vide* the annual Sunday supplement articles about the newest young jazz players or the resurgence in jazz interest or the latest jazz prince of charisma—encourage personality pieces at the expense of learned opinion. By now, surely, *The Jazz Tradition* should stand at the head of a shelf of similarly conceived books. It stands almost alone.

The "new and revised edition" is open to one serious complaint that might have been obviated had Williams altered the title to something like *The Jazz Tradition 1920–1970*. It's no surprise that musicians who have come along in the past 15 years aren't mentioned, but it's disappointing that Williams hasn't updated the chapters on those musicians about whom he was especially prescient. Last year, a lecture he delivered in New York on the postwar Count Basie orchestra forced me to reconsider my own views on the subject, but the essay on Basie still ends in the 1930s. His reservations about Charles Mingus suggest little familiarity with the tremendous impact Mingus's music has had on the best bands of the 1980s, notably those of David Murray and Henry Threadgill. At a time when the jazz press was sloganeering for John Coltrane, Williams saw equal if not greater originality in Ornette Coleman; time has vindicated that judgment, yet he has nothing to say about the extraordinary changes in Coleman's music since 1968.* He virtually ignores the later manifestations of Ellington, Davis, and Rollins, and of the whole issue of jazz repertory (a movement in which he has been a catalyst) and what it might tell us about the value of, say, Jelly Roll Morton's music when distinguished from Morton's recordings. It is unfair to rebuke a book for not being something it never attempted to be, but admirers who might be expecting fresh salvos from one of jazz criticism's most incisive minds should be forewarned. The Smithsonian's gain, evident in the invaluable recordings Williams has produced (a kind of *critique concrete*), is journalism's loss.

---

*His silence here is ironic, because Coleman is the one musician who best exemplifies Williams's observation that the composer is father to the improviser who is father to the composer, etc. Coleman was originally signed by a record company as a writer of intriguing tunes. These reflected and fomented his approach to improvisation, which culminated in his virtual abandonment of composition in favor of Free Jazz. In the '70s, however, he concentrated on composing—for large ensembles (including symphony orchestra) and small (including rock band). In obsessively notating every part, he spurred yet another school of improvisation, represented on his own records and those of such disciples as James Blood Ulmer and Ronald Shannon Jackson.

Although they are of the same generation, Whitney Balliett's approach to music criticism is the antithesis of Williams's. In recent years, he has attempted to organize his books with loosely fitting themes—*Alec Wilder & His Friends, Improvising, American Singers*—but they remain collections of *New Yorker* articles, consecutively presented. Except for his frequently caustic reviews and occasional diaries of jazz festivals (he annually covers Newport/Kool, an event with which he seems increasingly bored, but rarely ventures into the clubs), Balliett generally focuses his energies on musician profiles, a form he has perfected to a science and at which he has no peers in or out of jazz. They consist of introductory comments about the musician under study, a general critique of his or her style (Balliett rarely refers to specific recordings), and lengthy quoted recollections and observations that somehow manage to convey the voice of the artist as filtered through the sensibility of the interviewer.

Balliett is a miraculous writer. It has been said that you can read him even if you don't care for jazz, but that wasn't my initial response to his work. As a novice, I was attracted to his assertiveness and lyricism but confused by his metaphors, especially as they converged in his descriptions of a musician's "typical" instrumental style. Only after I was familiar with Pee Wee Russell's music, for example, could I savor this passage from *Such Sweet Thunder* (reprinted in revised form in *Improvising*): "In the lowest register, which he seems increasingly to prefer, he gets a hushed, edgeless sound. In the middle range, his tone becomes more explicit, suggesting soft, highly polished wood. . . . He often starts [a blues] in the lower (or chalumeau) register range with a delicate rush of notes that are intensely multiplied into a single, unbroken phrase that lasts the entire chorus. Thus he will begin with a pattern of winged double-time staccato notes that, moving steadily downward, will be abruptly pierced by adolescent falsetto jumps." He continues this description for another couple of hundred words, and if you know Russell's playing intimately each phrase rings true. But Balliett isn't describing a real performance; it's a mythical ur-Russell performance. Balliett's preference for the general over the specific governs his vision of the jazz art, in which style is character rather than a succession of isolated masterpieces.

Yet if Balliett is nonpareil in his prose portraits, his critical views are on occasion so idiosyncratic and hyperbolic that his neglect of detailed argument can be confounding. His current collection, *Jelly Roll, Jabbo, and Fats*, is one of his best and underscores his strengths and weaknesses. Its 16 essays, one on two formidable French critics (Hughes Panassie and Charles Delaunay), and the rest on musicians (four of them—Morton, Bechet, Young, and Coleman—among Williams's titans) are exemplary portraits. In some, Balliett supplements his own interview material with lengthy quotations from other writers and musicians, and this can be confusing. When he writes that Ornette Coleman "has said" something, are we to infer that Coleman said it to Balliett? The confusion stems, in part, from the tap dance Balliett has lately adopted to avoid the first-person pronoun.

Sometime during the 1970s, Balliett made the draconian decision to remove all the *I*'s from his writing. He not only eschews the pronoun in his current work, but has expelled it when revising his older pieces. At the same time, he has filtered out the metaphorical overdrive that occasionally clotted his early work. The new stuff is cleaner and fresher. Yet I miss that authoritative "I," and the scene-setting it was able to do, and the squally opinions it was willing to defend. The authority remains, but in its present omniscient state it has lost weight. Which may be why his more curious assertions ("Michael Moore is the best jazz bassist alive"*) are more suffered than contested. Surely his antagonistic comments on Max Roach and Art Blakey should be of greater interest than they are, considering the special brilliance he has brought to explicating drumming styles of the 1930s and, in *Jelly Roll, Jabbo, and Fats*, the 1920s (Tommy Benford, Freddie Moore, and Sonny Greer). Balliett the stylist and Balliett the critic often appear to be two men; the former dazzles you with a description of Cecil Taylor at work that is more vivid than any photograph, but the latter offers little about the value, historical place, or emotional impact of Taylor's music.

Listen to the opening gambit from his masterpiece on Lester Young (at least a dozen other passages in his new book are as good): "Very little about the tenor saxophonist Lester Young was unoriginal. He had protruding, heavy-lidded eyes, a square, slightly Oriental face, a tiny mustache, and a snaggletoothed smile. His walk was light and pigeon-toed, and his voice was soft. He was something of a dandy. He wore suits, knit ties, and collar pins. He wore ankle-length coats, and porkpie hats—on the back of his head when he was young, and pulled down low and evenly when he was older. He kept to himself, often speaking only when spoken to. When he played, he held his saxophone in front of him at a forty-five degree angle, like a canoeist about to plunge his paddle into the water. He had an airy, lissome tone and an elusive, lyrical way of phrasing that had never been heard before."

Balliett has written as evocatively about Henry Red Allen, Sidney Catlett, Earl Hines, Lee Konitz, and many others. Who today writes that warmly and poetically about artists in any other field? Jazz is lucky to have him, and Balliett must surely know that if his 11 volumes were filled with similar profiles of American writers or painters, his own literary stock would be all the higher. He is one of a handful of veteran critics from the 1950s still active, and he is still important because, instead of turning into a raconteur or consumer guide, he continues to find the energy to reimagine the musicians he most admires. His critical eye is lively and urgent. And infuriating. Read a little longer into the Lester Young essay and you come upon the notion that "most of" Young's imitators "could play his style better than he could himself" (no examples given), and the strange description of Young's clarinet sound as "nudging, murmuring." But that's the

---

*That sentence was excised when Balliett reprinted the essay on Moore in *American Musicians* (1986), an indispensable selection of his best work over 25 years.

Balliett conundrum: The descriptive writing is precise, inspired, and emotional; the critical writing is loose, literary, and cool.

Reading Williams and Balliett back to back, I found them surprisingly complementary. Williams makes connections, points his finger, thinks the big questions, identifies masterpieces. Balliett makes the ineffable explicit, visits homes, captures the lingo, poeticizes the prosaic underpinnings of art. Williams lectures; Balliett entertains. Though, of course, each frequently crosses over into the other's territory. You cannot read either of them without becoming a better listener. They have greatly enriched American criticism, and I wish it wasn't always another jazz critic saying so.

(August 1983)

MUSICOLOGIST

The Renaissance lasted 250 years, the Swing Era barely 10. Yet by any standard of aesthetic achievement, the latter embodied an authentic musical renaissance that, unprecedented and impossible to equal, is now the stuff of legend. From 1935, when Benny Goodman, little known beyond a coterie of jazz musicians, mined gold playing the music of Fletcher Henderson (a pioneering black orchestra leader), until the end of World War II, when diverse circumstances— including the draft, a cabaret tax that punished dancers, rationing, a recording ban initiated by the American Federation of Musicians, and a change in taste— wiped them out, big bands were the common coin of American music.

Think of it: hundreds of full-size orchestras playing a luxurious dance music that combined the talents of astonishing composers and improvisers, presented with flash and style, criss-crossing a nation that boasted almost as many ballrooms as bus depots. We lose ourselves in recollections of the abundance of talent, and forget for a moment that the improbable richness of the Swing Era was played out against a background of Depression and war. A few years ago there was a TV offer of recordings by the big bands that promised to bring back "the happiest years America has ever known"—popular music as the great anodyne. In the case of the Swing Era, though, pop endures as something a good deal more savory than a nostalgic drug. The best music of the decade embodied a brave and buoyant new art that has lost none of its power to surprise and gratify. As Gunther Schuller shows in his long awaited study, *The Swing Era: The Development of Jazz, 1933–1945*, that art can withstand scrutinous analysis, as well as comparisons to Europe's most vaunted classics.

Strangely, a comprehensive history of the Swing Era that connects the amplitude of music (indeed, of entertainment) to the dearth of *do re mi* has yet to be written. Notwithstanding useful surveys of the bands, notably George T. Simon's amiable fan's notes, *The Big Bands*, and Albert McCarthy's more critical history,

Big Band Jazz, and countless volumes about particular performers, the period has been less well analyzed than, say, the glory days of rock and roll. Nor is Schuller's mammoth volume much of an attempt at a rounded history; he's almost exclusively concerned with recordings. Yet, combining the disciplines of criticism and musicology, he probes deeper into the music—paying special attention to orchestral voicings—than anyone else has ever attempted. And because he has very likely listened to, analyzed, and performed more kinds of music than any other writer, he has come up with an aesthetic roadmap that, though controversial (critics have been raging over certain passages from the moment advance copies went out), is certain to influence the way the Swing Era is apprehended for years to come.

Schuller is himself an imposing presence in American music. A self-taught and prolific composer in many idioms, he has been a passionate advocate of other composers as well, among them Joplin (he conducted the debut recording of *Treemonisha*), Ellington, and bandleader Paul Whiteman. At 63, he has been an energetic booster for four decades, as musician, conductor, educator, and writer, while producing a massive catalogue of original music—including operas, ballets, symphonies, and chamber works. In the '50s, he coined the term "third-stream" to describe a music that consciously seeks to blend elements of jazz and the academy. In 1968, a year into his 10-year presidency of the New England Conservatory, he published the first volume in his jazz history, *Early Jazz: Its Roots and Musical Development,* a relatively compact but groundbreaking work, often referred to in *The Swing Era.* He promises at least one and possibly two more volumes in the series.

The plan of *The Swing Era* is straightforward. Although he acknowledges the importance of black bands that set the stage for Goodman's triumph, he begins with an obligatory, evenhanded look at the "King of Swing," then proceeds to investigate, often at considerable length, the leading black and white bands, the territory bands, the great soloists, and a few of the small combos. Within each chapter, he offers a general evaluation of the artist, then treks through the musician's discography session by session, illustrating dozens of passages from recordings with transcriptions and a variety of graphs. Schuller is always a musicologist first and a critic second—only when the nuts and bolts are sufficiently canny does he allow himself an emotional response. Thus, much of the writing is academic ("The chords in mm. 2 and 3 are in a sense a spinning out of the B-flat7 tonality through two passing chords [A-flat7 and G7] to the B-flat-related A-flat-m6 chord in m. 3"). Yet the jazz lover will find much here that is accessible, insightful, tart, and eloquent, if not always convincing. A 13-page measure-for-measure analysis of Ellington's "Reminiscing in Tempo," for example, is a useful corrective to the tendency not to tackle that difficult work at all. As an early attempt to supersede the limitations of the 78 rpm disc, the piece represented a major step in Ellington's development, but no amount of notation and analysis can disguise the monotony that is the work's major failing. Unfortunately, Schuller contends his appreciation at the expense of Ellington's later extended works; but, by heaven, his enthusiasm cannot be ignored.

Discussions of Jimmy Blanton's innovations on bass, of swing and dynamics, of the instrumental equations that made up Glenn Miller's trademark sound, of the piano styles of Earl Hines, Teddy Wilson, and Art Tatum, and of orchestras (Claude Hopkins, Edgar Hayes, Les Brown) that are rarely discussed at all, encourage you to approach familiar records in a new light and should prompt record labels to explore the dark corners of their vaults. Schuller enjoys playing devil's advocate, and some of the most surprising passages concern white bands (Larry Clinton, Bob Chester) that are hardly mentioned in most jazz histories. By the same token, he gives Helen Forrest and Cab Calloway their due as singers, though he underrates Jimmy Rushing and Louis Armstrong.

The Swing Era is hardly an unalloyed delight. Permeating his every chapter is a sour, quibbling condescension to musicians Schuller thinks have sold out and to other commentators with whom he has scores to settle. (How many readers will be able to fathom his very long footnote about French critic André Hodier?) He has little patience for the third stream that exists between jazz and pop, though in this regard a double standard emerges. Of the popular white bands, especially Goodman and Miller, he insists we credit them with bringing "an unprecedented and since then never equaled number of Americans as close to jazz as they were ever to be." Yet he is merciless when he suspects a black band of trying to cop some of that popular success. He concludes a remarkably misguided essay on Armstrong with the daydream that Armstrong (a wealthy man) should have been allowed to stay home on a government pension, rather than "scratch out a living as a good-natured buffoon, singing 'Blueberry Hill' and 'What a Wonderful World' night after night." One can readily imagine the colorful response Armstrong would have made to such an offer.

Schuller shares the musicologist's penchant for focusing on exquisite leaves and missing the majesty of the forest, as when he praises Eddie Sauter (his modulations are "certainly equal to Richard Strauss's") for his arrangements on vocals, but shrugs off his major works, including "Clarinet á la King," as pastiche. He states that Ellington "made no further attempts to grapple with conceptually larger forms" after 1943 (unlike Schuller himself, who cites two of his own pieces), never mentioning any of the works—"New World A-Coming," "The Tattooed Bride," "Harlem," "The Golden Broom and the Green Apple," among many others—that contradict him. He dismisses the Ellington small band recordings and two of his most extraordinary big band transformations of pop material, "Chloe" ("confused") and "The Sidewalks of New York" ("unworthy material").

But then, there's a lot of uncharacteristic loose talk here. Schuller writes, "In many ways, [clarinetist Frank] Teschemacher was the Ornette Coleman of the twenties," but fails to mention a single way. He writes that Ellington "never did make the transition to a language and grammar of jazz capable of producing music *on its own unique terms.*" (The emphasis is his.) And if, in 1939, Ben Webster was one "of the two or three leading masters of the saxophone," who was the other or the other two—Coleman Hawkins, Lester Young, Chu Berry, Johnny Hodges, Harry Carney, Benny Carter? In a footnote (of which there are dozens), he says first that Dizzy Gillespie "must" have been influenced by Rex Stewart, then that "he may not have been entirely unaware" of Stewart. He seems to have made no attempt to keep abreast of jazz reissues (obsolete catalogue numbers are cited) or scholarship: His statement "To read most of the histories and reference books on jazz is to gain the impression that jazz died around 1942" is so far from the truth as to be ludicrous. There are shameless tautologies, of which the most egregious is, "The very length of this chapter [on Benny Goodman] is a telling indication of the magnitude of Goodman's impact on the music of his time."

Far more surprising, for a scholar of Schuller's gifts, are the factual errors. I assume that gremlins, with whom I am intimately familiar, are responsible for renaming Jimmy McHugh "Johnny" and Bob Haggart "Habbart." But what is one to make of the accreditation of Ray Nance's trumpet solo on "Take the A Train" to Rex Stewart ("who, very tightly muted, delivers one of the most cohesive solos of his career")? That solo, one of the most celebrated in jazz history, made Nance famous. He confuses Les Hite with Leon Elkins (on Armstrong's "I'm a Ding Dong Daddy"); pointlessly argues against the "official" credit of "One O'Clock Jump" to Count Basie (the "official" credit goes to Durham-Page-Smith, as any record label will attest); names "Sophisticated Lady" as the first Ellington hit ("Mood Indigo" was a huge success two years earlier); argues that Coleman Hawkins never "dominated" the tenor world (he did so decisively between 1926 and 1936); credits Lawrence Brown for transforming "The Sheik of Araby" (ignoring Jack Teagarden's earlier transformation of "this somewhat whiny standard"); cites as "tragic" that no one asked Ellington "to compose a substantial ballet comprising, like Tchaikovsky's ballets, a number of 'exotic' cameo set-pieces, like 'Caravan' or 'Mood Indigo,' " ignoring *The River*, commissioned by the American Ballet Theater in 1970; and insists that Louis Armstrong wasn't a "household name" until the 1960s.

Still, once you note all the errors or misstatements, all the opinions likely to inflame your complexion and tax your blood pressure, the fact remains that in these 919 densely printed pages is a genuine and resolute vision of a musical phenomenon, screened by the temperament of a composer who can probe the issues of musical decision-making (the how and the why) with an intimacy denied most of us. Schuller proves, unhappily, that even the best-equipped musicologist can stub his foot in the dark as often as any musically illiterate critic, but he provides a close and unfamiliar look at the mechanics of jazz that cannot fail to strengthen the enthusiast's cognition. *The Swing Era* should probably not be read straight through, but absorbed in short doses with the relevant records at hand. Schuller is an original, obsessive listener; what makes him a great critical writer is his ability to let you hear and interpret through his ears.

(March 1989)

Index